THE EDGE
OF DOUBT

D1596562

DAVID P. MIRALDI

For Brendan, Thomas, and Rose

DOUBT

A feeling of uncertainty about the truth, reality, or nature of something
A general feeling of uncertainty, worry, or concern
Distrust or suspicion

Source: Dictionary.com

PREFACE

The criminal charges against Nancy Smith and Joseph Allen have been controversial from the moment that the first allegations surfaced. In writing this book, I have relied primarily upon trial transcripts, court filings, YouTube videos of court proceedings, police records, witness statements, newspaper accounts, and interviews (both on and off the record).

This book is one of narrative nonfiction. Like other works in this genre, the events described in this book are true, but some of the dialogue and thoughts of the characters have been re-created. I have tried to be as accurate as possible. I have provided chapter notes at the end of the book to document my sources and to identify the dialogue and thoughts that are surmised from other sources.

Because this book involves allegations of sexual abuse of children, I have changed the names of those children and their parents to protect their privacy.

PART ONE

CHAPTER 1
JUDGE LYNETT MCGOUGH
AUGUST 4, 1994

Her left hand trembled slightly as she grabbed the envelope. Opening it, the judge removed the verdict forms and checked them twice for inconsistencies, noisily flipping through the pages as she read them. With so much media attention, she could not afford any missteps, no matter how minor. She took a deep breath and surveyed her small courtroom—litigants and their attorneys sharing one large trial table, the victims' parents filling one spectator bench while the defendants' families and friends jammed into the other. For now, they were all silent and edgy, each side tormented by what they did not know but soon would.

In a moment, she'd announce the jury's decision in open court and lives would be forever changed. But for that short interval between her silent reading and her public pronouncement, the judge was caught in a powerful feeling, both exhilarating and humbling, something that she'd only experienced at times like this.

For Judge Lynett McGough, this criminal trial had been like no other. The police and the prosecutor had claimed that preschool children participating in the Lorain Head Start program had been periodically raped and molested by one of the school's female bus drivers and her male companion at an unknown location. By the bad luck of the draw, Judge McGough had been assigned this emotional, high-profile case where her every ruling would be scrutinized not just by the attorneys but by the community as a whole. It would have been a challenging case for any judge, but particularly for the county's only female judge, who was finishing her first term and battling for re-election.

Setting down the verdict forms, she asked the defendants to rise. They quickly complied, joined by their attorneys. The defendants were decidedly an odd pair. Joseph Allen, a middle-aged, African-American housepainter, was dressed in a loose-fitting short sleeve shirt and casual slacks. Nine days earlier, he had initially refused to shed his orange jail garb for civilian clothes, but had eventually relented after his attorney convinced him that jail clothing would mark him as a guilty man to the jury. The other defendant, Nancy Smith, was a neatly groomed white woman, dressed in a suit jacket and skirt. The thirty-seven-year-old mother of four teenagers stared at the wall above the judge, fear evident in her eyes.

The three attorneys were also studies in contrast. Still seated, the prosecutor, Jonathan Rosenbaum, was known for his blunt and slashing style—an attorney who didn't care if he offended or alienated others. In his early forties, the balding prosecutor seemed to bound about the courtroom as if constantly in search of prey. Well prepared and instinctively agile in cross-examination, Rosenbaum pounced on witnesses' mistakes and drove them home, often humiliating them in the process. Strong-willed and unwavering, he could win over reluctant jurors by the force of his personality.

Smith's attorney, Jack Bradley, possessed Hollywood good looks and an affable personality that could charm both jurors and clients alike. Now in his midforties, he had quickly become one of the most sought-after criminal defense attorneys in the county. The likeable Bradley connected with jurors, and his smooth style often caused jurors to overlook the holes in his defenses. However, during this trial, she had seen another side of him. An intense competitor, he'd become irate in chambers several times, erupting at Rosenbaum, who he claimed had failed to timely disclose trial witnesses and exculpatory evidence. Each time, she had sympathized with Bradley but refused to grant the mistrials he'd requested. Instead, she'd devised compromises that she believed permitted the prosecution's case to go forward without trampling upon the rights of the defendants. She was convinced that her skillful solutions had inexorably pushed this case to the finish line and off her docket.

Standing next to Joseph Allen was Joseph Grunda, the former Lorain County prosecutor, who'd been assigned to defend the indigent Allen. The sixty-one-year-old Grunda was lean and athletic looking—a street-smart lawyer who'd seen almost everything. In his navy blue suit, he looked authoritative, while his gray hair and tightly clipped mustache gave him the stature of a distinguished statesman. In the courtroom, he combined elements of both attorneys: at times, gruff and hard-hitting, while at others, controlled and beguiling with his smile and mischievous glances.

Holding the verdicts in both hands, the judge cleared her throat. "'In the matter of the State of Ohio versus Nancy Smith, we, the jury, find the defendant Nancy Smith guilty of count one of gross sexual imposition.'"

The judge could hear a collective gasp flow from Smith's followers and loud whispers of "yes" coming from the victims' families. Almost immediately, Nancy Smith broke into heavy sobs. Startled by the defendant's reaction, Judge McGough stopped reading the verdicts.

Before the judge could continue, Nancy Smith pointed at Joseph Allen and whimpered, "I never met this man. I never saw this man. I never touched those children. Ever." She turned to face Bradley and buried her head into his shoulder. Over Smith's muffled crying, the judge finished reading the verdicts. The jury had found her guilty on all six charges: two counts of gross sexual imposition, two counts of complicity to rape, attempted rape, and rape.

Picking up the verdict forms involving Joseph Allen, the judge announced eight guilty verdicts, five for rape. When she'd finished reading them all, Allen was looking at the floor and shaking his head, his demeanor quiet and stoic.

The judge then began polling each of the individual jurors to confirm that this was their verdict. When each had, the judge addressed them. "I know these cases were very difficult. This has been a long trial. I want to thank you again for your service. At this time, you are released from jury duty and are free to discuss this case with whomever you wish. Bailiff, please take the jurors to the jury room."

Although the judge pretended to watch the jurors as they filed from the room, she constantly glanced at Nancy Smith, who looked like she might collapse into an anguished heap at any moment. Determined to carry on, the judge kept her voice firm and resolute. "We are going to take a brief recess. I will ask that the sheriff deputies take both defendants to the basement holding facility. We will go forward with the sentencing in thirty minutes but we will give Ms. Smith a chance to compose herself before we do that."

Before a sheriff's deputy could escort Smith from the courtroom, she glared at the prosecutor. "I didn't touch those children and you know I didn't touch them." Smith's head drooped as she said her final words: "Oh my God."

The judge stood and turned. Before she could open the sliding door to her chambers, she heard the spiteful voice of a spectator talking to someone else in the courtroom. "Your mother did this to my daughter. She got what she deserved."

The judge had heard enough. She retreated into her chambers, shut the door, and lifted its only window about six inches above its ledge. She tapped a cigarette from a pack, lit it, and took a long drag. Smith's emotional outburst had been unnerving, but, in Judge McGough's experience, criminal defendants routinely maintained their innocence long after they'd been convicted. Why should this defendant be any different?

She was not surprised by the jury's guilty verdicts. Yes, the jurors could have dismissed the children's incredible accounts as products of their imagination and acquitted the defendants, but the jury had believed the children—that much was certain. But, of course, there was more than just the children's stories to support the verdicts.

This case was a parent's nightmare and a permanent stain on the community. How could these things have happened to children enrolled in the Lorain Head Start preschool program? At trial, four children, now five and six years old, had trooped forward like little soldiers and told the jury about the shocking things that had been done to them while they were supposed to be in school. They all testified that their bus driver, Nancy, had kept them on the bus and not allowed them to leave with the other children when they'd arrived for the school's afternoon session. Instead, she'd driven them to the home of a man named Joseph, where they were sexually molested and forced to do unspeakable things.

Judge McGough once again thought about the evidence that linked Nancy Smith to Joseph Allen. Although the defendants vehemently denied knowing each other, the prosecution had presented several witnesses who testified that they'd seen the two together. When they'd testified, she hadn't found any of them to be overly convincing, but it was the jury's role to assess their credibility, not hers. The jury had obviously believed them, and in the end, it all made sense. The only way Joseph Allen could have had access to the children was through a Head Start employee. The children had identified Nancy Smith as that employee. If Joseph Allen committed these crimes, then Nancy Smith had to be his gateway to the children. It was that simple.

As a judge, she'd developed an unshakable confidence in jurors and their collective ability to ferret out the truth. When twelve people from widely different backgrounds arrived at a unanimous decision, she trusted the result. This case would be no exception.

She decided to smoke another cigarette while she finalized her decisions about sentencing. As she exhaled the smoke slowly, she picked up a paper that outlined the potential sentences for each crime, something her law clerk had prepared in advance. As a mother of four, a former city prosecutor, and now a judge elected to protect everyday people, she had no doubt what she would do. The jury had concluded that Smith and Allen had committed horrible crimes and she would hand down maximum sentences.

She was well aware that many of her early critics believed that she was not qualified to be a judge, and at every stage of her first term, she had proven them wrong. This sentencing was just another opportunity to demonstrate that.

She'd come to the law later in life. At age thirty-eight, she'd graduated from law school, passed the bar exam, and begun her practice. Lawyers soon learned that she did not hesitate in taking on a variety of challenging cases. Criminal defense, divorce, personal injury, probate litigation—she shied away from nothing, eventually landing the job as North Ridgeville's city prosecutor and law director. After practicing law for only seven years, she'd surprised the legal community by seeking a newly created judgeship in Lorain County. During her campaign, she'd promised to be a judge who cared about victims of crime, particularly women and children. By her energy and hard work, she'd prevailed in a crowded field of Democratic hopefuls in the primary. A few months later, she'd defeated her Republican and independent opponents in the general election by garnering 44 percent of the vote, thus becoming the first woman ever to be elected judge in the county.

As a judge, she projected confidence and rapidly adapted to her new position. Mentored by one of the senior judges, she was counseled not to dither on decisions and to keep her docket moving. She consciously made rulings that pushed cases toward earlier trial dates, and if an attorney requested more time for anything, she was reluctant to grant it. Her steely blue eyes could wither an unprepared attorney—something she used effectively to communicate her impatience and reproach. Because she demanded so much of herself, she expected the same from others. However, her courtroom persona was in sharp contrast to the quiet woman who could spend hours watching birds and squirrels in her backyard sanctuary or cheering on her beloved Cleveland Indians.

She rubbed out her cigarette, closed the window, and called her bailiff to gather the attorneys and their clients. She was ready to proceed to sentencing and bring this long trial to an end.

After opening the sliding door that separated her chambers from the courtroom, she took her seat behind the bench. She surveyed the courtroom and found that it was packed with the same people as before. Peering down at the trial table, she glanced at Nancy Smith, who sat stiffly with her attorney. Smith was more composed than when she'd last seen her—no longer crying, but her face was puffy and red.

"I will begin with my sentencing of Nancy Smith."

Smith rose from her chair, helped by her attorney. The defendant looked straight ahead as her attorney guided her to a spot in front of the bench.

"Before I pronounce my sentence, what would you like me to consider in mitigation, Mr. Bradley?"

Bradley looked at his client and then at the judge. Usually smooth and unflappable, Bradley hesitated before responding. "Your Honor, this lady has never been in trouble in her life. She has never harmed any person in her entire life." Bradley stopped, searching for his next thought.

The judge set down her pen and rubbed her chin, waiting for him to continue. It was obvious that the verdict had deeply unsettled him.

"Your Honor, we ask that the Court not sentence her and that the Court grant her a new trial immediately. The jury obviously lost its way in this case."

The judge drummed her fingers on her legal pad. Although she didn't interrupt Bradley, this was not the time to request a new trial. Unlike Bradley, she hadn't been surprised by the verdicts and did not view them as grave miscarriages of justice as he apparently did.

"It was not fair to have a trial jointly with Joseph Allen. I asked for separate trials and I still believe that should have been done."

He was rehashing an old issue. The prosecutor had requested that Smith and Allen be tried together rather than separately—something within the judge's discretion after considering several factors. She'd allowed joinder and she would not reverse that now, particularly after she'd invested two weeks of her valuable time in a trial.

Joinder had made sense. It had promoted judicial economy and had protected the vulnerable children from being forced to testify twice. Bradley had argued that his client could not receive a fair trial if she shared the courtroom with a previously convicted child molester. Now he argued that this was the principal reason why she'd been found guilty. In effect, he was blaming her for his "innocent" client's conviction. She bristled at the suggestion but did not interrupt him.

"This lady has gone through a nightmare. She continues to go through a nightmare. I would ask that the Court grant us a new trial."

Judge McGough tapped the back of her pen against her notepad. She'd asked Bradley to offer his thoughts about mitigating circumstances and he'd taken it as an open invitation to attack her earlier ruling and ask for a new trial. What was he thinking? The prosecution had presented evidence on every element of the crimes and had obviously convinced the jurors. With her strong belief in the reliability of juries, she would not summarily cast this jury's verdict aside.

"Mr. Rosenbaum, do you wish to speak on this issue?"

Rosenbaum stood quickly and looked with disgust at Bradley. She knew his remarks would be sharp and direct. "This lady has had a fair trial. Her nightmare does not compare to the ordeal that these children and their parents have experienced and will continue to experience." His voice took on an exasperated air. "The evidence was overwhelming against her. Obviously, the jury didn't have much trouble. From this side of the table, we feel that she is guilty of the crimes charged and should suffer a heinous penalty for it."

Without ruling on the motion, the judge nodded and then looked to Nancy Smith. "Ms. Smith, this is your opportunity to address the court." Realizing that she had bypassed her attorney, the judge added, "Mr. Bradley, do you wish your client to speak at this time?"

Bradley nodded and a distraught Nancy Smith began to speak. "All I can tell you is I did not commit these crimes." Her voice shook and she could not hide her anguish. "I don't even know this man. I have never ever seen this man before. I have never gone with a black man."

The judge realized that Smith was going to repeat the same things that she had said on the witness stand—claims that the jury had rejected.

"I am a mother," Smith continued. "I just want my children. Oh God, I didn't do these things. I never touched those children. I never touched them. Never." There was no hiding her desperation. "That is all I can tell you. I never touched them. I never did. I never hurt them in any way. Oh please, I never did anything wrong in my life. I've always tried to be a good mother."

The judge responded, "Ms. Smith, the jury has found you guilty."

"But I didn't do it."

The judge had not intended to spar with the defendant, but she needed to inject some reality into their exchange. "There is little or no way that this codefendant could have had access to these children—"

Before the judge could say "without your help," Smith interrupted her with what was becoming a familiar mantra. "I didn't even know him, Judge. I swear on my life, I don't know this man. I have never seen this man. That is all I can tell you."

When Smith did not continue, the judge realized that she had nothing more to add. With the preliminaries out of the way, the judge cleared her throat before announcing the sentences. She looked at the defendant and said, "On count one, it will be the judgment of the law and the sentence of this Court that this defendant will serve a term of two years at the Ohio Reformatory for Women at Marysville.

"On count two, this defendant will serve a term of not less than five nor more than fifteen years." For the four remaining crimes, the judge also set minimum and maximum prison terms. When she'd finished, the total sentences amounted to a minimum of thirty years in prison and a maximum of ninety years.

Bradley helped his unsteady client return to her seat while Joseph Allen and his attorney, Joseph Grunda, rose to stand before the judge. Unlike Bradley, Grunda had realized that a jury could convict his client. The man had three strikes against him: he was a convicted child molester, he was black, and he hadn't testified in his own defense.

Grunda began, "My client has always maintained that he did not know Nancy Smith or any of these children. The first and only time he saw Nancy Smith or any of the children was in this courtroom. I understand that the jury found both of them guilty. Without a doubt, he knows none of these people. After all of our conferences together, I believe him. Based on that, I would ask the Court to impose minimum sentences for my client."

The judge looked at Rosenbaum, who was shaking his head. "Mr. Rosenbaum, do you wish to be heard on this?"

The prosecutor rose quickly and took a deep breath. "Your Honor, unfortunately, this is the second time that I've stood in a courtroom at the sentencing for this convicted jackal. He deserves the maximum sentences. He needs to be placed away so that he can never harm another child again."

The judge liked the prosecutor's brevity. "Mr. Rosenbaum, do any of the victims wish to be heard at this time?"

"It is my understanding that they do not, Your Honor."

"All right then," the judge said, and then shifted her gaze to Joseph Allen. "Mr. Allen, this is your chance to speak if it is not against the advice of your attorney. Do you want to be heard?" Allen nodded and said, "I'm standing here accused of crimes that I didn't commit, nor do I know the victims." He spoke slowly and calmly in a slow Southern drawl. "I wasn't present when these crimes occurred. I know I might have had a record, but I've cleaned up my life."

The judge knew that Joseph Allen had first come onto the radar of police investigating this case after he'd allegedly propositioned four runaway girls, ages thirteen through fifteen. She briefly considered confronting him with this bald contradiction but decided not to interrupt him.

"If I'd committed these crimes, I wouldn't have put this Court through a trial. I would have done pled to the charges. I have a daughter myself. I have a son myself. I have a grandson myself. I haven't abused them, and I never abused no one's kids. I never tied no one up."

Judge McGough sat impassively as Allen rambled on. He was conveniently ignoring that for three years he'd sexually abused a neighbor girl beginning when she was six years old. He'd pled guilty to that. Did he think she'd forgotten about his previous conviction?

He next launched into a recitation of his living arrangements at the time that the crimes allegedly occurred. The prosecution had claimed that he'd abused the children at least four times between January and early May 1993.

"I lived with my family until the middle of March of 1993. I didn't move into my apartment until after that. Now, how am I supposed to have done these horrible things from January to June when I wasn't even living there for most of that time?"

The judge raised her eyebrows before she cut him off. "Mr. Allen, your trial is over."

"Yes, I know."

The judge took a deep breath and launched into her sentencing. "The jury has found you guilty of a forcible rape of children as young as four years of age." She did not raise her voice, but disgust was evident from her tone and piercing stare. The jury had done its job and now she would do hers. When she'd completed her sentencing, she'd imposed five life sentences that were to be served one after the other—if such a thing were possible.

After advising both defendants of their right to appeal, the judge struck her gavel. "We are finished here today."

But as later events would reveal, this case was far from finished. It would surface and resurface for the next three decades, stoking controversy every time it did.

CHAPTER 2
DETECTIVE TOM CANTU
MAY 8, 1993

For the last half hour, Detective Tom Cantu had been trying to pry details from a reluctant and sometimes indifferent four-year-old victim. This came as no surprise. He'd read the report filed by the patrolman who'd interviewed the little girl and her family at the emergency room the night before. The victim had repeatedly claimed that she did not remember most of what had happened, forcing the officer to rely on the girl's mother and the emergency room nurse to provide the details.

A twenty-three-year veteran of the Lorain Police Department, Cantu was a detective in the Youth and Gangs Division, where he often investigated sexual molestation crimes against minors. A former marine, he'd returned home to a boring desk job at the steel mill. He'd craved more stimulating work as well as something that would allow him to help people. When he'd learned that the city was offering examinations for both new police officers and firefighters, he couldn't make up his mind which test to take. He'd flipped a coin and the rest was history.

Cantu prided himself on doing careful, methodical work and following police protocols. Over the years, that approach had worked, allowing him to solve countless cases and bring hundreds of criminals to justice. His dedication had not gone unnoticed. For the last two years, he'd been rated exceptional in his performance reviews.

It was only natural that he'd been assigned this investigation. In several well-publicized cases, he'd investigated and obtained convictions against teachers who had molested students under their charge. Although this new assignment did not involve a teacher, it did focus upon a school bus driver who had allegedly molested young children under her care. If a crime had been committed, he was determined to build a strong case that would result in a conviction and prison time for the offenders.

Earlier in the day, he'd read the patrolman's initial report and had been horrified by what it described. A child had been molested in someone's house instead of being delivered to the Head Start school. How could anyone do this to helpless, vulnerable children? Ten years ago, he'd have thought this almost impossible, but, today, similar crimes had been uncovered in day care centers across the country at an alarming rate. Masquerading as dedicated child-care workers, sexual deviants had somehow wormed their way into these places, abusing the very children they'd been entrusted with protecting. No part of the country had been immune to this cancer, and now it had allegedly happened in the city where he worked and was raising his family.

Cantu returned his attention to the victim, Nina Zorich. The shy four-year-old was a beautiful child with long, light brown hair and delicate features. She and her mother appeared to be Hispanic, but he wasn't sure. The little girl clutched the teddy bear that Cantu had given to her, talking to it in a hushed tone.

"So, Nina, tell me about this man, Joseph," Cantu prodded.

"I don't want to talk anymore. I want to play."

"Well, we've got to talk about this. Tell me how Joseph hurt you."

"I don't remember." Nina looked away from Cantu and directed her gaze at the teddy bear. Addressing it, she said, "Do you want to have a cookie?"

"Come on, Nina, tell him what you told me yesterday and what you said to the nurse at the hospital," her mother, Marge Bronson, interjected.

"I don't remember," Nina replied.

He'd tried to build a rapport with this child, but she didn't trust him and this interview was going nowhere. Cantu looked at the girl's mother, his eyes communicating concern. Like her daughter, the mother was very pretty. Her wavy dark hair was carefully coiffed, piled high on top of her head with bangs that extended beyond her eyebrows—like a country western star. Her dark brown eyes were her most arresting feature. Today, they shone with both intelligence and agitation.

Before Cantu could ask another question, her mother said, "Let me explain why she doesn't want to talk."

"Sure."

"This morning Nina told me that Joseph threatened to burn our house down if she told anyone what he did to her. He said he'd kill all the police, the doctors, her mommy and daddy."

Cantu squatted and looked directly into Nina's eyes before he spoke. "First of all, Joseph isn't going to hurt anybody or burn your house down. Okay? What Joseph did to you was very bad and you didn't do anything wrong. We're gonna make sure Joseph doesn't hurt or touch anybody again." Cantu stood and then sat down once more in a nearby chair. He turned his gaze to the mother. "What does she say happened?"

The mother did not answer immediately. She shook her head and glanced away from him. When she returned her gaze to him, he saw distress and anger. Cantu knew that look; he'd seen it often enough. Something terrible had happened, not just to her daughter, but to her as well. As a detective, he knew that her healing would not begin until the people who'd done the unthinkable had been caught and punished.

When the mother began to speak, she was edgy but relatively composed. "About a month ago, maybe longer, she didn't want to go to school. Even my neighbor noticed it. My neighbor says to me, 'God, I noticed Nina was so happy and then as soon as that bus pulled up, she went hysterical.'

"I didn't know what was wrong with her. One day, boom, the bus pulls up and I can't hold her. She wants to run away. That's when the bus driver, Nancy, asks, 'Is there something wrong? Does she think someone is doing something to her?'"

"The bus driver said that?" Cantu asked.

"Yeah. And I was, like, surprised. Why would she say something like that? It was weird, right? And I say, 'She was perfectly normal all this morning, but as soon as she saw you, she got all upset.'"

Cantu nodded, encouraging the mother to continue.

"This week, okay, she didn't have school on Monday so nothing happened then. She didn't want to go on Tuesday, so I let her stay home. She went on Wednesday. On Thursday, she threw another fit, but I was volunteering at the school that day, so when I got there, I asked the teacher if Nina was having any problems. The teacher said, 'Nina acts normal in class.' I told her that Nina didn't want to get on the bus today. The teacher acted real surprised, you know.

"Again, my neighbor saw it all. She says to me, 'You guys were out picking dandelions and when Nina seen that bus driver, she went crazy. What is wrong?' I tell her that I talked to Nina's teacher and she says there's no problem at school."

The mother took a deep breath before continuing. "Then on Friday, yesterday, she gets off the bus. I always give my kids a big hug and a kiss right when they get home. I'll ask them about school, but on Friday, Nina didn't want to talk about school. She just wanted to finish a movie, a Barney tape. So when it's over she says, 'You know, Mommy, since school was closed, we just went to Nancy's house again.' I knew immediately that something was wrong, but I had to play it, you know, play it cool."

"Is Nancy the bus driver?" Cantu asked.

"Yes."

"And how old would you say she is?"

"She has to be fortysomething 'cause she has two older kids."

"What about Joseph?"

"I don't even know. I know she has a boyfriend named Joseph."

"Who, Nancy?"

"Yeah, Nancy, 'cause she told me."

"Is Joseph a white guy?"

"He's black and Nina says he's on the bus sometimes."

Cantu glanced at Nina, who was no longer playing with the teddy bear. Instead, she was watching her mother, her expression calm and indecipherable.

"So I decide to keep things normal and go shopping with her and see if I can get the story out of her. While we're driving down Oberlin Avenue, she says, 'Yeah, we go over there sometimes before the school opens.' You see, she gets picked up at twelve thirty and school doesn't start until one thirty. They can sit on the bus for a half an hour. They've got all this time. You know what I'm trying to say?"

Cantu nodded.

"After school is over, she gets home in fifteen minutes. So I know that on the way to school, there's at least a half hour where the bus driver isn't picking up kids. You follow me?"

"Yeah."

"Nina says, 'We just always go over to Nancy's house and we play dolls and other games.' And I say, 'Oh, you do, and where do you go?' She tells me that they go in the basement. And I ask, 'Do you play the one game called doctors?' She says, 'Yes.' I go, 'Really?' At this point, I'm shaking. I'm flushed. I go, 'How do you play that game? I forgot because I haven't played that game for such a long time. Can you tell me how you play it?' She says, 'Well, all of us kids, we take off our clothes and then Joseph plays with us.' With this, I'm having a heart attack, you know."

Cantu nodded and then grimaced.

The mother looked at her daughter. "She just turned four. She can't make up a story like this."

"No," Cantu said, his voice soft.

"Right?" the mother asked, some agitation in her voice.

"No, that's exactly right."

"Then Nina says, 'You know what is really gross? His peepee.' I go, 'You seen his peepee?' She says, 'No, it was wrapped, but you know that little hole in the peepee, he put it in my mouth and he peed on me. But it tasted nasty and I spit it out and he squirted it on my face and then he put it on my panties and Nancy got really mad. But you know what, Mommy? It cleans up really fast. The other kids, they drink it, but I think it's really nasty.'

"By now, I'm having a real heart attack. But I think, let me take her to Hill's and see if she changes her story. I had a few things to buy there. At Hill's, she says that she can tell me more stories but she doesn't want anybody in the store to hear about them. Now I'm barely holding it together. So, then we go to Kmart, where I buy her some shoes and she tells me more."

"Mommy got me sandals too," Nina interjected for the first time. The little girl's right index finger touched her lips as if she were trying to remember something.

"Did he touch her vagina?" Cantu asked, looking at the mother.

"Yeah."

"With his penis?"

"Right. And she said she was crying today because he held her mouth and smacked her legs and stuck a branch inside of her."

"He stuck a branch?"

"Yeah. At this point, I just had to get her home. When we got in the door, I said, 'Mommy just wants to check you.' I took off her white T-shirt and I found something. I go, 'God, what's this?' And she says, 'That's a piece of the branch that Joseph left on me.' I put it away. I spread her legs and she goes, 'Yeah, he kisses me down there and he smacked me today 'cause he put the branch on my privates.'"

Cantu turned away from the mother. In unflinching words, she'd told him what had happened, and he needed a moment to regain his footing—like a man who'd been struck and staggered by a huge wave.

"What did this branch look like?" he finally asked.

"It's like a little piece of green leaf."

"Was anybody else around when this happened?"

"She says that there are other kids at the house. Sometimes they go upstairs into Nancy's bedroom, but sometimes she stays by herself with Joseph."

"Did she ever see him do this to anyone else?"

"I don't know. Ask her."

Using a quiet voice, Cantu directed his next question to Nina. "Did Nancy ever do anything to you?"

"She hits me," Nina replied.

"Why does she hit you?"

"Because I be bad."

"What?" Cantu asked.

"'Be bad.' She's saying because she's been bad," her mother explained.

"Where does she hit you?"

"On my legs and feet," the girl answered. Pointing to the microwave in the room, Nina said, "You've got TV here. Maybe."

"It's a microwave that the policemen use to heat up their food," her mother replied.

"You eat lunch?" Nina asked.

The girl was finally talking and Cantu wanted to capitalize on this. "Did Nancy ever touch you bad? Besides hitting you, did she do anything else to you, honey?"

"Um, she put a watch on me, a dirty watch," Nina answered.

Ignoring her response, Cantu asked, "What about Joseph? What did he do to you?"

"He put a book on my head," she replied, her voice small and barely audible.

Nina's mother intervened. "Okay, he put a book on your head. Tell him what he did. Tell him what you told Mommy and the nurses and Grandma."

Needing to control his own interview, Cantu jumped in. "Did he play games with you like doctor?" he suggested.

Before Nina could answer, her mother said, "When we were at the emergency room, Nina said, 'These are the good doctors, right? They're not going to hurt me like Joseph does when we play doctor?' I go, 'Oh, my God.'"

"Did Joseph ever give you milk and cookies and stuff like that?" Cantu asked.

"Uh-huh."

"When Joseph took you down into the basement, what did he do to you?"

"Hit me."

"What else did he do? What did you tell the doctors and nurses? You need to tell me so I can help you."

"Can I take this bear home with me?"

"Sure."

"Can I have something to drink?"

"Yeah, I will get you some pop if you want some."

"Pop? Popcorn?"

"I don't have any popcorn. Can you tell me about the bad things they did to you?"

"Can you take my picture?"

"Not right now. I'll do that later before you go. Why don't you tell me the bad things Joseph did to you."

"Tell him," her mother urged.

"I want another pop. I know something else."

"Tell me what else happened," Cantu said.

"He hit me with a branch and a stick right here," Nina said, pointing to her groin.

Cantu believed that he was finally making progress. If he kept his questions focused, Nina would answer them. He pulled out a diagram of a girl and asked her to circle the areas where Joseph had touched her. She circled around her genitalia and belly and explained that he touched her with his hand. Just when Cantu was ready to move on, the little girl said, "He touched my feet too."

Nina's mother had described Joseph's urinating on her daughter, and he wanted Nina to confirm this. Instead, Nina claimed that Joseph had urinated into a cup and asked her to drink it. She had taken a sip and then spit it out.

Cantu decided to make his next question narrow and direct. "Did Joseph ever pee on your face?"

Nina pointed to the side of her face. "He peed right here on my face."

Following the mother's outline, Cantu wanted to establish that Nancy and Joseph had argued after this had happened. "Why did Nancy and Joseph yell at each other?"

"Because he was bad and he kissed Chantel," Nina answered.

Cantu and the mother exchanged confused glances.

"That's what she keeps saying. Nancy yelled at him and she took a knife and said she was going to kill him for something he'd said. I have no idea who Chantel is," her mother explained.

"She took a gun and a knife," Nina volunteered.

"Tell him who dressed you after you played doctor with Joseph," her mother said.

"Nancy," Nina answered.

"Well, she told me sometimes it was Nancy and sometimes it was Nancy's son," her mother added.

"Can we go now?" Nina asked.

Cantu needed more information and he wanted to keep pressing forward while he still had the child's cooperation. "Just a few more questions, honey. Okay?"

The child didn't respond and Cantu took that as her consent. Over the next ten minutes, Nina confirmed that Joseph had kissed her on her "toota," rubbed his hands all over her body, and poked her in her buttocks. She told him that Nancy brought other children to the house: Alecia, Peter, and Marcus. Joseph had undressed and touched them all. When they were through, Nina now claimed that it was Nancy's son who had dressed them.

"Are they going to be arrested for this?" her mother asked.

"I'll find out who this bus driver is, identify her boyfriend, and try to get some statements from them. They're both facing felonies for this."

Cantu suddenly remembered another line of inquiry. Even if the child no longer wanted to answer questions, the mother could. "Before you go, fill me in on what the emergency doctor found in his physical exam."

"He couldn't see that anything was torn, but they found other things. I can't explain it, but they had findings. Both him and the nurse said that they would do a report and testify."

"Where did you take her?"

"Lorain Community Hospital."

"I don't want to bad-mouth the local hospitals, but if you want a thorough examination, take her to Rainbow Baby and Children's Hospital in Cleveland. I had a molestation case where they found nothing at the local hospital but discovered things when they did a more complete exam there. If the victim hadn't been seen there, we'd have had nothing. Okay? Will you do that?"

"Sure."

Cantu watched as the mother and daughter left the police conference room. One of the mother's statements continued to echo in his brain: Nina couldn't make up a story like this. He agreed. Four-year-old children normally did not lie. In this case, the explicit facts were well beyond the knowledge of a four-year-old child. Yes, children that young could get details wrong, but he was convinced that something horrible had happened to her.

As for the mother, he wasn't sure that he liked her. Something in her manner concerned him, but he couldn't identify what it was. However, whether he liked her was irrelevant. His mission was to protect children. This little girl had been molested, and he was determined to arrest the perpetrators and put them away.

CHAPTER 3
MAYOR ALEX OLEJKO

MAY 24, 1993

Mayor Alex Olejko was stunned by what he'd just learned from the distraught Hispanic woman sitting across from him. The seventy-one-year-old mayor had listened in disgust as Marge Bronson recounted how her young daughter, Nina, had been molested by a Head Start bus driver and a man named Joseph. Until Bronson and the child's grandmother had arrived that afternoon, he'd known nothing about this incident. The pair were incensed that no arrests had been made and they wanted justice now. Olejko understood her outrage.

Olejko, a retired steelworker, had spent a lifetime in politics—mainly as a member of the city council, but he had become mayor in 1984, when the previous mayor had died suddenly in a car crash and, as the president of the city council, he was next in line. He'd quickly adapted to the position, demonstrating both leadership and flair. Always a gregarious, outgoing man, he had bold dreams for his city, and his enthusiasm was contagious.

He could not believe that such a thing could happen to a young Hispanic child on his watch. He had a special relationship with Lorain's Puerto Rican community; he'd appointed many to positions of leadership in his administration. Olejko, the son of Polish immigrants, had become famous for his saying "There are only three places to be: heaven, Puerto Rico, or Lorain." And now, something horrible had happened in his beloved hometown.

"I know you're upset. I am too, but we need to get some answers from the detective in charge. I'm going to call Detective Cantu and get him up here. Okay?" Olejko picked up the receiver with his right hand, revealing the gnarled fingers that had been broken decades ago when he'd been a promising minor league catcher.

Bronson shook her head in disapproval. "He doesn't return my phone calls anymore. If you ask me, he doesn't know what he's doing."

For the first time, Bronson's mother, Margaret Ortiz, spoke. "Thank you, Mayor. I think that's a good idea."

A few minutes later, Detective Cantu arrived with a file folder in his right hand. After shaking hands with the mayor and nodding toward Bronson and Ortiz, he spied the chair farthest from the women and sat down. Cantu looked out the large glass windows toward the Black River and Lake Erie before fixing his eyes on the mayor.

Olejko decided to forgo any pleasantries with Cantu and get right to the point. "Tom," the mayor began, clearing his throat, "I've listened to Mrs. Bronson tell me about her daughter and the awful things that happened to her. She's obviously concerned that you haven't arrested the bus driver or anyone else. What's going on?"

Before Cantu could answer, Bronson blurted, "He hasn't arrested her because he knows her. I've been told they're friends." She drew out the word "friends" for emphasis.

Raising his hands in a peacemaking gesture, Olejko said, "Let's let Detective Cantu tell his side."

"First of all, let's set the record straight. I'm not friends with the bus driver," Cantu said, irritation creeping into his voice. "When I'm off duty, I sometimes work security at a local bingo game and I've seen Nancy Smith and her mother there. I've said hi to them a couple of times. That's it."

The mayor nodded at Cantu and glanced at the women. "Okay. Thanks for clarifying that, Tom. What about your investigation? Are you close to making any arrests?"

"Mayor, I need some solid evidence. I can't put cuffs on somebody just because Mrs. Bronson made these accusations. I've explained that to her. I need more."

"What about the emergency room report? The doctor told me he found signs of abuse—no penetration, but other signs," Bronson argued.

"That's not what's in the hospital record," Cantu replied, shaking his head to stress his point. "The ER doc didn't find any signs of trauma. That's why I told Mrs. Bronson to take her daughter into Cleveland for better testing. She did that and we're waiting for those reports."

"Wait a minute," Bronson said. "I took Nina there almost two weeks ago. I don't understand why you don't have those records yet. Even so, that doctor found things—you should get off your butt and talk to her." Bronson glared at Cantu and then looked to the mayor for support.

"I've got a call out to her, but we haven't connected yet," Cantu said, his voice and manner not convincing.

Despite his skepticism about the phone call, the mayor decided to press the detective about other areas of his investigation. "What have you discovered about the bus driver?"

Cantu told the mayor that he'd identified the bus driver as thirty-six-year-old Nancy Smith, a divorced mother with four teenagers. He explained that she had no criminal record and had an impressive work ethic, rarely missing work and holding down three jobs. When he'd confronted her about the allegations, she'd been shocked and vigorously denied any wrongdoing.

"That doesn't surprise me," Olejko countered. "They all say that."

"I know. That's why I'm trying to discover as much as I can about her," Cantu said, his tone defensive. "She says she doesn't date black men and doesn't have a boyfriend named Joseph. I've talked to people who know her, and so far, that checks out—but I'm still digging. She wouldn't be the first person to have a secret life."

"You've got to do more than just talk to her friends," Bronson said, not hiding her irritation.

Ignoring her interruption, Cantu continued, "That's not all. I checked her records at Head Start. She's on time with the kids, her mileage is always the same, an aide or parent rides the bus with her every day, the teachers take the kids off the bus, and this woman goes directly from the school to another job. Nothing suspicious there. I've also canvassed the neighborhoods around her home and the school. Nobody has seen a big yellow school bus parked on their street."

"You can't rely on the Head Start records. They're just covering their asses," Bronson said. "The buses don't always have aides on them. If they're telling you they do, then they're lying." Her voice remained loud and angry.

Cantu again disregarded her claim. "I'm going to the school tomorrow afternoon to talk to the kids who ride Mrs. Smith's bus. Mayor, I'm not leaving any stone unturned."

"You better talk to Marcus Logan and Melissa Warner. Nina says they were with her at that house and—"

Cantu interrupted, "That's another thing, Mayor. Her daughter tells a different story every time I talk to her. We're dealing with a little kid so I kind of expect that, but there are times when she denies anything ever happened to her. Other times, she says she can't remember any of the details."

"That's because Joseph threatened to kill her," Bronson said. "I told you that when we first met." Turning her attention to the mayor, she said, "You need to put somebody else in charge of this case."

"Tom's a good detective," Olejko said. "What else?"

"Mrs. Bronson's daughter says this happened at Nancy's house, which is frankly impossible seeing that Nancy and her kids live with her parents. Nancy's father is retired on disability and he and his wife rarely leave their house."

"See, he's on a first-name basis with this bitch," Bronson exclaimed. "They're buddy-buddy."

Bronson's words caused Cantu to flinch. "I don't like your attitude, Mrs. Bronson."

"I don't care what you like. Until you start doing your job, I'm going to call you out whenever I want to."

"Okay. Let's not allow this to get out of hand," the mayor said, knowing that it already had. "Now, Mrs. Bronson, I think Detective Cantu is working the case. You just have to give him more time."

"He doesn't believe us. That's the problem. He doesn't think anything happened. So, of course, he's not going to find anything—I don't care how much time you give him," Bronson said.

Cantu threw up his arms in exasperation. "Mayor, I'm going downstairs to see if Captain Rivera is around. Maybe she'll listen to him." His face flushed, Cantu rose from his chair and left.

The room was suddenly silent. For one of the few times in his life, the mayor couldn't think of anything to say. He opened a desk drawer as if searching for something and then looked up. Bronson and her mother were staring at him, their unhappy faces reflecting both anger and distrust.

"We'll sort this out. We will find out who did this and make arrests soon," the mayor finally said, brushing his hand through his slicked-back hair.

The women did not reply.

"If you'll excuse me for a moment, I need to talk to the safety director and I'll be right back." Standing abruptly, Olejko felt his lower-leg prosthesis dig into his stump, and pain shot up his spine. Trying not to limp, he walked past them and into the hallway, where he waited for the two detectives.

When the two policemen emerged from the elevator, the trio entered his office. This time, Captain Cel Rivera would try to appease Bronson. Rivera had been on the force for twenty-two years and had steadily climbed the ranks, eventually becoming the commander of the criminal investigation bureau which included overseeing all of the plainclothes detectives. When dealing with victims, he also evinced an empathy that was born from his own difficult childhood bouncing between an orphanage and foster homes.

Rivera began, "We understand your impatience, Mrs. Bronson. We are searching for answers. At this time, we don't know who this Joseph is and we don't know where this crime took place. We're working on it. Believe me, we're working on it. You just have to give us more time to do our jobs."

Bronson looked at her mother and rolled her eyes. "Okay, you do your investigation, but I'm going to find out what I can. I'll talk to those kids myself if I have to. I'm not going to sit around while these monsters are still out there."

Rivera took a deep breath before he responded. "I know how upset you must be. I would be too, but you can't do that. You'll jeopardize our investigation if you talk to these little kids or their parents. We can't have you feeding them any information. If you do, it will make their stories unreliable. Do you understand that?"

Mrs. Bronson nodded. "Okay, but you better get some answers and get them fast."

CHAPTER 4
FURTHER INVESTIGATION
JUNE 2, 1993

For the last ten days, Detective Cantu had been struggling to keep his probe from spiraling out of control. Despite her promise to stay out of his investigation, Marge Bronson had not. She'd meddled by reaching out to other parents and telling them that their children could be victims too. Then she and her fiancé had contacted the media, spilling sensational details that were aired on a local television station and published by a local newspaper. Despite this, Cantu hoped that he'd soon be able to draw some conclusions from this unwieldy jumble of accusations and denials. Soon he'd pick up Nancy Smith and drive her to the Bureau of Criminal Investigation in Richfield, Ohio, where she'd take a polygraph exam. Anxious to clear her name once and for all, Smith had agreed to the test.

Every time Cantu thought he had a handle on the Head Start case, something would unravel. The day after the tense conference with the mayor and Marge Bronson, he'd visited the Head Start school and met with all of the preschool children who rode on Nancy Smith's bus. Accompanied by a Head Start administrator, he'd questioned them as a group. All eleven children denied that Nancy had ever "touched them in a bad way," and none of them knew anything about a man named Joseph. Instead, they all said that they liked Nancy and thought she was "nice."

However, on the very day that Cantu had talked to these children, Marge Bronson had contacted the parents of Marcus Logan and Melissa Warner, two of the eleven children he'd questioned just hours earlier. With each parent, she'd divulged details of Nina's molestation and told them that, according to Nina, their children had been abused too. The concerned parents quizzed their children and later took them to the local hospital to be checked for signs of abuse.

Melissa's mother, Deborah Hanko, had contacted the Lorain police from Lorain Community Hospital that night, and, just before midnight, Patrolman Puza had met them there and gathered the initial information. Melissa and her mom told the uniformed officer that, on several occasions, Nancy Smith had driven Melissa by bus to a house where she'd been led to the basement with the other children. There, Joseph had urinated on her feet and had asked her to touch his penis. A fully clothed Nancy Smith had also forced her to touch her breasts. They'd played doctor and other games. To ensure Melissa's silence, Joseph had brandished a knife and threatened to hurt her if she ever told anyone.

Cantu's mind drifted back to his meeting with Melissa and her mother four days earlier. Deborah Hanko had expressed disappointment that it had taken Cantu several days to meet with them. However, once the interview began, the twenty-eight-year-old woman was pleasant throughout. She and her daughter were both pretty, sharing pensive brown eyes, brown hair, and a pale complexion. While the mother's hair was shoulder-length, Melissa's was cut short, almost like a boy's, with bangs that fell below her eyebrows.

Cantu first asked the girl to give him a more detailed description of the house. After he turned on his tape recorder, she provided details about its interior. Determined to exhaust her memory about the home, he asked, "What else do you remember about the inside of the house?"

"There were pictures of Nancy and Joseph together in the living room," she said.

"Okay, that's good. What else?"

"The basement walls were white and there were two beds down there," Melissa said. She paused and then tilted her head as if in thought. "They were hiding long guns in the basement. I think they were hiding them from the police."

Cantu ignored the girl's last statement. It made little sense. Instead, he asked, "What does Joseph look like, honey?"

"He's a black man."

Her mother interrupted, "I don't know if I should say this, but when I first talked to her, she said he was white. Now she says he's black."

Cantu nodded but did not repeat the question. Instead, he asked, "Young or old?"

"He's young."

"Anything else? Is he a nice-looking guy? Does he have a mustache or anything?"

"He got a mustache right here," Melissa said, pointing to a spot above her lip.

"What happened to you down in the basement?"

"They do nasty stuff."

"Uh-huh, tell me what they do to you."

"Nancy sticks a knife right here," the girl said, this time pointing to her neck.

"Did Joseph do anything to you?"

"Joseph didn't do anything to me. Only Nancy did that one thing," the girl said.

Cantu exchanged a confused glance with her mother. He had expected Melissa to tell him the same things that he'd read in Puza's report.

As if to get the investigation back on track, the mother said, "She told me that Joseph peed on her feet and that Nancy forced her to touch her chest."

"What about Joseph forcing her to touch his penis?" Cantu asked.

"Oh God, did he ask her to do that?" her mom exclaimed. "I thought it was just Nancy's chest."

Cantu was bewildered by the mother's reaction. This allegation was in Puza's report; the mother could not have forgotten that sordid detail. Trying to reconcile the two, Cantu concluded that Puza had misunderstood them at the hospital.

Thinking that he may have assumed too much from the earlier report, Cantu decided to confirm some basic points.

"Were there any other kids with you at Joseph's house?"

"My friends Alda, Alia, and Brian."

Cantu tried to act unsurprised at these new names. "How about Marcus? Was he ever there?"

Melissa nodded and smiled as if embarrassed by her omission. "Yeah, he's been there."

"How about Nina?"

"Yeah, her too."

"Melissa, how did you get to Joseph's house?"

"The other bus driver takes us," she replied.

"Who? Nancy?"

"No, Angel."

Cantu was even more confused. This was a new development.

Her mother tried to explain. "Angel takes her to school now."

"Okay," Cantu said, nodding and understanding the child's mix-up. "And how did you get to Joseph's house, honey?"

"School bus."

"All right. Now, who drove the school bus to Joseph's house?"

"Angel."

Both Cantu and her mother shook their heads. Melissa was mistaken and they would just leave it at that.

Signaling that the interview was coming to an end, Cantu reached to turn off his tape recorder. Before he could do so, the mother said, "Yesterday morning, we drove the streets by her school. Melissa pointed out Joseph's house to me."

Cantu's eyes lit up; this was the break he needed. The mother and daughter agreed to show him the house immediately. A few minutes later, they piled into his Crown Victoria, and as they approached the school, the mother told Cantu to turn onto Oakdale Avenue. When he did, Melissa pointed to a house.

"It's not that color, remember?" her mother said. Melissa then pointed to a peach-colored house at 1763 Oakdale Avenue and said that was where Joseph lived. Although he wanted to knock on the door right then and there, Cantu first took the two back to the station before heading out again to talk with the home's occupants.

Back at the station, he did some research and discovered that the house was owned by a forty-seven-year-old white male named Charles Ellis. Armed with that information, Cantu returned to the house and rang the front doorbell. Ellis opened the door, and after Cantu provided the owner with the reason for his visit, the owner welcomed him inside, apparently eager to clear his name. Cantu realized very quickly that the house's floor plan did not match Melissa's description, and after talking further with Ellis, he concluded that this house was not Joseph's.

Cantu's mind next cycled to his meeting with Marcus Logan and his father, Franklin. During that encounter, Cantu quickly learned that Marge Bronson had also reached out to the Logan family, warning them that Marcus had been at the house where Bronson's daughter had been sexually abused. When questioned by his father, Marcus had initially denied knowing Joseph or being harmed by him. However, sensing fear in his son's eyes, Franklin Logan had pressed the boy, interrogating him for more than two hours. The boy had eventually broken and admitted to the abuse. When Cantu met with Franklin Logan, the man was teeming with rage and anxiety.

After his father's relentless questioning, Marcus eventually told him that Nancy the bus driver had been secreting him away from his Head Start classroom for two years. Wearing a mask, she periodically came into his class and took three of them at a time to be with Joseph, whom he described as a black man with blue eyes and white spots on his body.

Once in Joseph's basement, they would play a game called "bad boys" and touch each other's private parts. Afterward, Marcus would be given milk, cookies, and candy. After Nancy walked the three children back to school, she would grab another three and take them to Joseph's. Marcus expanded the group of victims to include Head Start students named David, Brian, and Aleah.

Like Melissa, Marcus also claimed that he could point out Joseph's house. Hopeful that the youngster could identify the house, Cantu drove Marcus and his father to the school, where Marcus pointed out a different house, one on Fifteenth Street, almost directly across from the school. Later, after Cantu returned to that house, he again concluded that it was not Joseph's home. The owner was white and the floor plan did not match what Marcus had described. Cantu also canvassed the neighbors, none of whom had seen a school bus or children entering the house.

Although he didn't believe Marcus's claim that Nancy could take children out of the classroom, he checked with Head Start administrators to find out if this was possible. Salina Rush, the director, was adamant that a bus driver would never be allowed to do that—only parents or guardians were allowed.

Two days after Cantu's interviews with Marcus and Melissa, Marge Bronson and her fiancé contacted a local television station. That evening the local news broadcast began with an investigative report about the Head Start allegations. Although Cantu had not watched it, he'd heard that the news anchor had begun the broadcast in a sensational manner, claiming that small children in the Lorain Head Start program "were being stuck with pins and forced to drink urine." Marge Bronson, her face smudged to conceal her identity, had claimed that her daughter and others had been picked up by a Head Start school bus but had not been delivered to the school. Instead, they'd been taken to a house where they'd been sexually molested.

The broadcast switched to a clip of an investigative reporter walking up porch steps and knocking on a front door. When the door opened, the startled owner, Charles Ellis, listened as the reporter asked him about abusing small children in his home. The pesky reporter wedged a microphone between the door and its frame before it closed, providing listeners with the man's vehement denials. Nina Zorich, who had listened to the broadcast, told her mother that the white man's voice was that of Joseph. The little girl then insisted that Joseph was white and wore dark makeup to appear black.

Although he thought it impossible for things to get worse after the television news report, they did. Not to be outdone, the *Morning Journal*, Lorain's morning newspaper, ran an article about the allegations of child abuse engulfing the Head Start program. One unidentified parent, whom Cantu immediately recognized as Marge Bronson, was quoted as saying, "It was like someone put a knife in me. They did some pretty nasty things to these kids."

After that, he was deluged with calls from other parents of Head Start preschoolers. Cantu received reports from fifteen parents who believed that their children had also been molested. Not surprising, ten of the children did not ride on Nancy Smith's bus. In fact, one child had left the Head Start program before Nancy had been hired as a bus driver for the program.

It had been time-consuming to sort through the many claims, but he'd reviewed each story carefully and objectively. The children had accused a variety of people, not always Nancy and an unidentified male named Joseph. However, the common denominator was their claim that they'd been abused in some way while participating in the Lorain Head Start program. Their stories were as different as they were bizarre. Were the children's claims credible? Did these horrible things really happen? He was ready to reach a conclusion on those questions.

When Cantu arrived at Nancy Smith's home on Fourteenth Street, she opened the front door as soon as he pulled into the driveway. He got out and opened the front passenger door for her. She was wearing a light jacket on this brisk spring day, and after she fastened her seat belt, she rubbed her hands together as if to warm them.

"You nervous?" Cantu asked.

Smith looked at him as if unsure how to answer. "My friends say I'm crazy to do this without a lawyer. They've all heard stories about how the lie detector test can get it wrong. So, yeah, I'm a little nervous. But it's just because the test isn't foolproof."

Cantu knew that if Smith had retained a lawyer, her lawyer would have arranged for a confidential "preliminary" polygraph exam to find out if she could pass it before agreeing to one orchestrated by the police. If she had passed the privately arranged test, her attorney would have required the police to sign a stipulation that this test could be admitted into evidence in any criminal trial. The law was clear: a polygraph test was not deemed reliable enough to be considered by a jury unless the parties agreed to that in advance.

Cantu understood that a polygraph examination could result in a false positive simply because a person was extremely nervous about the test itself or about the accusations. Nevertheless, he believed that the test was accurate most of the time.

"Let me explain how the test works. The polygraph measures your vitals: your pulse, breathing, and galvanic skin response," Cantu explained.

"What's that last thing?" Smith asked.

"Your skin can momentarily become a better conductor of electricity when you get upset by a question. The machine can measure that," he said.

"Okay."

"The examiner will ask you some baseline questions, like your age, your job, and other things that should not upset you. He'll then ask you some questions about the children's allegations and see if your vital signs change when you answer them. If they do, it's an indication that you're not telling the truth. It's pretty straightforward."

That was all he wanted to say about the test. Although he was tempted to ask her more questions about the children's claims, he knew that would be a mistake. If she got comfortable talking to him about them, she might be more relaxed when she answered similar questions during the polygraph examination. Instead, he turned on the radio and they traveled in silence, listening to the music and, occasionally, venturing into awkward small talk.

Once they arrived at the bureau, he introduced Nancy Smith to the polygrapher, Jim Krakora, and waited outside the examination room until it was completed. After Krakora walked her out of the exam room and into the waiting area, Cantu entered the exam room with him and they closed the door.

"Well, what do you think?" Cantu asked.

"You want the bottom line, Tom?"

"Yeah, of course I do."

"She didn't do this any more than you or I did. She passed. I asked her a number of questions about sexually molesting children or helping someone else to do that and she denied it. According to the polygraph, there was nothing deceptive in her answers."

"Okay. That's what I wanted to know," Cantu responded.

Once he and Nancy Smith were in the car, she asked if she had passed. In a few days, he'd receive an official summary of the polygraph results and let her know then.

"I'm not allowed to release that information to you yet. Everything is preliminary."

He could see the disappointment in her eyes. "I know you talked to the examiner for a few minutes. What did he say?" she asked.

"I'm not supposed to discuss that with you, but let's just say that you did okay." He looked over at her and she nodded.

"What happens next?" she asked.

"I'll forward the test results to the county prosecutor along with my written investigation and then he'll decide whether we should close the investigation." As soon as the words left his mouth, he knew he'd said more than he should have.

As they drove in silence, Cantu drafted his summary in his head. Tomorrow, he'd report that the alleged victims had given widely inconsistent accounts—stories that could not be reconciled. After almost a month of investigation, he hadn't discovered any credible evidence of molestation or other crime.

Despite what the parents thought, the medical evidence was also inconclusive. The doctor at the Cleveland children's hospital had found some scar tissue that might or might not indicate that Nina Zorich had been sexually abused. However, the doctor had also explained that this scar tissue could have been formed months before the events alleged in his investigation, leaving open the possibility that others had abused her. As for Marcus Logan, the local hospital had found that he had tested positive for chlamydia, a sexually transmitted disease. However, the more sophisticated chlamydia test administered at the Cleveland hospital had come back negative. Nancy Smith had voluntarily submitted to the same test and the results were also negative. All tests and exams involving Melissa Warner were normal.

Cantu had investigated two houses as well as Nancy Smith's as the possible site for the abuse. None of them matched the children's descriptions and none were occupied by a single male. He seriously doubted whether "Joseph" existed.

And now Nancy Smith had passed the lie detector test. After their several meetings and her impassioned denials of any wrongdoing, he'd concluded that she was not the type of person who could hide her true feelings. He doubted that she could have suppressed her emotions to defeat the polygraph test.

Cantu had reached the end of the road. Although he had initially believed that Nina Zorich had been molested by her bus driver and "Joseph," he'd come full circle on that proposition. He now concluded that no abuse had happened at the school, on the bus, or at any alleged suspect's home. He was ready to close his investigation.

Little did he realize that in ten days, after a newspaper editorial called for arrests in the Head Start case, he would be "promoted" to a new position as a desk sergeant. As part of his "promotion," he would be relieved of any further duties involving the Head Start case, and a new detective would be assigned and directed to start "fresh."

CHAPTER 5
DETECTIVE ELADIO ANDUJAR
AUGUST 2, 1993

As the unmarked cruiser headed to the Nativity School in central Lorain, Detective Eladio Andujar looked at the five-year-old boy in the front passenger seat. Marcus Logan appeared excited, his feet dangling and kicking the bottom part of the seat. Brushing his hand across his short hair, Marcus returned Andujar's glance.

"Can I see your handcuffs?" the boy asked.

"Maybe later," Andujar replied.

The handsome boy's delicate features shifted from hopeful to disappointed. "Why not now?" he whined.

Not answering, Andujar kept his eyes on the road and sighed. He'd been working the Head Start case for ten weeks now and was no closer to solving it than his predecessor, Tom Cantu. The key to the case was locating the house where Joseph lived and had molested the children. If he could find that house, everything would fall into place—everything. Not only would he solve the case, but he would free the Lorain police from the shroud of failure that surrounded its investigation.

After they had driven several blocks, Andujar broke the silence and asked Marcus, "Are you going to help me find that bad man?"

"Yep."

"Once we get to the Head Start school, you and me, we're getting out of the car. And then you'll walk me over to Joseph's house. Okay?"

Marcus looked out his side window and seemed to nod in the affirmative.

"Is that a yes, my friend?" Andujar asked.

The thin boy turned his head toward Andujar and gave him a peeved expression that seemed to say, "You'll see."

Andujar shook his head and wondered why he even bothered with this kid. Since the investigation had begun, Marcus had identified two homes as being Joseph's. One had been a dead end, while the other was headed that way. Andujar suspected that Marcus's father, Franklin Logan, had played some part in both of the questionable leads. Perhaps if Andujar could work with the boy without his father's interference, he could get the boy to take him to Joseph's house.

While Tom Cantu was in charge of the investigation, Cantu had driven to the school with Marcus and his parents during their first meeting at the end of May 1993. Marcus had assured them that he could find Joseph's house. They'd driven to the Nativity School on Fifteenth Street, where the young boy had identified a house across from the school as Joseph's residence. Cantu had wisely asked Marcus to describe the interior of the house before he talked to its occupants.

After Cantu had driven them back to the station, he'd returned to the Fifteenth Street house, which was occupied by two white males, Donald Moffitt and his younger brother, Ken. Donald Moffit had immediately allowed Cantu to enter the house and check its layout, which did not match Marcus's description. No black males lived in the house and Cantu quickly ruled out this location as the site of the molestations.

The second apparent failure had occurred on Andujar's watch. In mid-June, Franklin Logan had contacted him, explaining that Marcus had lied when he'd suggested the first house as being Joseph's. Franklin Logan explained that Joseph had brainwashed his son and threatened to kill him if he ever cooperated with investigators. Joseph had told him to lie, and according to his father, Marcus had "lied his ass off" to protect Joseph.

Andujar remembered Mr. Logan's excited tone as he continued. "I told him that if he did not tell us about Joseph, Joseph would do the same things to his little sister that he'd done to him. I asked him if he wanted that to happen. This hit him pretty hard and he got this changed expression on his face. When I reassured him that he was safe now, he said he would show me Joseph's house." The father claimed that they had then driven through the school's neighborhood and Marcus had picked out a house on Lexington Avenue as being Joseph's.

Andujar and several detectives had immediately gone to work, putting the house under surveillance and taking surreptitious photographs of the owner, Richard Jones. When the detectives asked the Head Start victims to look at Jones's photograph in a photo lineup, the children, including Marcus, either identified the wrong person or said that Joseph wasn't among the photos.

When Andujar had talked to Richard Jones, Jones had maintained his innocence, telling the detective that he was a man of God and would never hurt a child. In fact, the neighborhood children called him Grandpa and he provided food to the needy. In addition, the house's interior did not match any of the children's various descriptions of Joseph's home—not by a long shot. However, this African-American male did have white splotches on his face; he lived within walking distance of the school; and his last name, "Jones," was similar to "Joseph."

Andujar then recalled an earlier conversation with Franklin Logan when the father had disclosed that he had been asking people around the Head Start school if they knew of a black male with white spots. Andujar suspected that Mr. Logan had zeroed in on the sixty-five-year-old Richard Jones after several people in the neighborhood told him that a black man with that description lived at 1928 Lexington Avenue. Mr. Logan had likely suggested the Jones house to his son, who'd then agreed that Joseph lived there. As unreliable as this lead seemed, Andujar was not ready to give up on it, especially when he had no others.

The detective believed that the boy had been constantly whipsawed by the suggestions of others, not just about the location of the house, but on other details as well. After he'd reviewed Cantu's reports, he'd learned that Marcus had originally claimed that Nancy Smith had entered his classroom wearing a mask of a black woman with gray hair. She'd taken Nina Zorich, Melissa Warner, and him out of the class and *walked* them to Joseph's home.

However, when Andujar had first interviewed him several weeks later, the boy said that he'd been *driven* there, sometimes in Nancy's bus and other times in her car. The boy had also given different descriptions of Joseph. At first, he'd maintained that Joseph was a mustached black man with blue eyes, partially bald, and with white patches on his face, but later changed that to a younger black man with black eyes. To Andujar's surprise, Marcus had also initially claimed that the molestations had been ongoing for two years. Later the boy fell in line with the other victims and said that he'd only visited Joseph's house three times.

Rather than dismiss the children's claims as false because of the inconsistencies and changes in their statements, Andujar remained determined to find the common threads that tied the victims' stories together. Children that age would, of course, mix fantasy with fact. This was to be expected, wasn't it? Despite some of their wild assertions, they uniformly maintained that Nancy Smith had sexually abused them and delivered them to Joseph's house, where he'd also molested them. That part of the case seemed well established. They'd also described things that young children would not know about unless they'd actually been sexually abused, giving greater credibility to their stories.

As a result, most of the puzzle had already been solved. The pressure was mounting to find Joseph and put the last pieces together. To the local community, that task seemed simple enough, but for the last three months, it had remained both elusive and exasperating.

He'd been encouraged when he'd talked to Marcus at his mother's house just ten days earlier. During that meeting, Marcus had seemed relaxed, particularly when they'd discussed Joseph. Because of that, Andujar had decided to show Marcus the photo lineup with Richard Jones one more time. Maybe this time the boy would feel comfortable enough to point out Joseph. He'd spread the six photos on a coffee table in the family's living room.

Andujar recalled the conversation.

"Do any of those men look like Joseph?"

"I have seen him before," the boy answered.

Andujar tried to mask his surprise. "You have seen him before?"

"He lives right by us."

At first Andujar was skeptical. "Oh really. Well, okay."

But then Marcus immediately pointed to the photograph of Richard Jones.

"He looks like Joseph? He looks like him?" Andujar asked, trying to keep his voice neutral.

"And my uncle took me to go see him."

"Huh? I don't understand."

Again, the boy emphatically pointed to the photograph of Richard Jones. "He is Joseph."

Andujar was confused. "Your uncle took you to go see him?"

"Uh-huh. He was gonna make sure if I remember him."

Although Marcus's reference to his uncle puzzled him, the detective decided to overlook it and keep pressing the boy on the identification. "That's Joseph?"

"Uh-huh."

"Are you sure?"

"Uh-huh."

"Is that the same Joseph you seen with Nancy?"

"Uh-huh."

Andujar grabbed the boy's hand. "Are you sure?"

The boy made eye contact with him. "Uh-huh. My mom says he got a son."

Ignoring the claim about a son, Andujar stared into the boy's eyes. "Okay. But are you sure that's the same Joseph?"

"Uh-huh."

"The one whose house you went to?"

"Uh-huh."

Pointing to the photo of Richard Jones again, Andujar said, "So you are sure that's Joseph, or did someone tell you that's Joseph?"

"This is Joseph." Although the boy hadn't answered his question directly, Andujar concluded that Marcus hadn't been coached on the identification.

After that interview, Andujar had decided that Richard Jones should remain a suspect. He'd arranged the meeting with Marcus today in order to investigate this further. What if the boy could walk him directly from the school to Jones's house on Lexington Avenue? That would add further proof that Richard Jones was Joseph. Without either of Marcus's parents hovering nearby to make suggestions, Andujar would have the perfect situation to plumb the boy's memory and maybe, just maybe, find Joseph.

Andujar parked the car on Fifteenth Street in front of the Head Start school. The block was dominated by the imposing Nativity of the Blessed Virgin Mary Roman Catholic Church, a church built earlier in the century to serve the Polish immigrants and their families who lived in the area. The church's former elementary school, a solid, three-story brick building, now housed the Head Start program after the neighborhood's demographics had changed and the parochial school had closed. After Andujar exited the car, he opened the front passenger door and Marcus scampered out. The boy was dressed in shorts and a T-shirt on this cloudy, humid day.

"Where should we start?" Andujar asked.

"We start here," Marcus said, pointing to the grassy lawn in front of the school. "Nancy always took my hand."

Andujar didn't know if this was an invitation for him to take the youngster's hand, but he didn't want anyone to think that he'd led the boy anywhere.

"Okay. Take me to the house. Which way?"

"We cross here," Marcus said. The boy looked casually for traffic and then stepped into the street. They passed the little sliver of land called Pulaski Park and headed south on Oakdale Avenue. Off to their right, the defunct Polish Club's crumbling parking lot bloomed with chicory and dandelions. The boy seemed confident as they reached the first intersection at Eighteenth Street.

"Now where?" Andujar asked.

"This way," the boy said, pointing to his left.

They walked another block until they reached the intersection of

Eighteenth Street and Garden Avenue. This time the boy appeared confused, looking from his left to his right and then turning around to survey where they'd just been. Andujar watched, saying nothing. Finally, Marcus said, "This way," and he turned left onto Garden Avenue.

The two-story houses that lined the street were no longer well maintained. After the original Polish immigrants had moved away or died, many of them had been sold to new owners who had turned them into rental properties. Marcus furrowed his brow as he stared at one house after the other.

"What are you looking for?" Andujar asked.

"I'm looking for K. K.'s house," Marcus said as if this should have been obvious to the detective.

"Who's K. K.?"

"He's my cousin and Joseph lives across the street from him."

"Marcus, I want you to look for Joseph's house, not K. K.'s house, okay?"

"I'm lost," the boy admitted. His head drooped as he stared at his feet. "Don't know where to go now."

Andujar let out a deep breath. This had been a long shot, he told himself. He grabbed Marcus's hand and they crossed Seventeenth Street into Pulaski Park. Crossing Fifteenth Street, they returned to his car.

The detective thought about taking Marcus back to his mother's house but decided to drive him past Richard Jones's house on Lexington Avenue. They drove in silence and Andujar watched the boy's expression as the car slowly passed the Jones house. Although Marcus was staring at it, he didn't say a word. If Marcus had actually pointed out this house to his father, Andujar was sure that the boy would speak out now.

After they traveled another block, Marcus spoke. "There it is," he said, pointing to a white house, a block closer to the school and on the opposite side of the street from the Jones home.

"Are you sure that's Joseph's house?" Andujar asked.

"Yeah, that's the one."

The detective was skeptical. "Why do you say that?"

"Because my cousin K. K. told my father that Joseph lives there," the boy replied.

This was another failure. How many more false leads would these children generate? By his count, this was the fourth house that a child had incorrectly identified as Joseph's. The number was five if one included Nancy Smith's residence. Andujar was through with Marcus.

"Okay. I'm going to drive you back home to your mom's house," Andujar said, his voice low and dejected.

In a few minutes, they were at Marcus's house on Ninth Street. Andujar walked the boy to his house, up the wobbly front porch steps, and knocked on the front door. Marcus's mom, Stella Gilliam, answered it quickly.

"Well?" she asked expectantly.

Andujar shook his head. "He couldn't take me to the house either by walking or in the car. It's obvious that your husband and his family have been taking Marcus into the area, making suggestions to him."

Marcus's mom shrugged her shoulders, tacitly admitting the truth of the detective's assertion.

"I know they think they're being helpful, but they're not. Tell them to stay out of this investigation. I don't want them taking Marcus down Lexington Avenue or any of the other streets near the school. Can you tell your husband that?"

"He's not my husband," she said as if that clarification distanced her from the detective's rebuke.

"Just tell Mr. Logan to stay out of the investigation."

"Okay."

As he drove back to the police station, Andujar believed he'd exhausted all of his leads. This final try with Marcus had only under-scored his desperation. How could he expect any of the children to guide him to Joseph's house? Besides lacking any sense of direction at that age, they'd been traumatized at the house too. He was no psychologist, but they'd want to repress those memories, wouldn't they?

Andujar was out of ideas. By now, he'd explored all of the possible claims stemming from the Head Start case. In the end, six children, including Marcus, had alleged sexual abuse at the hands of Nancy

Smith and Joseph. He'd done all he could to investigate each one, but unless he received new information, he was stymied.

Perhaps someone who knew Joseph would come forward and talk. Or maybe Joseph would make a mistake—brag about his activities or get caught with some other kids doing who knows what. Somehow, they'd eventually find him. If they didn't—well, he didn't want to think about that possibility.

CHAPTER 6
DETECTIVE JOEL MILLER
AUGUST 23 - NOVEMBER 4, 1993

Detective Joel Miller, another member of the department's Youth and Gangs Division, had watched as his colleagues experienced one disappointment after another while trying to crack the Head Start case. He'd assisted Detective Andujar a few times but had not been actively involved in the investigation. Miller was a ten-year member of the department and had joined the Youth and Gangs Division at the end of May 1993, several weeks after Detective Cantu had opened the investigation. He prided himself on thinking outside the box, making connections that others missed.

From Miller's vantage, Andujar had diligently worked the case. He'd reinterviewed the original children, questioned additional Head Start preschoolers, and painstakingly canvassed the neighborhoods around the Head Start school in search of Joseph's "house." In addition, he'd seen others in the department pitch in, including their boss, Captain Cel Rivera; Detectives Pete Rewak, Dennis Moskal, and Mark Carpentiere; and several uniformed officers. Despite the increased manpower, they'd made no progress after following every possible lead. As time dragged on, they'd all heard the whispering: competent detectives would have solved this case by now. Impatience reigned from the police chief to the mayor to the community at large, particularly the Head Start parents.

Today, Miller was not doing anything connected with the Head Start case. Instead, he was talking to Joseph Allen, a black, forty-year-old handyman/housepainter who'd been accused of propositioning four teenagers, ranging in age from thirteen to fifteen. The four white teens had run away from the Green Acres Children's Home on Saturday, August 21, and allegedly been told by another Green Acres teen that they could find refuge in Allen's one-floor cottage apartment located at Kennedy Plaza in central Lorain.

The four girls had left Green Acres in Oberlin, Ohio, around eleven that Saturday night and arrived at Allen's apartment a few hours later. The girls claimed that Allen had invited them inside, where they'd found a black woman and her two small children staying with him. The teens alleged that they'd partied with Allen for the rest of the evening, listening to loud music, using drugs, and drinking alcohol. One thirteen-year-old girl claimed that Allen had grabbed her and kissed her. He'd offered her money for sex, which she'd refused. He'd made similar offers to the other three girls, offering to pay up to $300 for sex. After refusing him, the girls had felt unsafe at his apartment and left. The following day, they'd contacted the Lorain police. At least that was their story.

Miller had left several notes at Allen's apartment after that, asking him to call him. Eventually, a few days later, Allen had phoned Detective Miller and agreed to stop at the Youth and Gangs Division for an interview that day. When Allen arrived, he was wearing work pants and a T-shirt. The man was solidly built around a six-foot frame, with broad shoulders and a wide chest.

"What's this all about?" Allen asked. His voice was deep and he spoke with a slow drawl.

Miller summarized what the girls had claimed. When he told Allen that the girls had accused him of offering money for sex, Allen scoffed at him.

"So that's what they said," Allen said. "They're lying."

"Well, what happened? Did they come to your place?"

"Yeah, they showed up. They said they had a pass from Green Acres."

"Why'd they come to your place?" Miller asked.

Ignoring his question, Allen said, "Soon as I found out that they'd run away, I called the police and told them to turn themselves in."

"What about the sex and the drugs?"

"It never happened," Allen replied. "I told them to leave."

Miller continued to press him on this, but Allen remained steadfast in his denials.

"Can I go?" Allen asked, his manner surly for the first time.

"For now," Miller told him. "My investigation is still ongoing."

Miller wouldn't seek charges against Allen at this time. The man hadn't engaged in sex with any of the underage girls—none of the runaways had accused him of that. Miller had more pressing matters to investigate and process. However, for the first time, Joseph Allen was on his radar.

October 22–27, 1993

For the second time in two months, an underage teen was making serious allegations against Joseph Allen. Hazel Parker, a fifteen-year-old girl, who had been in and out of the Green Acres home, claimed that she had stayed with Joseph Allen at his one-floor apartment in Kennedy Plaza after she and another girl, Melissa Walsh, had run away from Green Acres. Allen had supposedly picked them up from the Apollo Theater in Oberlin and driven them to his place. Parker alleged that they'd had sex many times at his apartment and in exchange, Allen had given her money, use of his phone, clothing, housing, and food. Although she admitted that some of the sex was consensual, she claimed that some was not. She also believed that Allen had given her two sexually transmitted diseases, chlamydia and gonorrhea. If that was not enough, she contended that Allen had dry humped her companion, Melissa Walsh, while they all shared a bed in the apartment.

Five days later, Miller caught up with Joseph Allen.

"So what's it this time?" Allen asked.

"It's about Hazel Parker," Miller said.

"Not her again," Allen replied.

"What do you mean?"

"I mean that girl just wants to get me into trouble. A couple of nights ago, I called the police on her after she took my car. She don't ask me or nothing. She just took the damn thing. She's paying me back. That's all."

"She's accusing you of having sex with her and giving her two sexually transmitted diseases," Miller responded. "She's only fifteen years old. You know that, right?"

After denying the sex allegations, Allen added, "I've got some diseases and my doctor told me I can't have sex, and believe me, I don't want to spread any disease." To Miller's surprise, Allen took off his shirt and showed him evidence of his "diseases." Miller could see white spots on parts of his body and a burn scar that also had white patches.

Miller's heart began to race as he realized what he may have discovered. Was this the Joseph that the Head Start children had described? Had he found the man who had eluded the department for five months?

"Do you mind if I take a few photographs of your body for my investigation?" Miller asked.

Allen shrugged and nodded, then completely undressed. Miller walked around Allen and snapped eleven photographs of the man's naked body, including several of his face.

After he'd finished with the photographs, Miller said, "That's it for now. You can go."

As soon as Joseph Allen had left, Miller grabbed the Head Start file. As he combed through Cantu's part of the investigation, he found that all the children had insisted the man's name was Joseph, except one. That boy had claimed that the molester's name was Allen. The boy's account had been dismissed because it did not fit with the other children's stories. But now it seemed to make perfect sense. Allen was the perpetrator's last name and Joseph was his first.

Miller was convinced that he was onto something. He checked the police archives to discover anything he could about this man. A year before, in May 1992, Joseph Allen had been accused of sexually abusing a four-year-old girl, but the investigation had been stalled due to a lack of evidence. However, the report had referenced an earlier incident. When Miller retrieved that file, he learned that Joseph Allen had been indicted for rape and gross sexual imposition of another young girl in 1985. He'd accepted a deal where the rape charge had been dropped and he'd pleaded guilty to sexual battery, a lesser charge. Allen had spent three years in prison for that crime.

Miller felt a sense of pride in what he'd pieced together. For the first time, the department had a solid suspect. If the Head Start children could identify Joseph Allen as the Joseph who had molested them, the case would be practically solved. Yes, they would need to tie down a few more details, but the foundation for a conviction would be in place.

October 28, 1993

Under normal circumstances, Miller would have handed his findings over to Andujar, who would have followed up with the victims and their parents. However, Andujar was on leave; his son was extremely ill and not expected to live. As a result, this was now Miller's investigation, and he would dictate the next moves.

Miller put together a photo lineup of six photographs, including Joseph Allen, and jumped into his car to visit the victims at their homes. By the end of the afternoon, he'd visited four homes with disappointing results. He now understood the obstacles that Cantu and Andujar had faced throughout their investigations: confusion, indifference, and short attention spans. Nina Zorich had pointed first to one photograph and then another, neither being Joseph Allen. Melissa Warner and Marcus Logan had claimed that Joseph was not in any of the photographs. Only Jessica Simpson, a victim brought to their attention later in the investigation, had pointed to Joseph Allen's photograph.

At each home, he'd studied the children's faces and demeanor. One girl seemed to look away when she stared at Allen's photo, another quickly moved on to the next photo, and a third appeared disinterested in the whole process. To Miller, these were all signs of fear.

The next morning, Marge Bronson, Nina's mom, called him. She explained that Nina had experienced nightmares the night before. In the morning, Nina had revealed that Joseph's photograph had been among the spread—the middle photo in the bottom row, which was where his photo had been placed. Miller quickly assembled another photo lineup with different people and drove to Nina's house. This time the little girl pointed to Joseph Allen without hesitation. He was very encouraged.

That afternoon, he contacted the parents of other children and asked them to come to the station to look at the photographs. Again, the results were not what he'd expected. Bret King, Justin Frank, and Jason Gilliam all claimed that Joseph was not among the photographs. Although Michael Osborne appeared to change his expression while staring at Joseph Allen's photo, he could not identify him. However, Michael's parents provided information that more than made up for their son's lackluster performance.

Michael Osborne's mother, Emily, pointed to Joseph Allen's photograph and told Miller that she'd seen him hanging around Nancy Smith's bus earlier in the year. She'd been holding her son's hand and he'd broken free of it when he'd spotted Joseph Allen and hightailed it back to another bus. Her husband also recognized Joseph Allen as a man who had attended a Head Start banquet last Christmas at DeLuca's Place in the Park. He said that he'd "partied" with Joseph that evening and claimed that Joseph had been with Nancy Smith.

After his parents reported these things, the boy became animated and volunteered that Joseph drove a green station wagon with a rack on top, just like the one his family owned. How the boy knew this, Miller did not ask. However, the detective did know that Allen owned an older-model, green station wagon with a rack on top—a vehicle that perfectly fit the boy's description. Like most detectives, he didn't believe in coincidences.

However, there were problems with young Michael's assertion. How and when did Michael spot Joseph Allen in his station wagon? The Head Start children, despite the differences in their stories, all agreed that Nancy had taken them to Joseph's house either in her bus, in her car, or on foot. The young boy's claim would be further challenged four years later, well after Joseph Allen had been convicted and sent to prison. At that time, the registration for Allen's vehicle was produced, and it showed that he'd purchased the green station wagon on June 3, 1993, a month after the last molestation had allegedly occurred.

Miller was more than heartened by the Osborne family's revelations, particularly the parents'. He was convinced that he had the right man, regardless of the children's reluctance to identify him as Joseph. Today, two credible adults had reviewed photographs and identified Joseph Allen as the man who had been with Nancy Smith or had loitered near her bus. They couldn't both be mistaken. And they had no reason to lie or embellish. What possible motive would they have to do that?

November 3, 1993

After the photo lineup with the children and their parents, Miller and Sergeant Russ Cambarare had tailed Joseph Allen off and on for several days. At one point, they'd followed him to a South Lorain grocery store, where he'd spoken with a girl, perhaps eight or nine years old, outside the store, but nothing had happened. The next day they'd asked him if he would agree to a polygraph examination to clear himself. He'd agreed.

Miller and Cambarare had driven Joseph Allen to Poly-Tech Associates in Akron, Ohio, for the test. On the way, Allen had been quiet and composed. Two weeks earlier, he'd agreed to and subjected himself to a polygraph examination that quizzed him about the Hazel

Parker rape allegations. According to the examiner, Allen had been deceptive in answering those questions, but Miller decided not to divulge that quite yet.

After the second test ended, Miller and Cambarare talked with the examiner. Again, the examiner concluded that Allen had been deceptive when answering the key questions.

"Well, Joe, it looks like you didn't do too well on the lie detector test," Miller said after he and Cambarare joined Allen again.

"What's that mean?" Allen asked.

"It means you're not telling the truth."

"I ain't never touched any of those kids you just asked me about. That test's wrong," Allen protested.

"Would you agree to come back to the station and talk to us about this? There's a lot of unanswered questions," Miller said.

"Yeah, I'll talk to you guys some more. I got nothin' to hide."

"Good. You know you don't have to speak with us," Cambarare added. "This is purely voluntary. You don't have to do this, you know that?"

Allen nodded.

"You hungry? We can buy you a hamburger at McDonald's if you are," Miller said.

"Yeah, I wouldn't mind getting a sandwich," Allen stated.

About an hour later, the two officers and Allen were at the Lorain police station. After walking into an interview room, the three sat at a table, Allen on one side while Miller and Cambarare took the other. Miller read Allen his Miranda rights and then slid a one-page summary of those rights to him. Allen picked it up, read it, and signed it.

"What do you know about the Head Start program?" Miller began.

"I don't know what Head Start is," Allen replied.

"So you're saying you don't even know where the Head Start school is?"

"No."

"Here, let me draw a map," Miller said, taking a blank piece of paper and roughing in the streets. "I'll put a star where the Head Start school is."

"I know the area. There's a church there, but I didn't know there was a school there too," Allen said.

Miller and Cambarare exchanged skeptical glances.

"Hey, Joe, you ever go to a party at DeLuca's Place in the Park?" Cambarare asked.

"Yeah, I been there. Went to a Christmas party at DeLuca's last year."

"What was it for?" Cambarare asked.

"It was for Catholic Charities. I get stuff from their store and sometimes I do odd jobs for them."

This time the two officers looked at each other and nodded. This was confirmation of Mr. Osborne's claim.

"We don't want to bullshit you, Joe, but we've got a lot of evidence tying you to these crimes against these kids," Miller said.

Allen did not reply but shook his head.

Miller continued, "We've got kids from the Head Start school who've picked your photo from a lineup. Not just one kid, but multiple kids. They say you did some really bad stuff to them. Do you deny it?"

"Yeah, I deny it," Allen said, his voice defiant for the first time. "I don't do that kind of stuff."

"We've got more. We've located parents who saw you standing near a Head Start bus that Nancy Smith drives. You know who Nancy Smith is, don't you?"

"No, I don't. I never heard of her before."

"All the kids say that she drove them to your house, where you molested them. Does that jog your memory a little?"

"No, it don't. I didn't do nothing to those kids."

"We know you like little kids. You were in prison for that."

"That's a long story," Allen responded.

"What about Chellie Short? We got a complaint that you abused that little girl just last year," Miller stated.

"People get mad at me for all kinds of stuff. They want to get even and I get blamed for all kinds of crazy shit."

Miller and Cambarare looked at each other again. Cambarare motioned with his head that he wanted to talk outside. Miller announced a short break, and the two left the room and talked in the hall. They decided that Allen was not going to admit to anything even if they questioned him all day and night. Maybe they could find things in his apartment that would show he was the Head Start child molester.

When they returned, Miller said, "I'm guessing that you wouldn't mind if we searched your apartment."

"Go ahead and search it. Ain't nothing there that shouldn't be."

"Will you sign this paper so we can search your house?"

"Yeah, I'll sign it."

"Anybody live there with you?" Cambarare asked.

"There's this woman named Blackie who stays at the house some-times. She helps take care of me when I'm sick. She's got two little kids. That's about it."

"Is she there now?"

"No."

"We might have questions for you as we go through the house. We want you to go with us. Is that okay?"

Allen nodded.

For the next three hours, Miller, Cambarare, and Detective Pete Rewak went through the house, taking items that they believed supported their case against Allen. They removed stuffed animals, toy cars, Batman and Mickey Mouse sheets, children's music and books, a Halloween mask, a coloring book, and assorted children's clothing. Allen claimed that he had obtained these things either from Catholic Charities or from a friend who managed an apartment complex and permitted Allen to take property after tenants had abandoned it.

They also confiscated notes between Allen and Hazel Parker and other female friends. Allen refused to comment on any of these communications. In a kitchen drawer, they found two photographs of a bedroom decorated with balloons and crepe paper streamers. Allen claimed that his mother had sent those pictures to him. They asked Allen about a *High Society* adult magazine and Allen gave the police the name of a friend who'd given it to him. Allen had also saved several newspapers, including a *Morning Journal* dated June 23, 1993, in which an article about Head Start had been a front-page story. Allen said that he collected newspapers and later sold them for money. All told, the officers took fifty-one items from Allen's apartment.

The officers believed that they'd solidified their case when they'd discovered all of the child-oriented items at Allen's apartment, convinced that these items would ultimately link Allen to the Head Start children. In so doing, they were ignoring Allen's claim that a woman and her two small children occasionally lived in the apartment with him—something that two of the Green Acre runaways had also reported to Miller when he had investigated their claim a month earlier. The next step was to find out if any of the Head Start children could identify these items. If they could, their case would only get much stronger.

November 4, 1993

That morning, Miller and Cambarare phoned the parents of the victims. They explained that they had apprehended a man who could be Joseph and had seized a number of his possessions in a search of his apartment. They wanted to see if the children could identify Joseph from a lineup of suspects and whether they could recognize any of the things taken from the suspect's residence. Although it was difficult, the detectives deflected the parents' questions, and soon they'd arranged for seven of the alleged victims and their parents to be at the station by eleven o'clock.

The process would be orderly and involve one child at a time. First, the police would take an individual child into the room that held the seized property. They'd ask the child whether they remembered various objects in the house while the seized items remained out of sight in a closed black plastic bag. If a child seemed to remember a particular item, they'd pull the object from the bag and ask the child if this was the item from the house. After that, the child would go to the viewing room with its mirrored-glass wall and try to identify Joseph. They'd allow parents to accompany their child if the child seemed too frightened or confused to go alone.

The questions involving the seized items followed a set litany. Did Joseph wear a mask? Did Joseph have any teddy bears at his house? Toy cars? Bad books? Children's bedsheets? Not surprisingly, when the detective suggested an item, the child often remembered seeing it at Joseph's house. Likewise, after the object was retrieved from the plastic bag, the child confirmed that this was the very item that they'd seen before.

In the viewing room, the results were mixed. Miller stayed in the background while Captain Cel Rivera and Sergeant Russ Cambarare interacted with the children. Two boys identified Joseph with little hesitation while four others pointed to the wrong person. Nina Zorich struggled to identify Joseph, but after reassurances from her mother, she eventually told everyone that Joseph was wearing a green shirt. In fact, Joseph Allen was wearing a long-sleeved, green plaid shirt.

"Don't worry, Nina, we will put that bad man in jail forever," Cambarare told her.

"Yeah, now you can go out and play outside and not worry," her mom added before they left.

Both Emily Osborne and her husband quickly identified Joseph Allen as the Joseph whom they had seen months earlier.

Detective Rewak was charged with the responsibility of documenting what had happened during the lineup. In his report, he described in detail the body movements and facial expressions of the four who had failed to identify Joseph Allen. One appeared "withdrawn," two looked down at their feet when Joseph stepped forward, and still another seemed frightened from the moment she entered the viewing room. The implication was clear: the children who could not identify Joseph were too scared to do so.

During all of this, one officer had videotaped the proceeding with his recently purchased video camera. Excited by his new toy, he'd asked and received permission from the police chief to record the event. As the camera's red light blinked, he captured almost everything that happened during the forty-five-minute session: the expressions of the children, the comments of their parents, the reassurances from the police, and the appearance of the men in the lineup. Almost four years later, a local newspaper would learn of this video, seek its disclosure, and obtain a copy. When it was viewed by those not connected with the official Head Start investigation, many found it disturbing. Instead of looking frightened, the children appeared befuddled, showing no signs of recognizing the man who had allegedly abused and terrorized them. But that would be later—after Nancy Smith and Joseph Allen had been convicted and were relegated to the inmate's life of drudgery and deprivation.

CHAPTER 7
THE ARRAIGNMENT
NOVEMBER 17, 1993

The Lorain County Courthouse stood on the far end of the city square, sullen and solitary, oak leaves swirling about its foundation. Constructed over one hundred years earlier, the three-story sandstone building had once held a single, ornate courtroom complete with a balcony for spectators. But over the years, the county had grown, the number of judges had multiplied from one to five, and the once grand building had been subdivided again and again until it had lost its original splendor.

Arraignments were scheduled this morning in front of Judge Kosma Glavas, the most recently elected judge, who, because of his junior status, was relegated to the smallest courtroom. About a dozen people, all recently indicted, would make their first appearance in the courtroom and enter a formal plea to the charges pending against them. Among this group were Nancy Smith and Joseph Allen.

The interior of the courthouse always took on a more frantic appearance on arraignment days. On this morning, the hallway outside Judge Glavas's courtroom was teeming with people, some standing and creating obstacles for those trying to pass through. Others sat on a long bench that ran along one wall. Most of those sitting were women: mothers, wives, or girlfriends of the accused, surrounded by their bedraggled children. Many wanted to grab a word with a defense attorney before they disappeared into the courtroom. All in all, they were a sad and desperate group.

Filled with family of the accused, the courtroom was frequently crowded during an arraignment. However, due to the nature of the Head Start case, Judge Glavas's courtroom was packed, including some who stood against the back wall. Among them were reporters and photographers, eager to provide their readers with the latest details about this explosive case. Two other groups were also in attendance, both fervently invested in the case for different reasons. Due to the limited seating, Nancy Smith's siblings and the parents of the Head Start children were sitting in close proximity to one another. Determined to exert pressure at every stage of the case, the Head Start parents were there to do just that, while Smith's family had come to provide moral support for her. Neither group wanted to be overheard by the other, and, as a result, they each sat in silence—edgy with anticipation and ready to lash out at the other if the opportunity arose.

If Joseph Allen and Nancy Smith knew each other, they showed no signs of recognition as they looked about Judge Glavas's courtroom. Dressed neatly in jacket and slacks, Smith sat and waited with her attorney, Jack Bradley, at a trial table. Bradley had arranged for Smith's arraignment to be the first one that morning. To the outside world, Smith's face held a vacant, exhausted stare, but inside, she was struggling to contain the panic and the tears that could escape at any moment.

Watched over by two sheriff's deputies, Joseph Allen sat handcuffed alongside eight other prisoners. Because of the cramped quarters, these men sat in the jury box, their bright orange jumpsuits providing a vivid contrast to the otherwise drab courtroom. Allen, too, looked subdued, but otherwise his face was impossible to read.

Things had moved rapidly after the lineup at the Lorain police station. Within a week, the prosecutor's office had presented the police findings to a grand jury, who'd determined that there was probable cause to believe that Nancy Smith and Joseph Allen had committed these crimes. This was not a finding that either was guilty, but only that they would have to stand and answer to the charges at trial.

Cameras came to the ready position when Nancy Smith's case was announced. They began clicking after she and Bradley stood to face the judge. Unable to control her tears, Smith stood as Bradley told the judge that his client waived a reading of the indictment and pled not guilty to all charges.

One of the Head Start parents yelled, "Child rapist."

"You'll rot in hell," one of Smith's relatives shouted back.

Judge Glavas raised his gavel and pounded it on his bench. "There will be no further outbursts in my courtroom. If anyone interrupts these proceedings again, they will be forcibly removed. Do I make myself clear?"

Unfazed by the commotion, the clerk pulled the top page from the pad in front of her, revealing at random the name of one of the county's five judges. She announced that Smith's case was assigned to Judge Lynett McGough. Because Smith had raised bond upon her arrest and the judge did not increase it, she was free to go. She lowered her head and, shepherded by Bradley, walked briskly out of the courtroom.

A few minutes later, Joseph Allen stood before Judge Glavas without an attorney. Not only had Allen been accused of sex crimes involving the Head Start children, but he'd also been charged with opportuning prostitution from two of the four teenage runaways who'd ended up at his apartment several months earlier. Before Judge Glavas could ask Allen about his financial ability to hire an attorney, Marge Bronson began cursing the defendant.

Pointing at Bronson, the judge ordered her out of the courtroom. She did not wait for a sheriff's deputy to escort her. Instead, she stood and walked to the exit, shouting one parting shot before opening the door: "Everybody's going to pay for what they did."

After she left, the judge continued quizzing Allen about his assets and quickly determined that he was indigent and entitled to a court-appointed lawyer. The judge appointed Joseph R. Grunda, the former Lorain County prosecutor, to represent him. Allen's bond had previously been set at $250,000 and Judge Glavas refused to lower it. Without the means to purchase a bond, Allen would return to jail. Like Smith's, his case would also be added to Judge McGough's docket.

Greg White, Lorain County's prosecutor, had assigned the Head Start cases to Jonathan Rosenbaum, his chief criminal assistant. For the last few months, Rosenbaum had been in contact with the Lorain police periodically as they had gathered evidence in their investigation. He was the obvious choice to handle the case as it moved forward.

If the Lorain police expected Rosenbaum to secure a conviction, Detective Miller and his fellow detectives needed to shore up several weaknesses. It was crucial that the investigators continue to search for the home where the molestations had occurred. Although they'd found Joseph, they hadn't discovered where he'd interacted with Smith and the Head Start children. In describing Joseph's residence, all of the children reported that the house contained a basement as well as a second floor. Some even reported a swing set outside. Allen's cottage apartment was built on a slab with no basement or upstairs and there was no swing set anywhere near it. It seemed evident that the children had not been molested there. Unless they solved this part of the puzzle, they could expect defense counsel to exploit this at trial and it could lead to acquittals.

Their failure to find the site of the crime also presented another problem when the case was tried. If the children had never been inside Allen's apartment, how could they have seen the items confiscated from it during the police search? A jury would have to believe that Allen ferried these items between his apartment and the unidentified house where he'd molested the children. Although not impossible, this was a stretch and could create reasonable doubt.

Besides the mystery of the other house, the Lorain police had scant evidence that Nancy Smith and Joseph Allen knew one another. At the time of the arraignment, that connection hinged on the testimony of Emily Osborne and her husband, Michael. The husband claimed that Allen had been with Nancy Smith at the Head Start Christmas party, but if others at the party could not verify this, the jury would likely think that he was mistaken. That would leave them with only Emily Osborne's story that she'd seen Joseph Allen loitering near Nancy Smith's bus. That did not establish that the two were acquainted and would cast doubt on the entire case. The Lorain police had to redouble their efforts to find more people who had seen the two together.

But they had time. The case would probably not be tried for another six months, maybe longer. During that time, they needed to gather more evidence to strengthen their case. On that effort hinged the ultimate outcome—convictions or acquittals.

CHAPTER 8
LETTER TO JUDGE MCGOUGH
MARCH 31, 1994

Judge Lynett McGough set the letter on her desk and grimaced. It was another letter from a dissatisfied criminal defendant asking her to remove a court-appointed attorney. This time it was Joseph Allen.

She never knew who drafted these letters. She suspected that one or two inmates at the Lorain County Jail probably prepared most of them. In any event, the letter was printed neatly and the grammar and punctuation were sound. The tone was respectful; Allen had addressed the letter to "Dear Honorable Judge."

Allen did not ramble in his letter but went straight to the point:

> *The reason for this letter is I am terminating my court appointed attorney, Joseph Grunda, as of now. I don't want him representing me anymore. Please remove him from my case and appoint me another attorney to represent me in this case.*

Before the case had been assigned to her, the arraigning judge, Judge Kosma Glavas, had appointed an experienced criminal defense attorney to represent him, not an inexperienced attorney who'd recently graduated from law school. That was five months ago and

Grunda was well into the case. Replacing him now would force another attorney to start at the very beginning. Before she would take any action, she would review the court file and see if Grunda had been diligent in his representation.

Opening the folder, she looked at his filings. She quickly concluded that he'd done the appropriate things. He'd sought the discovery of the prosecution's witnesses, exculpatory evidence, and results of tests—all of those things a good criminal defense attorney would request. When the prosecutor had been late in providing this information, he'd filed a motion to compel.

From her vantage point, she believed that Grunda had gone above and beyond what she usually saw from court-appointed attorneys. He'd filed a motion to review grand jury documents, sought a change of venue due to pretrial publicity, asked her to spend county money to hire a private investigator, filed a motion to reduce bond, and filed a motion to dismiss based on the prosecutor's inability to prove that the crime had occurred in Lorain County. She'd denied the motions to dismiss, to reduce bond, and to view the grand jury documents. However, she'd held in abeyance her ruling on the motion to change location until they actually began empaneling a jury.

As she read the second paragraph of Allen's letter, she saw that he was unhappy with her as well:

> *It is necessary that he be removed because he does not care about my rights nor does this court. I have done nothing to be treated this way. I have been falsely accused of this crime and the court knows that I'm innocent and this court has failed to protect my rights.*

Several factors had probably prompted Allen's letter. Although Grunda was being thorough with his filings, he probably was not communicating with his client. She'd fax Grunda a copy of Allen's letter and he would likely talk to his client at his first opportunity. She suspected that after some attention, Allen would be satisfied to continue with his current attorney. She also assumed that Allen was upset because she'd not reduced his bond at a hearing last week. That meant that Allen remained in jail while Nancy Smith (whose bond had been set lower than Allen's) was free. He'd probably seen that as just another example of a judge who didn't care about a black man's rights.

The letter ended with something that sounded like a motion to compel, requesting that the prosecutor divulge his evidence against him. Whoever had written this for Allen ended the letter with this demand:

> *Requesting a motion for discovery. The prosecutor's evidence is ineffective and inconclusive. Therefore, it has become necessary to file a motion to compel discovery. Criminal Rule 16.*

THANK YOU

As far as Judge McGough was concerned, these last few lines confirmed that Grunda was not communicating with his client. Grunda had already filed a motion demanding this crucial information and she'd ruled on it, setting a deadline for the prosecutor to comply. How could Allen claim that she didn't care about his rights? She'd just enforced them.

It was her experience that court-appointed attorneys filed all of the usual documents aimed at discovering the principal parts of the prosecutor's case. However, they normally did not develop their own exculpatory evidence—finding witnesses who could dispute the prosecutor's claims. This was hard work for very little pay. Many of these witnesses lived on society's fringe. They could be poor and uneducated; some had criminal records of their own. It usually took several meetings to adequately prepare one of them for a courtroom appearance. Whether Grunda was finding and developing his own witnesses, she didn't know. That was neither her concern nor her job. She'd eventually grant Grunda's motion to hire a private investigator, but she'd limit the expense to four hundred dollars and wait several months before authorizing the expenditure.

CHAPTER 9
ATTORNEY JACK BRADLEY
JULY 10, 1994

t was a Sunday afternoon and Jack Bradley was in his office. As a busy criminal defense attorney, he had no other choice. From Monday through Friday, he hustled from one courtroom to the next, handling arraignments, pretrials, and sentencings. His daytime schedule barely left time to meet with clients, leading to late-afternoon appointments that often spilled into the early evening.

And that was when he wasn't in trial. When that happened, the trial took over his life, controlling his every waking thought and hijacking his dreams while he tried to sleep. There was always the frenetic work before trial: last-minute motions and a marshaling of the most persuasive facts to include in his opening statement and closing argument. Once in trial, he had to orchestrate the defense and react to his opponent's surprises, while always appearing calm and confident to the jury. And if he lost the high-stakes battle for his client's freedom, he'd be haunted by what he should have done but hadn't. Trials were all-consuming, uncontrollable, and, by their very nature, unpredictable. They were why most attorneys avoided the courtroom.

Between these two demanding worlds, Bradley needed to carve out uninterrupted hours where he could review documents, draft a motion, or silently strategize about a case. However, this Sunday he wouldn't do any of those things. Instead, he'd promised Nancy Smith that they would have a long talk about her upcoming trial.

As he waited for Nancy to arrive, Bradley reflected upon his seventeen years as an attorney. Despite the pressure and the chaos of his work, he couldn't picture himself doing anything else. For as long as he could remember, he'd always wanted to be a lawyer. After earning his bachelor's degree from Case Western Reserve University, he couldn't afford to go directly to law school. Instead, he'd taught fourth-graders at a Lorain elementary school for several years to finance his education at Cleveland State's law school.

Once he'd passed the bar, he'd started his practice from scratch. In those early years, he sometimes waited in the back of the Lorain Municipal Court, hoping that the judge would appoint him to represent an indigent defendant. But he was hardworking, nimble, and personable—traits that served him well when trying cases and in negotiating plea deals outside of the courtroom. Now when local people thought of a talented criminal defense attorney, they thought of him.

He, unfortunately, had a murder trial that would take place almost immediately before Smith's trial. While he was involved in the murder defense, his investigator, Lenny Gerace, a former Lorain police narcotics detective, would be interviewing witnesses and making preparations for the next trial. With Gerace's assistance, he was confident that he'd be ready for the second trial.

Bradley liked Nancy Smith and he was convinced of her innocence. She was understandably consumed by fear as her trial date drew near. Who wouldn't be? To calm her, he'd arranged this meeting to explain what would likely happen at trial—not just the mechanics, but what each side would present as evidence. Over the years, he'd discovered that clients appreciated knowing this up front. He would make no promises to her other than that he would do his best. She'd have to be satisfied with that.

He'd handled every type of criminal case during his career, but this case was different, and it worried him. A hysteria surrounded these allegations, and jurors were human beings who could be swept away by their emotions. With its allegations of sexual molestation of preschool children, this case would foster fear, disgust, and outrage.

Somehow, he'd need to overcome this emotional onslaught and convince the jury that the children's testimony was unreliable and wholly inconsistent with who his client was—a devoted mother who would never injure anyone, particularly a child. But he didn't deceive himself. Anything could happen at this trial—anything.

To compound this uncertainty, he wouldn't know what the children would claim until after they'd been called to the witness stand. Under the antiquated criminal rules in effect in Ohio in 1994, he wasn't allowed to have a copy of their earlier statements until they'd finished answering the prosecutor's questions. After that, it was always a frantic rush to read the statement or listen to a cassette tape and then develop questions for cross-examination. Although the judge would recess the jury while he did his review, he only had a short time. Bradley knew that an effective cross-examination required careful preparation, and this slapdash approach severely hampered his efforts, but it was all he had.

This was even more frustrating because other states had changed this rule and allowed "open discovery," a system where prosecutors were required to provide witness statements and police reports before trial. In Ohio, some prosecutors were releasing this information out of a sense of fairness, thus creating a patchwork of different rules depending on the county or the court. Like his counterparts across the country, Bradley believed that open discovery, with its robust disclosure of evidence, made it less likely for a defendant to be wrongfully convicted. However, with open discovery, defense counsel would be better prepared, increasing the chances that a guilty defendant could be acquitted. Nonetheless, when the criminal justice system had to choose between these two outcomes, it strove to prevent innocent people from being convicted—at least in theory.

Bradley's opponent, Jonathan Rosenbaum, released only what was absolutely required by the law. He and other prosecuting attorneys like him were known as "strictly by the book" prosecutors. Like poker players, most prosecutors held witness statements close to the vest, showing them only when it came time to play them.

Bradley's thoughts were interrupted when he heard someone walking into his waiting room. He left his office and found Nancy

Smith standing in the waiting area. He waved for her to follow him back to his office. As he watched her, Bradley saw a woman trying to hide her anxiety but unable to do so convincingly. She smiled and let out a deep breath as she lowered herself into a chair. However, her façade of calm quickly dissolved.

"I'm not sure I can take this much longer," she said. "I'm not sleeping at night. I keep asking myself: What happens if the jury doesn't believe me?" Smith's chin began to quiver and she tried to fight back the tears. Regaining control for a moment, she answered her own question. "I go to prison and my children lose their mother. Jack, I'm so scared."

Bradley studied his client's anguished face. There were dark shadows under her eyes that her makeup could not hide. Her eyes bored into him, imploring him to give her some reassuring words.

"We have to trust the system, Nancy. We have to believe that twelve jurors will use their common sense and conclude these charges are ludicrous," he replied.

"Jack, I swear to God I don't know that other man. That's the truth," she said, her voice shaking.

"I believe you, Nancy, and a jury will too," he said, maintaining eye contact with her. He knew that this statement broke one of his cardinal rules: never tell your clients how a jury will decide their case. However, she seemed so distraught that he wanted to reassure her.

"So how is the case going?" she asked, the desperation in her voice reduced to urgency.

Bradley sighed inwardly as he contemplated his reply. This was the most common question that clients asked and the most difficult one to answer. Until the testimony and evidence unfolded in the courtroom, the question was unanswerable. Again, he needed to provide his client with hope.

"I think it's going well," he answered. "You know—about as well as could be expected." Before she could quiz him further, he asked, "Were you able to compile that list of additional witnesses for me?"

"Just like you asked, I've got a list of more people from Head Start who want to testify for me," she said, handing him a sheet of wrinkled paper with names, addresses, and phone numbers.

"That's good. I need to update my witness list in a few days and I'll include these." What Bradley did not say was that he had to avoid marginal, duplicative witnesses. For trial, he would choose only those who were knowledgeable, articulate, and made a good appearance. He would cherry-pick the best from their witness list.

"This is hard on my children, too," Smith confided. "None of us feel like leaving the house. People openly stare at us, and their eyes are so accusing. How could they really think that I'd do these horrible things?"

"It's times like this when you find out who really are your friends. I hate to say it, but that's true," Bradley said, his voice quiet and soothing.

His words failed to have a calming effect. "I don't understand how I can go on trial and they don't have to tell me exactly when and where I supposedly did these terrible things." For the first time, she exhibited some anger in her voice.

Bradley agreed. The prosecutor had filed a bill of particulars that was supposed to provide him with the details of the crimes. As to Nancy Smith, the bill alleged that she'd engaged in sexual acts with Marcus Logan and then delivered that boy and Nina Zorich to Joseph Allen, who'd raped them. It also claimed that she had forced another boy, Jason Gilbert, to lick her breasts. The prosecutor claimed that these crimes had occurred sometime between January and June 1993 at an unknown location, a vagueness that made it impossible for either defendant to provide a definite alibi.

"They know I didn't do these things. I passed a lie detector test," Smith said.

"Yes, you did, but the second test was deemed inconclusive."

"But I never failed them."

"Don't you remember what Prosecutor Rosenbaum said about that at the last pretrial?"

Smith shook her head. She'd obviously forgotten. Noting her confusion, Bradley said, "The prosecutor suggested that you have a split personality. Apparently, he and the second polygraph examiner discussed this possibility. No medical evidence of that, of course, just this unsubstantiated claim that you have two completely different people living inside your head. And that's why you passed the first lie detector test. You were the nice Nancy that day, not the bad one."

"How can anyone say that?" she asked, trying to hold back the tears. "At my age, I'm supposed to have suddenly developed multiple personalities." She stopped talking and wiped a tear from her cheek. After regaining her composure, she said, "They investigated me for seven months before they charged me. In all that time, they must have found some evidence that I didn't do these things. Can they just keep that stuff to themselves?"

It was a good question that had no easy or quick answer. Yes, the US Constitution required a prosecutor to turn over any evidence that was exculpatory—so said the US Supreme Court in the case of *Brady v. Maryland*. Simply put, the prosecution had to disclose any evidence that could exonerate the accused or reduce their punishment. However, its application was tricky. The evidence had to be so important that its introduction would probably change the outcome of the case.

In addition, it was the prosecutor who determined what was exculpatory, further complicating the application of the rule. What might appear exculpatory to a defense attorney might not be viewed that way by a prosecutor. They had different perspectives and saw the evidence through different lenses. However, it was the prosecutor alone who determined what was disclosed, without receiving any input from either the judge or the defense counsel. Throughout the country, the law placed prosecutors in a conflicted position. On the one hand, they were supposed to zealously prosecute their cases, while on the other, they were asked to undermine these very cases by ferreting out evidence that was favorable to the defendant and delivering it to the defendant's attorney.

Bradley knew that this was too complicated to explain to his client. Instead, he told her that the prosecutor had identified some evidence as exculpatory. Digging through his file, he pulled out a document labeled "Discovery" and read from it. "Here's what the prosecutor says is favorable to our defense. 'Joseph Allen had an explanation for every item seized by the police from his apartment. Some of the child victims identified people other than Joseph Allen in the photo lineups. Some children identified locations as the site of the molestation that were not accurate. The children have not been able to direct the police to the location where these incidents occurred.'"

"That's not much, is it?" Smith responded.

"They also provided us with a witness list that's a mile long. I want you to look at these names and tell me if you recognize any of them and, if so, what they may know about the case."

"There have to be more than fifty names here," Smith said.

"Sixty-nine actually. I counted them. They'll only call a fraction of them, but we won't know which ones," Bradley responded. It was a game that both prosecutors and defense attorneys played. Bradley's witness list would be equally long.

For the next half hour, he and Smith reviewed the list of names, and when she could, she told Bradley what she knew about the people. After that was completed, he ended the meeting and walked her to the waiting room, where they parted.

When Bradley came back to his desk, he returned the discovery document to its file folder. However, something in the document was out of place. A phrase, listed between the names of prosecution witnesses James Williams and Michael Osborne, read: "The videotape of the lineup conducted with children, defendant, and other subjects." And that was it. The state did not explain why this information was included in its witness list, nor did it suggest that the videotape might be exculpatory. It just dangled there—something without context or meaning, something to be overlooked and ignored.

CHAPTER 10
THE TRIAL BEGINS
JULY 25, 1994

J udge McGough opened the sliding panel door that separated her chambers from her courtroom. Looking down from her bench, she saw three attorneys fidgeting at the trial table, their file folders, loose papers, and yellow pads scattered about them. Nancy Smith and Joseph Allen sat next to their respective attorneys, while two Lorain police detectives flanked Jonathan Rosenbaum. Before the trial began, she would rule on two motions and perhaps resolve other last-minute issues raised by the attorneys. She and the attorneys routinely viewed this time as the warm-up to the main event. However, today's pretrial rulings would have a critical impact on the case's ultimate outcome.

The prosecutor wanted to combine the trials of Nancy Smith and Joseph Allen. Unless the judge allowed this joinder, each defendant would have a separate trial with different juries at different times. Jack Bradley was also seeking a continuance on behalf of his client, Nancy Smith. The judge had reviewed his motion. Truth be told, she'd already set aside this week to try this case and Bradley would have to present some compelling arguments to persuade her to delay this trial for a third time.

She decided to address the joinder motion first. The two cases had many of the same issues involving the Head Start children, but Joseph Allen had also been charged with opportuning prostitution—allegations based on the accusations of the teenage runaways. In his motion, the prosecutor had agreed to separate those claims and try them later. With those charges out of the way, the prosecutor argued that the remaining claims against Joseph Allen arose out of the same facts as those involving Nancy Smith. He'd also reminded the judge that joinder would protect the young children from the ordeal of testifying twice. It went unsaid that joinder would also allow the judge to avoid an extra trial—something she favored whenever possible.

"What is your position on joinder, Mr. Bradley?" she asked.

Bradley knew that consolidating the two cases posed grave dangers to his client. The prosecutor planned to introduce proof that Joseph Allen had pled guilty to molesting a six-year-old girl nine years ago. If that wasn't damaging enough, the prosecutor also intended to call the victim to show that Allen had lured her in the same way that he'd allegedly enticed the Head Start children. Nancy Smith's case would be tainted by this evidence, too, even after the judge provided a "curative instruction" warning the jurors not to consider it when deciding Nancy Smith's fate.

Bradley began, "I filed a motion against this. As I stated in my brief, it would be totally unfair to force Nancy Smith to be tried alongside a convicted felon. There will be evidence presented against Mr. Allen that a jury would not hear if my client were tried separately. I can also foresee that Mr. Allen's defense will not be consistent with ours."

While Bradley was talking, Rosenbaum shook his head vigorously.

"We have a problem here, Mr. Rosenbaum?" the judge asked as she raised her eyebrows.

"No, Your Honor," Rosenbaum replied.

"Mr. Bradley?"

"Not that I know of, Your Honor."

"Okay, then," the judge said. She demanded civility between attorneys in her courtroom and this case would be no different. She'd raised four children by maintaining structure and discipline; she'd do the same with attorneys practicing before her.

From the judge's standpoint, Bradley's arguments were too vague and speculative to sway her. "I understand some of your concerns, Mr. Bradley, however I'm going to allow joinder. Your client's case and Mr. Allen's case involve the same victims, the same time frame, and, specifically in your client's case, allegations that she aided and abetted Joseph Allen. I think these cases are appropriate to consolidate. Not only does that serve judicial economy but it saves these very young victims from testifying twice."

The judge had referred to the children as victims, not as *alleged* victims nor as very young *witnesses*. Like a discordant note, this terminology jarred both Bradley and Grunda, but neither thought it prudent to mention it. No judge liked to be corrected—particularly about their choice of words.

There was another possible ground to oppose joinder, but it was not raised. Nine years earlier, Jack Bradley had served as Joseph Allen's court-appointed attorney when Allen had pled guilty to the charges of child molestation. Was it a conflict of interest for Bradley to continue as counsel for Nancy Smith if both Smith and Allen were tried at the same time? Could Bradley have used this information to convince the judge to deny joinder? Two years later, this issue would be raised, but Judge McGough would refuse to grant a new trial for this and other reasons.

After ruling on the State's motion for joinder, Judge McGough turned to Nancy Smith's motion for a continuance. It was no secret that Bradley had been in trial the previous week; however, that was not the basis for his motion. "Do you wish to be heard on your motion?" she asked.

"Yes, Your Honor. At two thirty on Friday afternoon, just three days ago, we received by fax a supplemental witness list naming five additional witnesses: Marty Howard, Willie Mae Smith, Dr. Richards, Kathy Cole, and Nicole Cole."

"I know who Dr. Richards is, but who are the other four?" the judge asked, directing her gaze at the prosecutor. The judge apparently did not know Dr. Richards very well. The physician at Rainbow Babies and Children's Hospital who examined children for sexual abuse was Dr. Amy Richardson. "Richardson" had become "Richards" in the prosecutor's filing.

Rosenbaum stood. "Mr. Howard provided Joseph Allen with some of the items taken from his house during the police search. Willie Mae Smith is someone who saw Mr. Allen around the Head Start school. The Coles are mother and daughter. One is a bus driver for Head Start and the other is a bus aide. Nancy Smith knows who they are. They will testify that they saw Mr. Allen hanging around the Head Start grounds."

Rosenbaum paused and looked at the two detectives for confirmation. When they nodded, he continued, "Dr. Richards is a woman who examined Nina Zorich for signs of abuse." His voice took on an air of indignation. "Mr. Bradley had notice of this witness. Her medical records were disclosed in discovery several months ago. If Mr. Bradley had requested to see those records back then, he'd have them now. Anyway, he asked me for her records this morning and I am providing them."

"All right, here's what we'll do. If Mr. Rosenbaum will give me a copy of the doctor's records, I'll have my staff make two copies. After Dr. Richards testifies on direct for Mr. Rosenbaum, we'll take a brief recess and I'll give both defense counsel an opportunity to review those records and report. That should give the defense attorneys adequate time to prepare their questions. The motion for a continuance is denied." The judge paused for a moment and then as an afterthought said, "It's my understanding that Dr. Richards won't be testifying until Wednesday anyway."

Bradley looked at Grunda and shook his head ever so slightly. The judge's ruling angered him, but what could he do? It was the kind of ruling that came from a judge who, as an attorney, had tried very few cases. A seasoned litigator knew that cross-examinations required time and research to be effective, particularly when the witness was a physician. To think otherwise was naïve. Even the four lay witnesses would be difficult to cross-examine when he had no opportunity to talk to them in advance or to find out more about their backgrounds.

However, both the judge and the two defense attorneys failed to ask one critical question: When had the prosecutor or his investigators learned that the four lay witnesses had relevant testimony and were potential witnesses? If asked, the prosecutor could not have claimed that these witnesses were recently discovered. The Lorain police had talked to Marty Howard on November 5, 1993; Willie Mae Smith on November 9, 1993; and Kathy Cole on November 16, 1993—all nine months before the trial. If this had been asked and disclosed, the judge could have asked the prosecutor a more probing question: Why did he wait until two and a half days before trial to disclose these witnesses to the defense?

In deciding whether to grant the continuance, the judge had merely tried to gauge the importance of these new witnesses. Everything Rosenbaum had reported about them was true. The Coles and Willie Mae Smith were prepared to testify that they'd seen Joseph Allen around the school. However, there was more to the story. Willie Mae Smith was also going to testify that she'd seen Joseph Allen on Nancy Smith's bus. Both defendants intended to defend themselves by claiming that they did not know each other. As far as the defendants knew, the prosecution had no witnesses who could show any connection between them. However, several other witnesses, embedded in the prosecutor's long witness list, would also testify that they'd seen the defendants together, undermining the cornerstone of this defense.

"Anything else?" the judge asked.

"Yes, Elizabeth Powell, also known as Angel Powell, is not on the prosecutor's witness list," Bradley said. "And I understand the prosecutor is going to call her."

"I believe Elizabeth Powell is on my list," Rosenbaum said. "Judge, you should know that Mr. Bradley sent an investigator to talk to her."

"For the record, this witness refused to talk to us. She said she was trying to work something out with Mr. Rosenbaum," Bradley explained.

"Anyway, Elizabeth Powell is not a new witness. She was his client's bus aide for several weeks before his client was told to stay away from work. I'm so sick and tired of people trying to create surprise out of nothing," Rosenbaum snapped.

"Is she on the list?" Bradley demanded.

"I believe she is."

"Well, find her and then we won't have any problems, Jon. You're sick and tired. I'm sick and tired. Find her on the list," Bradley challenged.

The judge intervened. "Look, is Ms. Powell on the list?" she asked, looking at Rosenbaum, who was scrambling through his file. When he continued searching, she said, "Let's don't take any more time on this right now. We can look at this again after jury selection. Okay?"

"Whether she is or not, I'm including her. She's someone he's aware of. He knew about her. There's no surprise here," Rosenbaum said with a tone of finality, as if he were the judge making the ruling.

Bradley was correct: Elizabeth Powell was not on the prosecutor's witness list. None of the prosecutor's four filings included her name. Rosenbaum was also right: Elizabeth Powell was not a surprise witness. Because Powell had worked on Smith's bus for about a month before Bronson made her initial allegations, Bradley's investigator had tried to interview her before trial but she had refused to talk to him. However, Powell's testimony would be far more damaging to Nancy's defense than they could have imagined at this point. In that sense, she would be a surprise.

The judge sighed. The trial had not yet begun and two of the attorneys were already at each other's throats. "Anything else, counsel?" the judge asked.

"Judge, I'd just like to request that the prosecutor provide me with witness statements, tape-recorded statements, whatever I'm entitled to," Bradley said. "I plan to ask for an *in camera* inspection of statements after each and every witness testifies on direct examination." Although the two Lorain detectives looked confused by the Latin phrase "*in camera*," the attorneys and judge were not. It was simply a legal term for a private review in the judge's chambers.

"Mr. Rosenbaum, I think you are well aware of the defendant's right to review witness statements at that time. Are there any statements?"

"Define 'statements,'" Rosenbaum said.

The judge looked at Rosenbaum quizzically. He was an experienced litigator and obviously knew what was required. "Either written or tape-recorded statements," she said.

"There are tapes of everyone," the prosecutor admitted.

"Then we will need those tapes and the appropriate tape recorders to play them," she said.

Rosenbaum nodded.

"And if there is any exculpatory evidence either in the prosecutor's files or the detectives' files, then these should be turned over to the defense immediately."

After waiting a few seconds and receiving no reply, the judge cleared her throat. "We'll recess for a few minutes and then I'll have the bailiff bring in the prospective jurors. Let's reconvene at ten o'clock."

CHAPTER 11
JURY SELECTION
JULY 25, 1994

I n state courtrooms across Ohio, attorneys are usually given wide latitude to question prospective jurors, often without time limits. This allows both sides to probe would-be jurors to unmask potential biases, develop a rapport, and gently indoctrinate them about their case. But that did not happen in Judge McGough's courtroom. Early in her term, she'd watched as attorneys wasted precious time with their repetitiveness and disorganization, particularly during jury selection. She respected the work of seasoned trial attorneys, but the inexperienced ones, those who rarely tried a case, were the culprits, and their bumbling drew her ire. As a result, she'd decided to conduct much of the juror questioning herself, regardless of the experience of the litigators involved. It was not unprecedented; federal judges handled jury selection without much input from the attorneys.

Because Judge McGough's courtroom was small, she cleared it of all spectators in order to accommodate the forty or so people who'd been summoned to serve as possible jurors. Soon, twelve people were seated in the jury box, with the remainder bunched together on the two spectator benches in the back. After introducing each attorney, she asked them to introduce their clients to the assembled group.

With the preliminaries out of the way, she launched into group questions where she explained the concept of reasonable doubt, the presumption of a defendant's innocence, their obligation to follow the law, their responsibility to assess the credibility of witnesses, and the state's duty to prove each and every element of the crimes charged. After each explanation, she asked the panel if they understood what she'd said, to which the twelve dutifully nodded.

Because Joseph Allen's attorney, Joseph Grunda, had sought a change of venue, Judge McGough asked the group about their prior knowledge of the case based on media coverage. Several jurors indicated that they had some information about the case from the newspaper articles. After quizzing each one individually, she ended the queries by asking, "If you are chosen as a juror in this case, can you set aside what you have read or heard and base your decision solely on the evidence and testimony that comes to you in this courtroom?" They all said that they could.

As Rosenbaum and Bradley listened to these questions and answers, they knew that the judge's inquiries were superficial. During jury selection, experienced attorneys asked open-ended questions to gauge a prospective juror's feelings on a subject. Once jurors begin talking, an attorney has a much better chance of evaluating them. The judge's leading questions elicited nothing more than a yes-or-no answer, revealing little of a person's inner beliefs. Of course, jurors would claim that they could set everything else aside and be fair when asked that pointed question. The issue was whether one side was beginning the case with a head start, even a slight one. The only way to find out was to ask prying questions that forced the jurors to reveal themselves.

Although the judge could stop him if he revisited a subject that she'd covered, Bradley considered whether he should dig deeper into the pretrial publicity when he addressed the group. As he was jotting this down on his legal pad, he heard the judge ask: "Would you agree with me that the charges here are terrible?" The panel nodded. He'd often posed this question to would-be jurors in prior cases, but it was different when he, as the defense attorney, asked this. However, when the judge inquired, this question seemed to communicate that she was personally repulsed by what these defendants had done.

The judge continued, "And they evoke in all of us a response that ranges from anger to disgust, these are terrible charges?" Again, the panel nodded and an uncomfortable sense of dread crept into Bradley's gut.

"Is there anything about the charges alone that would cause you to begin the case with a preconceived notion?" she asked. Everyone shook their heads. Bradley relaxed; perhaps he was overreacting to this line of questioning.

"We all have an absolute revulsion when we hear about cases that involve the abuse of children," the judge intoned. "Would you all agree?" Again, Bradley tensed. How much longer would the judge stay on this topic?

"But wouldn't you all agree with me that it is equally important that if people are not guilty of child abuse, that they be found not guilty?" she asked. The panel again nodded.

And so it went for an additional half hour as Judge McGough asked pointed questions to the group. When she'd finished, she looked at the attorneys. "I'll ask all counsel at this time, please don't cover these topics again." Then, addressing the prosecutor, she said, "Mr. Rosenbaum, your opportunity to inquire."

The prosecutor rose and nodded to the prospective jurors. "Good morning, ladies and gentlemen," Rosenbaum began. He was greeted with a chorus of good mornings from the panel. "As you might guess, the reason we ask all of these questions is because we're looking for jurors that can do the best they can."

Following the lengthy questioning by the judge, the prospective jurors were ready to listen to the prosecutor. After scanning all of their faces, he began solemnly, "If we don't get twelve people who are going to do the job we give them as jurors, the whole criminal justice system fails. When that happens, we don't need police, we don't need lawyers, we don't need courthouses, and we don't need the law. All these things lead up to your role, which is to put it all together. And if you don't do that, it's wasted, right?"

The jurors nodded. They were supposed to agree with him, weren't they?

Both Grunda and Bradley had heard variations of this theme from other prosecutors, but Rosenbaum's opening gambit was both blunt and bold—a direct challenge to the jury. He was signaling to them that if they didn't do their duty, countless hours of police and prosecutorial work would be thrown away. Did they have the toughness to finish the hard work done by others? He stopped short of telling them that it was their job to convict, but the implication was clear.

His next task was to condition the panel to view his case favorably and to defuse its weaknesses. Talented trial attorneys can do this seamlessly. In this case, Rosenbaum would present very young witnesses who claimed that they were victims of a variety of strange sexual acts. Some of what they said made no sense, and this strangeness extended beyond the bizarre sexual acts that they would describe.

"Is there anyone here that has a hard time believing that someone would molest a child?" Rosenbaum asked the panel as a group. No one said anything or raised a hand in response.

"Does anybody find this fact so weird that they can't believe it to be true?" Again no one responded.

"Let me put it this way: Sometimes sexual acts between human beings, whether it be adults and children or adults and adults, are pretty bizarre by our standards. Do you feel that some people have tastes that just can't be accounted for? Mrs. Hersh, what do you think?"

"I feel the same," she responded.

No longer content with group questions, the prosecutor asked this question selectively to individual jurors. "I mean, we know that no matter how sickening, these things could go on, right?" Each prospective juror agreed. Rosenbaum was conditioning the jurors to accept the improbable, making the impossible possible.

He then asked them if they believed that four-year-old children had the ability to identify someone who had abused them. They did. "Was it possible that Head Start students, kids who lacked self-confidence, were more likely to be targeted for molestation?" When asked, several jurors agreed to keep an open mind on this.

By the time Rosenbaum completed his questioning, he'd planted seeds that sexual predators do inexplicable things to satisfy their strange cravings. He'd also suggested that disadvantaged children could be targeted by predators. He'd personally engaged with each of them and obtained commitments that these allegations were possible and to be taken seriously. More important, the judge had never curtailed his questioning and defense counsel had never objected to any of his inquiries, even those that were so fact-specific that an objection might have been sustained.

Jack Bradley rose and stood before the panel. He seemed confident and eager to interact with them. He was a Lorain boy, comfortable with everyday people, and, as a result, talking to jurors came naturally to him. After some preliminary questions, he wanted to take away some of the prosecutor's early gains.

"Do you think that there's ever a situation where a child might make a false accusation about being sexually abused?"

Like Rosenbaum, he singled out individual jurors to answer this question. Each one agreed that it was possible. One even suggested that a child might "be intimidated" to make a false claim. However, there were already signs that the jurors were not going to easily dismiss a child's assertion of sexual molestation.

"So you have a three-year-old and a four-year-old. Do they ever have fantasies?" Bradley asked one prospective male juror.

"Yes."

"How about something as serious as sexual abuse?"

"I imagine it could happen," the man said.

"Do you think this would be rare?"

"Yeah."

"Why?"

"Because I teach them to tell the truth and we're always asking questions about things like that."

If the case had involved the claims of one or two children, jurors would have been more likely to dismiss the story as wholly fantastical. However, if a handful of children claimed that they had been sexually abused by these defendants, jurors would find it increasingly difficult to conclude that the stories were made up. At that age, children could not talk among themselves to invent a common story, could they?

Bradley attempted to suggest another reason for the false claims. "Is it possible that a child is abused and transfers that blame onto someone else?" One panel member conceded that "kids make things up and could do this," but none of the prospective jurors seemed overly excited by this suggestion. Neither Bradley nor Grunda had hired an expert witness to support this theory.

Trying another tack, Bradley asked, "There's so much graphic stuff on cable television. Is it possible that children can be exposed to this and then have it affect their little minds? What do you think about that, Mrs. Culver?"

"I think children are shielded from these television shows, but I suppose they could. Who's to say?" she answered, quickly breaking eye contact with Bradley.

He posed that same question to several other prospective jurors and received equally tepid responses. However, when he asked them whether the police could make a mistake, they all readily acknowledged that this could happen. After another fifteen minutes of questioning, Bradley finished and the judge told Grunda that he could inquire.

The former prosecutor began by reminding the panel that the case was not about "these kids" against two adults, but the State of Ohio, with all of its power, against two defendants. By now, the group had been questioned by the judge and two attorneys and were tiring of the process. Unless Grunda engaged with them on an individual basis, they were likely to allow their minds to drift.

"You understand that children may have practiced their testimony with adults many times before they get on the witness stand?" Grunda asked the group. It was an important idea but one that needed to be reinforced by peppering individual prospective jurors with the question. If he had reminded the panel that he'd served as Lorain County's prosecutor for twelve years, they might have accepted his suggestion that prosecutors often rehearsed children's testimony several times before trial. But he did not.

"You agree with me that sometimes a person who gives a false story, after saying it and repeating it many times, may eventually come to believe that the story is true?" By this question, he had suggested a mechanism by which the children could appear convincing when they were, in fact, not telling the truth. Again, he did not reinforce the point by seeking comments or opinions from any member of the panel.

"You understand that a child can be manipulated by older people? Any of you doubt this? It could be an adult, parent, friend, or even a law enforcement officer?" This was another powerful suggestion, but, because he abandoned the point after the group nodded, the idea never had an opportunity to sink its roots into their minds. After five more minutes of group questions, Grunda concluded his inquiries.

Because all three attorneys had finished their questioning, they would now have the opportunity to excuse individual jurors for any reason by exercising their peremptory challenges. The prosecutor had eight peremptory challenges, while each defendant had four. Rosenbaum waived his first challenge, but Bradley used his. With one of the twelve dismissed, the bailiff called another prospective juror to be questioned.

Judge McGough asked the new person, Edward Minney, the same questions that she had posed earlier in the trial to the panel but also incorporated questions that had been asked by the prosecutor and defense attorneys. Her questions were leading and Mr. Minney answered them with a perfunctory yes or no. Satisfied that she had covered all of the important questions, the judge said to the attorneys, "Mr. Rosenbaum and all counsel, very briefly, please."

Agitated, Rosenbaum rose. "May we approach the bench, Your Honor?" Once all the attorneys were gathered in front of the judge, Rosenbaum said, "If we are going to be able to function like lawyers in this case, then we've got to take a pause. This is an important case to all of us with kids. You may have asked some of the questions that we have touched upon, but I'm not going to rush here. If you are going to take away my right to question prospective jurors, then you might as well take it away entirely."

This was not the first time that attorneys had objected to Judge McGough's efforts to speed up a trial, but, before today, the unhappy attorneys had always been respectful to her. The prosecutor's brazenness momentarily unnerved her, but she quickly decided that if she showed any weakness, she would lose control of the trial.

In the firmest voice she could muster, she said, "That's what I can do if I have to." She expected this would silence the dissenting prosecutor, but it had the opposite effect.

"I don't think so," he said with equal authority. "We can appeal this and that's what's going to happen." This was a threat. No judge wanted to try a lengthy case and have it appealed and reversed on a technicality. Rosenbaum continued, "We have a right to interact with this jury. If you are going to just repeat my questions because you're in a hurry, maybe you ought to do it all."

The judge's blue eyes blazed as she sought to contain her anger. "This man has heard all of the questions. I want to give you limited voir dire," the judge said, using the legal term for the jury selection process.

"He has not," Rosenbaum snapped back. "The fact that he's heard the questions doesn't mean a thing."

"The law gives me the right to question prospective jurors. And I have the right to do it entirely by myself."

"Then I wish you'd just say that and we could be done with it," he said.

The judge was through sparring with the prosecutor. "Your voir dire, Mr. Rosenbaum," she responded in a tone that said, "Take it or leave it."

Although the judge never backed down during this exchange with Rosenbaum, she did not limit any of the attorneys from asking questions for the remainder of the selection process. Four jurors were eventually excused, and it took another hour of questioning to find their replacements. By the end of the process, twelve jurors (six men and six women) and two alternates had been selected.

The preliminaries were over. A jury would begin the process of ferreting out truth from lies. Upon that rested the fates of the defendants.

CHAPTER 12
OPENING STATEMENTS
JULY 25, 1994

"Ladies and gentlemen, each party will now tell you what they think the evidence will be. These are called opening statements. What the attorneys say is not evidence but simply a preview or outline of their respective cases," Judge McGough said. She was pleased that the trial had moved so quickly into this next stage. With a little luck, the prosecution might also have time to call a few witnesses before she sent the jury home for the day.

In outlining the case to the jury, the prosecutor had the advantage. He knew who would testify for the State and what they were likely to say. Defense counsel, on the other hand, were like children peering through the slats of a wooden fence, seeing only a portion of the baseball field. The defense attorneys knew only what had been disclosed in the bill of particulars and what they had uncovered from talking to people on the case's periphery. This group included the Head Start employees friendly to Nancy Smith and parents whose children were not part of the probe. They'd sent investigators to talk to the alleged victims' parents, but some had refused to talk, and those who had, hadn't divulged much.

Defense attorneys could defer their opening statements until after the prosecution's case had concluded, but this was almost never done.

Both Bradley and Grunda would give their opening statements now, recognizing that they needed to counter Rosenbaum's narrative early on.

Rosenbaum began, "The attorneys for the defense are not the only people who appreciate that children are impressionable and may repeat what they hear. I think you'll find that the police investigated this case as best as humanly possible to avoid any type of contamination that the children would get from other children."

However, case contamination can occur in ways other than children talking between themselves. It happens when parents talk to each other, if media coverage discloses details of the accusations, or if police and parents improperly question children. Rosenbaum's opening salvo was strong, suggesting that the charges were the result of a careful, deliberate investigation.

He next assured the jury that the prosecutorial team understood the gravity of the charges and would not have proceeded in this case unless it had good cause. "No one here has any desire to convict the wrong person. That will not protect the children of our community, which I think is everybody's goal in this courtroom."

Like any good trial lawyer, he also decided to use his opening statement to disclose a weakness in his case, namely his inability to tell the jurors when these crimes precisely happened. He continued, "These events occurred sometime between January of 1993 and June of 1993. Of course, we are dealing with kids who were threatened with violence if they told.

"The kids began to act out. A lot of children were doing things that we know children shouldn't know about." Although attorneys are required to stick to reporting facts in opening statements, Rosenbaum ventured into argument: "They couldn't have learned this from watching cable TV."

The children's bizarre sexual conduct would become a key component to the prosecution's case. Every parent who testified would claim that their child exhibited some aberrant behavior. However, the police records did not fully bear this out. Several of the parents had never reported these actions to the police when the allegations first surfaced.

Rosenbaum paused and surveyed the jurors' faces before returning to his presentation. "The children were interviewed and reinterviewed. The police did so in a manner that attempted to have them tell us what happened, not for us to suggest things to them." Several years later, psychologists and psychiatrists, experts in child interview techniques, would listen to the taped interviews and reach the opposite conclusion. These experts, four in total, would find that the Lorain police had broken almost all of the fundamental rules for questioning young children about potential sexual abuse. These departures were not deliberate but the result of the interviewers' lack of training and experience.

Rosenbaum continued, "The way this case came to light, I think, also confirms what these children have to say. And you will find that it can't be rumor spreading or as a result of witness contamination.

"The children came forward eventually due to inappropriate behavior. They all said that Nancy Smith took them to Joseph's house. No one knew who Joseph was. One boy said his name was Allen. This defendant's name turns out to be Joseph Allen.

"All the kids said that Joseph was ugly and had some skin problems. Some said he was a black man with white spots. Others said he was a white man who wore black makeup." Again, Rosenbaum divulged a weakness in his case and deftly defused it.

"Joseph Allen was interviewed by Detective Miller as a suspect in another case. Allen said he can't engage in sex with people. 'I have diseases,' he said. 'Let me show you my body.' Guess what? He had scars on his body where the pigmentation was light, and he had white spots." Rosenbaum was telling a story, the best way to engage with an audience, and he had the jury's full attention. "And guess who happened to have white spots and guess whose name is Joseph and whose last name is Allen?"

Rosenbaum explained that the children were reinterviewed and asked to pick Joseph Allen from a lineup. "Some pick him out. Other kids look at him, panic, and identify everyone but him. Some of the kids, we'll be honest, couldn't say that's him." Again, Rosenbaum had disclosed a weakness in his case and attempted to neutralize it. He continued, "Everybody could identify Nancy."

He next prepared the jury for the children's testimony, not only its content but its unpredictability. "If the kids don't panic on the stand, they'll tell you about the bizarre and sick acts: tying them up, prodding them, pushing things into their private parts, being stuck with needles, picture taking, oral sex, attempted or possible anal sex."

After this shocking claim, he introduced another weakness in his case. "Nancy participated and transported them to this unknown location. We still don't know where it is."

He would end with what was probably the prosecution's most compelling evidence. After telling the jury that Joseph Allen lived alone, Rosenbaum revealed that the police had found peculiar things at his house. "There are no children living in his home, but he has toys and a mask. He has clothing for little children. He has a pornographic book that has a picture of someone shooting a hole in someone's head. He has a large dress. For some reason, he has photographs of a room decorated for a children's party."

These were, indeed, strange things to be found in the home of a middle-aged, single man, but he did host women friends who came to his apartment with their children.

Rosenbaum lowered his voice. "Nina Zorich volunteered that the eyes on the mask light up. And the mask does have eyes that light up. She told the police about that before she ever saw it. The kids also drew a picture of the belt that Joseph tied them up with. The police found a belt that fits that description. Another kid told police that Joseph Allen vowed to wear a dress and come to his house to kill him if he ever told about what went on there. The police found a dress in Joseph's house that was large enough for him to wear.

"They told us about these things before Joseph was ever identified. That means nobody put this stuff into their heads." Anyone listening to the prosecutor's opening statement knew that this evidence was persuasive. These things could not be a coincidence. It lifted the children's stories from the incredible to the truthful.

Detective Miller's written report about the Halloween mask told a slightly different story. The detective had asked Nina Zorich if Joseph had ever worn a Halloween mask with black hair. When she said that he had, Miller also asked her if the eyes did anything. Although Rosenbaum had implied that Nina's mask identification had been spontaneous, it had, in fact, been prompted and had occurred after Allen was a suspect.

Almost as an afterthought, Rosenbaum told the jury that the State would present evidence proving that Nancy Smith knew Joseph Allen. He did not outline what that evidence was nor suggest who would testify about it—only that it was coming. As a result, the defense would have no opportunity to prepare for it until it happened.

Experienced trial attorneys recognize that a case can be won in the opening statement. Studies show that a juror's first impression rarely changes after the opening statement. The prosecutor's opening statement had been as skillful as it had been forceful. Certain that both defendants were child molesters, he'd delivered an opening statement that provided a convincing blueprint for their conviction.

To counter what they'd just heard, the defendants' attorneys needed to deliver concise, hard-hitting opening statements of their own. Bradley began his presentation in a folksy, conversational way.

"Let me tell you about Nancy Smith. She is a thirty-seven-year-old single mother with four teenage children. At the time that these allegations arose, she and her children lived with her parents. Her mother passed away a few months ago and they still live with her father. She is a graduate of Lorain High School." His intent was to show the jury that his client was an average citizen just like them, incapable of harming small children.

Bradley then launched into a detailed summary of his client's average workday. He explained how she juggled three jobs: driving Head Start children to the school's morning session, transporting senior citizens to the YMCA immediately after that, returning to the Head Start school to pick up the morning children, driving the afternoon Head Start children to school, starting a third job to drive elementary students to the YMCA, and then returning to the Head Start school to take the afternoon children back to their homes. Nancy Smith was engaged from seven thirty a.m. to five p.m., scurrying from one job to the next. After describing his client's daily routine, Bradley told the jurors, "Again, don't hold me to all of the details."

By documenting Nancy Smith's busy day, Bradley was suggesting that she was far too busy to carve out an hour or so to do the things she was accused of. Besides the hour that the children were allegedly at Joseph's house, the prosecution needed to show that the children were in Nancy Smith's custody for the entire afternoon. On the days of the alleged abuse, the children claimed that they never entered the school for the afternoon session that ran from one thirty to five.

Bradley could have challenged the prosecutor to prove that the Head Start children were with his client the entire time that they should have been in school. Would the prosecutor tell them how she managed this? She'd obviously have had to skip her afternoon job at the YMCA. Did she? Would the prosecution provide records to show that she had? If so, would these records match the children's absentee records from the Head Start program?

After chronicling Nancy Smith's day, Bradley revealed that Head Start required a bus aide to assist his client on her route. In addition, Head Start parents often rode the bus with her. Once the bus arrived at the school, the schoolteachers met the buses and gathered the children from them. Bradley was outlining one of the cornerstones of his defense. How could the children have been secreted away from the school under the noses of a bus aide, a parent rider, and teachers who met the bus? Were the bus aides and teachers somehow complicit in Nancy Smith's scheme or simply incompetent in discharging their duties?

Central to both Smith's and Allen's defense was the claim that they didn't know each other. Just that morning, he'd learned that three of the prosecution's eleventh-hour witnesses would tell the jury that they'd seen Joseph Allen hanging around the Head Start school. Bradley didn't know what these people would claim or if additional "linkage" witnesses were buried in the prosecution's long witness list. These things weighed on Bradley as he moved on to discussing this evidence, and he decided to be careful—better to underpromise and overdeliver than to do the opposite.

"There may be witnesses that come in here to say that my client, Nancy Smith, knows this man," Bradley said as he pointed to Joseph

Allen. "The prosecution may present witnesses who say that they think they may have seen this man in the vicinity of the Head Start school or may have seen a black man on her bus, but I think that they're mistaken. I think that they are wrong.

"You're going to decide whether or not the State has established beyond a reasonable doubt that Nancy Smith had any type of relationship with this man." He would be better able to argue this point in his closing argument after he'd heard all of the evidence on the point. With that, he sat down, to be replaced by Grunda.

Standing before the assembled twelve, Grunda began, "Quite frankly, at this point, I do not know what the evidence will show in this case." This might have been acceptable if he'd been addressing the judge or a group of attorneys who knew that prosecutors rarely disclosed the details of their cases. However, it set the wrong tone for this jury. They'd heard the prosecutor talk about the peculiar things found in Joseph Allen's apartment and they wanted to know if any of this could be explained.

"The little we know about this case is this: Joseph Allen did not know that woman until they got charged. I believe that the evidence will show that Nancy Smith never brought anyone over to see my client." Grunda then explained that Allen lived in a one-floor unit in public housing located on Broadway, the main commercial street in Lorain, Ohio. His neighbors never saw a woman dropping children off at his place nor a big yellow bus parked near his unit.

"There will be evidence that Sandra Caban, a woman friend, lived there with Joseph Allen off and on between January and June of 1993. This was not an intimate relationship. He provided Sandra Caban with a place to stay and she kept some clothes there.

"You will also learn that my client has nieces and nephews who come to visit him and he has toys for them. The evidence will be that he had nothing to do with these Head Start children. None of these children were at his apartment or anyplace where he went. You will find that he is innocent of having anything to do with these children."

As it would later develop, Grunda would not call any witnesses to establish any of these assertions. Sandra Caban would not testify, nor would any of Joseph Allen's brothers testify about visits with their children at Joseph's apartment where they played with toys.

If cases were won or lost based on the opening statements, the defendants were in trouble.

CHAPTER 13
THE STATE'S CASE BEGINS
JULY 25, 1994

First impressions are as important in trials as they are among individuals meeting for the first time. For that reason, a party's first witness is carefully selected. Rosenbaum's choice, Emily Osborne, was a surprise. Although she had worked for two months at Head Start and her son attended the program there, she did not appear to have any meaningful connection to the case. Her son, Michael, was not identified as one of the alleged victims. For the defense attorneys, it was difficult to see how her testimony could significantly advance the prosecutor's case.

In her early thirties, Mrs. Osborne was a solidly built, attractive woman with long blond hair. She was articulate in a blunt way, an intelligent woman who would likely connect with the predominately white jury. And she did have things to say that fit squarely within Rosenbaum's narrative. Better yet, she had moved to Boise, Idaho, five weeks before trial. Even if the defendants' investigators had tried to locate her, they would not have been able to talk to her in person.

After being sworn, Mrs. Osborne explained that she was married, had one son—Michael Osborne III—and had worked at Head Start for about two months as a bus aide from December 1992 until sometime in February 1993. She had also served as secretary to the Head Start board, taking and typing its minutes. For the last five weeks, she and her family had lived in Boise at her sister's house. As she answered these preliminary questions, the witness's voice grew stronger. She appeared to be a stable, responsible woman who by a twist of fate had found herself on the witness stand in this sensational case.

"Now, did there come a point where you noticed some sort of behavior change in Michael?" Rosenbaum asked, wasting no time in getting to the crux of the examination.

Clearing her throat, Mrs. Osborne said, "Sometime in December of 1992, Michael came home from school and he was very, very quiet, which is not like Michael at all. He is very, very talkative." The witness looked at the jury before she continued with her story.

"Michael came in and went straight to his bedroom and shut the door. And that is unusual too. He never shuts the door.

"Well, I gave him a few minutes, oh, maybe twenty-five minutes, and he didn't come out. I figured he was changing his clothes, getting something else on. So, I went downstairs and I didn't knock on the door, I just opened it."

Rosenbaum was careful not to interrupt Mrs. Osborne. She was telling her story in a straightforward way and had the jury's full attention—not an easy feat after they'd spent a long day being questioned during jury selection and listening to opening statements.

"And he had his pants down and he was on top of a big bear that was about two and a half or three feet tall. I didn't get angry with him or anything. I just asked him, 'What are you doing?' And he looked at me and said, 'I'm humping.' And I said, 'You're what?' And he goes, 'I'm humping.' I said, 'Well, where did you learn that from?'"

Knowing where this was headed, Bradley objected. To answer this question, Mrs. Osborne would have to repeat her son's response—something known as hearsay. And this type of hearsay was inadmissible. However, the judge overruled him. After Rosenbaum told her to continue, she said, "And I asked him where he learned that and he said, 'From a guy at school.' And I said, 'What guy?' And he said, 'Joseph.' And I said, 'Who is Joseph?' He goes, 'You know, he works there.'"

Mrs. Osborne told the jury that Michael described Joseph as a black

man. Because Mrs. Osborne was an aide on the same bus that transported her son to school, he promised to point out Joseph when they
arrived at the Nativity School. She explained that the Head Start
program held its half-day programs at Nativity, but the full-day
program was hosted at City Center, a few miles away. Once the bus
arrived at Nativity, Michael transferred from a bus driven by a man
named Abraham to a bus operated by Nancy that took him to the full-
day program at City Center. Over the next few days, Michael was
unable to point out Joseph as he walked from one bus to the next one.
However, on the Friday before the Christmas break, she had an
encounter with Joseph.

She explained that the buses were lined up with Nancy's in front
and Abraham's in the third position. She watched as Michael walked
toward Nancy's bus until he reached the back of her bus, ready to
board. After that, she turned and went back onto her bus.

"The next thing I know, he comes running over to me and he was
shaking like a leaf. And I asked him what was wrong. And he told me,
he says, 'Joseph grabbed me.' And I come running off the bus with him
and he points to this man and says, 'He grabbed me by the arm.'"

"Did you have a confrontation with this man?" Rosenbaum asked.

"Yes, with Joseph."

"Is that man in the courtroom today?"

"Yes."

"Can you point him out?"

"Right there in the green shirt."

"Let the record reflect that the witness has identified the defendant," Rosenbaum said.

Over the next few minutes, Mrs. Osborne told the jury that Joseph
was standing by a tree and fence, away from the buses, when she saw
him. She marched over to him and told him to stay away from her son,
promising that either she or her husband would take action if he ever
tried anything like that again. She also claimed that she'd seen Joseph
around the school about "a half a dozen" other times.

Pointing toward Joseph Allen, Rosenbaum cemented the identification by asking, "Is there any doubt in your mind that this is the man
that Michael identified as grabbing his arm?"

"Not at all," Mrs. Osborne replied resolutely. "Michael was scared to death of him. You know, there was no doubt in my mind whatsoever. Michael had no hesitation in pointing him out."

"Has Michael told you of any other encounters that he's had with Joseph?"

Mrs. Osborne looked down at her lap. "He's been very sketchy. He's afraid," she explained. "Sometimes he's willing to talk about these things, but his story changes a lot as far as when. The only thing that he was really adamant about is that encounter."

Emily Osborne had given the prosecution a potent beginning. She'd painted a picture of a sick and perverted man snatching little children, almost at will, as preoccupied adults were busy doing other things. How could the jurors not fear this large black man sitting just a few feet away from them? However, Mrs. Osborne was not through; she had one more salvo to deliver.

In his opening statement, Rosenbaum had disclosed that not all of the children had been able to identify Joseph Allen in the police lineup. With Mrs. Osborne's help, Rosenbaum would turn this weakness into a strength. Rosenbaum asked her to describe what happened when Michael was placed in the observation room.

"They were standing in a line and Michael picked out everybody but him. He went all around him. I mean, every single time. He was brought into the room I believe three or four times. And he went every single time, everybody but him, even though they put Mr. Allen in different positions in the lineup."

Mrs. Osborne also described what happened the last time Michael was asked to identify Joseph Allen.

"There were five guys and Allen was the fourth one from the right. They had the first guy step forward and everyone just right down the line. Michael didn't react. He was saying, 'Yeah, maybe, no, yeah, oh, that's him.'" Mrs. Osborne paused as if remembering the event more clearly. She continued, "And then Joseph stepped forward and Michael jumped back like this and says, 'That's not him.' And I was like, 'Are you sure, Michael?' He started crying. He got all teary and ran out of the room."

With that, Rosenbaum concluded his direct examination. After being asked about prior statements, the prosecutor told Bradley and the judge that there were none for this witness. The defense attorneys would have to fashion their cross-examinations based on what they'd just heard and nothing more.

However, there was more—a lot more. When the videotape of this police lineup was viewed three years later after a public records request, it told a different story. For the thirteen minutes that Michael Osborne was in the observation room, Mrs. Osborne was with her son for only two and a half minutes. The videotape showed Michael identifying three of the five men as Joseph, and never identifying Joseph *and* another man. More shocking, Michael never ran out of the room frightened and crying. In the tape, the boy appeared calm throughout. In fact, at one point, Michael had playfully picked up the dead microphone and mimicked one of the detectives, pretending to ask one of the men in the lineup to step forward. The videotape was in sharp contrast to Mrs. Osborne's testimony. And she would be the only witness to talk about the lineup.

If the criminal rules had permitted the defense attorneys to have access to the Lorain police reports, Bradley and Grunda could have destroyed this witness in short order. But the rules did not allow it. As a result, they did not know that when Detective Cantu first talked to Mrs. Osborne on May 28, 1993, she'd only reported her son's humping. She'd never mentioned anything about a confrontation with Joseph.

Five months later, on October 30, 1993, after Mrs. Osborne and her son had viewed a photo lineup of suspects, she'd told Detective Miller a different story about Joseph. She claimed that she had been holding Michael's hand when he spotted Joseph standing by Nancy Smith's bus. The boy had broken free from her grasp and run away. After she'd caught up with him, he'd said, "I'm not going back to Nancy's bus until that stranger leaves." In her earlier story, she hadn't accused Joseph of grabbing her son, nor had she described any angry encounter with him. Her account had apparently evolved over the past nine months.

Bradley began his cross-examination like a boxer jabbing and probing for his opponent's weak spot. He spent several minutes quizzing Mrs. Osborne about her son's bus drivers for the various legs of his rides but did not succeed in contradicting any part of her story. He also suggested that Mrs. Osborne had been fired from her job, but she denied it, claiming that she had fractured her ankle and could not move about on the buses. He sought to gain an admission that a bus aide was always present on a bus along with the driver. However, she parried that by saying "almost always."

He eventually jumped to the arm-grabbing incident.

"And then you had an encounter with this Joseph where he'd tried to grab your son at the Head Start program?"

"Not tried. He did," Mrs. Osborne protested.

"You saw that?"

"No, my son said so. He was still holding his arm and his arm was red."

"Then at that point you called the police?"

"No, I didn't."

Bradley had landed his first real blow, but there was another potential follow-up question. If this incident had happened just before Christmas, presumably Michael was wearing a heavy winter jacket. How then could Mrs. Osborne have seen that his arm was red? Did she have X-ray vision?

Bradley continued, "You went to the Head Start program and reported this incident?"

"I talked to someone. Yes, I did," she countered. "I talked to Glen. I don't know his last name." Mrs. Osborne was referring to Glen Thaler, the director for transportation at Head Start, who would be one of Bradley's key witnesses. Thaler was scheduled to tell the jury that the program's safeguards made it virtually impossible for Nancy Smith to drive away from the school with several children still on board.

"And you told Glen that there is this Joseph who is hanging around the school and that he's taught your son how to hump and also grabbed his arm?"

"No, we did not talk about the humping," she said. "I mentioned the arm, but I wasn't sure about what Michael was saying about the humping."

"So you didn't tell him about that?"

"No, I didn't."

"Nothing further with this witness," Bradley said. He'd found a weakness in her story and exploited it. There was no reason to allow her to wriggle out of it. He'd ended on a high note.

Grunda stood and looked at his legal pad. Part of Mrs. Osborne's account troubled him and made him suspicious. After the incident, Mrs. Osborne had allegedly seen Joseph Allen by a fence, away from the buses. But she had watched as her son walked toward Nancy Smith's bus, following him to the back portion of Nancy's bus. How could Joseph have grabbed her son by Nancy's bus and then be found standing near a tree just a few moments later?

Explaining the discrepancy, Mrs. Osborne said, "My son was one of the children that doesn't always go straight onto the bus. He'd run around in front of the buses and play."

"But you were there?"

"Yes, I was."

"You were watching him?"

"Yes."

"You did not see Joseph?"

"No, I didn't."

Quickly moving to another topic, Grunda asked, "And you also say that your son changes stories a lot?"

"Yes."

"And he doesn't always tell the truth, does he?"

"He doesn't tell big lies or anything like that. He just makes—"

"Makes stories up?"

"Yeah, makes stories up like little kids. They sit there and they play with their cars."

"What about you?"

"What about me?"

"Do you make up stories?"

"No, I do not."

"Do you tell the truth?"

"Not when I'm—" She stopped. "I make up stories to my son to tell him a story, a bedtime story and stuff."

Grunda sensed that he was onto something. "Do you tell the truth all the time?"

"As far as I understand, when it is very important, yes. I mean, I'm not going to say I don't lie. Yes, I do lie."

In fact, Mrs. Osborne lied to doctors in order to obtain narcotic pain medications. Neither Grunda nor Bradley was aware of Mrs. Osborne's struggle against opioid addiction at various times in her life. This, too, would surface several years after the trial was over and would call into question her ability to perceive things accurately at the time of the arm-grabbing incident and the police lineup. Like the defense attorneys, the jurors would know nothing about this.

On redirect, Rosenbaum tried to establish where Joseph was located when he grabbed Michael. Mrs. Osborne conceded that she only knew where Joseph was standing when she stormed out of her bus to confront him.

When neither defense attorney had any follow-up questions to Rosenbaum's latest line of inquiry, the judge told Mrs. Osborne that she could step down. With careful questioning of the prospective jurors and a concise and compelling opening statement, the prosecutor had likely won the first day. Despite several stumbles during cross-examination, the State's first witness had done much to support the prosecutor's theory of the case. Just as the prosecutor had claimed in his opening, the abuse came to light only when children began acting out in sexual ways. In addition, the children were scared of Joseph Allen. Despite what the defense claimed, Mrs. Osborne—a competent, credible adult—had seen Joseph Allen loitering about the school when Head Start children were boarding and exiting buses. Allen had come very close to snatching a five-year-old boy as he was about to get onto Nancy Smith's bus.

The prosecution had laid the foundation for a strong case, but each trial has its own ebbs and flows. Both Grunda and Bradley were not ready to panic. They only had to establish reasonable doubt to secure an acquittal. But was that really true in a case like this?

Although that was the law, jurors in child molestation cases often find it hard to apply a reasonable doubt standard. Subconsciously, they usually want more proof that the defendant did not commit the crime. What could be worse than acquitting someone who would victimize children again?

CHAPTER 14
TRIAL DAY TWO
JULY 26, 1994

The second day of trial found the courtroom's spectator benches packed again. Gone were the prospective jurors who had waited patiently for their names to be called. In their place, local newspaper reporters sat poised, while the families of the alleged victims and the defendants eyed each other uneasily. Absent from the courtroom were any individuals who might be called to testify. The day before, the judge had granted Bradley's motion to separate witnesses, which forbade prospective witnesses from sitting in the courtroom until they'd completed their testimony.

Before the bailiff escorted the jurors into the courtroom, the judge needed to determine if the prosecution's next witness, six-year-old Michael Osborne III, was competent to testify. To do so, Judge McGough would ask him a series of questions to gauge his intelligence, but more important, to determine if he understood his obligation to tell the truth. Michael sat in the witness chair, tapping his feet together and staring at his mother, who sat in the front row of the spectator benches. The handsome boy looked like a pint-size rock musician, with a mane of long blond curls that extended to his shoulders.

The previous morning, Grunda had informed prospective jurors that the prosecutor routinely rehearsed its child witnesses before they testified. The prosecutor also prepped the children by asking them the same types of questions that the judge would later ask them to gauge their competency. After Judge McGough asked Michael several questions about himself and his interests, she asked him what color her jacket was. Michael told her that it was white with black and green stripes.

"Now, Michael, if I told you that I had a red jacket on, would I be telling the truth or would I be telling a lie?"

"A lie."

"And if you come into court, are you going to tell the truth?"

"Um-hum."

"Is that the right thing to do?"

"The right thing to do is to tell the truth."

"And what happens if you don't tell the truth?"

Michael paused for a moment before responding. Most children answered this question by saying that it was bad to tell a lie or they'd get in trouble if they didn't tell the truth. However, Michael seemed flummoxed by the question.

"Um, um, the people, I mean Nancy, I mean the people, the people are going to get—" Again, he paused. "Nancy and Joseph are going to get arrested."

Ignoring his jumbled response, the judge assisted him by asking a leading question. "Well, if you don't tell the truth, do you think you might get in trouble?"

"Humm."

Again, leading him, the judge asked, "Do you think if you told a lie today, that would be a bad thing?"

"I wouldn't tell a lie today."

"Okay. I'm going to find that the child is competent and we will hear his testimony," the judge concluded.

After the jury was ushered into the courtroom, Rosenbaum began his questioning. After Michael answered some background questions, he initially denied that he'd attended Head Start or traveled to Head Start on a bus. Rosenbaum took a different approach. He pointed toward Nancy Smith and asked Michael if he knew who she was. Michael identified her as Nancy, his bus driver.

Rosenbaum did not risk asking Michael to identify Joseph Allen in the courtroom. Instead, he asked, "Do you know the man's name who is sitting behind me in the green shirt?"

Although Michael had failed to identify Joseph Allen in police lineups eight months earlier, he replied, "It's a—what—that's Joseph."

"Can you tell us anything about Joseph?"

"Well, he grabbed me on the arm and I can't remember."

Leading the witness, Rosenbaum asked, "Can you tell us if it scared you when he grabbed your arm?"

"It really scared me."

After a series of questions where Michael was unable to say where he was standing at the time he was grabbed, Rosenbaum switched to another topic.

"Do you remember if he did anything else bad to you?"

"Uh-huh."

"Do you ever remember saying 'humping'?" Rosenbaum suggested.

"No."

The prosecutor had taken this witness as far as he could. "Okay, I have no other questions, Your Honor."

Before Bradley began his cross-examination, he asked to review any prior statements of Michael Osborne. Rosenbaum held up a cassette that was labeled "Michael Osborne" and dated May 28, 1993, approximately three weeks after the police began their investigation. As was the protocol, the judge recessed the trial to allow them all to listen to the tape in her chambers.

As they listened to the tape, they heard Emily Osborne's voice as she answered Detective Cantu's questions. Both she and her son were responding to the detective's queries, but mainly Mrs. Osborne. Although her voice was a surprise, the substance of her statements was even more shocking. She made assertions in her taped statement that were far different from those in her courtroom testimony the previous day. The tape also provided an inside look at the police interviews, and it revealed techniques that were to be avoided when questioning children about potential sexual abuse.

Rosenbaum claimed that he had never reviewed Cantu's investigative work prior to trial, including his taped interviews with the children and their parents. He would later say that he only listened to the tapes of the detectives who had solved the case (Andujar and Miller) and considered Cantu's investigation "trash." Because Cantu had labeled the cassette as an interview with Michael Osborne, Rosenbaum claimed that he didn't know that it also included Emily Osborne's statements.

This assertion revealed a more serious problem. If Rosenbaum had never reviewed Cantu's tapes or any part of Cantu's investigation, had anyone in the prosecutor's office done this? Under a rule set down by the US Supreme Court, the prosecution has the constitutional duty to disclose any exculpatory evidence that is in its possession or that of the police. How could the prosecution discharge this obligation if it had never examined Cantu's work and the recorded statements it generated?

Bradley believed that he had been sandbagged. Barely able to suppress his anger, he said, "Judge, I'm asking for a mistrial. In the alternative, I'm asking that this tape be played to the jury so they can hear how this investigation was conducted. If this tape is any indication, then this case is a travesty."

The judge drummed her fingers on her desk as she contemplated the request. A mistrial meant dismissing the jury and starting over with a new panel at a later date, something all judges wanted to avoid. She needed to weigh her alternatives. The prosecution had broken a rule, but could the situation be rectified without sending everyone home? Mrs. Osborne had just testified the afternoon before and she was available to be cross-examined again.

As she pondered her response, the judge asked Grunda about his position. He agreed with Bradley that a mistrial was warranted. As a former Lorain County prosecutor, he was deeply troubled by what he'd just heard on this tape. As a prosecutor, he had declined to bring charges when he felt the police investigation was tainted and undependable.

"You've got to start all over, because the way the police conducted its investigation was totally wrong. I mean, the mother tells the child what to say and what not to say and the police officer is there. The

State—and I'm not blaming Mr. Rosenbaum—the State did not get a thorough understanding of how this investigation was conducted." The implication was clear: after the mistrial, the prosecutor should reexamine this case and drop the charges.

However, in the end, Grunda overshot his mark. "This tape completely exonerates my client." Although Michael Osborne had denied any knowledge of a man named Joseph in the taped interview, Grunda's conclusion was an exaggeration. The prosecutor had other child witnesses who would testify that Joseph Allen had molested them.

The judge gave Rosenbaum his chance to respond. He did not approve of the detective's methods and agreed that the tape should have been identified with both Emily and Michael Osborne's names, and should have been given to the defendants the day before, immediately after Mrs. Osborne had testified on direct, as required by the rules.

"This witness is still here. We're talking court time, maybe an hour's worth of business court time. There's no reason to have a mistrial. Mrs. Osborne should be recalled to the stand. She could be cross-examined and there is no prejudice to the defense," Rosenbaum suggested.

The judge nodded, but she would give Bradley one more chance to change her mind. Bradley argued that "the rules are the rules" and they needed to be followed. He maintained that the dynamics of cross-examination change when a witness leaves the stand, has time to reconsider her testimony, and then is recalled.

The judge was not moved by Bradley's final argument and agreed with Rosenbaum. "You can cross-examine her on the inconsistencies in her taped statement and protect your client's rights. Mr. Bradley and Mr. Grunda, you can use parts of the tape during your cross-examination if you wish."

Despite the judge's encouragement, the defendants' attorneys could not easily play the tape in front of the jury when they lacked the means to locate specific portions on it. When a witness says something at trial that conflicts with a previous statement, a cross-examining attorney confronts the witness about the two different versions. When one of those versions is on tape, an attorney needs an index in order to cue the tape to find the relevant two or three sentences. If the defense attorneys had been given the taped statement in advance, they could have done this or directed a court reporter to prepare a written transcript of the statement.

Either method would have provided them with a more effective tool to unmask Emily Osborne. Instead, they would have to rely on a less precise way. Bradley and Grunda would ask her if she *remembered* making a particular statement during the taped interview. Because the jurors had not listened to the tape, they would not know whether the cross-examining attorney was accurately paraphrasing the witness's earlier statement. Because of that uncertainty, jurors might believe that the witness was being unfairly attacked, and it would lessen the effectiveness of the cross-examination.

Bradley's first job was to refresh the jury about Mrs. Osborne's earlier testimony. She again said that a black man named Joseph had taught her son to hump, something she discovered in December 1992. Once more, she claimed that Joseph had grabbed her son a few days after this revelation and that she'd reported this incident to Head Start's Glen Thaler.

"Did you tell anyone else?" Bradley asked.

"Yes, I told my attorney," she replied.

This response should have set off alarm bells in both defense attorneys' heads, but it did not. Trial attorneys don't always listen carefully to a witness's answer because, in the heat of battle, they are busy formulating their next question. This was one of those situations.

Why would Mrs. Osborne have told an attorney about this episode? Was she contemplating a civil lawsuit against Head Start? Did she hope to reap a financial reward if she could prove that Michael had been molested while under the preschool's supervision? She was never asked any of these questions. When a witness has a financial interest in the outcome of a case, the law allows an opposing attorney to develop this evidence to prove bias.

Bradley was focused, instead, on another significant inconsistency in her testimony. In her taped interview, Mrs. Osborne claimed that Michael first began humping about two or three weeks before the interview, which was taped on May 28, 1993. Yesterday, she'd claimed this happened in December 1992. When he asked her about this discrepancy, she struggled to explain it. First, she claimed that Michael's behavior had started in December and gradually become more prevalent in May. Later, she claimed that his strange behavior had happened once in December, then stopped, then restarted in May. In the end, she conceded that whatever she said on tape was what she'd said.

Bradley moved on to another important change in her story. "Didn't you suggest to your son on the tape that it was Nancy's boyfriend, an older white guy, who taught him how to do this on the bus?"

"I remember saying that and that's what Michael told me at first."

"What was Nancy's boyfriend's name?"

"Charlie."

"And that's what your son then agreed to?"

"For a while, yes."

"So it went from Charlie to a black guy named Joseph?"

"He was afraid to say it was Joseph," she explained.

"Weren't you and the detective suggesting other names to your son? Why would you do that?" Bradley's implication was clear: she and the detective had contaminated the investigation by feeding Michael names.

"Because Michael brought up those names at our house before this," she said, trying to defuse this problem.

"On the tape, you also suggested a black guy named John Mincy as someone who may have taught Michael this behavior?"

"Yeah, we talked about John," she conceded.

"Who is John Mincy?"

"He was a bus aide who worked on Nancy's bus for a short while. He also babysat for me."

Bradley had one more point. "You wanted to provide Detective Cantu with all of the important details, didn't you?"

"Yes."

"I've listened to the entire tape, Mrs. Osborne. Nowhere in your statement did you tell Detective Cantu that Joseph grabbed your son's arm at the school. Isn't that true?"

"I don't remember," she replied.

Bradley stared at Mrs. Osborne for a few moments, expecting her to explain her answer, but she didn't. "Okay then, no further questions."

Rising slowly from his chair, Grunda looked at the witness through his half-frame glasses, almost squinting. Although Mrs. Osborne and Cantu had suggested to Michael that Joseph had taught him how to hump, Michael had steadfastly denied knowing anyone named Joseph during the interview. This would be the crux of his cross-examination.

"Mrs. Osborne, your testimony yesterday was that a man named Joseph taught your son how to hump. That's what your son allegedly told you, correct?"

"Yes. My son is the one who said the name Joseph, first at home and at the police station."

"If I told you that the taped interview tells a different story, would you like to listen to the tape to refresh your recollection? Would that help you?"

"It still wouldn't make any difference. He may not have mentioned Joseph at the police station, but I know that he said Joseph's name at home," she countered.

"Your Honor, I would like the tape played."

Rosenbaum quickly objected. "He knows that's improper. If he wants to play it for this witness outside the presence of the jury, I have no objection."

The judge agreed with Rosenbaum. "If you'd like to play the tape for the witness outside the presence of the jury, you may."

"I'd rather the jury hear it, Your Honor."

Of course, the defense attorneys wanted the tape to be heard in its entirety. Not only did it reveal a witness who had changed part of her story and invented a new one, but it showed a flawed police interview, rampant with leading questions and suggested answers to an impressionable five-year-old child.

Although the defense was permitted to play a selected part of the tape to disclose an inconsistent statement, the rules of evidence did not allow it to play the entire recording in open court. However, if a witness claimed a lack of memory, that witness could have their memory refreshed by listening to the entire statement in private. In refusing to play the full tape to the jury, the judge was following well-established law.

Despite this, there was another rule that would have permitted the judge to side with the defendants and allow the jury to hear the complete interview. The judge had listened to the tape in its entirety. If it contained exculpatory evidence, then she had the power to fashion almost any remedy to counteract the prosecutor's failure to provide the tape earlier, notwithstanding the prosecutor's claimed ignorance of its subject matter. If either of the defense attorneys had made this argument, the judge could have ordered the tape to be played in its entirety.

Grunda continued, "In the taped interview, didn't your son say that he learned about sex on the bus?"

"Yes."

"Didn't he say on the tape that he learned how to hump from a boy named Gregory?"

"Yes, that's the little boy that rode the bus with him."

"And isn't it true that when your son was asked if he knew a Joseph, he said no?"

"Yeah, he denied Joseph a few times and then at home he would say—"

"No, I'm talking about the taped interview."

"Okay. At the police station, I think yes."

"And isn't it true that he denied that Joseph ever taught him how to hump?"

"Yes."

Convinced that Mrs. Osborne was lying, Grunda wanted to suggest her motive to the jury. "Isn't it true, Mrs. Osborne, you didn't get involved in this case until you'd heard about these stories and you wanted some publicity?"

"No, it's not. I can bring my attorney in."

If Grunda wanted to provide the jury with a motive, Mrs. Osborne had just handed one to him. The next question should have been: Why do you have an attorney?

Instead, he asked, "Isn't it true that on May 28, 1993, your son denied ever knowing a black man named Joseph?"

"At the police station, yes. In front of my attorney, no." For the third time that day, Mrs. Osborne had mentioned her attorney, and for the third time, she received a free pass. "Yes, at the police station he thought Joseph was there," Mrs. Osborne persisted, suggesting for the first time that her son believed that Joseph was lurking somewhere in the police station.

Playing to the jury, Grunda decided to ask blunt questions that he knew Mrs. Osborne would deny. "Isn't it true, Mrs. Osborne, that you've been making suggestions to your son as to what happened to him from December 1992 to the present?"

"No, it is not."

"How many times did you go over the story of what he should say in this courtroom?"

"None."

"Never?"

"Never."

Turning to face the jurors, Grunda feigned surprise. "Never did that?"

"Never."

"Well, wouldn't you agree that your son's memory was the freshest when he gave the police interview on May 28?"

"That he openly talked about, yes."

Grunda sat down. Both he and Bradley believed that they'd undermined the credibility of the prosecution's first witness. If the entire tape had been played, the police investigation would have been discredited (and perhaps disgraced), but the prosecution had been saved from that fate.

Rosenbaum declined to ask Mrs. Osborne any questions to rehabilitate her and she was excused from the stand. The judge did permit her to sit in the courtroom while the defense attorneys cross-examined her son.

A few minutes later, Michael Osborne was recalled to the stand. The young boy looked apprehensive as he chewed a big wad of gum.

After his mother's testimony, there was something anticlimactic about the questions that would be addressed to him.

The young boy repeated what he'd told Rosenbaum, including one phrase that was identical to his direct testimony—that "his mom came flying out" of her bus to confront Joseph. When asked whether this happened at Nativity or City Center, Michael claimed to have forgotten and then ventured, "Cityview." His mother had testified that this had occurred at Nativity. Bradley decided to sit down.

Grunda asked a few questions, but the boy seemed intimidated. Not wishing to add to the boy's discomfort, Grunda asked several innocuous questions and ended his exam.

As the trial neared the noon hour, Rosenbaum elected to call two "short witnesses," people whose testimony would likely take very little time. The first was Willie Mae Smith, one of the witnesses he had disclosed several days before trial. Instead of merely testifying that she'd observed Joseph Allen around the school, the fifty-six-year-old grandmother claimed that, on one occasion, she'd seen Joseph Allen on Nancy Smith's morning bus, helping children onto it and then seating them once aboard. Two of Willie Mae's grandchildren attended Head Start and lived with her. Both Bradley and Grunda were convinced that Willie Mae was wrong, mistaking Joseph Allen for John Mincy, a black man who occasionally worked as Nancy's bus aide.

Rosenbaum closed his exam by asking Willie Mae if she was on probation. (He was under an obligation to disclose felony convictions of his witnesses.) Admitting that she was, Willie Mae explained that she had been "cussing" out the police when they'd come to her house to investigate "her kids." Rosenbaum ignored her response and asked her pointedly if she'd been convicted of possessing criminal tools, a fourth-degree felony, to which she agreed she had.

On cross-examination, Willie Mae volunteered that Nancy Smith was a "real nice lady" who "was nice to the kids. They loved her." When the police had first talked to Willie Mae, they had asked her if either of her two grandsons had reported anything unusual about Nancy, i.e., whether they had been abused. They had not.

The defense chipped away at her recollection. She could not identify the season when she'd seen Joseph Allen working as a bus aide.

She also conceded that she'd only looked at his face for about one or two seconds on one occasion. Although she continued to say that she'd seen Joseph Allen on Smith's bus, by the end of the cross-examination, that seemed unlikely.

The State's final witness that morning was Marlon Howard. A plumber by trade, Mr. Howard had formerly managed apartments in Elyria. He was acquainted with Joseph Allen through a mutual friend. He testified that after a tenant had moved out and abandoned all of his property, Mr. Howard had invited Joseph Allen and his friend to take what they wanted: "furniture, clothes, everything."

The jury was left to guess about the relevance of this testimony. Mr. Howard was a foundational witness. His testimony would apparently tie in with other evidence later in the case.

The judge realized that her court time would be unnecessarily wasted if she had to continually call a recess after a prosecution witness testified. She was convinced that there was a better way to allow the defense attorneys to review a witness's prior taped statement. Once the jury had left, she asked the prosecutor, "Mr. Rosenbaum, wouldn't it be more efficient if you provided the defense with the tapes in advance of the witness's testimony?"

"What would you suggest, Your Honor?" Rosenbaum asked.

"Can you give them all of the tapes for each witness you plan to call now?"

"I don't want to turn over any tape before I've listened to it. I could release a few at a time after I've reviewed them."

"I think that would be preferable to what we're doing now—having the jury wait an hour between a direct and cross-examination. Will you do that?"

"Yes."

"I'm going to give everyone the afternoon off. Mr. Rosenbaum, I expect you to deliver some tapes to the defense attorneys after you've reviewed them today. Any objection from defense counsel?"

"That would be an improvement," Bradley said.

"Okay. I'll see everyone tomorrow morning."

CHAPTER 15
TRIAL DAY THREE
JULY 27, 1994

The third day of trial would belong to Elizabeth Marie Powell, a former Head Start employee. Four years later, she would say, "I don't want nothing to do with this case. It ruined my life." But on this day, Ms. Powell, whose nickname was Angel, would be a linchpin in the prosecution's case against Nancy Smith and Joseph Allen. She would provide incriminating testimony that the two knew each other and she'd tell how, on one harrowing day, she'd brandished a tire iron and chased Joseph Allen off of Smith's Head Start bus while the children's screams filled the air.

Before Powell took the stand, Bradley sensed trouble. As he'd told the judge two days earlier, Powell had refused to talk to his investigator, claiming that she'd "worked something out" with the prosecutor. He'd also complained that Rosenbaum had never formally included Powell on his witness list, an allegation that the prosecutor had denied. Bradley concluded that whatever Powell was going to say, it wouldn't be good.

Powell had worked for Head Start from November 1992 until the end of May 1993. She'd sought a bus driver position there after she'd been laid off as a heavy equipment operator in the construction industry. During her time with Head Start, she'd worked as both an aide and a bus driver. In April 1993, she'd been Nancy Smith's aide.

When the police first began investigating the Head Start allegations, several of the children claimed that Angel had either driven them to Joseph's house or been there when they'd arrived. As a result, the Lorain police had interviewed her several times and she'd taken two polygraph tests. On June 17, 1993, Detective Andujar had questioned her for almost two hours at her home, taping the interview. Rosenbaum had given that tape to Bradley the previous afternoon to allow the defense attorneys to review it prior to her testimony. Because the tape was a copy, it was staticky and the voices were sometimes muffled. Despite the recording's poor quality, the defense attorneys had heard enough to suspect that Powell did not like Nancy Smith. Her interview was rife with resentment and grievances against Smith, and this spelled trouble.

The twenty-seven-year-old Powell had visited the courtroom a week earlier with Emily Osborne and her son to meet with the prosecutor. Before she took the stand today, she'd insisted that no photographs be taken of her during her examination.

As was his style, Rosenbaum quickly dispensed with the background questions and asked the witness to describe her experiences as Nancy Smith's bus aide.

"Did you happen to observe how the kids interacted with Nancy Smith?"

"They would pull away from her. They did not want her to touch them. She would try to reach over and hug them, and they would pull away from her. Sometimes they would cry about it." This was in sharp contrast to what Willie Mae Smith had told the jury the day before.

Powell claimed to have witnessed this behavior with four children who would all testify in the criminal case: Marcus Logan, Nina Zorich, Michael Osborne, and Jason Gilbert. After Nancy Smith had been relieved of her bus driver duties, Powell had noticed a marked change in the children's demeanor. They "seemed more happy" and "they would talk and laugh." Powell was not surprised by this. Nancy Smith "was very harsh with them at times, and sometimes she was very mean."

"Did she ever swear at them in your presence?" Rosenbaum asked.

"Yes, she did."

Powell was also irked by Smith's disdain for the Head Start rules. Smith "sometimes frequently" operated her bus "without an aide." In addition, Powell claimed that Smith routinely stopped at a corner store to buy a soda pop before delivering the children to the school. Smith would dash into the store while Powell stayed with the children. During one such stop in mid-April, a black man had attempted to board the bus.

"He came up to the steps, and I picked up the tire iron that was on the bus. I told him if he came up another step, I was going to knock him off the steps. I asked him would he please leave the bus."

"What happened then?"

"He would not get off the bus. He kept mumbling. And I could hardly make out anything he said. The only word I could understand was 'Nancy.'

"And I told him, 'Nancy is in the store. Get off the bus.'

"He would not get off the bus. And I told him if he did not get off the bus, I was going to hit him with the tire iron.

"And the kids all started screaming, 'Hit him. Hit him.' They ran toward the back of the bus, and they were egging me on to wallop this man."

Rosenbaum nodded. "What happened then?"

"I pushed him off the bus. I shut the door and locked it. And he walked into the store, and, the next thing I know, he came out with Nancy, arm in arm."

According to Powell, when Nancy Smith opened the bus door, she told Powell that the man's son was on the bus. When Powell still refused to let him board the bus, she heard Smith tell the man to meet her down the street and wait.

Powell told the jury that she had never seen the man before that day. In October 1993, the police had asked her to try to identify him from a lineup of photographs. At that time, she'd been unable to positively identify him, although she'd found one photograph that looked like him.

With each successive question, Rosenbaum had gradually heightened the drama with this witness. Staring intently at her, he asked, "Now, today, for the first time, did you see someone that you can identify as the black man that tried to get on the bus that was with Defendant Smith?"

All eyes were on Powell when she answered. "Yes, sir, I did."

"Is he in the courtroom today?"

"Yes, sir, he is." Powell raised her right arm and pointed her finger at Joseph Allen.

Rosenbaum could have ended his examination here on a high note, but he could not resist taking the witness down two additional paths. "Ms. Powell, while a bus aide for Defendant Smith, did you ever hear the children say anything sexually inappropriate or surprising for a young child?"

"Yes, I did. I heard Marcus Logan ask Melissa Warner—"

"Objection," shouted Bradley.

The three attorneys converged on the judge's bench. Bradley argued that this was hearsay and had no relevance to either defendant. Rosenbaum argued that it was another example of the children "acting out" after being abused by the defendants. The defense counsel argued that whatever he said could have been learned at home, from overhearing older children, or in countless other social settings. The judge sided with Rosenbaum but asked him to provide a foundation that would give the jurors the context of the remarks.

"How old were these children?"

"Between four and five."

"Will you tell the Court and the jury what you overheard?"

Both defense attorneys objected, only to be overruled again by the judge.

"It was Marcus Logan, and he said this to Melissa Warner: 'Suck my penis.'"

"And what did you do about that?"

"When I dropped him off at his house, I told his father what he'd said."

Rosenbaum moved quickly to his final point. Again, without attempting to develop a foundation for his question, he asked, "Now, did you overhear on the bus radio that Defendant Smith had taken some kids on an outing in the woods and that the kids were lost?"

Bradley and Grunda immediately objected, Bradley throwing his pen onto the trial table to emphasize his anger. Besides leading the witness, the question assumed facts that were not in evidence, namely that Nancy Smith had wandered off with Head Start children to some unauthorized place. Although Judge McGough allowed Rosenbaum to develop the point, Powell was unable to say that the voice she'd heard on the radio was Nancy Smith's or that the alert was in regard to any of the children who rode on Nancy's bus.

Bradley was livid. "I ask for a mistrial again. I ask for a mistrial and a hearing."

"Denied. Let's continue with the questioning."

When Rosenbaum told the judge that he had no further questions, the jury was dismissed. Bradley stood. "Judge, I want to remain calm, but I am upset—extremely upset." Bradley complained that the prosecutor had waited until late afternoon yesterday to turn over any of the witness tapes to them. He claimed that the prosecutor had dumped eight hours of tapes at his doorstep, depriving him of sufficient time to review them. He asked for more time to review those tapes, particularly the two-hour tape of Elizabeth Powell.

Judge McGough bristled at the request. "Mr. Bradley, you are not entitled to the tapes until after a witness testifies on direct examination," she said, reminding him that he was fortunate to have received the tapes in advance, irrespective of the inconvenience.

"Then I will give them all back," Bradley said defiantly. If the judge would not accommodate him, he'd force the judge to return to the old procedure. He'd listen to the tapes in chambers after a direct examination, while the jury and the rest of the participants waited.

"I would like to be heard," Rosenbaum said.

"No," the judge snapped.

Ignoring the judge, Rosenbaum continued, "He has eight hours of tapes, but some are for tomorrow, not for today."

"Mr. Rosenbaum, sit," the judge commanded. The judge explained that she was upset because the defense attorneys had not listened to the tapes between eight thirty and ten that morning, before she brought the jury back into the courtroom.

"We didn't know what order the prosecutor was going to call the witnesses," Bradley complained.

"How much time?" the judge asked, sensing that another trial day was being squandered.

"An hour and a half," Bradley replied.

"I'll tell you what. You've got ten minutes."

Before the judge could dismiss them, Bradley said, "I want to renew my motion for a mistrial based on Mr. Rosenbaum's improper question about the lost children. It—"

"It wasn't an improper question," Rosenbaum interrupted.

"Judge, can I finish? I'm tired of Mr. Rosenbaum interrupting me at will."

"Histrionics," Rosenbaum said, shaking his head.

"It just happens to be polite," Bradley answered.

"Throwing things on the table is histrionics," Rosenbaum said, reminding Bradley of his earlier behavior in front of the jury.

"Asking a stupid question that you know—"

"It was not a stupid question," Rosenbaum said.

"She lied," Bradley countered.

Rosenbaum persisted. "It was not a stupid question. She lost those kids in the woods."

"Gentlemen, you may be seated," the judge said, interrupting them. "Your motion for a mistrial is denied. The State will provide the defense with every other tape of every other witness. We are in recess for ten minutes."

A few minutes later, the judge came back into the courtroom. Noting that it was lunchtime, the judge told everyone to return in an hour. Grunda and Bradley would get the time they'd requested, but at the expense of lunch. For the next hour, they listened to the tape involving Elizabeth Powell, occasionally rewinding it as they attempted to understand barely audible portions. At one forty-five, the judge told them to conclude their work.

When the trial resumed, Bradley began by trying to establish that the Head Start program had safeguards in place that would have prevented Smith from secreting children away from the school. Powell fought him at every turn, claiming that Smith often operated her bus without aides or failed to pick up a parent monitor when circumstances warranted it. Bradley eventually saw the futility of developing these points with a hostile witness and turned his attention to the most damaging part of Powell's testimony—Joseph Allen's attempt to force his way onto Nancy Smith's bus.

Over the break, Bradley had talked to his client about Powell's testimony. Smith, visibly upset, explained that there had been an incident on the bus, but it had not involved Joseph Allen. According to her, the man involved in the confrontation was the father of Cameron Taylor, a Head Start student. While Smith was in the store, the father had tried to enter the bus to see if his son was on board. Because Smith knew the father, she'd tried to intercede on his behalf when she'd returned.

After listening to the tape, Bradley was convinced that the tape backed up his client. Despite the tape's poor audio quality, he heard Powell tell the detective that the man who'd boarded the bus claimed to be Cameron Taylor's father, but she couldn't confirm it because she'd never met him before. When Bradley asked her about her earlier statement, she denied it. She now claimed that she'd met Cameron's father before that incident and knew what he looked like. Pointing her right index finger toward Joseph Allen, she reinforced her earlier testimony. "It was the man right there who tried to get on the bus. And today, when I saw him in person, I am for certain. I will stake my life on it."

If Powell's taped statement had been transcribed, Bradley could have settled the matter by reading the relevant part to her, word for word. Likewise, if Bradley could have magically cued the tape to her earlier statement, the jurors could have heard for themselves what Powell had told the police a year earlier. But neither of those options was available, and for now, the jury was left to guess about Powell, her previous story, and her credibility.

In her police interview, Powell could not hide her resentment of Nancy Smith. Would she attempt to sugarcoat these earlier remarks when confronted with them? She did not. She told the jury that the

Head Start management had given Smith special privileges and had allowed her to get "away with murder." Despite revealing her animosity, these comments still aided the State's case. She'd accused a permissive Head Start administration of failing to control Smith and that assertion fit squarely within the prosecution's theory of the case.

After Bradley finished his cross-exam, Grunda followed up on Powell's hostility toward Nancy Smith. "Isn't it true that in that taped statement, you claimed that Nancy was trying to get you fired?"

"Yes sir."

"You don't like Nancy very much, do you?"

"What does that have to do with this case, sir?"

"Do you like Nancy?"

"I'm indifferent to Nancy." Turning his head toward the jury, Grunda theatrically rolled his eyes in disbelief.

After Grunda sat down, Rosenbaum opted not to ask Powell any more questions—either the jurors believed her or they didn't. Up until this point, Rosenbaum had presented witnesses whose primary purpose was to prove either that Joseph Allen had prowled around Nancy Smith's bus or that the two defendants knew each other. In the next phase, he would ask the Head Start children and their parents to reveal the horrors allegedly done to these preschoolers.

Rosenbaum's next witness, Ann Gilbert, was a parent of Jason Gilbert, an alleged victim. The married mother of two worked as an admitting registrar at a local hospital. Like Emily Osborne, Mrs. Gilbert seemed to be a stable, hardworking, concerned parent— someone the jurors could relate to. She told the jury that her son began exhibiting strange behavior in February 1993. When she read a newspaper article about the allegations surrounding the Lorain Head Start program in May 1993, she put "two and two together."

Mrs. Gilbert explained that in February, Jason had complained that his "butt was burning" and that he "didn't want to ride the bus." He'd also experienced nightmares, waking, crying, and telling his mom that the police were after him. She'd also caught him in a sexual act with his younger foster brother. When she'd entered Jason's room, she'd seen him with his pants pulled down, lying on top of the other child. He'd also put a toy gun in his own mouth and said, "Pow." Because he'd never behaved like this before, Mrs. Gilbert searched for a reason. The explanation finally came after she read the disturbing newspaper article about child abuse at Head Start.

When Mrs. Gilbert had questioned her son about this possibility, he'd told her that "Nancy's boyfriend [had] hurt him in the butt with a stick." Eventually, he'd told her that the man's name was Joe. Armed with this information, she'd contacted the police.

Rosenbaum was not a lawyer who wasted anyone's time, particularly a jury's. After eliciting this essential information, Rosenbaum ended the examination. Because it was after four p.m., the judge elected to dismiss the jury for the day. The defense would have to wait until the next day to cross-examine Mrs. Gilbert. As a result, the day ended on another high note for the prosecution.

CHAPTER 16
TRIAL DAY FOUR: MORNING SESSION

JULY 28, 1994

When Judge McGough arrived at the courthouse at seven thirty, all was quiet as she walked through the hall toward her office. Upon entering her chambers, she slid open the door that separated her private area from the very public courtroom. The courtroom was almost dark, its shaded windows blocking most of the outside light. In the near darkness, she could just make out the exhibits that were haphazardly arranged on a table in front of her bench. She'd intended to sit at her desk and sign some entries on other cases, but, instead, she paused, shook her head, and sighed.

She'd expected emotions to run high in her courtroom; she could control that. But yesterday, a prosecution witness, Angel Powell, had claimed that she'd been threatened in the hallway by one of Nancy Smith's followers. Not to be outdone, the defense alleged that someone associated with the victims' families had been relaying testimony delivered in the courtroom to other prosecution witnesses waiting to testify—a clear violation of the judge's order requiring a separation of witnesses. Barely able to suppress her anger, she'd demanded that the attorneys control their clients, including their families and their friends.

When she saw someone open the courtroom door, she hurriedly shut the sliding panel, slamming it against the door frame. She walked over to her large desk, sat down, and attended to the paperwork that lay stacked on the desk's surface. After forty-five minutes, her bailiff entered to report that jurors, attorneys, and clients were all present. The judge nodded and scrawled her signature on one last entry before rising to enter the courtroom.

When the trial resumed at eight thirty, Bradley began his cross-examination of Mrs. Gilbert. Polite and amiable, Bradley tried to show that Mrs. Gilbert had been wrong when she'd attributed her son's changed behavior to sexual abuse at the preschool.

He asked a series of questions to probe this. Hadn't she originally believed that her son's burning sensation had been the result of poor hygiene? She had. Hadn't the problem with the foster child occurred several times over several months? It had, and Jason had been punished for it. Hadn't she asked Jason where he'd learned that behavior? She had, and he hadn't provided an answer despite her best efforts to learn this from him.

Bradley decided to close his examination with questions developed from what he'd heard on her son's taped interview with Detective Andujar one year earlier. Mrs. Gilbert agreed that her son had been interviewed in early July 1993 and that she'd recently listened to the tape.

"Are you aware that when your son was asked if anybody hurt him, he said no?"

"Yes."

"And you are aware when he was asked if Nancy placed a stick in him, or anybody placed a stick in him, he said no?"

"Yes."

"He was asked if anybody told him not to tell and he said no?"

"Yes."

"And he also told the detective that nobody had ever put tape over his mouth, right?"

"Right."

"And, at that interview, he said he did not know a person named Joseph?"

"Yes."

When Grunda examined Mrs. Gilbert, he picked up on Bradley's last question.

"And he didn't know who Joseph was, did he?"

"He didn't know him by Joseph. He knew him by Joe," she said defensively.

"After he was asked many, many times about Joseph and Joe, he claimed that he didn't know him, is that right?"

"Yes." This time there was resignation in her one-word answer.

To bolster his flagging witness, Rosenbaum tried to undo the damage caused by her last answer. "Now, Mr. Grunda suggested that your son was asked about Joseph many, many times. Is that correct?"

"I can just recall once," she said, backtracking from her earlier answer.

Upon further questioning, Mrs. Gilbert claimed that her son had told them about a man named Joseph before they contacted the police —again, blunting her son's denials captured on the tape. With Rosenbaum's careful questions, she also suggested that her son's denials were the result of his initial discomfort and unfamiliarity with the detectives.

As he headed for his final questions on redirect, Rosenbaum asked, "Now, do you feel, as Jason's mother, that you can tell when he's telling the truth and when he's not?"

"Yep."

"Do you feel that what Jason says about Joseph and Nancy actually happened?"

Bradley and Grunda yelled their objections in unison.

"Sustained."

Switching gears, Rosenbaum asked Mrs. Gilbert if Head Start officials ever called when Jason was absent from school. They did not. Likewise, if she put her son on the bus and he did not show up at the school, would someone notify her? No one would. With that final point, Rosenbaum sat down. Neither defense attorney had additional questions.

"Please call your next witness, Mr. Rosenbaum," the judge said.

Although Michael Osborne had testified about an encounter with

Joseph Allen two days earlier, the jury's first opportunity to hear directly from a child about the alleged abuse would come from the State's next witness, Jason Gilbert, now six years old. Like Michael, Judge McGough would have to assess whether he was competent to testify. It was a low bar, but it was one that Jason would barely clear.

Jason Gilbert was a thin boy with even features. Something about the boy evoked pathos. Perhaps it was his too-large dress shirt that hung limply over his narrow shoulders or his straight brown hair that drooped over his forehead. Whatever it was, he seemed overwhelmed by his surroundings as he sat in the witness chair waiting for the judge to question him outside the presence of the jury.

"What happens if you tell a lie, Jason? What do you think would happen?" the judge asked.

"It's a lie," the boy replied.

"What would happen?"

"It's a lie," the befuddled boy repeated, his voice barely audible.

"I'm sorry. I can't understand you."

"It's a lie," he said, not raising his voice.

"It's what? You would tell a lie? Why would you tell a lie?" the judge asked, startled by his response.

"Because."

"Why would you do that?"

Jason did not reply.

The judge asked him about his nervousness and whether he could answer questions in a courtroom filled with people. She then returned to his understanding of the truth. "Will you tell the truth if you are here?" she asked.

The little boy nodded.

"Or will you tell a lie if you're here?"

"Truth."

The judge wanted to make sure that Jason realized that he was not to guess at questions when he did not know the answer.

"And, if somebody asks you a question that doesn't make sense or you don't understand, then what would you do?"

The question stumped the boy and he could only say, "Hmm?"

"Do you know what you are supposed to do?"

"What?" he asked, expecting and hoping that the judge would provide the answer.

"If that happens, can you say, 'I don't understand'? Would you be willing to do that?"

Jason shook his head.

The judge tried to suppress her surprise and asked again. "If somebody said something and you don't understand, could you tell them? Can you say, 'I don't understand'? Can you say that?"

Realizing that no was the wrong answer, Jason reversed course. He nodded.

Like all children his age, Jason wanted to please his adult questioner and had changed his answer when he understood that his first response was not what the adult desired. The scientific literature warned police, social workers, and psychologists not to repeat questions for this very reason. It was a classic way for a child's story to become tainted and it had just happened in the courtroom, except no one apparently realized it.

The judge continued, "Because, you know, if people ask you questions, you're not allowed to guess. Is that okay?"

He again nodded.

Testing him, the judge asked, "What happens if we ask you a question, and you don't know the answer? Then what?"

"It's a lie," the boy responded, again showing that he didn't understand what the judge had been trying to teach him.

Undaunted, the judge again explained that he was to tell the attorneys if he did not understand a question or did not know the answer. Eventually, he seemed to grasp the concept. The judge asked the attorneys if they had any additional questions that they wanted her to ask him.

"I would still like to have some clarification on whether he knows what happens if you lie," Bradley said.

"Jason, if you tell a lie, what do you think happens?"

"It's a . . ."

"It's what?"

"It's the truth," the boy suggested.

Ignoring his response, the judge led him to the correct answer. "Is it bad?"

"Huh?"

"Is it bad?"

"Uh-huh."

"Okay. I'm going to allow you, Mr. Rosenbaum, to proceed with this witness."

"I object for the record," Bradley said, knowing that the appellate courts vested trial judges with almost unlimited power to determine a child's competency and rarely, if ever, reversed them on this basis.

"I understand," the judge said, perhaps revealing her own misgivings about letting the boy testify. However, in the end, she'd let the jury decide what weight to give his testimony, if any. After the verdict, jurors would later tell newspaper reporters that they'd found the defendants guilty almost entirely because of the children's compelling testimony. And the first one to convince them would be Jason Gilbert.

Jason and the other children posed special challenges for both the prosecutor and the defense attorneys. The prosecutor's direct exam had to be carefully crafted. That meant he needed to ask pointed questions that could be answered in just a few words, and he had to avoid open-ended questions that could lead to bizarre and disjointed responses. Although leading questions were normally forbidden during a direct examination, judges made an exception when dealing with children. The questioning attorney was given some leeway in their use, particularly when necessary to keep the examination on track or to change subjects.

How much latitude depended on the discretion of the individual trial judge. In this case, it seemed likely that Judge McGough would give the prosecutor great leeway. As her first term had progressed, she'd seemingly relished her growing reputation as a "tough on crime" judge. In addition, the victims in this case were children, and as a judge, she was determined to protect them in any way possible.

The young witnesses presented different problems for the defense attorneys. If they constantly objected to the prosecutor's leading questions, the jury might penalize them for trying to keep important testimony from them. When they questioned the children, they could not come across as heavy-handed or intimidating—or even worse, clever and tricky.

Rosenbaum began by asking Jason some questions about himself and his family. After that, Jason identified both Nancy Smith and Joseph Allen in the courtroom. From there, Rosenbaum relied primarily on leading questions to develop Jason's testimony: Did people take their clothes off while you were there? Did Joseph ever take his clothes off? Did you ever see Nancy with her clothes off? In response to each question, Jason nodded.

If a question required Jason to provide a number, he routinely defaulted to five. How many times had he seen Joseph with his clothes off? Five. How many times for Nancy? Five. How many times did Joseph put a stick in his butt? Five. How many times had Nancy touched his penis? Five.

After Rosenbaum elicited that Joseph had touched Jason on his "butt," he asked, "Did he touch you anywhere else?"

"Umm, umm, on my titties."

Rosenbaum asked him that question several more times, altering the wording slightly to avoid an objection. Each time, Jason could not think of a new body part. Rosenbaum switched to a different subject. What parts of the body was Jason forced to touch on either Joseph or Nancy? When Jason testified that he'd been forced to touch Joseph's penis, Rosenbaum seized on this: "Did Joseph ever touch your penis?"

"Yeah."

Jason claimed that he'd also been forced to touch Joseph's butt and Nancy's chest, including licking it. She'd also forced him to kiss her on the mouth.

Using a leading question to switch topics, Rosenbaum asked, "Did you ever see a gun at Joseph's house?"

Jason nodded.

"Can you tell everybody what happened with this gun?"

"Put it off and shoot me."

"Who put the gun where?" Rosenbaum asked, expecting Jason to say that Joseph had threatened him with it.

"Under Joseph's bed."

"And what did Joseph do with the gun?"

"Put it in my mouth and shot me," the boy answered.

"He put it in your mouth?" Rosenbaum asked, trying not to sound confused.

Jason nodded.

"Did he shoot?" Rosenbaum asked, unsure what the boy would say next.

Jason nodded.

"Did the gun go 'boom' and did it hurt?"

Again, the boy nodded.

"You are sure?" Rosenbaum asked, hoping that the boy would tell the jury that Joseph had threatened to harm him with the gun if he ever told anyone about what happened at his house.

"Yeah."

Trying to direct him to another answer, Rosenbaum asked, "Did he say anything to you when he put the gun in your mouth?"

"No."

Despite the boy's seeming inability to grasp what he was supposed to say, Rosenbaum persevered by asking the question again but in a slightly different way. "Did he tell you to do anything when he put the gun in your mouth?"

"Tie me up on the bed."

"Before that, before we get to that, I want to ask you a little more about the gun. I want to ask you if you remember Joseph saying anything when he put the gun in your mouth. Do you remember if he said anything?" Rosenbaum asked for the third time.

The boy finally nodded.

"What did he say?" Rosenbaum asked.

"Nintendo."

"Nintendo?" Rosenbaum asked, as if he had misunderstood the boy.

The boy nodded.

"It was a Nintendo gun?" Rosenbaum asked, finally processing this unexpected turn in the questioning.

"Yeah."

"Let me ask you one more time: Did Joseph say anything when he put the Nintendo gun in your mouth? Yes or no? Or do you remember?"

"No," the boy replied, leaving the jury to guess which of the prosecutor's two questions the boy had actually answered.

Rosenbaum finally gave up on the question. Undeterred, the prosecutor moved to other topics and was able to elicit testimony that Joseph had placed tape over Jason's mouth, tied him on a bed with rope, and taken his photograph while he was in that vulnerable position.

In his opening statement, the prosecutor had confidently declared that the police had found things in Allen's apartment that had been described by the children before Allen had ever been a suspect. Rosenbaum would now begin developing this critical part of his case.

"Can you tell us what he used to tie you up?" the prosecutor asked.

"A rope."

"Can you tell everybody what the rope looked like?"

"Uh, uh—I don't know." The boy looked bewildered.

The prosecutor paused and then marched to the table that held his trial exhibits. "I want to hand you something that I put a number five on. Have you ever seen this before, Jason?"

The boy nodded.

"What is that?"

"A rope."

"Is that the rope that you were tied up with?" Rosenbaum asked.

"Yeah," Jason agreed.

Without the prosecutor's help, could Jason have identified the rope as the one he claimed had bound him and the other children? The prosecutor's last question had suggested the answer and, as such, could have been classified as an improper leading question. Despite the judge's discretion to permit leading questions with young children, would she have sustained an objection to leading questions on a critical piece of evidence?

Neither Grunda nor Bradley would ever know because they did not object. If they had, they would have discovered how much "rope" the judge was willing to give Rosenbaum in this regard. Even if the judge had denied their objection (which was likely), it would have alerted the jury that the prosecutor was steering the witness to make the identification.

Jason also testified that he had seen Batman sheets and toy cars at Joseph's house. Rosenbaum showed him these items, now marked as exhibits, and the boy confirmed that these were the same ones that he'd seen at Joseph's place. In fact, he remembered all of the cars that were shown to him.

Of all the items seized, the Halloween mask was the most distinctive item that the children had allegedly described before the search. Probably for that reason, Rosembaum chose to close his examination with this item.

"Did Joseph ever wear anything that was scary?"

Jason nodded.

"What was that?"

"A gun."

"Okay. But did he wear anything?" Rosenbaum persisted. "Did he ever put anything on that might have scared you?"

"Batman," the boy replied.

Unable to get Jason to recall the mask from his memory, Rosenbaum literally took matters into his own hands, picked up the mask, and showed it to the boy. "Have you ever seen this before?"

The boy nodded.

"What is it?"

"It's a scary—"

"Did anybody ever wear this?"

The boy nodded again.

"Who?"

"Joseph."

"I have no other questions, Your Honor."

Bradley stood and smiled at Jason, who refused to look at him. Somehow, he had to show the jury that this boy's story could not be trusted, that it had been formed from months of adult suggestions and manipulations.

"You liked it at Head Start?" he began.

The boy nodded. When asked to name his classmates, Jason looked puzzled and then recalled only Nina and Marcus, two of the other children who would testify at the trial. Bradley asked a series of leading questions during which the boy admitted that another adult was on the school bus as an aide, that he and two others remained on the school bus when it arrived at the school, and, after all of the children had exited, Nancy drove them to Joseph's house in the bus, where it remained parked throughout their stay. By exposing these facts, the defense believed that it would show the prosecution's scenario was as unlikely as it was fantastical. They thought that, unlike a diner at a restaurant, the jurors could not choose their facts à la carte. They either bought them all or bought none of them. Bradley and Grunda were convinced that if they drew out the craziest parts of the children's stories, the prosecution's case would crumble.

"Weren't you afraid that you were going to get in trouble?" Bradley asked.

"No."

"What happened after you left Joseph's house? Did Nancy take you into the school?"

"No."

"You would just walk in, you and Marcus and Nina?"

"Yeah."

"And would you see your teacher?"

"Yeah."

Bradley did not hide his incredulity as he asked his next question. "And did your teacher just say, 'Hello. Glad you are here, Jason'?"

"Yeah."

Glancing at the jurors, Bradley raised his eyebrows and shook his head ever so slightly. He searched their faces for some clue that they were with him. They had to be. How could they not? Feeling emboldened, he decided to take a risk with the boy.

"You are not afraid of Nancy, are you?"

The boy nodded.

"Why?"

"Because."

"Tell me why you are afraid of Nancy."

"Because."

"Is that what you were told? You are supposed to be afraid of Nancy?"

"Yeah."

He should have ended this line of questioning here, but he ventured one more. "She is not such a bad lady, is she?" Bradley persisted.

Jason nodded.

"She is?"

"Yep."

Unable to gain that admission, Bradley returned Jason to his account of the visits to Joseph's house.

"What was the bus aide doing when you were at Joseph's? Did the bus aide wait on the bus or did the bus aide come into the house?"

"Come into the house."

The prosecutor claimed that Nancy took the children to Joseph whenever she did not have an aide or parent on the bus. Would this inconsistency register with the jury?

"Did the bus aide do anything bad to you at Joseph's?"

"Yeah."

"Was it a she or a he?"

"He."

"A he?"

The boy nodded.

"And who was the bus aide?"

"Hmm?" Jason again looked baffled.

"Who was the bus aide? Do you know his name?"

The boy nodded, his brain searching for the right answer.

"What was his name?" Bradley pressed.

"Joseph."

The boy's answer startled everyone. Allen had never worked for Head Start as an aide or in any other capacity. Bradley wanted to capitalize on this bizarre claim.

"All the time?"

"Yeah."

"He was on the bus every day?"

"Yeah."

"Every single day?"

"Yep. Yeah."

"Really?"

"Yep."

"That is the truth?"

The boy nodded.

"He would give you to your sister?" Bradley asked, referring to the job of the bus aide to deliver a child to a responsible person—in this case, Jason's sixteen-year-old sister.

"Yep."

At that moment, Judge McGough decided to interrupt Bradley and give the boy a breather.

"Mr. Bradley, let's break for a minute." With concern in her eyes, she looked at the boy. Noting that he was standing in front of the witness chair, she asked, "Jason, are you okay standing up? Do you want to sit back in your chair? You've been standing a pretty long time." As if he were a toddler, she pointed to the witness chair and asked, "Do you want to crawl back up there? Are you doing okay?"

"Yep."

Bradley was miffed by the judge's intrusion; she had killed his momentum. Her fawning over Jason had done more to rehabilitate the young boy than anything the prosecutor could have done in a redirect examination.

As if sensing his impatience and irritation, the judge said, "You may proceed, Mr. Bradley."

Bradley chose to end his exam by reminding Jason that he'd given a completely different account to the police. Pointing to Detective Andujar, Bradley asked if he'd talked to him. The boy nodded.

"Is he your friend?"

"Yeah."

"How many times did you meet with him?"

"Five."

"Five times with him also?" Bradley repeated, hoping the jury would recognize the pattern. "Do you remember telling him that Nancy never touched you?"

"No."

"You don't remember saying that to him."

The boy shook his head.

"Do you remember telling him that Nancy never put a stick in your butt?"

"No."

"Do you remember telling him that nobody touched your private parts?"

This time the boy answered differently. "Yeah," he admitted.

Bradley repeated the question for emphasis and the boy nodded.

"Were you telling him the truth then?"

"Yeah."

He ended on that strong point and ceded the floor to Grunda. Grunda wanted to develop Jason's claim that a bus aide had accompanied them into Joseph's house. He wanted to see where this would lead. With a six-year-old witness, he didn't have much to lose if things went awry.

"Do you remember an aide by the name of Angel?"

"Yeah."

Jason also admitted that Angel was on the bus with Joseph and that when they arrived at Joseph's house, she went inside with them and not Nancy.

"Did she take off her clothes too?"

The boy hesitated for a moment before answering no.

"So Angel went into the house. And it was Angel who made you do all those bad things, huh?"

"Yeah."

"Nothing further."

Rosenbaum declined to ask Jason any more questions and decided to regroup with his next witness, Franklin Logan, the father of Marcus Logan.

CHAPTER 17
TRIAL DAY FOUR: AFTERNOON SESSION

JULY 28, 1994

Franklin Logan raised his right hand and swore to the tell the truth. The twenty-nine-year-old Logan was a handsome African-American male with fine features, short-cropped hair, and a well-trimmed mustache. Thin and athletic-looking, Logan appeared confident and eager to talk to the jury. At the outset of his testimony, Logan told the jury that he had married Marcus's mother about a year earlier and worked at Ford building minivans.

Rosenbaum quickly turned his questions to Logan's son, Marcus. After establishing the years that his son had been in the Head Start program, Rosenbaum asked, "Have you noticed any changes in his behavior or his attitude about Head Start?"

"Marcus used to be very outgoing, playful. He used to have a lot of friends. And now he pretty much keeps to himself."

"Did you notice any problems at home?" Rosenbaum asked.

"While he was at his grandmother's house, we found him on top of his younger sister with all of his clothes off. Both of them."

"When was this?"

"I'd say between March and April."

This fit squarely into Rosenbaum's opening narrative that some

Head Start children had mysteriously begun to "act out" in the spring of 1993, a harrowing clue that they'd been sexually molested.

The jury had already heard about Michael Osborne's humping his teddy bear and Jason Gilbert's sitting atop his younger foster brother with his pants down. However, there was a difference between Logan's testimony and that of the other two parents. Despite repeated interactions between the Logan family and the police for a year and a half, Marcus's alleged behavior with his younger sister had never been documented in any reports authored by Detective Cantu, Andujar, or Miller. This was in stark contrast to the other two boys, whose unusual sexual conduct had been documented in the police reports after their parents had told the detectives about their behavior early in the investigation.

Nevertheless, with this third parental claim of aberrant behavior, Rosenbaum was meticulously proving his case. Something sordid had triggered this abnormal conduct, and the reasons sat several feet from the jury—Nancy Smith and Joseph Allen.

Rosenbaum asked Mr. Logan how he'd learned of the allegations swirling about the Head Start program. Logan claimed that he'd learned this from his son, who'd told his mom about a detective's visit to the school. Rosenbaum's next question was quite specific.

"Prior to that, did you have any contact with any of the other parents?"

"No."

However, something important had been left unsaid—something that happened immediately after the detective's visit. Either that day or the next, Marge Bronson had phoned Marcus's mother and provided details about Nina's molestation. More important, Mrs. Bronson had suggested that a doctor examine Marcus for evidence of sexual abuse. According to Bronson's daughter, Marcus had been taken to the same house, where they'd both been molested.

Mr. Logan testified that he'd asked Marcus if anything had happened to him at school. Marcus then told him about a "man named Joseph" and what he'd done to him. He'd also "implied that his bus driver was there." When asked to describe Joseph, Marcus had said that he was a black man with white spots on his hands.

However, Mr. Logan left out a few important things. Upon being questioned, Marcus had initially denied that anything bad had happened to him. Convinced that his son was holding something back, Mr. Logan had interrogated his son for two hours until his son finally said that he'd been abused.

Rosenbaum established one final point with Franklin Logan. The elder Logan admitted that he'd interfered in the police investigation and pressured his son to wrongly identify Richard Jones as Joseph. Because the defense attorneys knew about Marcus's false identification (through a recorded statement that they'd just received), they would exploit this to undermine the boy's credibility about anything he said.

"Is there a tape where Marcus describes to the police this other person that you showed him?"

"Yes, there is."

"Did Marcus, though, tell you that this was not the Joseph who had abused him?"

"Yes, he did."

By taking full responsibility, Mr. Logan had defused a potential landmine and made his son's forthcoming testimony more believable. For Rosenbaum, it had been a skillful piece of lawyering. He'd anticipated a potential attack and blunted it.

Although Bradley and Grunda knew about Marcus's role in falsely accusing Richard Jones, they were unaware that he'd also incorrectly picked out two other homes as being Joseph's. As a result, the jury would never know the full extent of Marcus's unreliability.

Bradley's primary goal during this cross-examination was to show that Marcus had provided his father with several different descriptions of Joseph.

This started out well.

"When your son first described this person, he said he had blue eyes, correct?"

"This is correct."

However, when Bradley tried to show that Marcus had wrongly picked Richard Jones as Joseph, Mr. Logan gave him pushback. Although Marcus had described Richard Jones to the police, Mr. Logan insisted that Marcus had "never identified him as Joseph." It was a nonsensical answer, but it stalled Bradley's thrust.

Moving on, Bradley wanted to demonstrate that Marcus had said that his classmates David, Brian, Aleah, and Brittany had also been at Joseph's house. It was a claim that no one else ever corroborated. Mr. Logan confirmed that Marcus had said this.

"You testified that the children received shots in their butts when they were there?" Bradley asked.

"Yes."

"And that these shots made them bleed?"

"I didn't know about that. I know that they were given shots," Mr. Logan responded.

"Was this on more than one occasion?"

"I'm not aware of that. I know at least once he told me that he was given shots and alcohol and marijuana."

For the first time, Bradley sensed that the witness was about to stumble.

"And marijuana?"

"Yeah."

"And alcohol?"

"Mm-hmm."

"So he actually smoked marijuana?"

"He told me that he did."

"Did you ever notice him coming home with either an odor of marijuana around him or an odor of alcohol?"

"I noticed him coming home with an odor of alcohol and a staggering motion." Mr. Logan realized that he needed to retract his last statement. "I did not smell alcohol. I joked with him about that," he said. For the next minute, Bradley and Mr. Logan jousted about whether he'd initially testified that he'd smelled alcohol on his son's breath.

"Did Marcus say how he got to Joseph's house?"

"They were taken by Nancy's car. However, I believe that he said one time that a bus was involved."

"So of the three trips, two were by car and one was by bus?"

"Yes."

Mr. Logan did not disclose that Marcus had initially claimed that he'd walked to Joseph's house with Nancy and the others.

Marcus's current version of the story was also problematic. Could Marcus have been transported to the school by bus and then driven to Joseph's house in Nancy's car? Before starting her route, Smith picked up the bus at a parking lot in Sheffield Village and left her car there. That parking lot (and her car) were four and half miles from the Head Start school.

Bradley had one final point. The State maintained that the children had been molested between January and June 1993. After listening to the taped interview, Bradley had found something that was inconsistent with that scenario.

"Didn't you tell the police that Marcus had told you that this had been going on for a couple of years?"

"Yes."

Bradley raised his eyebrows and looked at the jury in case they didn't grasp the significance of the father's answer. Bradley asked several more questions before sitting down. After Grunda finished his questioning, the prosecutor announced that he would call Marcus Logan as his next witness. The jury was cleared from the courtroom and the judge questioned the six-year-old, finding him competent to testify.

Rosenbaum's direct examination of Marcus Logan was almost flawless. The prosecutor kept things crisp by using a combination of leading questions and questions that could be answered with one word or with a short phrase. In this way, Marcus identified things found in Joseph Allen's apartment: the mask, toy cars, Batman sheets, and a photo of a bloody head. However, Marcus did make a few missteps.

The prosecutor next wanted Marcus to identify the pink dress seized at Joseph's apartment. "Does Joseph always wear men's clothes?" the prosecutor asked. Experienced litigators can ask leading questions by phrasing them to prompt a negative response.

"Yes," Marcus said as he chewed a big wad of gum.

Rosenbaum switched to the direct approach. "Did you ever see him in any ladies' clothes?" the prosecutor asked.

"No."

Later, Marcus failed to describe Joseph Allen as a man with spots on his body.

"Now, does Joseph have spots on his body?"

"No."

"Does he have dots?"

"No."

Rosenbaum tried for his third and final time to elicit the response he wanted. "Does he have parts of him or little parts that are a slightly different color?"

"No."

"Are you sure?"

"Yes."

Rosenbaum gave up and switched topics. Over the next few minutes, the prosecutor asked a series of questions that outlined the sexual abuse involving Marcus, both acts done to him and things he had been forced to do to the defendants. Anyone who had listened to the boy's earlier taped statements could hear how much his vocabulary had improved over the last year. Where before he'd described the male sex organ as his "privates" or "peepee," he now said "penis"—suggesting that over the months, someone had worked with him in telling his story. He also now knew the word "vagina" and used it effortlessly in his testimony.

Rosenbaum ended the examination with an emotional flourish, using a series of leading questions to heighten the drama.

"Are you sure that this person here in the blue shirt is Joseph?"

"Yes."

"Do you not want to look at him?"

"No."

"Are you afraid?"

"Yes."

"Are you ashamed?"

"Yes."

"Do you not want to look at Nancy?"

"No."

"Are you afraid of Nancy?"

"Yes."

"Are you ashamed of what happened with Nancy?"

"Yes."

"I have no further questions, Your Honor." Rosenbaum could have whispered his last words; the courtroom was completely silent.

The defense attorneys now had the unenviable job of cross-examining this cute six-year-old boy who'd just described how he'd been abused: oral sex, anal sex, and being forced to kiss both defendants in ways that were both crude and outrageous. He'd told about being stuck with a needle in his buttocks and being forced to drink urine from a cup. Somehow, Bradley and Grunda had to convince the jury that none of this was true.

Despite Rosenbaum's effort to shield Marcus from the fallout from his false identification of Richard Jones, that was where Bradley would begin. At the break, he'd requested, and the judge had ordered, that Detective Andujar return to the station and gather the six photographs that Marcus had been shown when he'd identified Jones.

Armed with them, Bradley would begin his cross-examination with the false identification. The boy had lied to the police; he could show that. But Bradley wanted to go deeper. He wanted to explore why Marcus had lied. Perhaps that would be the key that would unlock the case for this jury.

After reacquainting Marcus with the photographs and confirming that he'd picked out Richard Jones as Joseph, Bradley asked, "You lied to the police when you told them that this was Joseph, didn't you?"

"Yes," Marcus said as he looked down at his feet.

"Were you trying to make your dad happy?"

"No."

"Then why did you lie to the police and tell them that this man was Joseph?"

"Because I was scared."

"Why were you scared of this man?" Bradley asked as he pointed to the photograph of Richard Jones.

"I don't know."

"What were you scared of when you picked out this man as Joseph?"

"I don't know," the boy repeated.

Bradley also wanted to explore why Marcus had initially reported that other children had gone to Joseph's house when he now claimed that they had not. He began by confirming that only Melissa, Nina, and Jason had gone to Joseph's house with him.

"You also told the police that Brian went. Do you remember telling them that?"

"Yes."

"Did you lie when you told them that Brian went?"

"Yes."

"Why did you have to lie to the police about Brian?"

"I was scared."

"And you also told them that David went, didn't you?"

"Yes."

"And did David go with you?"

"Yes."

"So David went with you to Joseph's?" Bradley asked, surprise registering in his voice.

"Yes."

"Why didn't you name David when I just asked you to name all of the kids who went to Joseph's house? You were supposed to be telling us the truth."

Marcus did not respond.

"So you are lying about David, aren't you, Marcus?"

"Yes."

Like a parent chastising his child, Bradley wanted to emphasize his point and receive an explanation for this bad behavior.

"You know, you're not supposed to lie when you are up here, are you?" Bradley asked, pointing to the witness chair.

"Yes."

"Why did you lie about David when you are up here?"

"I don't know." Marcus's lips were quivering and he looked about the courtroom as if searching for an escape route.

"You shouldn't lie when you are up here, should you?"

"No." By now, tears were streaming down the boy's cheeks.

"Okay," Bradley said. In his zeal to unmask the boy, he'd turned Marcus into an object of sympathy.

The judge intervened and handed the boy a tissue. "Do you need to take a break?" she asked him.

"Yes," he replied meekly.

The judge decided to take the afternoon recess. When questioning resumed, it would be anticlimactic. However, Bradley had raised the ultimate question—why? If these crimes had been committed, why would a child lie about the details? It made no sense.

For the defense attorneys, the more logical conclusion was that these horrible things had never happened. It explained why one child's story differed from another's and why the same child's story changed and evolved over time.

Bradley and Grunda were also troubled by something else. The police and the prosecutor seemed determined to believe the children regardless of what they said or how often they altered their stories. Why was that? Were there forces afoot that simply defied explanation? If so, how could they defend against that?

CHAPTER 18
TRIAL DAY FIVE
JULY 29, 1994

When the trial resumed on Friday afternoon, it would belong to Marge Bronson, the mother whose impassioned pleas to the police had ignited their exhaustive investigation. Both the prosecution and the defense knew that she was a crucial witness—perhaps one of the trial's key witnesses. Today, she would speak directly to the jurors and tell them in graphic detail about the horrible things that the defendants had done to her daughter. If the jury believed her, guilty verdicts would almost certainly follow. But that was the question: Would she appear credible?

Under Criminal Rule 16, a prosecutor was required to disclose a witness's felony convictions to the defense, who in turn could reveal them to the jury. The law reasoned that this information had a bearing on a witness's credibility and in some cases, it was enough for the jury to doubt or disregard someone's testimony on that basis alone.

Marge Bronson was a convicted felon, but the jury would never know this.

When Bradley raised this issue two months later as he sought a new trial, he argued that Rosenbaum should have discovered Bronson's conviction and revealed it to him. Rosenbaum countered by explaining that he'd asked the witness about any convictions and she'd assured him that her record was clean. He also asserted that Bradley should have known about her conviction because he'd handled the appeal of a codefendant in the same case that involved Mrs. Bronson. In her own defense, Mrs. Bronson said that she didn't know that she'd been convicted of anything. She'd made a deal to testify against a codefendant (her ex-boyfriend) and thought the federal authorities had dropped all charges against her. Somehow, she'd forgotten that she'd pled guilty to one count of conspiracy to distribute cocaine and had been sentenced to one year in prison. Her prison time had been suspended and replaced with six months of house arrest and three years of probation. In an ironic twist, her probation had ended just a few days before her testimony in this case.

Despite all of the finger-pointing and denials about the conviction, one thing was certain: these jurors would never know anything about it or the circumstances surrounding it. They'd be unaware that she'd been accused of selling cocaine to federal government agents and receiving large amounts of cocaine at the same home where she was raising her children.

On this day, what the jurors saw was an attractive, well-groomed brunette—a law-abiding single mom who was doing her best to raise three small children. They'd soon discover that she was also a persuasive communicator—a woman who could mesmerize her audience by providing attention-grabbing details while, at the same time, revealing her inner emotions as she chronicled events.

Rosenbaum could have called Marge Bronson as his first trial witness, but he'd held back. Perhaps he'd anticipated that the defense would try to cast her as the ringleader of a witch hunt—the person who'd convinced other parents that the defendants had done abominable things to their children too. By having her testify on the fifth day, Rosenbaum was minimizing her role in the case.

Rosenbaum began his questioning by asking her about her daughter and her early experience at Head Start. He soon directed her to tell the disturbing story of her daughter's abuse. Except for providing more details, Marge Bronson recounted much the same story that she'd reported to Detective Cantu fifteen months earlier. She told the jury that, for several months, Nina had to be coaxed to board the Head Start bus. On May 7, 1993, Nina had come home on the bus but claimed that she hadn't gone to school, but instead had been taken to a house where she'd been sexually abused. Mrs. Bronson's voice became more agitated as she recounted her conversation with Nina that evening.

"And she goes, 'But, Mommy, when we were at Nancy's and Joseph's house, and we had to play the doctor game, they said I was a good girl, but you know what they did to me, Mommy? They tied my hands up, and they put tape over my mouth, and they stuck this stick inside of me. Then I couldn't breathe no more.

"'And then God said that I died, and I went up to heaven. And God said that he wasn't ready for me, so he threw me back down. Then I woke up. But that stick they stuck inside of me, it really hurted. But if I was a good girl, how come they did that to me?'"

By quoting her daughter, Mrs. Bronson was telling a compelling story, but her daughter's out-of-court statements were hearsay and probably inadmissible. Although an Ohio evidence rule allowed someone like Mrs. Bronson to repeat a small child's hearsay statements in sexual abuse cases, this special rule was only triggered if the child was unable or unwilling to testify and other requirements were met. Because Nina Zorich was scheduled to testify, this rule did not apply, at least not yet. However, neither defense attorney objected to these hearsay statements and Mrs. Bronson was free to "quote" her daughter without any check.

Continuing her daughter's account, Mrs. Bronson said, "'Well, Joseph didn't want to hear me scream all the time, so he used to cover my mouth up with tape.'

"And then after that, I said, 'Are you sure, Nina? Are you sure?' Because, you know, I couldn't believe what I was hearing."

Mrs. Bronson looked at the jury. "And I'm questioning her for a couple hours, because this is really hard stuff. I didn't want to make accusations about somebody if it wasn't really true."

To demonstrate that she could corroborate her daughter's story with physical evidence, Mrs. Bronson told the jury that she'd found a leaf on the inside of her daughter's T-shirt, evidence that Joseph had stuck her with a stick. Before giving her daughter a bath, she claimed to have seen vaginal discharge. The emergency room physician who'd examined Nina that night was never called to confirm the mother's claim.

"And she goes, 'That is how come I don't want to take a bath. I don't want to smell clean. Because if I smell dirty, Nancy and Joseph won't touch me.' And she showed me exactly how they put the stick in there.

"I flipped. I started going crazy. I lost it at that time.

"And she goes, 'Oh, Mommy, don't cry. Don't send me back to that bad school. Nancy and Joseph said that if I told you, that you're going to die. You're going to have a heart attack and you're not going to live and I'm going to lose my mommy.'

"And I had to collect myself and calm down and gather myself up for her. But at the same time, I was just horrified. I was just dying.

"And then about ten o'clock that night, that is when I took her to the hospital."

With almost no prompting from the prosecutor, Marge Bronson had told the jury a dreadful tale. With her powers of description and knack for incorporating dialogue into her story, she'd transported them back in time to the moment when she'd uncovered her daughter's nightmare.

Directing her to another topic, Rosenbaum asked, "Now, prior to all this, did you notice anything unusual about Nina's clothing?"

Mrs. Bronson told the jury that in February, Nina had come home from school wearing nylon panties. She thought that this was odd because all of her daughter's underwear was made from cotton.

"And I'm just taking off her underwear, getting her ready for the bathtub, and I go, 'Nina, how come you have all these bruises right here on your leg?' And she goes, 'Oh, I just got those today at school playing the games we have.'

"So I'm thinking, 'Okay.'

"So I give her a bath and I notice that her vagina was red and irritated. And I didn't think much of it, because I thought, maybe, because little girls don't wipe good or something like that.

"But she had the wrong pair of underwear. I didn't know where they came from."

When Mrs. Bronson paused, Rosenbaum asked if she'd given the panties to the police and she indicated that she had.

"I would ask you to look at the contents of that plastic envelope. State's Exhibit Fourteen. Do you recognize that?"

"Yes, these are the pair of underwear that Nina had on."

Not only had Mrs. Bronson told the jury about abuse that had happened on May 7, but she'd laid the groundwork for abuse that may have occurred three months earlier in February. How else could one explain the strange underwear and the injuries to her daughter's body?

Mrs. Bronson had more to say. She told the jury that Nina began hiding in the closet, taking her dolls in there and removing their clothes.

"And I walked in there and I caught her, and she was humping on one of her dolls."

At other times, the mother would eavesdrop on her daughter when she was in the closet with her Barbie dolls.

"And she would take off all her clothes and she would lay there and say, 'Okay, now, you guys can do it.' And she would just go talking about sexual things. And I was listening to her outside the door talking nasty to her dolls."

After the abuse had been discovered, Mrs. Bronson related how her daughter had French kissed her one day after she'd crawled onto her lap.

"And all of a sudden, she opened her mouth and started French kissing me. And I'm like, 'Nina, what are you doing?' And she goes, 'Well, Auntie Nancy showed me how to kiss like that. That is how you're supposed to kiss.'

"And I go, 'No, honey, that is not how you're supposed to kiss.'

"And she says, 'Well, Auntie Nancy said she had to show us how to kiss like that, because we had to kiss her boyfriend Joseph like that.' And then I said, 'No.'"

In his final series of questions, Rosenbaum asked Mrs. Bronson about her relationship with Detective Cantu. She claimed that things had started well but deteriorated.

"Did Detective Cantu ever tell you to contact the other parents?" Rosenbaum asked.

"Yes."

Detective Cantu's records do not document this alleged conversation, and the notes of a social worker who met with Mrs. Bronson on May 28, 1993, reveal a different story. Mrs. Bronson told the social worker, Sandy Kelly, that she'd met with two parents and told them what had happened to Nina and to their own children. In her report, Ms. Kelly stated that Mrs. Bronson had "expressed amazement" that Detective Cantu had "threatened to have her arrested if she continued to interfere with his investigation." Ms. Kelly also warned her that her actions could "[do] more harm than good."

However, when describing her motives, Mrs. Bronson maintained that she'd talked to the parents "because [she] was just a concerned parent." She'd reached out to the newspapers for the same reason.

After that, Rosenbaum ended his questioning. Bradley asked the judge for a short recess in order to organize his thoughts for his cross-examination.

"We'll take five minutes," Judge McGough said as she directed the bailiff to take the jurors to the jury room.

Although this was not as much time as Bradley would have liked, the judge had accommodated him in other ways today. She'd ruled against the prosecutor when he'd tried to call another Head Start student, Amanda Lilly, as a witness. The little girl was prepared to say that Nancy Smith had touched her inappropriately while on the bus. The judge had ruled that these claims were too dissimilar to those upon which charges had been brought but that, depending on the evidence, Rosenbaum could offer her as a rebuttal witness.

The judge had also delayed the trial for over an hour to allow Bradley to talk to Dr. Amy Richardson by phone. Two days earlier, the prosecutor had supplemented his discovery to advise the defense that "Dr. A. Richards [Richardson] has information that the State feels is inadmissible but possibly could be used in an attempt to impeach Margie Bronson." Earlier that afternoon, Bradley and the doctor had talked. While Mrs. Bronson was testifying, Dr. Richardson had faxed Nina Zorich's medical records to Bradley via the court's fax machine.

Now Bradley needed time to read them in silence and prepare his questions accordingly.

Dr. Richardson's records showed that on May 27, 1993, Marge Bronson's boyfriend had called Dr. Richardson's office in order to get a copy of her medical report because he wanted to give it to an investigative reporter for a local television station. Dr. Richardson had refused and had insisted that Mrs. Bronson meet with her the following day to warn her that releasing the records could jeopardize the integrity of the police investigation.

After establishing that this meeting took place, Bradley asked Mrs. Bronson, "And Dr. Richardson talked to you about not releasing this information to the news media, is that correct?"

"Correct, but—"

"Because she told you that this could possibly contaminate the investigation, is that correct?"

"Yes, but I wanted the reports for my lawyer."

This time Bradley pounced on the revelation.

"Oh, you had a lawyer?" he asked.

"And I still do."

"A Cleveland lawyer?"

"Yes, I do."

"So you can sue Head Start?"

"I don't think that concerns you right now."

"So you can sue Head Start?"

"It's none of your business," Mrs. Bronson snapped.

"I'm asking you a question. So you can sue Head Start?" Bradley persisted.

"Does it matter?"

"Answer the question, please."

"I'm not sure."

At this point, both Emily Osborne and Marge Bronson had disclosed that they had retained attorneys, presumably to seek money damages from Head Start when the criminal case was over. When they'd testified, Ann Gilbert and Franklin Logan hadn't been asked that question. Had all the parents hired attorneys to sue Head Start? If so, had they done so almost immediately after learning of the abuse allegations?

For the next five minutes, Bradley questioned Mrs. Bronson, seeking admissions that she had tainted the investigation in a number of ways. Had she discussed the details of the allegations with other parents? Had she allowed her daughter to be present when she talked to the detectives? Had she ignored Dr. Richardson's admonition to avoid the media? Mrs. Bronson admitted to doing all of these things. But what did it mean?

Witness contamination was not something within the common knowledge of jurors. What was it exactly? What difference did it make if an adult discussed allegations of abuse in front of a child? Could one child's story cause other children to make false accusations? Did it make the entire investigation unreliable?

The defense needed a witness who could answer these questions. Perhaps that person was an experienced law enforcement investigator or a psychologist who understood how children's memories were shaped and molded. Was either Bradley or Grunda planning to call such a witness? They weren't. The problem was that they hadn't understood the scope of the contamination until they'd listened to the taped statements of the parents and children. And by then, it was too late. The trial was well underway. By denying them prior access to these statements, the law (and the prosecutor to the extent that the tapes were exculpatory) had placed the defendants and their attorneys in a deep hole, one that threatened to swallow them in its recesses.

Despite their late arrival, the taped interviews were still the grist for Bradley's questioning. Bradley decided to confront Mrs. Bronson with some of her daughter's early allegations that the police and prosecutor had eventually abandoned. While driving near the school with her mother, Nina had seen a white man cutting his lawn and had told her mother that she'd just spotted Joseph.

"And she told you that this man was Joseph, and she wanted to leave, right?"

"She said it looked like him."

"And then that same man was on television because he was questioned by the investigative reporter, wasn't he?"

"Because he looked like one of the persons that was there at the house."

"One of the adults that was there?" Bradley asked.

"Along with these two," Mrs. Bronson said, looking at Joseph Allen and Nancy Smith at the trial table.

Bradley seized on this. "So there were other adults there besides the two defendants?"

"I'm sure of it," she replied firmly.

"And, as a matter of fact, you told Detective Cantu that Nancy's daughter was there?"

"Yes, she was."

"And you also told Detective Cantu that Nancy's son was there?"

"Yes, I did."

"And that they were involved in this also, didn't you?"

"Yes, I did."

"And that Nancy's mother was there, also?"

"Yes."

If the jurors were paying attention, they should have been deeply disturbed by these answers. The police had not arrested or charged any of these people, yet Mrs. Bronson maintained that all four of them had somehow been a part of this evil enterprise. Would a rational person believe this?

Toward the end of his cross-examination, Bradley began to point out little discrepancies in Mrs. Bronson's direct testimony. After Mrs. Bronson had accused Nancy Smith of molestation, her daughter had allegedly referred to her as Auntie Nancy. To Bradley, this seemed so crazy that it couldn't possibly be true.

"So you are telling me after she reported sexual abuse, she was calling her Auntie Nancy?"

"Yes, because that is what Auntie Nancy, which is not her aunt, told her to do."

"So after she disclosed to you this traumatic event about being sexually abused, she still called this lady Auntie Nancy?"

"Lord knows why."

"Called her Auntie Nancy?"

"Because she told her to, yes."

When he concluded his cross-examination, Bradley asked the judge to play the four audiotapes that involved Nina Zorich and Marge Bronson to the jury, arguing that they touched on the mother's credibility and demonstrated how she had contaminated the investigation by making suggestions and allegations in front of her daughter. Rosenbaum objected, pointing out that the tapes did not remotely touch on her credibility.

The judge sided with the prosecutor. "I'm not going to do that."

Grunda kept his cross-examination short. He confirmed that Nina never arrived home late at night and was never dropped off in a car.

Turning to her daughter's evolving descriptions of Joseph, he asked, "And, if I'm not mistaken, she indicated to you that Joseph was a white man, correct?"

"No. He would paint himself black and have white spots on him."

Grunda manufactured a confused look. "Didn't you say on direct that she said he was a white man? He was covered up with black and had white spots on him?"

Sensing that he was trapping her, Mrs. Bronson replied, "Didn't I answer it earlier?"

"Not to me. Isn't that true?"

"She said that he was black or white and had white spots on his body."

"Now you are changing. He was white or black?"

"Either way. She said he painted himself and he had white spots on his body," Mrs. Bronson replied.

Grunda tried a different tack. "And this man who was cutting the grass outside, was he white or black?"

"White."

"Thank you. And she thought this was Joseph, is that correct?"

"Yep."

Grunda concluded with a simple question: "Where did she say that these bad things had happened?"

"In a junky basement and in a bedroom upstairs."

To emphasize her answer, Grunda repeated it. "In the basement. Junky basement, correct?"

"Correct."

He would remind the jury in his closing argument that there was no basement or upstairs in Joseph Allen's apartment. After a few more questions, he sat down.

The judge asked Rosenbaum whether he wanted to ask the witness any more questions on redirect.

"No, ma'am," he replied.

A few minutes later, the judge adjourned for the day. The first week of the trial was over.

CHAPTER 19
TRIAL DAY SIX
AUGUST 1, 1994

On this day, Rosenbaum planned to call more alleged victims and, at some point, add the testimony of Detective Joel Miller to break up the repetitiveness. His first three witnesses would be Head Start children, all girls: Nina Zorich, Melissa Warner, and Jessica Simpson. His strategy was clear: he would overwhelm the jury with child victims. The more children who testified, the more difficult it would be for this jury to believe that the children's claims were based on imagination and not fact. With a little luck, he would conclude the day with Kelsey Calvin, the girl whose claims of sexual molestation had sent Joseph Allen to prison nine years earlier. Unlike the small children whom he'd prodded and coaxed thus far during the trial, she was now twenty-one years old and could fully describe what had happened to her.

Of the three girls from Head Start, Jessica Simpson refused to answer any questions posed to her by Judge McGough during her competency evaluation. As a result, the judge had no choice but to rule that the little girl was incompetent to testify. However, both Nina Zorich and Melissa Warner cleared the competency hurdle. Like the child witnesses who had preceded them, these girls were unable to provide a free-flowing narrative. Instead, they responded to the prosecutor's pointed questions with a shake of the head, a shrug of the shoulders, or a yes-or-no answer. Occasionally, they answered with a phrase, or, very rarely, with an entire sentence.

Using this method, Rosenbaum nudged Nina Zorich to confirm all of the sexual molestation claims, not just those involving her but those that she'd witnessed concerning the other children. He also insisted that she demonstrate how a person French kissed, something her mother claimed that she'd learned from Nancy Smith. The little girl refused several times, but the prosecutor persisted until she began crying.

As if he was working through a checklist, he also verified that she'd been stuck with a needle and stick, spanked, restrained with rope, and gagged with tape. He also asked her to identify things taken from Allen's apartment: the rope, the Halloween mask, and a photograph.

As they'd done with previous child witnesses, the defense counsel pointed out discrepancies between their trial testimony and their earlier statements. Although Nina Zorich had testified that she'd been driven to Joseph's house in his car during her direct exam, on cross-examination, she reverted back to what she'd initially told the police, namely that she'd been taken there by bus, a much less likely scenario. In a new wrinkle, she also claimed that Nancy Smith had taken all of the Head Start children to Hill's or Kmart, where they'd viewed toys but didn't buy any. Later, she said that they'd dined at a restaurant. Both claims were far-fetched and were not supported by any corroborating testimony. She also insisted that she and others had also been taken to Nancy's house, where her son and daughter had been present, allegations debunked by Detective Cantu in the first weeks of the investigation.

Melissa Warner's testimony followed the same pattern. Although neither defendant had been charged with any crimes involving Melissa, she testified that Nancy Smith had taken her to Joseph's house with the other children. Melissa said that she'd never removed any of her clothing there, but she claimed that Nancy Smith had rubbed her slacks in her vaginal area.

On cross-examination, Bradley confronted her with her earlier taped statement where she'd claimed that a bus driver named Angel had driven her to Joseph's house, not Nancy. He also developed another unlikely part of her story. On direct exam she'd insisted that no one had accompanied her back to her classroom after she'd been returned to the school. Bradley asked her to expand on that, and she explained that she'd walked by herself to the playground, where she'd joined her classmates. Although her teacher had watched her arrive, she supposedly never asked the girl any questions.

However, something was happening in the courtroom that went beyond the words spoken. Yes, the children, with the aid of the prosecutor, offered up their dreadful stories. And on the other side, the defense attorneys zeroed in on details that ranged from the improbable to the crazy. Those things were visible on the surface. However, beneath that, other circumstances, powerful and silent, were shaping the jurors' minds.

Quite simply, the children's presence produced an overpowering emotional response from the adults who listened to them tell their stories. Part of that reaction was caused by the children's appearance. They were all good-looking youngsters, ranging from the cute to the beautiful. Another factor was their innocent demeanor. As they were questioned, their shyness and bewilderment were palpable. They spoke softly and jurors strained to hear their words. Marcus Logan and Nina Zorich cried during their testimony, Nina several times. How could the jurors not feel an instinctive need to protect these children?

But it went beyond the children's appearance and demeanor. It was also how other adults responded to them. Jurors could see that authority figures believed them. The children's stories had convinced the police who'd persevered for over six months to locate Joseph. Once the case had been transferred to the prosecutor's office, assistant prosecutor Rosenbaum had taken over where the detectives had left off.

And when the jurors watched Judge McGough interact with the children, they saw a woman very solicitous to their needs. During Nina Zorich's testimony, the judge had intervened over a half dozen times, giving her water and tissues and frequently asking her if she was okay. At one point, she'd volunteered that the girl didn't have to respond to a question if she was not sure of her answer. Besides offering breaks and water to Melissa Warner, the judge, at one point, had intervened and taken over the girl's questioning. She'd also ruled in favor of the prosecutor when one of his leading questions had coaxed the witness to alter her answer.

Rosenbaum had asked, "Now, I want to ask you again. Did you ever have to touch Nancy anywhere?"

As she had done before, Melissa shook her head.

"I would like to hand you this doll, which is supposed to be a grown-up girl doll. Do you want to look at it? Can you show me on that doll where you had to touch Nancy?"

Bradley objected. "She has already indicated twice she didn't touch Nancy, now he is asking a leading question."

The judge summarily ruled against him. "This is a six-year-old child. Overruled," she said in a voice that teetered between exasperation and indignation.

The judge obviously wanted to encourage the children to feel comfortable in her courtroom. However, if too attentive and protective, she could signal something more—her belief that the children were telling the truth about the core facts.

And then there was the media—newspaper reporters scribbling notes and photographers snapping pictures of the participants. The jurors understood that this case was very significant and their decision would be front-page news. They, too, were in the spotlight, and the community would ultimately judge them. Would there be public outrage if they acquitted the defendants? All of these things swirled about in the courtroom, influencing the jurors in ways they did not know or did not fully realize.

Rosenbaum's next witness was Detective Joel Miller, another authority figure who did not doubt the children's story. Miller would provide two critical pieces to the prosecutor's case. He'd tell them how the defendant fit the children's description of Joseph and then how the items found in Joseph Allen's apartment cemented the identification.

Rosenbaum carefully avoided asking the detective to talk about the two investigations that had first brought Joseph Allen to his attention. Miller simply said that he'd "run across" Allen as a suspect in another case. During that other investigation, Miller explained that Allen had "willingly showed [him] his body." Without any context, the comment was puzzling, but things got weirder as Miller began identifying eight photographs that he'd taken of Allen's body. These photos captured a variety of Allen's skin conditions: a pockmarked face; burn scars on his shoulder and stomach; and white spots on his penis, legs, right ankle, knees, and buttocks. One photograph showed a scar on Allen's right hand.

Did these skin conditions match what the children had described earlier? Only two of the children had talked about Allen's white spots during taped interviews. Nina Zorich had explained that the "white" Joseph had failed to apply black makeup completely over his face and hands, leaving white spots there. Marcus Logan had described big white spots all over Joseph's body—causing Joseph to look almost Caucasian. In confirming that the spots were large, Marcus had provided a strange, nonsensical explanation. "Big, 'cause my cousin said he seen him at Cedar Point." However, according to Marcus, not all of the spots were large. The backs of Joseph's hands were covered in white "dots."

Although Joseph Allen was a black man with white spots and burns on his body, several things did not match the descriptions that Marcus and Nina had provided to Detective Cantu early in the investigation. The two children had described Joseph as having white spots or dots on his hands; Joseph Allen did not. Likewise, no one could say that Joseph Allen was "almost white" as Marcus had claimed. Allen was a dark-skinned African-American and would never have been confused for a Caucasian.

Detective Miller readily admitted that he'd never listened to Cantu's taped interviews but had relied almost exclusively upon the reports authored by Detective Andujar. He'd shied away from anything Detective Cantu had generated because "he had it so messed up." As a result, he was unaware of the children's earlier descriptions.

The remainder of Miller's direct examination focused on the items that he'd seized from Joseph Allen's apartment. Through this witness, Rosenbaum intended to make good on his promise that the children had described these things before Joseph Allen had been a suspect. Although Miller identified a Halloween mask, bedsheets, children's toys, a pink dress, children's tapes, a belt, and a violent photograph of a man being shot, he did not deliver on Rosenbaum's promise that the children had described these things before Joseph Allen had been arrested. Instead, the detective said the opposite.

Referring to Marcus Logan and the all-important Halloween mask, Rosenbaum asked, "My question is: Did he mention or describe the mask *before* you showed it to him?"

"The children, no. No. No, they didn't," Miller said, his answer surprising Rosenbaum. Thus, according to the detective in charge of quizzing the children about these seized items, none of the children— including Marcus—had described the mask before the police showed it to them.

Rosenbaum tried to regroup. "Okay. All right. So you showed them that mask and asked them if they could identify it?"

"Right."

As Miller answered more questions, it became evident that the detective had used that same procedure when questioning the children about the other items. He would ask them if they remembered a partic- ular item from Joseph's house, such as a belt, a magazine, or a mask. If they said that they did, then he'd show them the item, and, invariably, they'd say that they'd seen it at Joseph's place. With four- and five- year-old children, this method was highly suggestive and not what Rosenbaum had promised in his opening.

However, the prosecutor was undaunted. He had several other ways to demonstrate that the seized property belonged to the same Joseph who'd molested the children.

"Were any of the children able to tell you that something was missing from the mask, like the lights with snake eyes?" Rosenbaum asked, leaving no doubt what he wanted his witness to comment upon.

Miller then told the jury that, without any suggestion from him, Nina Zorich had spontaneously pointed out that the mask's eyes should light up. He'd previously removed the mask's lightbulbs before showing it to the children. The implication was clear: the only way Nina could have known about the electrified eyes was if she'd previ- ously seen this exact mask at Joseph's house.

However, Miller's report told a slightly different story. He'd asked Nina pointedly if Joseph had ever "wor[n] a Halloween mask with black hair." When she'd said that he had, she was shown the mask, which she identified as Joseph's. Miller then had asked her "if the eyes did anything on the mask." He'd directed her to look at the eyes, and only then had she commented on them. Because Ohio law did not require the prosecutor to turn over official police reports like Miller's, the defense attorneys (and the jury) were unaware of these details.

At the request of the police, Nina had also drawn a picture of the rope that Joseph had used to tie up the children. Miller told the jury that Nina's picture depicted a rope that looked eerily like the belt that they'd taken from Joseph's apartment. For some reason, the prosecutor did not produce Nina's picture for Miller to identify.

However, the most dramatic claim centered on a pink dress located in Allen's apartment. While Nina was looking at the seized items, she'd allegedly told Miller that Joseph had worn a pink dress. She said that Joseph had also vowed to wear it as a disguise and kill her parents if she ever disclosed what he'd done to her. Remembering a pink dress in Joseph's apartment during his first search, Miller obtained a search warrant to retrieve it. Later, after he'd seized it, Nina identified it as Joseph's dress.

The other items, while not specifically referenced by the children, were identified. This included children's bedsheets, two photographs of a bedroom decorated for a party, children's toys, and children's tapes. The prosecution hoped that these items, in the home of a man who supposedly lived alone, marked Joseph Allen as a pedophile. He owned them either to entertain children or to entice them into his home.

When Rosenbaum finished his direct exam, he'd accomplished what he'd set out to do. Several of the seized items had been connected to the children's Joseph. If believed, this testimony provided the vital corroboration necessary to establish guilt beyond a reasonable doubt.

Bradley asked for a sidebar outside the hearing of the jury. "I would like to see Miller's affidavit for the search warrant before I do my cross-examination," he said, directing his comment toward the prosecutor.

Rosenbaum did not have a copy in his file but promised to get it. While he did that, the judge took a brief recess.

When the trial resumed, Bradley stood ten feet from Detective Miller, holding a legal pad in his left hand and the recently retrieved search warrant in the other. Bradley planned to knock the detective off his stride at the outset.

In his opening statement, Rosenbaum had touted Miller as the clever detective, the one who had connected seemingly disparate pieces of evidence and solved a crime that had baffled his more experienced colleagues. In particular, he'd highlighted Miller's ingenuity in realizing that Head Start student Justin Frank had provided a critical clue when the boy had told investigators that the molester's name was Allen. While other detectives had disregarded the boy's story because all the other children knew the man as Joseph, Miller had realized that the boy had not been wrong—Justin merely knew the man by his last name.

Justin Frank was one of a handful of Head Start students who had provided the police with allegations of sexual abuse, but whose stories were so inconsistent with the others that they had not been incorporated into the case. Justin, like others in this group, would never be called to testify. In his police interview, the boy claimed that he had been abused on the bus by a man named Allen on the last day of school, May 27, 1993. This was sixteen days after Nancy Smith had been relieved of her bus driving duties. The boy had claimed that his bus driver was Sammy and that the molester looked like a Hispanic neighbor named Al. Despite all of these incompatible facts, both Rosenbaum in his opening statement and Miller on his direct examination had cherry-picked Justin's hearsay statement about the molester's name to fortify the case against Joseph Allen.

Because the Lorain police reports involving Justin's story had never been turned over to the defense, Bradley was unaware of these contradictory allegations. Nevertheless, Nancy Smith had provided him with information that would serve as the grist for his cross-examination about this statement.

Bradley's first questions to the detective seemed innocuous, simply restating some of Miller's earlier testimony. After briefly summarizing how he'd become involved in the search for Joseph, the detective repeated his conclusion that Justin Frank had correctly identified the molester by his last name of Allen. Bradley also had the detective confirm that the crimes against the Head Start students occurred sometime between January and June 1993. With both doors closed, Bradley sprang his trap.

"Did Justin Frank ride Nancy Smith's bus during that time frame?"

"I don't know," Miller said, trying not to show any surprise or dread at the question. "I know this boy was enrolled at Head Start in the 1992–1993 school year."

"Would it be significant to your investigation to know that Justin Frank was only on Nancy Smith's bus from September until Christmas break in 1992?"

"Yes."

"Because that would predate any of the allegations in this criminal case?" Bradley asked, his voice indignant.

"Yes."

"And that would be significant?"

"Yes," Miller said as he shifted uneasily in the witness chair.

Despite not having access to Justin's complete story, Bradley had shown that Justin would not have been in a position to provide any reliable information about the molester—not even the molester's name.

Building on this, Bradley confirmed that Miller had not assisted Detective Andujar in reinterviewing the children when Cantu had been relieved of his duties. Miller also admitted that he'd never bothered to listen to any of the taped interviews before trial, apparently believing it unnecessary to know what the children and parents had said earlier in the investigation. Even after the trial began, Miller claimed that he'd only listened to one or two of the tapes, "sort of hit or miss." Unlike either Cantu or Andujar, Miller had not taped any of his conversations with the children or their parents, an investigatory technique that Bradley tried to suggest was careless at best and suspicious at worst.

"And why didn't you tape any of your statements?"

"That is not my style of interviewing," the detective answered coolly.

"You don't use tapes?" Bradley repeated the question to register his surprise.

"Same style FBI uses. I just write everything down so I have it," Miller said.

Bradley hoped the jury could see through the detective's bluster. Taped statements obviously verified a witness's exact words. Anything less left an investigator open to claims of inaccuracy or invention.

Switching topics, he asked, "Where is the picture that Nina Zorich drew? You know, the one of the rope that looks like the belt you took from Joseph Allen's house?" Because it had not been introduced into evidence, Bradley guessed it had been lost.

"I don't have it, but I wish I did."

"Why do you wish that?"

"For evidence," the detective said, trying to hide his embarrassment.

"What happened to this important piece of evidence?"

"It got lost in the shuffle," Miller admitted.

Bradley looked at the jury and raised his eyebrows as if to say, "Can you believe that?" Sensing that the witness was slightly off balance, Bradley confronted him with the questionable method by which children had identified the items seized from Allen's apartment. After reviewing the process with him, Bradley queried, "It would be fair to say that none of the items that you took from Joseph Allen's house were specifically described by the children until *after* you got the items out of his residence, isn't that correct?"

"That would be correct."

Bradley nodded and looked to the jury, trying to emphasize the importance of that answer. Miller's statement had baldly contradicted Rosenbaum's assertion in his opening statement.

"By the way, did you show any of the children's clothing to the parents?"

Miller looked confused for a moment. "This clothing here?" he asked, pointing to the items seized at Allen's apartment.

"Yes, that clothing."

"I think I showed them a sock or something to see if they could find a match—you know, if a kid lost it," Miller said.

"None of the clothing matched any of those children?"

"No, it didn't."

In a similar vein, Bradley asked, "Did you take the children over to Joseph's apartment to find out if this was the place where they'd been taken?"

"No, I didn't," Miller said.

"Did anyone take them over there?" Bradley pressed.

"I don't believe that was the house where it happened, Jack—Mr. Bradley," the detective stammered.

"I'm not asking you what you believe. Did anybody take them there?"

"No."

"Why don't you believe this is the residence?" Bradley asked, highlighting a significant flaw in the prosecution's case.

"I believe there is a basement in the residence. I believe there might have been a couple of residences based on what the kids said," Miller explained. His answer begged more important questions: How could Joseph Allen, a man living in poverty, reside in or have access to several dwellings in addition to his apartment? If the crimes did not occur in Allen's apartment, who owned the homes where they happened? Were the police still searching for other accomplices? In all likelihood, Miller had no answer to these questions, which would have highlighted the superficiality of his investigation.

Instead, Bradley pulled the search warrant from his left hand and appeared to be studying it. When he'd first received it, he'd immediately felt that he could discredit Miller by the affidavit he'd signed to obtain the warrant. In the affidavit, Miller had not claimed that Nina Zorich had seen a pink dress at Joseph's house, but only a dress. Because Miller had testified that Nina had told him about a pink dress, this inconsistency made Miller vulnerable to a claim that he'd amplified the girl's description to make the connection more convincing. When confronted with the discrepancy, Miller blamed others.

"I didn't draw up the affidavit," Miller said.

"But you read it before you signed it, didn't you?"

"Yes."

When Bradley sat down, he felt that he'd made significant inroads into the prosecution's case. He'd secured an admission that none of the children had described the seized items before they'd been taken from Allen's apartment. He'd also challenged the accuracy of Miller's direct testimony and revealed the superficiality and sloppiness of the detective's investigation.

When Grunda questioned Miller, he focused on the two photographs that he'd seized at the apartment. They both depicted a bedroom decorated for a birthday party with balloons and other festive things. He admitted that Allen had explained that his mother had sent him the pictures from her home in Alabama. Later, when Allen sought a new trial, his mother would sign an affidavit swearing to this, but she did not travel to Ohio to testify at her son's trial. Grunda also confirmed that the photos had not been taken in Allen's Lorain apartment. Miller also admitted that Allen had claimed during his interviews that a woman and a child had stayed with him while he was sick.

Rosenbaum chose not to ask any additional questions of Miller on redirect. Whatever gains the defense had achieved with Miller would be short-lived. Rosenbaum's final witness for the day would be Kelsey Calvin, the person who'd accused Joseph Allen of molesting her a decade earlier.

When Rosenbaum told the court that Kelsey Calvin would be his next witness, Bradley immediately asked for a sidebar conference. Ever since the judge had allowed the two cases to be tried together, he'd dreaded this moment. Although aimed theoretically at Joseph Allen, Calvin's testimony could sink both defendants.

The law strictly prohibited a prosecutor from introducing evidence of a defendant's past crimes to demonstrate that the defendant had a tendency to commit those crimes again. However, there was an exception to this rule. Evidence of prior bad acts was admissible if it tended to prove something else—motive, opportunity, preparation, identity, or plan. If the prosecutor provided notice to the defense that he intended to prove one of these things, the judge would decide if the exception applied. Prior to trial, Rosenbaum had given written notice that he intended to call Ms. Calvin to prove a similar preparation and plan.

The question was whether Judge McGough would permit it.

Because evidence of a prior similar crime can overpower a jury, judges are cautioned to allow it only after a careful consideration of its relevance, reliability, and potential for prejudice.

Bradley's first thought was to try to insulate his client from this testimony. "Judge, I know this witness has nothing to do with my client and I would ask that you instruct the jury that her testimony should not be considered in any way to determine the guilt or innocence of Nancy Smith."

"I can't agree with that instruction. It is far too broad," Rosenbaum said.

Sensing this would be a lengthy discussion, the judge recessed the jury. When they'd left, she asked, "Mr. Rosenbaum, let's talk about *State versus Allen* and why you believe you can use prior-acts testimony at all."

"It is the State's contention that Mr. Allen used a similar method of operation with Kelsey Calvin when she was a child. Mr. Allen was convicted of molesting her. He gave her toys, a birthday party, decorations—all to entice her. This evidence goes to his knowledge and identity. She will testify about things that will be very similar to what happened to the Head Start children."

Grunda should have been prepared on this issue. Instead, he seemed to be caught flat-footed. "The only thing I know is that he was charged with a couple of things and he pled guilty. There was no trial."

The judge said, "There doesn't need to be a trial if there is a plea."

The judge was correct, but the exception went farther. It did not require that the prior conduct result in a conviction or a plea, but only that the testimony be reliable.

Grunda now expanded on his objection. "We don't know what Mr. Allen's motive was back then. As I understand it, there was a plea bargain in this matter and he pled to avoid going to trial. And that doesn't mean that he was guilty of similar acts in that particular case. This is one-sided and I don't think it should be allowed."

Because it was a plea bargain, Grunda was questioning the reliability of the witness's proposed testimony. Allen had been charged with the little girl's rape. At that time, he'd maintained that the girl's story was a fabrication, something her mother had invented after they had broken off their relationship. However, his court-appointed attorney at the time, Jack Bradley, had advised him that if convicted of rape, he could spend decades in prison. He'd agreed to plead guilty to the lesser crime of sexual battery and receive a much shorter sentence. He'd had a change of heart about his plea once imprisoned, but the judge had denied him post-conviction relief, concluding that his guilty plea had been both voluntary and knowing.

Evidence of prior bad acts was particularly relevant when the perpetrator's identity was disputed, as it was in this case. Joseph Allen had denied having any contact with these children. If Allen's modus operandi a decade ago matched that of the "Head Start Joseph," then this evidence would be relevant and very helpful to the jury. However, Grunda had not forced the prosecutor to show in detail how the crimes a decade ago were similar to the ones currently before the court. Because the danger of prejudice was so great, the law required the similarities to be striking—so idiosyncratic that they were like a behavioral fingerprint.

Ten years earlier, Allen had acted alone and had focused on one child. He'd allegedly enticed Kelsey Calvin with toys and treats and then molested her—not uncommon tactics for a pedophile. However, the "Joseph" whom the children described worked with an accomplice and had three or four children at his place at the same time. He'd also allegedly prodded them with sticks, injected them with a needle, placed tape over their mouths, urinated on them, played games with them like "doctor" and "bad boy," forced them to drink urine from a cup, and tied them to a tree. In many ways, Kelsey Calvin's testimony would not match that of the Head Start children and arguably did not reveal the same behavioral fingerprint.

Because Kelsey Calvin's testimony was potentially ruinous for both defendants, Grunda should have been prepared with a written legal memorandum on this issue. In it, he needed to remind the judge that, to be admissible, Joseph Allen's conduct ten years earlier had to be so similar to "Joseph's" behavior in this case that it showed that they were likely one and the same person. Before the witness testified, he should have demanded the opportunity to voir dire her (questioning the witness outside the presence of the jury) to develop the dissimilarities. If the behaviors were not strikingly similar, Grunda would have had grounds to exclude Calvin's testimony in its entirety.

And it was not just Grunda who failed Allen at this critical juncture. Judge McGough was the gatekeeper for all the evidence and had the responsibility of safeguarding Allen's right to a fair trial. Unless the prosecutor established that Allen's prior conduct was eerily similar to "Joseph's," she was duty-bound to exclude any evidence that showed he was merely the *type* of person who might commit this crime. On her own authority, she could have ordered the jury dismissed while the witness was questioned on these points.

Even if the witness had been questioned privately, it remains an open question whether Judge McGough would have ruled to exclude Calvin's testimony. However, Grunda never forced the issue. After he finished his short argument, the judge said, "If Ms. Calvin's testimony is as Mr. Rosenbaum has indicated, then I will allow it on a question-by-question basis." She also indicated that she would instruct the jury that Calvin's testimony about Allen's specific behavior could only be used for the limited purpose of identifying Allen as the perpetrator in the Head Start case. The jurors could not consider her testimony as proof of Allen's guilt or innocence in this case. As to the claims against Nancy Smith, she would tell the jury that Calvin's testimony only related to Allen's case.

When the jury returned, the judge provided them with the limiting directive. Although based on a standardized jury instruction, it was filled with so much legal jargon that it was almost incomprehensible. Even if the instruction had been clearer, it probably wouldn't have made any difference. Jurors cannot compartmentalize evidence and they will apply it as they deem appropriate in spite of an instruction to the contrary. As events would soon show, the reasonable doubt that the defense attorneys had so painstakingly developed would erode with each word Kelsey Calvin spoke, regardless of her testimony's restricted purpose.

Kelsey Calvin seemed composed as she sat in the witness chair. She looked about the courtroom, spotted Joseph Allen, and stared at him for a moment, her disdain for the man clear from that brief glance. After she'd answered some background questions, the jury learned that Ms. Calvin was twenty-one years old, a single mom with four children, and employed as a waitress. She testified that she'd first met "Joe" when she was six and he was painting a house two doors from her residence. She admitted that Allen knew her mother and that Allen and her mother were intimate.

"How well do you know this man?"

"Very well."

"Has he ever been convicted of molesting you as a child?"

When Ms. Calvin said that he had, Rosenbaum asked her about the circumstances. The witness told the jury that when she was six, Allen had asked her if she wanted some toys to entice her into his house. After giving her a soft drink, he sat on a couch and bade her to come and sit on his lap, where he started "grinding with [her] on his lap."

While at his house, Ms. Calvin played with toys, and on future occasions, she returned because he promised to give her candy, pop, and chips. Twice he decorated his house with balloons for her birthday. At these parties, he would undress her and then lie on top of her and touch her.

"Did he ever tie you up?" Rosenbaum suggested.

She explained that he'd used belts and extension cords to bind her. Rosenbaum was drawing a connection between Calvin's experience and the ones described by several of the Head Start children. Rosenbaum next handed her two photographs of a bedroom decorated for a party, taken from a drawer in Allen's apartment.

"Do you recognize that specific room?"

"No."

"Have you seen a room decorated similarly, in a like manner?"

Ms. Calvin told the jurors that Allen had decorated a room like that for her parties, although there was nothing distinctive about the decorations.

"Now, were there any other sexual acts that Mr. Allen committed upon you as a child?"

She said that there were and she detailed what Allen had done to her after he bathed her and placed her on his bed. She also claimed that the abuse had lasted for three years, until she was nine years old. With that, Rosenbaum completed his direct exam.

Because this evidence was not directed toward Nancy Smith, Bradley declined to cross-examine the witness. He wanted to distance himself as much as he could from what she'd just said. If the witness was going to be discredited, it would be Grunda's job.

As pivotal as this witness was, Grunda seemed to lack a plan for impeaching her. He began by asking her if she and her mother still occasionally slept at Allen's apartment when they had no place else to stay. She denied this.

Surprised by her response, he asked her questions about the ages of her children, eliciting testimony that she'd had her first child when she was only fourteen years old and had given birth to four more children, one of whom had died in infancy. Ms. Calvin had been taken from her mother and placed in Green Acres Children's Home, and later into foster care. She had never been married. It appeared that Grunda hoped to discredit her based on her troubled and promiscuous teenage years. Throughout the cross-examination, Ms. Calvin did not lose her composure or show impatience.

Finally, Rosenbaum had heard enough. "Is this in any way relevant to this case? She has sat through his attempt to impugn her, but I think enough is enough," he said.

The judge asked the attorneys to approach.

"What is the relevancy?" she asked Grunda, her blues eyes intent and piercing.

"I want to show that she had a room at Allen's house and that her mother lived there," Grunda explained.

"She's already told you that she never lived with him, so what's the purpose of all of this?" the judge asked.

"I think I will establish it."

"It's got nothing to do with her testimony about what happened to her at age six," the judge replied, her voice as impatient as Rosenbaum's.

"I don't know that this happened to her at six. She first met him at six," Grunda protested.

"Let's move on."

Grunda decided to ask the witness about the relationship between Joseph Allen and her mother. Ms. Calvin would only say her mother had sex with Allen one time "to [her] knowledge." She did eventually admit that her mother, her sisters, and she were always welcome at Allen's home if they needed a place to stay. Finally, Grunda decided to hazard several questions about the alleged molestation.

"So five or six years after this happened, you told the police about this?" he asked, hoping to show that her allegations were less reliable because of the delay in reporting them.

"No. I told some people about it when I was put in the hospital for overdosing on drugs when I was nine years old." This answer seemed to be inconsistent with the dates of the criminal case against Allen. Ms. Calvin had been twelve years old when Allen was indicted.

Regardless, Grunda hadn't expected the witness's admission regarding her drug use. Believing that he could discredit her with this revelation, he asked, "Are you still taking drugs?"

"No," she said.

Grunda nodded and looked at the jury. "No further questions."

His cross-examination had been rambling and lackluster, but his last question had provided Rosenbaum with an opening that the prosecutor seized.

"Why did you overdose on drugs, take that bottle of pills when you were nine years old?" Rosenbaum asked. The question had nothing to do with the defendant's prior bad acts, the sole reason Kelsey Calvin had been permitted to testify. However, Grunda had stumbled onto the topic of her drug use, and under the law, he had "opened the door." Now Rosenbaum was allowed to inquire about it.

Ms. Calvin looked at her hands before answering. After that momentary pause, she said, "Because I was tired of Joseph touching me. I was tired of him making me do things that I felt that I had no business doing. I was tired of him hurting me. I didn't want to live anymore, because I was just tired of it."

And that was how the day ended.

CHAPTER 20
TRIAL DAY SEVEN: EARLY MORNING SESSION
AUGUST 2, 1994

In a surprising move, Rosenbaum would call just one more witness before resting his case that morning, and it would not be a doctor. Although the State had alleged that Allen had penetrated and stuck several children with a stick, the prosecutor would present no medical evidence to corroborate this. He'd named Dr. Amy Richardson as one of his eleventh-hour witnesses and he'd withstood Bradley's attempt to disallow her due to that late notice. Dr. Richardson had examined Nina Zorich and Marcus Logan in May and June 1993 and was well qualified to detect signs of physical abuse. However, after Rosenbaum had talked to her in preparation for her trial testimony, he decided not to have her testify.

What danger did she present? Would she be too tentative with her opinions when Rosenbaum questioned her? Would she concede something damaging on cross-examination if the defense asked just the right question? It probably was a combination of both. Bradley and Grunda had copies of her findings and her report. They knew that she'd warned Marge Bronson not to go to the media because it would contaminate the investigation. Thus far, the jury did not understand how investigations could become unreliable when specifics of the alleged crime were shared between parents or with the public at large.

Had she testified, Dr. Richardson could have explained this and cast doubt on the integrity of the detectives' work.

Thus, it fell to Detective Eladio Andujar to serve as the prosecutor's closer. He would be a safe choice—someone who would tie up loose ends and defend the investigation at the same time. Andujar had been a patrolman for five years before becoming a detective in the Youth Bureau in November 1992. He'd been the lead detective on the Head Start case from mid-June 1993 until his son had been hospitalized in November 1993. After his son's death, he'd taken bereavement time and returned to his job a few weeks before Christmas.

Detective Andujar told the jury that he'd taken over the case from Detective Cantu because Cantu had experienced conflicts with the "complainants in this case." It was more than simple conflicts that had led to Cantu's dismissal. As Cantu's final reports indicated, he'd eventually doubted that the crimes had occurred and did not believe that a molester named Joseph existed. Quite simply, he'd no longer trusted the children's accounts.

Rosenbaum wanted Andujar to tell the jury that Cantu's investigation, although flawed, had led to no contamination. The detective explained that while it is not good practice to have parents present during an initial child interview, their involvement did not necessarily mean that the interview was tainted. If a parent was simply repeating what a child had said previously, then that was permissible. It was only when the parent introduced new information that the process became corrupted.

This was the extent to which Andujar understood contamination, and it probably represented what the judge and attorneys knew as well. However, Andujar's explanation was both simplistic and incomplete. A child interview can become unreliable by a whole host of factors: leading questions, questions repeated until the child changes an answer, the interviewer's belief in the truth of the allegations, and the interviewer's failure to explore answers that are inconsistent with the child's initial story. Someone like Dr. Richardson could have fleshed this out in detail.

Andujar also made a basic assumption that a parent who spoke for their child was accurately repeating what that child had actually said.

However, other factors could cause a parent to provide untrustworthy information. A parent with a psychologically unstable personality could invent, exaggerate, or imagine events. One who craved attention or was motivated by financial gain would also be undependable. Did any of the parents fit one of these profiles? If they did, the police weren't trying to find out.

Rosenbaum wanted the jury to have confidence in the children's identification of Joseph Allen as their molester. Both Marcus Logan and Nina Zorich had initially identified different individuals as Joseph. Andujar excused Marcus's misidentification as the product of fatherly pressure, while he vouched for Nina Zorich's ability to identify the defendant.

"And did Nina, in your presence, pick Mr. Allen's picture from a photo spread?" Rosenbaum asked.

"She picked Joseph Allen."

Rosenbaum did not ask Andujar when this had happened, and this was for good reason. Andujar had been on leave when Joseph Allen had first become a suspect, and the detective had no contact with the alleged victims at that time. The first time Nina was shown a photo spread including Joseph Allen was on October 28, 1993, when Detective Miller came to her house. To everyone's disappointment, she'd picked out two other men (Claude Carter and Richard Adkins) from the photo lineup as Joseph.

Rosenbaum completed the exam by asking Andujar to identify the nylon panties that Marge Bronson had given to him during the investigation. She'd testified earlier that her daughter had worn them home from Head Start and they weren't hers. With that, Rosenbaum ended the exam.

Bradley realized that his cross-examination of Andujar would be his final opportunity to highlight the shortcomings of the police investigation. He began by attacking Nina Zorich's identification. Unaware of her initial failure to identify Joseph Allen, he took a different path.

"You also know that the *Lorain Journal* and other newspapers printed Joseph Allen's photograph in the newspaper shortly after his arrest. You know that?"

"Yes."

"And your photo spread wasn't conducted with Nina Zorich until after that time, was it?" Bradley guessed.

"Correct."

"That is not contamination?" Bradley asked, his voice incredulous.

Rosenbaum stood up and provided what, in legal terms, is known as a speaking objection—something guised as an objection that in reality provides the witness with an answer. "Your Honor, I object. There should be some evidence that establishes that someone saw this photograph before there was any contamination." If Andujar was listening to Rosenbaum, he'd have known exactly how to answer the contamination question.

In cross-examination, attorneys are given wide latitude to test the witness's testimony, and Bradley's question was proper. Andujar could have answered Bradley's question with a simple no and explained his answer. Exercising her discretion, the judge told Bradley to rephrase the question.

Bradley did just that, and Andujar sidestepped the contamination issue by saying he would have to know where Allen's photo was located in the newspaper.

Moving to a new topic, Bradley asked, "Did you ever take a look at State's Exhibit Four?"

"Yes."

"What is it?"

"It is a newspaper that has an article that says, 'Dispute Blows on Head Start Case.'"

During Detective Miller's initial search of Joseph's apartment, he'd found this news article and seized it. Miller had apparently grabbed it because he thought Joseph Allen, like some criminals, collected newspaper articles about the crimes he'd committed.

"What does that article have to do with this case?" Bradley asked Andujar.

"I don't know. I didn't read it."

"Well, read it, and tell us what it has to do with the case," Bradley said, challenging him.

Over the next minute, Andujar read the article, which described an administrative dispute involving the Head Start program. When he'd finished, Andujar tried to look undaunted. "The article has nothing to do with this case," he said, his voice flat. Bradley glanced at the jury to gauge their response; none of the jurors reacted in any visible way.

For the remainder of his cross-examination, Bradley attempted to demonstrate that the police had bungled the investigation. Andujar cooperated somewhat by initially criticizing Cantu for interviewing the children and allowing the parents to do most of the talking.

Bradley wanted to expose Andujar's inexperience and lack of training. Andujar had been a detective for only seven months when he'd taken over the Head Start investigation. Prior to that, he'd received specialized training in child abuse cases during a four-day course and that was the extent of it.

Bradley sought to test his knowledge. "And I'm sure, as part of that course, you talked about working macro cases?"

"I'm not sure what you're talking about," Andujar responded.

"Do you understand what a macro case is?"

"I've heard of it. It doesn't come to mind right now," the detective said, looking momentarily confused until he remembered the term. "Meaning many victims?" the detective asked uncertainly.

"Yes, cases where you have many victims accusing—"

"One or two people of sexual abuse," Andujar said, finishing the attorney's question.

Andujar believed that his four-day training had "probably covered that during one eight-hour course." However, when asked what he'd learned, the detective could remember only that a detective was "to interview the children alone from their parents."

"And that wasn't done in the beginning of this case?" Bradley said, prodding.

"Correct, but I feel that they weren't contaminated," Andujar countered.

"But you don't know, do you?"

Andujar defended the integrity of the investigation, spouting the familiar mantra that the children's stories had been validated because they'd remembered many of the items that the police had seized at Joseph Allen's apartment. Bradley did not challenge this. He assumed that the jury recalled his cross-examination of Detective Miller, where the detective had asked the children about an item before they'd been asked to identify it.

For the final ten minutes, Bradley and Andujar sparred over whether the initial misidentifications by Marcus Logan and Nina Zorich showed that their testimony was so contaminated as to be unreliable. They also rehashed whether Marge Bronson's appeal to the media had tainted the investigation. For the jury, they'd heard it all before.

When it was Grunda's turn to cross-examine the detective, he focused on the investigators' inability to locate the house where the crimes had allegedly occurred. Because the prosecutor was required to prove that the crimes occurred in Ohio, Grunda tried to suggest that the children might have been transported as far as Michigan, molested, and then returned back to Lorain. If so, an Ohio court would have no jurisdiction over the matter. It was a far-fetched theory that probably bewildered the jury. Andujar insisted that the children had singularly maintained that they'd been taken to a house located near the school.

Taking no chances, Rosenbaum asked Andujar on redirect, "You know from your investigation, regardless of where the actual sex abuse took place, that the events that led up to it began and ended in Lorain County, right?"

When the witness agreed, Rosenbaum asked no further questions, and a few moments later, he rested his case. Rosenbaum tendered all of his exhibits and the court admitted them. Each of the defense attorneys made a motion for acquittal claiming that the prosecutor had not presented sufficient evidence to allow the jury to decide the issue. Judge McGough summarily rejected their motions.

Things were moving quickly now. Bradley would present his witnesses on behalf of Nancy Smith. It was possible that he, too, could finish his defense by the end of the day.

CHAPTER 21
TRIAL DAY SEVEN: THE DEFENSE BEGINS
AUGUST 2, 1994

For the remainder of the day, Bradley would call a series of witnesses who he hoped would convince the jury that his client had been wrongly accused or, at the very least, raise reasonable doubt about her guilt. The people who would testify had two things in common: they knew Nancy Smith, and they did not believe that she was capable of ever molesting a child. When Bradley asked them questions, they each testified in a lucid and convincing manner. However, when Rosenbaum interrogated them, they were no match for the seasoned prosecutor. Soon they would become flustered, and by the time they'd completed their testimony, they'd appear either foolish or wildly inaccurate.

Michael Taylor, a thirty-three-year-old father of a Head Start student, was the first to testify. He admitted that he'd grown up in the same neighborhood as Nancy Smith and knew her. He would attempt to counter Elizabeth "Angel" Powell's testimony that when Smith had run into a store to buy a soft drink, Joseph Allen had tried to board the Head Start bus and she'd driven him away with a crowbar. Taylor was prepared to tell the jury that he was the man in Angel's story, not Joseph Allen, and nothing like that had happened.

Taylor explained that the evening before the incident, he'd had a bit too much to drink and had gotten into an argument with his wife, left the house, and spent the night at his parents' nearby home. The next morning, before he went to work at the steel mill, he spotted the Head Start bus at a corner store and decided to poke his head in the bus to say good-bye to his son, Cameron.

"I look on the bus, and Angel says, 'Get off my bus. Get off my bus.' All crazy and she grabs the handle and closes the door on my face.

"I said to myself, 'What's up with this?' It trips me out. She knows who I am.

"I went in the store, and Nancy was getting a pop. I told her that Angel slammed the door on me and got all hysterical. And Nancy started laughing.

"And we walk out of this store, get to the bus, and Nancy said, 'What's going on? What is the matter?'

"And Angel, all of a sudden, Angel recognizes me or whatever.

"Nancy says, 'You remember Cameron's dad?' And Angel apologizes and she laughs it off.

"And ever since then, when they pick my son up for school or bring him back, Nancy comes to the door or lets the window down, and she'll laugh and say, 'Get off my bus, get off my bus.'

"It was funny there for a time."

Taylor's story was in stark contrast to what the jury had heard a few days earlier. However, it largely matched Angel's first taped statement provided to Detective Andujar when she'd told him that the man who attempted to board her bus claimed to be Cameron Taylor's father. At that time, she said that she couldn't confirm this because she'd never met him before.

When it was Rosenbaum's opportunity to cross-examine Taylor, he was prepared. "Mr. Taylor, do you have a record of any kind?"

"I'm going to court, a driver's license thing."

"I'm not talking about a driver's license. I'm talking about a felony."

"Right. I have one thing."

Taylor's felony conviction should have been disclosed in his direct exam. Failing that, Taylor should have admitted it as soon as Rosenbaum inquired, but he hadn't. Taylor explained that he'd been convicted of welfare fraud after he'd received welfare and unemployment benefits at the same time. He'd been caught and "was in the process of paying [the] money back."

"So you lied to welfare about how much you made?"

"No, no. I didn't lie to welfare."

"What you are saying is, you knowingly cheated welfare?"

"Right, I did that."

For the next fifteen minutes, Rosenbaum challenged Taylor's memory on details. Was Nancy ever the aide while Angel drove the bus? Yes. Rosenbaum told him that had never happened. How did he know that Nancy would be in the store when the bus was stopped in front of it? Common sense. Rosenbaum responded that common sense would also say that people don't molest children. Why did he think that Angel knew him? Because she'd seen him bring his boy to the bus. How did he know that she was capable of recognizing his face away from his house? Because if Taylor saw someone, he could remember them if he saw them someplace else. Rosembaum sarcastically complimented him on his "wonderful memory." Why didn't Taylor report Nancy for leaving the bus to go to the store? Not his place.

After a while, Rosenbaum's constant challenges began to wear Taylor down.

"She is shopping in the store, even though she is supposed to be on the bus. And you don't know where she takes your kids, do you, during the day?" Rosenbaum asked.

"Supposedly to school and back home."

"Supposedly to school and back home," Rosenbaum repeated. "You don't know where they are going, do you?"

Taylor attempted to fend off the implications embedded in the question. "I questioned my son thoroughly on this," Taylor answered, knowing that Rosenbaum was referring to the sexual abuse allegations.

"The bottom line is: You really have no knowledge of where your kids went on that bus during the day, do you?"

"Bottom line, nobody knows anything to be exactly sure. No one can really say unless they are there."

"Exactly."

Rosenbaum had skillfully switched the focus to topics that Taylor had never testified about. He hadn't tried to vouch for the whereabouts of his child after he'd been picked up on the bus.

"And you tell your child to obey the bus driver and the aide?" Rosenbaum asked, transforming a defense witness into one of his own.

"Yes, sir, I have."

"So you trusted these people to do the right thing?"

"Like any parent, yes. You trust them with that responsibility."

After a number of confrontations with Rosenbaum, the witness was tiring of continually fencing with the better-armed prosecutor.

"When was it that you came forward and told Mr. Bradley that you were the parent that wasn't allowed on the bus?"

"Last week after I read about it in the paper, you know, about the person who wasn't allowed on the bus and was threatened with a crowbar—"

Rosenbaum cut him off. "Was that you who was threatened with a crowbar?"

"No, sir, it was not."

"That wasn't you?"

"No, sir, it was not."

The jury, like the witness, could conclude that there were two episodes near the store—one involving Mr. Taylor and another with Joseph Allen that involved a crowbar. Taylor was in no position to dispute the possibility of two separate events. He hadn't listened to Angel Powell's taped statement, so he had no way of knowing that the "two" events were one and the same and that the crowbar was an embellishment to her original story. Rosenbaum's questions had overpowered him, as they would Bradley's next witness, Audrey Witt.

Mrs. Witt had been a teacher at Head Start for thirteen years and taught both a morning class that started at eight thirty and an afternoon class that began at one thirty She was familiar with the procedures for loading and unloading the children from the school buses. She told the jury that the teachers collected their students when all eight buses had arrived. The teachers routinely retrieved them from the buses and led them as a group into their classroom.

"Are children ever left on the bus in the afternoon?"

"No."

In the morning, some children would remain on a bus if they were going to City Center for the all-day program. But this was not the case for the afternoon children, which included the alleged victims. They all came inside.

Mrs. Witt also explained that if a child had an accident at school, that child would be given dry clothing, including new underwear. Bradley believed that this would explain why Nina Zorich had arrived home one day with different underwear.

"Were you outside the school building each time the children were brought to school or left the school?"

"Yes."

"I want you to look at this gentleman right here," Bradley said as he glanced at Allen and addressed him. "Would you stand up, please?" Returning his attention to Mrs. Witt, Bradley asked, "Have you ever seen that man around the Head Start school?"

"No."

"Did anyone ever report this man as hanging around the Head Start school?"

"No."

When Bradley sat down, Mrs. Witt was not prepared for the onslaught that awaited her from the prosecutor.

"Would it be wrong for a bus driver to take the kids to a park before school and deviate from her route?"

Mrs. Witt had expected questions about what she'd just testified about, and this question startled her.

"I haven't heard of that," she said.

"Did I ask you if you ever heard of it?" Rosenbaum said, irritation evident in his voice.

Mrs. Witt instinctively recoiled. She hadn't meant to upset anyone by her answer. "I'm sorry," she said, looking down at her folded hands.

"Would it be wrong, ma'am?" the prosecutor asked, his face stern.

"I—I don't know," she stammered.

"You don't know."

"That's right," she replied, unable to hide her bewilderment.

"Okay. Would it be wrong for a bus driver to leave her bus and go to the store and do some personal shopping while the kids are waiting on the bus?" Rosenbaum asked, escalating Nancy Smith's infraction from buying a can of pop to purchasing a number of personal items.

"Yes, that would be wrong."

"Even if there was an aide on the bus?"

"Yes. That would be wrong."

"And you have no knowledge of Nancy Smith ever doing anything like that, do you?"

"No, I do not."

"And she wouldn't do that, would she, in your opinion?"

Grunda objected. Lay witnesses are generally not allowed to offer their own opinions. Their testimony should be limited to factual matters.

"Overruled," Judge McGough said.

Mrs. Witt testified that she did not believe that Nancy Smith would get off the bus for a personal errand. When Rosenbaum told her that Smith had, he wondered if this would change Mrs. Witt's opinion of Smith. At first, Mrs. Witt said that it might affect her estimation of how well Smith did her job, but it wouldn't affect her feelings about her as a person. After more wrangling, Rosenbaum brought her to the point that this knowledge would change her view of Smith.

Rosenbaum's strategy was becoming evident. He was castigating Nancy Smith for inconsequential departures from her responsibilities, elevating them to reckless derelictions of her duties as a bus driver. He was telling the jury that if she could "get away" with these things, then she was untrustworthy and capable of more serious departures like molesting the children. It was quite a jump, but the earnestness with which he presented this evidence made it appear plausible.

He would next attack Mrs. Witt's claim that the teachers took all the children off the buses. Rosenbaum established that around two hundred children arrived on the eight buses. Mrs. Witt told Rosenbaum that she would check four buses while her aide would check the other four. She also volunteered that she liked to talk to the bus drivers when the children arrived and occasionally took children from other classes with her. These self-inflicted admissions gave the impression that the process was disorderly and lax.

When Rosenbaum suggested that the atmosphere was one of confusion, Mrs. Witt backpedaled. The buses emptied one at a time, she explained, and there were ample teachers to collect the children. However, Mrs. Witt did not know whether Nancy Smith drove the all-day children to City Center in the morning and could not say if all the children exited from her bus.

"And you personally verified that the right kids were left on her bus?"

"I got my children off."

For the prosecution to gain convictions, Rosenbaum needed to convince the jury that children were left on the bus and then taken to Joseph's house. Mrs. Witt was telling them that this couldn't happen. Which of them would persuade the jury? In what would be an unfair contest, poor Mrs. Witt was overmatched.

"You are saying this is an infallible system?" Rosenbaum asked.

"Yes."

"Two hundred kids getting off these buses. You don't know who is on there. You don't remember at this time if Nancy Smith drove to City Center or what kids should have stayed on her bus or not, and the system is infallible. Never a mistake made?"

Mrs. Witt winced as Rosenbaum waited for her answer. "I think there are mistakes made in everything."

"Then the system is fallible?"

Mrs. Witt desperately wanted to help Nancy Smith, but, instead, she felt herself falling down a deep hole—one that threatened to swallow her completely. She tried to sidestep the unrelenting prosecutor. "I'm not the only person out there to see all the kids off," she protested.

"Did you understand my question when I asked: Is the system infallible?"

"No, I guess not," Mrs. Witt answered weakly.

But even this concession was not enough to satisfy the prosecutor. "You are a teacher. What part of my question did you not understand when I asked: Is the system infallible?"

"I think you are implying that there is some failure in it?"

"I didn't imply anything. I asked you a simple question: Is the system infallible?"

Mrs. Witt did not reply. If she hadn't felt so shattered and discomposed, she might have reminded the prosecutor that almost no system was fail-safe. However, not even that was the issue. The question was whether four students (Nina Zorich, Marcus Logan, Melissa Warner, and Jason Gilbert) *all* could have been left on one afternoon-arriving bus under the noses of their teachers and aides.

Rosenbaum pushed for an answer. "You said yes. Do you want to change your answer?"

By now, Mrs. Witt was flummoxed. "You lost me. I must be the dumbest person, but you lost me," she replied, her words not "lost" on the jury.

Rosenbaum cleared his throat. "Let me ask you one more time, ma'am. Is the system infallible?"

Bradley stared helplessly at his witness. When he'd talked to her about testifying, she'd spoken with confidence and intelligence; he'd never envisioned the debacle unfolding before him. He objected in hopes that Mrs. Witt could collect herself. "What system is he talking about?"

Judge McGough intervened. "Ms. Witt, do you understand the question?"

"Something about children on the bus and going to another center or something?" she replied.

"No. You testified that you have a system wherein children are brought to Nativity, exit the school bus, go to their classrooms, and that you have a system that you utilize every day," the judge explained.

"Right," Mrs. Witt said.

"Mr. Rosenbaum's question to you was: Is that system infallible?"

"Yes, I guess," Mrs. Witt answered, hoping that this answer would finally end things.

"Yes, you guess?" Rosenbaum repeated her answer as a question.

"Mm-hmm."

"Well, is the answer yes?"

"I don't know, and I have to guess. Well, let's just say I don't know."

"Thank you."

"You're welcome."

Mrs. Witt's cross-examination did not get any easier. Rosenbaum accused her of wanting to clear Nancy Smith because anything less would result in an embarrassing stain on the Head Start program. "You have a defensive attitude about this, don't you?" he asked.

"No, if there is an attitude, it's the way you keep digging at me. I'm already a nervous wreck," she replied.

When an attorney badgers a witness on cross-examination, jurors often identify and sympathize with everyday people like Mrs. Witt who find themselves in the strange world of the courtroom for the first time. However, in this case involving child molestation, the jurors were being asked to scrutinize every witness and they may have welcomed the prosecutor's tough questions.

Rosenbaum headed into his final questions. "If a trusted driver took a couple of kids off a bus before it got to Nativity School, would you know about it?"

This was not the prosecutor's theory in this case. Nancy Smith had allegedly left the children on the bus *after* it arrived at the school. From there, they walked, rode in a car, or were transported by bus to Joseph's house—variations that depended on a particular child's account. None of the children had testified that Smith had dropped them off at Joseph's house and continued on her route. In fact, all of the children had testified that Smith had been with them at Joseph's house at all times.

"Objection," Bradley said.

"Overruled."

Regardless of how the judge ruled, if Bradley had supported his objection with an explanation, the jury and the witness would have been alerted to something important—namely that the prosecutor had suggested a scenario for which there was no evidence.

Mrs. Witt considered the question before answering.

"Did you understand my question? Would you know if a bus driver took a student off the bus before they arrived at the school?"

"Yes," she said.

"How?"

"Sometimes—"

Rosenbaum cut her off. "How? Not sometimes."

"Children would come in and say something."

"How would you know that?"

Mrs. Witt did not answer him.

"That is not a guarantee, is it?"

"I'm sure there would be some other way of finding out."

Of course there was. Usually, an aide or a parent was on the bus, and they would either forbid it or report it. However, that answer escaped Mrs. Witt under the duress of the prosecutor's blistering questions.

"A threatened child, of course, would come forward, right?" Rosenbaum asked.

Mrs. Witt made no response.

"I have no other questions."

Bradley's other witnesses fared almost as poorly as Mrs. Witt. Another teacher, Denise Ray, also testified about the procedure of getting the children off the buses. She volunteered, however, that a bus driver could keep a child on the bus as a "timeout" if the child was being disciplined. This was later contradicted by another bus driver, Eddie Soto, who testified that he did not have that power and any person who claimed that he did would be "lying." To the jury, these contradictions revealed an underlying dysfunction at Head Start, a belief the prosecutor wanted to foster.

Whenever witnesses testified in absolutes, Rosenbaum made them look ridiculous. When one teacher claimed that she was positive that Joseph Allen had never loitered about the school, Rosenbaum asked her if she remembered every person that she had ever encountered in her entire life. When another claimed that he was familiar with the car that Nancy Smith drove, Rosenbaum asked if it was possible that she owned another one too. When the witness repeatedly refused to admit that possibility, he lost credibility with the jury.

More than a dozen fellow employees and friends had offered to testify on Nancy Smith's behalf. The seven bus drivers, aides, and teacher who did take the stand struggled against Rosenbaum's aggressive questioning. Whether any of the others would have fared any better would remain an open question after the trial. However, Bradley hoped that Glen Thaler, Head Start's transportation manager, would provide the type of testimony he desperately needed. Thaler was a career military man who, upon discharge, had taken this job. He was not the type of person who could be easily cowed. If his testimony went as planned, he would provide Nancy Smith with an alibi for at least one of the alleged incidents.

The only specific day that the prosecution alleged that the defendants molested the children was May 7, 1993. When Nina Zorich had returned home that day, she'd told her mother that she'd gone to Nancy's house because school was closed. Bradley wasted no time in establishing the alibi. Thaler first explained that he actually worked for the Lorain County Community Action Agency, an entity that provided transportation services for Head Start and other charitable organizations.

"Can you tell us what Nancy's duties were during the first and second weeks of May 1993?"

"Nancy was delivering meals most of the time for Meals on Wheels. She drove the bus for Head Start only twice during those days: the seven thirty run in the morning and five o'clock run in the afternoon."

"Did she pick up the afternoon children to take them to Nativity during those two weeks?"

"No. The afternoon children were picked up by a different person."

"Did you review your records to verify what you have just testified to?"

"Yes, sir."

"Do your records verify this?"

"Explicitly."

Should Thaler have been directed to bring those records? Their presence in the jury room would have been a stubborn reminder that Nancy Smith had been elsewhere on May 7, 1993, a critical date in the prosecution's case. More important, their absence raised doubts about

Thaler's testimony. If the records demonstrated what he'd just said, why didn't he bring them?

Bradley ended his exam with a question that he hoped would discredit Emily Osborne.

"Did anyone ever report to you that their son had been grabbed trying to get onto a bus during the 1992–93 school year?"

"No, sir, no one did."

Rosenbaum tested the witness on a number of issues. Could Nancy Smith have driven the bus by Hot Waters to show the children boats on Lake Erie? No. Anyone who testified to this would be lying? Correct. How would you know if Nancy Smith stopped her bus to let children off before she reached the school? Neighbors would report this. Was he informed of a parent being pushed off her bus? No. If someone reported that this happened, they would be lying? Probably yes. Is it permissible for a bus aide to get off the bus to buy a can of pop? Yes, as long as the bus driver was still on the bus.

Rosenbaum would close by suggesting that Thaler was protecting his own reputation by his testimony.

"Are you personally embarrassed by this whole investigation, the allegations against your driver?"

"No, sir."

"You are the man in charge."

"Yes, sir."

"This happened on your watch."

"Yes, sir."

"And you feel no responsibility?" Rosenbaum pressed.

"I mean, how can I be responsible?"

"Because maybe your drivers aren't where—"

"If there's truth, yes, I would feel bad. But if there is no truth, no. I wouldn't."

"There is no truth to it?"

"No, sir."

"There is no truth whatsoever?"

"No, sir."

"So you have resolved in your mind that this is a bunch of bunk?"

"I wouldn't say a bunch of bunk."

"Then what is it?"

"I call it infatuation of somebody's mind," Thaler said, using stilted language that would not resonate with the jury.

"Of somebody's mind?" Rosenbaum asked, raising his eyebrows in mock confusion.

"Those people making the allegation."

"So if there are twenty people making the allegation, it would still be an infatuation?" Rosenbaum asked, lingering on the final word.

"Until proven, yes, sir."

"I'm asking you."

"Until proven, yes, sir. I'm not the jury. I'm not the judge."

"It's not going to look good for you if this case is proven," Rosenbaum persisted.

"Very possible."

Thaler had stood up to Rosenbaum, but the prosecutor had given the jury a way to disregard his testimony if they wanted to.

Bradley's second-to-last witness was Mary Molnar, who was the child-care coordinator for the Lorain Family YMCA. She'd hired Nancy Smith to transport children from the local schools to the YMCA for the after-school program. For the last two years, Smith had worked weekdays from two thirty until four in the afternoon and had been her most dependable driver. The implication was clear: if Smith was shuttling children to the YMCA in the afternoons, she could not have been molesting the alleged victims at the same time as claimed by the prosecutor.

Molnar claimed that Nancy Smith handled this schedule throughout the school year, but she would occasionally miss if she was required to work longer hours for the Meals on Wheels program. If this happened, she explained, Glen Thaler would call her and send another bus driver in her place. Like Thaler, Molnar testified from memory about Smith's attendance.

When Rosenbaum asked her what days Nancy Smith missed, Molnar said that she would have to check her time cards.

"You cannot say how many days she missed, can you?"

"I'm not superhuman. I can review a time card and it's on there," Molnar said, looking desperately toward Bradley for help. She'd later claim that she'd given Nancy Smith's time cards to Bradley before the trial, and when she'd testified for him on direct, she was surprised that he hadn't asked her to refer to them during her testimony.

"So you are saying today, without checking any records, that you are confident that she could not have committed these crimes?" Rosenbaum said, his tone sarcastic.

"I have not been told the time frame when this was committed."

"So what is the point of your testimony?" Rosenbaum challenged.

"That Mrs. Smith was employed with us. She started at two thirty and was off at four o'clock."

"The days that she showed up, the days that she wasn't sick, right?"

Mrs. Molnar looked down at her lap. "Mm-hmm."

"And you have no idea how many days those were?"

"If you would like, I can get her time cards." Again, she looked to Bradley for help.

"Were you asked to bring her time cards? Were you?" Rosenbaum demanded.

Molnar didn't know how to answer this question. How could she bring the time cards when she thought that she'd already given them to Bradley? She could mention that Bradley had possession of them, but what if he had a reason for withholding them? "No," she said in a small voice.

"Did you think it was important before you came here?" The confused woman took in a deep breath of air, which Rosenbaum construed as a smile. "Is this funny?"

"No," the admonished woman answered.

"You don't know if there were times when she showed up at Head Start and was sick for your job, do you?"

"No."

"You don't know what days she was absent due to illness from your job, do you?" Rosenbaum asked again, changing the words ever so slightly.

"Not at this moment in time."

Rosenbaum had created the opening that he needed to neutralize Molnar's testimony. He could argue that Nancy Smith had molested the children during an afternoon when she'd called in sick from her job at the YMCA. Without the time cards to disprove him, Rosenbaum had provided the jurors with a scenario that would allow them to convict Smith.

Mary Molnar was upset as she walked out of the courtroom. She'd never had an individualized preparation session with Bradley before she'd testified. Instead, a few days earlier, he'd talked to a group of Smith's friends, including her, outside the courtroom for about ten minutes, reviewing the types of information that he'd be eliciting from them. However, they'd never discussed the potential questions that Rosenbaum would ask on cross-examination, nor were they alerted to his relentless manner. As a result, she hadn't been ready and she'd paid the price. She hoped that the other witnesses fared better than she had.

CHAPTER 22
TRIAL DAY SEVEN: NANCY SMITH TESTIFIES
AUGUST 2, 1994

L ike a besieged city, Nancy Smith had watched as her defenses had been breached one at a time, and only one barricade remained—Nancy Smith herself. Each of her witnesses had answered Bradley's questions competently, only to either stumble or crumble under the prosecutor's fierce questioning. Smith was now in the unenviable position of being her own last best chance. For someone facing years in prison, it was a terrifying place to be.

Smith began by telling the jurors about herself. At the time that the allegations arose, she lived with her parents and two of her four children on West Fourteenth Street in Lorain, a middle-class neighborhood not far from the city's largest park and Lake Erie. Bradley quickly switched gears and pointed his finger at Joseph Allen.

"Do you know this man?"

"No. I do not know that man," she said, her voice resolute and steady.

"Have you ever met him before in your life?"

"No."

"Have you ever talked to him?"

"I have never met that man anywhere in my life. I have never talked to him. I have never seen him anywhere."

Those three questions and her denials were the crux of her defense. If the jurors believed her, they would not convict her.

Because the jury had heard disjointed snippets of Smith's work schedule throughout the trial, Bradley next questioned her in detail about her average workday. Over the next few minutes, she talked about juggling jobs transporting Head Start students, senior citizens, and elementary school children, and making deliveries for Meals on Wheels. When asked about driving Head Start students from Nativity to City Center, she unnecessarily played into one of the prosecution's theories, revealing that, at the beginning of the year, "kids were just getting on anybody's bus" when switching to go to the other location. Although she later said that it "was real confusing until it got straightened out," she had reinforced Rosenbaum's claims that disorder reigned when children exited the buses and that the administrators were either lax or incompetent in implementing a reliable system.

Bradley tried to steer her back on course. "Did that ever involve any of the afternoon children?"

"No."

Parroting the testimony of Glen Thaler, Smith testified that she did not pick up the afternoon Head Start children during the first two weeks of May 1993. She was involved in the Meals on Wheels program and could not have diverted the children to Joseph's house on May 7, as claimed by Nina Zorich and her mother.

After finishing the questions about her jobs, Bradley turned to the prosecutor's claims that she had made personal stops and deviated from her bus route. Smith claimed that she only stopped once at the corner store to purchase a soda. At the time, Angel was driving and she was the aide. In addition to this stop, she occasionally allowed Audrey Taylor, a parent volunteer, to get off the bus at a corner store to do her own personal shopping.

She also admitted that she drove the bus by the Lorain Municipal Pier, known as Hot Waters, allowing the children to see the boats and the lake. She explained that her route included West Erie Avenue and this drive-by amounted to just a short detour of several blocks before she returned to West Erie. She also confirmed that she stopped once at her own house to change her jeans after they unexpectedly became soiled due to her period.

Bradley returned the questioning to his client's personal life. "Did you have a boyfriend during the '92–'93 school year?"

"Yes, I did."

"What was his name?"

"Charlie Thomas."

She further explained that they had dated for six years and had broken up in July 1993. If the former boyfriend had also testified, the jurors would have had confirmation of this, but he was not called.

"Ever tell anybody that you had a boyfriend named Joseph?"

"No, I never had a boyfriend named Joseph."

Bradley closed his direct examination by eliciting answers about his client's cooperation with the police during the investigation. He turned to her arrest in November 1993.

Clutching and rubbing her hands together in her lap, she said, "And they came to my home. There were three or four of them—detectives and police officers. They came into my home. They told me I was under arrest."

"Was anybody else there?"

As Smith relived the scene, her voice began to tremble. "My children were there. Three of them. They took me out the side door and handcuffed me in front of my children and took me to jail."

"For what?"

"They said for gross sexual imposition."

After Bradley listed the alleged victims, he asked, "What, if anything, have you done to them in a sexual manner?"

"I have never touched any of those children in a sexual manner at all. Ever. I was their bus driver and that was it. I drove them. I picked them up and I took them to school and drove them home.

"I have never ever touched anybody's child. I am a mother. I have four children that I have raised, that I am raising, and I never touched my own children. Why would I do this to somebody else's?"

Nancy Smith fought to hold back her tears. "I'm sorry," she finally said, sniffling, "but this has ruined my life. I have never touched any of these people's children. And to be accused of this is terrible. It's terrible because I am a mother."

Bradley asked her a few more questions and then sat down. The judge called a brief recess, and when the trial resumed, Rosenbaum rose from his seat to cross-examine Smith.

Rosenbaum began by naming the child accusers, one by one, and asking Smith if they were "good kids." She said that they were.

"And all of these good kids have identified you, have they not, as the person that did these things to them and took them to his house?"

Smith took in a deep breath. "That's what I've been told."

"They trusted you?"

"They have no reason not to trust me," Smith replied.

"Their parents supported you?"

"Yes."

"You were in a position of authority in their lives?"

"I was their bus driver," she said, aware that Rosenbaum was trying to take her someplace she didn't want to go.

"And that gives you some authority?"

"It gives me the authority to have them sit in their seats," she said.

"To tell them what to do?" Rosenbaum prodded.

"Well, I couldn't tell them exactly what to do."

Rosenbaum moved on to another topic. "So you admit going to Lakeview Park and Hot Waters, right?"

Smith was quick to minimize these deviations. "I drove through. I never stopped."

"Was this on your route?"

"Yes, it was."

The prosecutor and Smith wrangled over this issue until she admitted that it was near her route but not on it. He also grilled her about Audrey Taylor, the parent volunteer, who exited the bus at a corner store.

"You let her off before the end of your route?"

"Right."

"And I take it no one ever called Mr. Thaler and said, 'Hey, you got a bus down by Hot Waters. You got a bus going through the park, or you got a bus letting a lady off to do her grocery shopping.' Am I right?"

"No."

"Well, so much for his neighbor theory then, right?" Rosenbaum snapped, referring to Thaler's testimony that people would call Head Start if they saw one of its buses stopping at an unusual place.

Bradley objected to Rosenbaum's comment on the evidence and the judge sustained it, but the jury had heard it.

The prosecutor continued to harp on Smith's stops before reaching the school as if this were the crime for which she was accused.

"I've stopped at the store more than once," Smith finally admitted. "But I only left the bus once and that was when I was an aide at the time. The other times, I would send a parent volunteer to make the purchase."

Rosenbaum would close by attempting to neutralize Smith's emotional testimony that, as a mother, she was incapable of molesting a child.

"Now, you aren't saying because you are the mother of children that you are incapable of committing a crime, are you?"

"Yes, I am," she said, defiance in her posture and words.

As was his style, Rosenbaum would magnify the witness's answer to make it appear ridiculous. "So what you are saying is that people that have children cannot commit crimes?" He looked at the jury and shook his head in mock disbelief.

"No, I'm not saying that."

"Well, what are you saying?"

"I'm saying that people that have children, I find it hard to believe that they go out and molest somebody else's child."

Toying with Smith, Rosenbaum asked, "Well, wouldn't you find it hard to believe that people without children would do such a thing?"

"Well, I can't answer that. I don't know," Smith said.

"Unfortunately, some mothers do molest other people's children, right?"

"I don't know," Smith muttered.

"Objection, not relevant," Bradley said.

"Overruled."

"Now, there is one thing worse than being accused of a heinous crime like this, isn't there?" Rosenbaum asked, pausing and locking his eyes with Smith's. "And that would be if a person were convicted of that crime, correct?" The prosecutor's meaning was clear. He was suggesting that the defendant's protestations were nothing more than self-serving attempts to save herself from a guilty verdict and prison time.

"Yes," Smith said. However, there was something worse than being convicted of a horrible crime. The criminal justice system's worst fate belonged to innocent people who were found guilty of crimes that they hadn't committed.

"And at all times relevant to this investigation, you were the bus driver of Melissa Warner, Amanda Lilly, Marcus Logan, Nina Zorich, Jessica Simpson, and Jason Gilbert?" Rosenbaum asked, rattling off the names of six children, two of whom had never testified in the case and never would.

"Yes."

The attorneys skirmished with redirect and recross examinations, but none of the questions or answers had much of an impact on what Smith had already said. Either the jurors would believe her or they would not.

"Please call your next witness," the judge said.

"Your Honor, at this time, Nancy Smith rests, subject to the introduction of her exhibits."

Although Bradley had other people willing and anxious to testify on Nancy Smith's behalf, he made the decision to rest his case after his client completed her testimony. From Bradley's perspective, Smith had presented herself as a sincere and decent individual. He believed that her emotional story had resonated with the jurors and that she had done well in fending off Rosenbaum's questions. She had established reasonable doubt and he would end on a high note.

Later, he would be second-guessed, particularly for not calling the bus aides and parent volunteers who rode his client's bus during the 1992–93 school year. Susan Coates and Sherry Hagerman were her aides during the first four months of 1993. Volunteer parents Kymberly Spangler and Audrey Taylor also rode Smith's bus, off and on, for much of that year. All were eager to testify about what they'd observed, namely that Nancy Smith was good with the children and never did anything inappropriate with them. Although none of them could vouch for Smith's behavior for the entire school year, their cumulative testimony would have established that Smith was rarely alone with the children and they'd never seen any of the kids shrink away from her—ever.

However, there was more to the analysis. Would they too have been bludgeoned by Rosenbaum's piercing questions? Could the prosecutor have twisted their words to suggest that disorder reigned when the children were discharged from the buses? In the end, was their testimony worth the risk?

Although they were also available, Bradley did not offer the Head Start attendance records concerning the alleged victims. If, in fact, Nancy Smith had kept three or four of the children on the bus instead of dropping them off at the school, the attendance records should have reflected that the children were all absent on the same day. The records showed no such pattern, and, as such, supported her claim of innocence.

After Bradley announced that he'd rested, the judge turned to the other defense attorney. "Mr. Grunda?" she asked, his name now a question.

"We rest," Grunda said, his tone polite and understated.

No one had expected Grunda to call his client to the stand. With his prior conviction and his statements to the police during the investigation, Joseph Allen would fare poorly against the prosecutor's relentless cross-examination. However, Rosenbaum had placed into evidence the incriminating items seized from Allen's apartment—children's toys, clothing, bedsheets, and music—and they begged for an explanation. Was there no one who could tell the jury why Allen had these things in his apartment?

In his opening statement, Grunda had mentioned a woman and her child who'd lived with and cared for Allen while he was sick. That could explain the presence of many of these items. Allen's two brothers and their children also lived nearby. Had Allen kept toys on hand to allow his nieces and nephews to play with them when they visited?

Allen had obtained many of these items from a donation center operated by Catholic Charities. When there, Allen had usually been accompanied by a woman named Eileen Andrews who had two daughters, ages seven and twelve. Did Allen plan to give some of these things to Andrews's daughters? The jury would never know. When the defense presented no alternate explanation, the police and the alleged victims controlled the narrative.

The judge looked at her watch. It was almost three thirty. She addressed the jury. "Ladies and gentlemen, at this time, we are going to recess for the day. There may be some rebuttal testimony tomorrow and then I expect the attorneys will give their closing arguments and you will get the case after that."

Their faces solemn, the jurors stood and slowly emptied from the jury box. The attorneys scrutinized those faces, looking for any telltale clue about their inner thoughts, but their expressions were unreadable. They always were.

CHAPTER 23
TRIAL DAYS EIGHT AND NINE
AUGUST 3 AND AUGUST 4, 1994

Sitting on a bench outside the courtroom, Kathy Cole and her daughter, Donnetta Cole Taylor, watched as Rosenbaum and the two detectives approached them, the men's wing-tip shoes clicking on the linoleum floor as they strode with purpose. The prosecutor had subpoenaed the two women as rebuttal witnesses and they had arrived at eight that morning as instructed. After the prosecutor introduced himself, he asked the women to follow him to the courtroom. He opened the single frame door, stepped in, and beckoned them to follow him, which they did.

"Take a good look at the black man sitting at the big table," Rosenbaum told the two women.

For several seconds, they stared at Joseph Allen, who sat on one side of the table, while Nancy Smith sat on the other, her head bowed. They hoped Smith would not glance up at them. She'd been a fellow employee at Head Start and they liked her. For the last five years, Cole had been a bus driver for the program, while her daughter had worked there as a bus aide when allegations swirled around Smith. Neither wanted to testify, but almost a year earlier, a detective had shown them Joseph Allen's photograph and they'd said that they'd seen him loitering about the school a few times. And now here they were.

"Come back into the hall and let's talk about your testimony. I only have a few minutes," Rosenbaum said, his eyes intense.

They dutifully followed him from the courtroom and sat on a bench while the prosecutor and the two detectives remained standing.

Cole fidgeted on the uncomfortable wooden bench and shook her head before she spoke. "I'm sorry, but the man in there doesn't look like the man I identified in the photograph," she told Rosenbaum. "He looks like a totally different person." She held out her hands with her palms facing up in a placating gesture.

Rosenbaum's face took on a look of betrayal and then he grabbed a file folder from one of the detectives. Breathing heavily, he rifled through its contents until he found the photograph of Joseph Allen. "This is the photograph that the police showed you back in November of 1993." He held the photo inches from Cole's face and jabbed at it with his index finger. "Study it. This is Joseph Allen. You told us that you saw this man around the Nativity School several times, didn't you?" His voice was forceful and he glared at her.

"I did, but the man in the courtroom doesn't look like this photograph," Cole protested.

"That's not what I'm asking you," Rosenbaum said, unable to contain his irritation. "Can you just say that the man you saw hanging around the school is the same man you identified in the photograph? I'm asking you to do one simple thing. It's a yes-or-no question."

Cole hadn't expected the prosecutor to continue to press her after she'd disclosed her uncertainty. Maybe he'd misunderstood her. "The man in the photograph doesn't look like the man in the courtroom," Cole repeated.

"Let me keep this simple: Is the guy in the photograph the person you saw around the school? Just say, 'Yes. This is the guy I saw around the school.' That's it."

How could she testify when she was so unsure of her identification? She would try again. "He looks so different now when I actually see him in person. I'm not sure he was the one around the school."

"Goddamn it, you will answer the way I want you to answer," Rosenbaum shot. Holding up the photograph, Rosenbaum asked, "Did you identify the man in this photograph as someone you'd seen hanging around the school? You just have to say yes or no to my question and nothing more. I need to know if you can do that before we go into that courtroom."

"I can say this is the photograph I picked out."

"If I ask you to point him out in the courtroom, can you do that?"

"No, I told you I can't."

Rosenbaum nodded and then turned to Donnetta Taylor. "Can you look at the photograph and say that's the man you saw around Nativity?"

Taylor nodded. Rosenbaum turned quickly and disappeared into the courtroom, leaving his witnesses in the hall.

"What just happened?" Cole said to her daughter.

"I don't know," she said.

As the prosecutor walked to the trial table, Judge McGough was seated, drumming her fingers on the ledge separating her bench from the courtroom below. She gave Rosenbaum an exasperated look but said nothing. She cleared her throat and then asked, "Are we ready to proceed, counsel?"

Bradley jumped up. "I would like to reopen my case. I discovered another witness last night and I would like her to testify before the prosecutor calls his rebuttal witnesses."

"Explain," Judge McGough said.

Bradley did just that. After the trial had recessed yesterday, he'd spoken with a group of his client's followers who were waiting in the hall. He'd asked if any of them knew the name of Nina Zorich's Head Start teacher. When one person did, he asked her to call that teacher and have her call him at home. After supper, he'd received a call from Roberta Price, one of Nina's teachers. Bradley asked her if Nina Zorich had ever had an accident at school and whether she'd gone home in clean underwear supplied by the school. Mrs. Price had answered yes to both questions and Bradley wanted the jury to receive that information.

Because of the late notice, the judge allowed Rosenbaum to question the witness out of the presence of the jury in order to understand her testimony and develop his cross-examination when the jury returned. After he asked thirty or so questions, the judge cut him off and told the bailiff to bring in the jury.

Roberta Price seemed calm as she surveyed her new surroundings. She smiled at Bradley when he began questioning her. She explained that she and another woman taught the afternoon class that included Nina Zorich and Marcus Logan. She told the jury that she remembered one specific incident where Nina Zorich had soiled her clothes after having an accident. She'd given the girl clean panties, placed the soiled panties in a plastic bag, written a note to Nina's mother, and given them to Nina. She testified that she did not know whether the note and soiled underwear "ever made it home."

Bradley's final question was an attempt to counter the parents' claim that their children were behaving strangely, apparently acting out because of sexual abuse. "Did you ever notice any unusual conduct on the part of Nina or Marcus?"

"No. They were happy, normal children. When they came into the classroom, they joined in all of the activities. And Marcus, he was very active. I guess he watched videos at home and he would dance and sing all afternoon. And Nina played with the other children. And they were just happy children, just like the other children in the class."

"Thank you. No further questions," Bradley said.

Rosenbaum stood and squinted at his yellow pad for just a moment. He stomped away from the trial table and stood in the middle of the courtroom at a place where he could see both the witness and the jurors. He scowled at Mrs. Price.

"Do happy, normal four-year-old children have knowledge of the mechanics of sex?"

"Some of them do," Mrs. Price said calmly.

"And you're saying that is normal?" he asked, mischaracterizing her answer.

"No, I'm not saying that's normal. Some do and some don't. Some children are aware from television."

"Does a normal four-year-old child ask a classmate to suck his penis?" Rosenbaum asked, trying to intimidate the witness with this jarring question.

"No."

"How about humping their stepbrothers and sisters?"

"Well no. I guess not," Mrs. Price said, squirming in her seat and looking shocked by the prosecutor's graphic questions.

Rosenbaum quizzed Mrs. Price about each of the alleged victims who were in her class, their attendance, and their behavior.

"These kids came to class every day. They were never absent. Is that what you're saying?" the prosecutor asked.

"Marcus mostly always was in school."

"'Mostly always' doesn't cut it," he snapped.

"He came to school," Mrs. Price replied.

For the next five minutes, the prosecutor tested Price's knowledge about her students and their behavior. Despite his abrasiveness, Mrs. Price never lost her composure. When she finished, Bradley rested his case for the second time. The prosecutor told the judge that he had three rebuttal witnesses to present.

After all of his bluster and anger in the hallway, Rosenbaum showed no displeasure with Kathy Cole or Donnetta Taylor when he questioned them in front of the jury. Both identified the photograph of Joseph Allen as the same man whom they'd seen about the school. Upon his prompting, they both admitted that they could not identify the man in the courtroom as the person they'd seen near Nativity School.

For his final rebuttal witness, Rosenbaum recalled Elizabeth "Angel" Powell to the witness stand. Throughout the trial, the defense had elicited testimony from the detectives and others that, early in the investigation, several children had claimed that Angel Powell was the bus driver who'd delivered them to Joseph's house or had actually been there. Bradley and Grunda were trying to lay the foundation for one of the classic criminal defense strategies: setting up a straw man as the perpetrator of the crime to create reasonable doubt regarding the defendants. If the defense attorneys had hoped to argue this in their closing arguments, Powell's testimony shut off that avenue. She testified and provided proof that she was in Tennessee at her grandfather's funeral on May 7, 1993, the only specific day that Nina Zorich had claimed that she'd been abused at Joseph's house.

Powell's testimony cleared her of being an abuser on that day and probably on any other, but she dealt Bradley and Nancy Smith an unexpected blow when Bradley cross-examined her, throwing into doubt Glen Thaler's claim that Smith was not driving the afternoon children to school during the first two weeks of May.

Bradley's questions began innocently enough. "I take it that you did not drive the bus on May third, 1993?"

"No, sir, I did not."

"May fourth, 1993?"

"No, sir, I did not."

"You were off that whole week?"

"I was on the bus, but Ms. Smith drove."

"Well, the Head Start records show that she did not."

Rosenbaum quickly stood and offered an objection. "There are no records in this case."

"True," the judge agreed.

Bradley then summarized Thaler's testimony on this point for the witness.

"Sir, Nancy did not do the Meals on Wheels until after I came back. When I came back on the thirteenth, I was told that she was pulled from the bus only two days before, on Tuesday the eleventh."

Powell's statement significantly undermined Smith's alibi. Had Smith driven the bus on May 7 to pick up the afternoon children? The jury now had conflicting evidence. Bradley did his best to undo the damage, eventually gaining an admission that Powell had not consulted any records before her testimony, but her claim had staggered him and cast doubt on Smith's alibi.

Rosenbaum told the judge that he had no more rebuttal witnesses and rested. With that, the judge recessed the jury for the morning break. When the jurors returned, the attorneys would deliver their closing arguments.

During her first term, Judge McGough had angered attorneys by limiting the time for both opening statements and closing arguments, believing that these constraints promoted greater efficiency in her courtroom. Addressing the attorneys, she said, "Each defense attorney will be allotted fifteen minutes for closing argument and the prosecutor will be given thirty minutes." After ten days of trial, this time restriction was wholly inadequate for the defense. Although trial judges have great latitude to control the length of closing argument, that power is not unlimited. Based on the complexity of the case, its duration, and the number of witnesses, the law requires that the time allotted must be reasonable; otherwise, it violates the Sixth Amendment to the US Constitution.

Neither defense attorney sought more time, apparently convinced that the judge would not grant it. Nonetheless, they could have raised the constitutional argument to pressure the judge to give them more time. And if she still did not budge, they could have formally objected and preserved the error for the court of appeals to evaluate after the verdict.

This format favored the prosecution. Rosenbaum would have thirty minutes to sum up his case to the jury, double the time allotted to each defense attorney. When the defendants' time was combined, it was theoretically the same; however, Bradley and Grunda were not going to divvy up the evidence and coordinate their remarks. They obviously represented different defendants. They did not know what the other would say or how persuasively the other would say it. As a result, there would be overlaps and, more important, there would be significant omissions. That was a given.

Maybe the time allotted wouldn't make a difference. If the three attorneys were simply going to rehash the trial testimony, they were unlikely to change any juror's mind. However, if one of them reached below the surface and suggested connections and inferences that had eluded the jurors, he could win the case in his closing argument. It was why a closing argument could be a game changer.

Once the closing arguments began, it was Rosenbaum who presented the jurors with a new way of analyzing the evidence. He provided them with a key to unlocking and understanding the children's often confusing and conflicting testimony. He told them to focus on the demeanor of the children when they testified. "How do these kids fake shame and humiliation?" he asked. Several jurors nodded, apparently moved by this suggestion.

He then magically turned the case's biggest weakness into a strength. "What you saw were humiliated and scarred children, who sometimes told the truth and sometimes lied." Then after a dramatic pause, he provided the jury with an empowering suggestion. "But you can tell the difference," he suggested. "When they told you that they were molested, they were telling the truth. You could see that."

How could the defense counter this? Without an expert to explain how the children's memories could be shaped and molded, it was nearly impossible. Instead, both Bradley and Grunda told the jury that the children's testimony was unreliable, citing the two times that they had identified someone else as their molester. "What does that tell you?" Bradley asked them. "It tells you how easy it is to mold the mind of a child, to contaminate it. Somehow, those kids made those identifications based on information provided by their parents."

Grunda was sharply critical of the Lorain police. "The Head Start parents were pressing them, contacting television and newspapers, complaining to anyone they could. The Lorain police were desperate. They had to find somebody and they chose Joseph Allen even though the evidence did not fit. His one-floor apartment where they found all this 'stuff' is not the place that the children described as the location of the crimes. They still can't tell you where these horrible things happened. Think about that for a moment."

After another recess, Judge McGough read the jury charges to the panel. The jurors retreated into the jury room and began their deliberations. When they hadn't reached a verdict by five o'clock, the judge sent them home for the evening. When they reconvened the next day, they finished their work around nine thirty in the morning after six and a half hours of deliberation over two days.

In the end, the jurors believed the children. They found the defendants guilty on all counts.

CHAPTER 24
POSTMORTEM
AUGUST 9, 1994

Jack Bradley sat at his desk with legal books, notes, and a yellow legal pad scattered across its surface. He picked up the legal pad, stared at the blank page, hit the pad gently on the desk surface, and shoved it away from him. The pad traveled about two feet before it collided with several volumes of leather-bound *Ohio State Reports* that he'd been reading the evening before. One week had passed since the jury had returned guilty verdicts against Nancy Smith and Joseph Allen, and it seemed as unreal today as it had back then.

How had it happened? Every attorney makes mistakes during a trial. When the case is won, the blunders are quickly forgotten and the attorney only remembers the clever and quasi-brilliant maneuvers that produced the victory. When the case is lost, however, errors are magnified and so is the tendency to blame oneself, the judge, the jury, and the witnesses who stumbled during their testimony.

Bradley was his own worst critic, but others were talking behind his back as well. Why hadn't he called more Head Start employees? Why hadn't he hired an expert to explain how children's minds could be manipulated? Why hadn't he introduced the children's attendance records? Would any of these moves have made a difference? In his closing, Grunda had argued that the prosecutor should have offered the attendance record to prove that the alleged victims were all absent on the same day. The jury hadn't been persuaded by this argument. If he had introduced these records, would the jury still have disregarded them? He had no doubt that Rosenbaum would have claimed that they were after-the-fact inventions.

As he continued with his postmortem, Bradley thought of the multiple grievances he had against Judge McGough, the leading one being her decision to consolidate Nancy Smith's case with Joseph Allen's. If tried separately, Smith's jury would never have heard Kelsey Calvin's testimony. As soon as the jurors learned that Joseph Allen had been convicted of child molestation ten years earlier, it gave them confidence to convict him again, and his client's fate was unfortunately tied to Allen's. The judge's decision to spare the children from testifying twice had ignored the overwhelming prejudice that this decision caused his client.

Bradley was also still bristling over the judge's refusal to punish the prosecutor for the late disclosure of witnesses and the tardy release of exculpatory evidence. And then to be limited to fifteen minutes in closing argument when his client could spend the rest of her life in prison—that was more than he could bear.

And then there were the jurors. How could they not have been troubled by the prosecutor's case? According to one juror who'd been interviewed by a newspaper reporter, the jury had not believed either of the prosecutor's two adult linkage witnesses, Elizabeth "Angel" Powell and Willie Mae Smith. Shouldn't the jurors have required some credible testimony from witnesses (other than the children) that the two defendants knew one another? How was that not reasonable doubt?

Weren't they also troubled by the inability of the police to locate the place where the crimes had allegedly occurred? Weren't they suspicious when the children's descriptions of Joseph varied from a white man to a black man, or from a young man to an older man? How could they ignore that the children had misidentified two prior suspects as Joseph? Bradley tried to remember the faces of the jurors. As he did, he was convinced that he'd drawn twelve gullible people who'd blindly followed the prosecutor wherever he'd chosen to lead them.

It galled him that the jurors hadn't forced the prosecutor to prove his case beyond a reasonable doubt. Instead, they'd apparently reversed things and put the burden on him to establish that his client couldn't possibly have committed the crimes. The prosecutor had encouraged this wrongheaded thinking by suggesting that the defendants' witnesses needed to show that Head Start procedures were infallible, that Nancy Smith had an aide or parent on her bus every single minute, that Nancy Smith had never called in sick for her afternoon job at the YMCA, and so on.

He wasn't confident that Judge McGough would order a new trial. Because she had sentenced both defendants as harshly as the law allowed, she probably wholeheartedly agreed with the jury's decision. If she had entertained some doubts, her sentences would have been milder to reflect her misgivings. She was also unlikely to admit that any of her rulings had led to an unfair trial. That was just human nature.

Regardless, he would file a motion seeking a new trial and/or a judgment of acquittal. If the judge denied that motion, his next recourse would be the court of appeals. Neither option filled him with much hope. Even when a trial judge committed errors, the court of appeals often labored long and hard to deem the mistakes "harmless" and affirm the jury's decision.

He reached for his legal pad and brought it directly in front of him. Picking up a pen, he began to write.

CHAPTER 25
MOTION FOR A NEW TRIAL
DECEMBER 2, 1994
FOUR MONTHS AFTER CONVICTION

Judge Lynett McGough had read Bradley's motion for a new trial, his briefs, and his supporting documents, as well as the prosecutor's scathing responses. Well, she hadn't read everything. In support of his motion, Bradley had filed eleven transcribed children's statements and a lengthy New Jersey case that she'd skimmed. The children's statements were over two hundred pages while the legal opinion was forty-six. She was a busy judge with a demanding docket. It was Bradley's job to get to the nub—not hers to wade through pages and pages until she found a relevant nugget.

But this was an important case. She would give Bradley a chance to persuade her during an oral hearing that would begin in just a few minutes. Rosenbaum would be there and he'd serve as the counterpoint to anything Bradley would say. However, she would be more than just a passive listener. She intended to ask some tough questions to both attorneys—but primarily to Bradley. If his client was entitled to a new trial due to "irregularities in the proceedings," he would need to convince her.

After the two attorneys checked in with her bailiff, she joined them in the courtroom. The room was empty, a stark contrast to the last time they'd convened here four months ago. She asked Bradley to provide her with an opening statement, one that would outline his major contentions. As he talked, she grew impatient as he revisited her decision to consolidate the two cases.

"If there is nothing new here, let's move on to your next point, please."

"That would be the late disclosure of exculpatory evidence," Bradley said. He criticized the prosecutor for waiting until the second day of trial to tell him about Dr. Richardson's concerns about contamination and for not providing the children's statements earlier.

"I want to make the record very, very clear here because I recessed the jury to allow you the time to talk to Dr. Richardson. And you talked to her on my phone in my office, isn't that correct?" the judge asked, her voice stern.

"Yes."

"And I gave you the time to review the records that she faxed to you. I also specifically asked you if you wanted to call her as your witness after the prosecutor told you that he wasn't going to. And you declined." The judge believed that she had done her best to accommodate the defense and she wanted the record to reflect that.

"I would have hired my own expert if I'd had this information earlier," Bradley explained. She understood what he was implying. Bradley would have retained his own expert, his own "hired gun," that he could control on the stand. She was not sympathetic.

"You had the opportunity to review Dr. Richardson's records in the prosecutor's office for months. Did you go there and look at them?" the judge asked.

"No. I thought those records only showed the testing results for chlamydia and my client had tested negative for that disease. So I wasn't concerned."

That was enough for the judge to make up her mind on that issue. "Let's move on," she ordered.

Bradley explained that his client had been prejudiced because the judge had not held a "taint" hearing before the trial. Based on a recently decided New Jersey case, Bradley argued that the trial court was required to determine if the children's testimony was reliable or if it had been tainted by improper interviewing techniques employed by parents, police officers, or social workers. The judge was not bound to follow anything but Ohio law, and as a result, she hadn't planned to give the New Jersey case much weight, but she would listen politely. She soon realized that even if she had followed this out-of-state ruling, a defense attorney was required to make a motion before trial and request it. This, Bradley had not done.

"Did you file a motion?" the judge asked.

"No, I didn't."

"Okay," the judge said in a tone that suggested that she'd heard enough.

"It's not that simple, Judge. These tapes were exculpatory and we should have received them before trial. If I'd known how horrible the interviewing was, I would have filed a motion on this, but I didn't get these recordings until the second day of trial. Likewise, if I'd known before trial that Dr. Richardson was concerned that the investigation had become contaminated by Mrs. Bronson's actions, I would have included that in my motion."

"Well, you could have filed this motion without the tapes and requested copies of any tapes or statements at that time. This motion needs to be raised before trial, is that a fair statement?"

"Well, I agree that there should be pretrial hearings on the issue of contamination."

"Made at the request of the defense, right?"

"Made at the request of the defense," Bradley conceded.

Rosenbaum, who had been uncharacteristically quiet, spoke. "This New Jersey case says that the trial court can look at corroborating evidence to determine if the children's testimony is reliable. And we supplied all kinds of evidence, like the mask, the sheets, the rope, the toys, the magazine. These things made the children's accounts credible and the jury agreed."

"It's more than that," Bradley argued. "If a parent or police officer asks leading questions to a four-year-old, that can shape a child's memory. Even by repeating the question, a child will eventually change an answer to please the adult. According to the New Jersey case, that is contamination. And all those things occurred in the Head Start interviews."

"I'd like to move on," the judge said.

"Can I just say one more thing?" Rosenbaum asked. Before the judge could answer, he continued, "Let's forget the interviewing techniques for a minute. If we want to buy into Mr. Bradley's theory, everybody else who testified in this case—and I mean the adults—have to be liars. The parents were lying when they reported what their kids told them. The parents were lying when they said that their kids were acting out sexually. The detectives were lying when they claimed that the kids described things in Joseph's house before they actually saw them."

"What else?" the judge asked.

Bradley told the judge that the prosecutor should have disclosed that Marge Bronson had a felony conviction. This issue had been thoroughly briefed in both Bradley's motion and Rosenbaum's reply. The judge had read the affidavits that Rosenbaum had supplied, including one from a co-conspirator whom Bradley had represented in the same case involving Bronson. Although Bradley had not been involved in the trial, he had been hired to handle the co-conspirator's appeal.

Rosenbaum weighed in. "Mr. Bradley apparently had knowledge of her conviction. If that's the situation, then there is no harm or prejudice whatsoever and it should not be considered as a basis for a new trial." Rosenbaum paused for a moment and then looked at Bradley. "We're saying that he knew and just sat on that information."

The judge wanted an answer on this. It was a serious allegation. "Do you wish to respond, Mr. Bradley?"

"No, Your Honor."

The judge had expected a denial or, at the very least, a statement that he was unaware of the conviction based on his on-again, off-again representation of the co-conspirator. Bradley's silence, however, resolved this issue in favor of the prosecutor.

No one was apparently troubled that the prosecutor's excuses had no bearing on Joseph Grunda's right to know of Bronson's felony conviction during his defense of Joseph Allen. However, Grunda had been relieved of his court appointment after the verdict and the judge had appointed another attorney to file an appeal on Allen's behalf.

"Okay then," the judge said. "Do you have any new evidence for me to consider?"

"I'm going to call Kathy Cole and Donnetta Taylor."

Before the hearing, Judge McGough had read their affidavits attached to one of Bradley's filings. Cole claimed that Rosenbaum had cursed at her when she'd been unable to confirm that Joseph Allen, the man sitting in the courtroom, was the same person she'd seen hanging around the Head Start school. More important, she felt that he had pressured her to identify him in the courtroom after she'd told him that she couldn't. In his brief, Rosenbaum had admitted that he'd been very angry with the witness, but only because he'd expected her to testify consistently with her earlier statement to the police. The judge was anxious to explore this issue—suborned testimony was a valid basis for a new trial and she wanted to know if this had happened.

After Kathy Cole was brought into the courtroom and sworn to tell the truth, she explained that the police had shown her a photograph of Joseph Allen soon after he'd been arrested and she'd told them that she'd seen him around the school. However, when she saw Allen in person in the courtroom, he looked so different that she could not say that was the same person.

"Mr. Rosenbaum said, well, you know, he's had his hair cut and he's had a shave and this and that since the picture was taken," she further explained.

"Did you feel Mr. Rosenbaum was asking you to lie?" Bradley asked.

"Yes, I did."

When the prosecutor stood to cross-examine her, he held her affidavit in his hand and his eyes were burning with indignation. "Show me in this affidavit where you said I asked you to lie."

"You told me—"

"Show me in the affidavit."

"You told me—"

The two fenced on this question until the judge intervened. "Please answer his question."

"No, it's not," Cole finally answered.

"So you left that out of the affidavit and brought that in today, right?" Rosenbaum asked.

"No, sir, I—"

"I see, so it's in the affidavit?"

"You won't let me explain anything."

Again, the judge required the witness to answer the question, and again she admitted that she had not made that claim in her affidavit.

Rosenbaum established that he'd called her house the evening before her scheduled testimony and, although she was home, she'd told her daughter to tell him that she was not there. When he met with her in the courthouse, he'd initially asked her to identify the man in the courtroom as the person whom she'd seen loitering about the school. When she'd refused, he'd abruptly stormed away, retrieved the photo of Joseph Allen from the courtroom, returned to her, and asked her if she could say that the man in the photo had been at the school.

"And you wouldn't identify the guy in the picture right away, would you, because you thought it wasn't the same man?"

"Yes."

"And not until I got upset did you agree that the man in the picture was the man that you identified in your statement seven months ago?"

"Yes."

After asking several more questions, Rosenbaum asked the most important one. "And you did not lie in court?"

"No."

"And nowhere in that affidavit did you say that you felt that I asked you to lie, but today you brought that forth to make it even stronger, correct?"

Cole did not respond. The judge prodded her. "Is that correct?"

"I felt he was prompting me to say things that I couldn't say."

"The only thing you were asked to say in court was the truth, right?" the prosecutor asked, taking over the questioning again.

Cole looked defeated. "Yes," she replied.

"And you believe that Nancy Smith did not do these things and you wanted to defend her?"

"Yes."

The judge then asked the definitive question again. "Is there anything that you testified to that was not true?"

"To the best of my knowledge, no."

The judge had her answer. Although Donnetta Taylor later testified that Rosenbaum had yelled and cursed at her mother in the courtroom stairwell, both she and her mother had nevertheless testified truthfully, and despite his angry outburst, Rosenbaum had never asked them to lie.

"We'll now go to closing remarks," the judge said.

Bradley asked the judge to consider the transcribed children's statements as new evidence. He argued that the coercive interrogation techniques described in the New Jersey case were present in the Head Start interviews.

"Let's look at the first interview of Jason Gilbert." Bradley held the statement in his hand and began reading. "The detective asked, 'Did anybody hurt you with a stick?' Jason said, 'No.' The interviewer asked again, 'Did anybody hurt you with a stick?' Again, Jason said no. The detective persisted and asked, 'Did Nancy have a stick?' This time Jason said yes. 'What kind of stick?' the detective asked. Jason replied, 'A Popsicle stick.' The detective suggested, 'Wasn't it a plastic stick?' After that, Jason changed his answer. 'Yeah, plastic stick.' Then the detective asked, 'What did she do with it?' And Jason said, 'Nothing.'

"Before you know it, Jason Gilbert is coming into this courtroom saying that someone stuck a stick in his behind. So from an interview that happened on July seventh of 1993, he's coming into the courtroom a year later and saying that he was actually hurt with a stick. How does that transition happen? Is it because the kids were initially afraid? Or is it because these ideas were planted in their minds because of improper interviewing techniques?"

"I have the transcripts, Mr. Bradley," the judge said. She didn't need him to read any additional excerpts.

"What the New Jersey case tells us is that when you question the children improperly, it contaminates the entire investigation. And it happened in this case, Judge. And we need to bring Nancy Smith back here, have a pretrial hearing with these tapes, and give her a new trial."

"Why isn't this a more appropriate subject for the court of appeals?" the judge asked.

"Because you know that there were irregularities in this case that led to her conviction—the late disclosure of witnesses, the revelation during the trial that the parents were present during the interviews of the children. It's those types of things that caused this trial to be unfair."

"You didn't ask for a pretrial hearing on this contamination issue," the judge reminded him.

"Because the prosecutor never turned over the tapes to me before trial. Those tapes were exculpatory. I was entitled to them long before any witnesses testified. Judge, you have the opportunity to ensure that proper procedures are in place in child molestation cases. You can do that by ordering a new trial and conducting a contamination hearing after that."

The underpinnings of the New Jersey case were also critically important. That court's decision had reviewed scientific articles about coercive questioning and its effect on children's memories. These studies showed that once an interviewer taints a child's memory by suggestive questioning, the distortion is permanent. The memory becomes as real to the child as any other. It explained why the jurors in the Head Start case were convinced that the children were telling the truth. The court also stated that all child interviews should be video-taped, not just to allow for a judicial review but to curb an investigator from using suggestive questioning.

In his closing remarks, Rosenbaum criticized Bradley for failing to ask for a pretrial hearing to determine whether the interviews were tainted. However, the New Jersey case had said that, to be entitled to a hearing, the defendant needed to show "some evidence" that the alleged victims' statements were the result of coercive interviewing techniques. Without any of the statements in his possession, how could Bradley have produced that threshold evidence or even known that the statements were seriously compromised?

The judge closed the hearing by promising to review portions of the transcript and to render her opinion in two weeks. When Judge McGough did announce her decision two months later, she denied the motion for a new trial.

Bradley would file an appeal with the Ohio Ninth District Court of Appeals and raise many of the same arguments presented in this motion. Joseph Allen, through a new court-appointed attorney, would likewise file an appeal. After extensions and delays and oral arguments, the court of appeals would rule in January 1996 just as Judge McGough had. The defendants had received a fair trial and they were to serve out their sentences. Later, the Ohio Supreme Court would decline to accept either case for review. When no attorney filed a writ of habeas corpus in the federal courts on their behalf, all traditional avenues of appeal either had been exhausted or were now closed to them.

Their future was bleak. The criminal justice system had run its course. They'd either spend half a lifetime in prison or die there. Of course, there was always the possibility of parole. But to show that they'd reformed, they'd need to tell the parole board that they'd committed the crimes and felt remorse for the harm they'd caused. Would the lure of freedom induce them to take this path? If the alternative was a lifetime in prison, who knew?

PART TWO

CHAPTER 26
PAUL FACINELLI

MAY 12, 1996
ONE YEAR AND NINE MONTHS AFTER
CONVICTION

T rue to his habit, columnist Paul Facinelli skimmed the letters to the editor as he sat in his kitchen, sipping coffee on this Sunday morning. For the past seven years, his thrice-weekly columns had sparked discussion and sometimes angry reactions among the *Chronicle-Telegram*'s thirty-three thousand subscribers. When a column struck a raw nerve with one of them, they sometimes retaliated with a letter to the editor, hoping that their spirited response would provide the comeuppance that this journalist so richly deserved.

Facinelli had joined the *Chronicle*'s staff in 1986 as the newspaper's Sunday editor. However, after a few years, the Elyria-based newspaper had asked him to write a column, and soon thereafter, he'd become something of a sensation. His articles teased and shocked the paper's readers every Monday, Wednesday, and Friday. The newspaper unfailingly placed his pieces in the far-left column of the paper's Local section in an effort to make his articles easier to find. But to many of the newspaper's more conservative readers, this far-left location seemed apt.

Born in the coal-mining town of Hazleton, Pennsylvania in 1945, Facinelli had been a math whiz as a kid and earned a scholarship to

Penn State with an eye toward earning an engineering degree. He soon learned that engineering was not his calling, dropped out, and joined the navy. It was as a military reporter that he discovered his passion for journalism. After his discharge, he earned a bachelor's degree in journalism from Syracuse University. From there, he landed a job as a sports writer with the *Akron Beacon Journal*, interviewing sports stars such as Billie Jean King and Muhammad Ali. Thinking that he wanted to teach journalism at the college level, he earned a master's degree from Kent State University and taught for a short time at a Florida university before coming back to northeastern Ohio and joining the *Chronicle*.

Facinelli returned his attention to the letters to the editor, where his eye caught one written by Raymond Kandt, a man who seemed to pen letters to the paper several times a year. Facinelli was mildly curious about the man but had never been inquisitive enough to look into his background. Over the years, the enigmatic Kandt had written letters on a variety of topics: Russian bomb shelters, high school test scores, the effects of Prohibition, global warming, and the Iran-Contra affair. Apparently a bright and well-read man, Kandt authored letters that were thought-provoking, witty, and flawlessly crafted—something Facinelli admired. Despite the eclectic nature of Kandt's opinions, Facinelli recognized a unifying underpinning in all of his messages—a call to think critically and to dig for the truth.

Kandt's current letter, the one that had caught Facinelli's attention, dealt with the Head Start case and was unfavorable to both Lorain County prosecutor Greg White and his chief criminal assistant, Jonathan Rosenbaum. Kandt's letter was a reaction to Prosecutor White's public statement that he could not bring charges "in good conscience" against a man accused of sexually abusing a five-year-old child after the suspect had passed a lie detector test. "How fair, how honest, how commendable," Kandt wrote of the prosecutor's decision, sarcasm dripping from his words. However, he reminded readers that Nancy Smith had also passed a polygraph test, but this "was not given any consideration by the prosecution."

Turning to the Head Start case in general, Kandt told readers that one woman and her parent helpers "had induced" small children to imagine the most "improbable bizarre acts at places unknown." These fantasies, "done under a cloak of invisibility," became the basis of sexual abuse allegations that had culminated in convictions that left "the scales of justice bent into an unrecognizable shape." Kandt ended his letter by asking Greg White to exercise his "good conscience" again and reverse the convictions of two innocent people—Nancy Smith and Joseph Allen.

Setting down the newspaper, Facinelli thought about what he'd just read. Like most people, he hadn't followed the Head Start trial closely when it dominated headlines two years earlier and, not surprisingly, had not formed strong feelings about it. The prevailing opinion was that the pair were guilty and it was time for the few critics to move on. A jury had listened to all of the evidence, deliberated conscientiously, and reached a unanimous decision. Wasn't the United States criminal justice system overwhelmingly skewed in favor of the accused? In his head, Facinelli ticked off many of the law's time-honored safeguards: the presumption of innocence, proof beyond a reasonable doubt, due process, the right to counsel, Miranda rights, and so on.

But here was Raymond Kandt, railing against verdicts that he claimed were the epitome of injustice. How could Facinelli not be intrigued? There was enough content here for a column, but was there more?

The following day, when he arrived at the *Chronicle*, he headed to the newspaper's archives and located the computer file that contained the pieces on the Head Start case. Many of the articles were written by Michael Higgins, the courthouse-beat reporter. To his surprise, he came across two earlier letters penned by Raymond Kandt about the case.

The first one had been written in 1994, about four months after the trial. In it, Kandt questioned the accuracy of the Head Start children's hearsay statements as recounted by Detective Joel Miller and others in their trial testimony. The inquisitive Kandt referenced studies described in a book, *The Real World of Child Interrogations* by psychologist Ralph Underwager. These studies showed that adult interrogators were shockingly inept at repeating what small children had told them about an alleged sexual abuse. This had become apparent after comparing the children's taped statements against what the adults claimed that the children had said. Kandt warned that "when there are no tapes, such errors may abound." He urged that, in all criminal cases, children's hearsay statements should be excluded unless they were "buttressed by taped interviews or other evidence."

Kandt had Facinelli's full attention. Facinelli jotted down the name of the book; he would read it.

Kandt told readers that he was deeply troubled by Detective Miller's failure to tape-record the children's statements about "the rather innocuous items" found in Joseph Allen's apartment. According to Detective Miller, the children had described many of the seized items before they'd seen them. Because the detective did not tape any of these conversations, the jury had to rely on Miller's recollection of the children's statements, something the studies had shown could be decidedly inaccurate.

Facinelli was impressed by Kandt's apparent mastery of the case facts and trial testimony. The writer claimed that, beyond Miller's testimony, the prosecution failed to present any other corroborating evidence: "no other witnesses to the supposed activities of Nancy Smith and Joseph Allen, no buildings where the abuse was said to have occurred," and no physical or medical evidence of the children's claimed injuries. Kandt concluded his letter with a simple question: How might the outcome have differed if the interviews had been taped? Facinelli nodded as he pondered that question too.

Facinelli next turned to a Kandt letter published a year after Smith and Allen had been convicted. Again, Kandt had pointed out some nonsensical facts and derided the children's claims as ludicrous.

Facinelli didn't know enough about the Head Start case to draw any conclusions from these letters. However, the writer had not just criticized the prosecutor's case, he'd ridiculed it as absurd. For Facinelli, this was impossible to ignore.

After skimming the other articles in the file, Facinelli sought out Michael Higgins, the *Chronicle*'s courthouse-beat writer. Higgins confirmed that the Head Start case had been a hotly contested trial and one that could have ended in either acquittals or convictions. He told Facinelli that one of the defense attorneys had sought mistrials on several occasions, claiming that exculpatory information was provided so late as to prejudice the defense. Both defense attorneys had argued that the children's testimony had been contaminated because of improper interviewing techniques and media coverage, and was not reliable. Equally distressing, the children's earlier statements often contradicted their trial testimony. Higgins confirmed that the case had been appealed and the appellate court had found no error. The beat reporter thought it likely that the defendants would remain in prison for a long time.

"What about these letters by Raymond Kandt? What do you know about him?" Facinelli asked.

"I don't know anything about him, but I do remember that when the staff called him to verify that these were his letters, he told us that he'd read the complete trial transcript as well as almost everything in the court file."

Facinelli raised his eyebrows and nodded. "No doubt a retiree with lots of time on his hands."

"Yeah, but still," Miller replied.

Changing gears, Facinelli asked, "If I were to do an investigatory piece on this case, where would I start?" Facinelli asked.

"The case was appealed, so there's a complete trial transcript on file at the clerk's office. That's a public record and accessible," Higgins said. "My guess is that both of the defense attorneys will talk to you, maybe even let you copy parts of their files. As for Rosenbaum, he can be abrasive with reporters."

"I'm going to do a little digging on my own," Facinelli said. "I think this is worth investigating, don't you?"

Higgins smiled and nodded. "Let me know if you need some assistance. I could introduce you to Jack Bradley, the defense attorney. I've talked to him a couple of times. He's approachable."

After thanking Higgins, Facinelli walked back to his desk. Somehow, he knew he would do this story. Little did he know that this decision would change his life in ways he could not imagine at the time. Regardless of the consequences, he would dig deep and confront the community with what he found.

CHAPTER 27
THE EXPERTS

SEPTEMBER 4, 1996
TWO YEARS AFTER CONVICTION

Paul Facinelli waited expectantly as Melvin Guyer cleared his throat on the other end of the phone line. Two weeks earlier, Facinelli had sent eleven transcribed statements of the Head Start children to both Guyer and another psychologist, Ralph Underwager. Both men had national reputations for evaluating the reliability of children's statements in child sex abuse cases. The two men were often hired by the defense to assess whether the police had followed proper protocols when interviewing the young accusers. When Facinelli had asked them to review the statements, both had agreed to do so at no charge. Facinelli had provided no background information about the case, sending only the transcripts of the interviews.

"If people were convicted based on these interviews, it is an affront to justice," Guyer began. Lacking the technology to tape-record the conversation, Facinelli began writing feverishly, trying to take down Guyer's precise words. Guyer continued, "These children were clearly tainted by the interviewing process."

"They were both found guilty of all charges," Facinelli disclosed. "They're currently in prison serving very long sentences."

Guyer sighed. "That's very unfortunate. I see this all too often—

convictions based on contaminated interviews. And, sadly, it happens all over the country."

Facinelli had been impressed with Guyer's credentials. The expert had earned a PhD in psychology and a law degree from the University of Michigan, where he was a tenured professor in its psychology department. He'd written and lectured extensively on child interrogations.

Over the last two months, Facinelli had himself read several books on the subject. These included Ralph Underwager's book, mentioned in Raymond Kandt's letter to the editor, and a book by Richard Gardner, *Sex Abuse Hysteria: Salem Witch Trials Revisited*. He'd also obtained a manual published by the National Center for Prosecution of Child Abuse that set forth guidelines for prosecutors when handling child sex abuse cases.

Facinelli had read these books before he'd delved into the Head Start documents. He'd had little difficulty gaining access to the trial transcript, the children's statements, and some police reports. After contacting Jack Bradley, Facinelli had reviewed these documents in Bradley's office. Bradley had also allowed him to copy whatever documents Facinelli believed would be important to his investigation.

Based on what Facinelli had gleaned from his prior reading, he'd been alarmed when he tackled the children's statements. Granted, he was no expert in child questioning, but it seemed that the Head Start interrogators had violated almost every rule designed to safeguard the interviewing process. Now his heart quickened as Guyer confirmed what he'd suspected.

"I don't know how much you know about this subject," Guyer continued.

"A little," Facinelli responded, downplaying his research.

"At this age, children's memories can be molded by their questioners. You see, children want to please adults. They gain their self-esteem based on how parents and other adults react to them. When they're questioned, children will figure out quickly what the right answer is— the one that they believe will satisfy the questioner."

From his reading, Facinelli knew this, but he did not interrupt Guyer.

"Kids that age are very intuitive. If you repeat a question, they'll assume that they've answered it incorrectly and change their answer. If someone asks a leading question, the child will usually agree and often build upon it. Once false information is reinforced enough, the child will believe it to be true and will appear honest and sincere when questioned about it. Once the child learns the story, fantasy becomes reality."

From his reading, Facinelli was aware that children's memories could be shaped in this way. However, he was anxious to direct Guyer to the specifics of this case. "I'm really curious to know your thoughts about the interviews I sent you," he said.

"These are some of the worst interviews I've ever reviewed," Guyer said, his voice more incredulous than indignant. "All of the interviews are horrible. In each interview, there are clear examples of coercive techniques. There is a high incidence of suggestibility and inappropriate questioning. They're really outrageous."

Facinelli was struck by how Guyer phrased his comments in both academic jargon and blunt English. Facinelli guessed that Guyer would be a good communicator if he testified before a jury.

Guyer continued, "To answer your question, let me begin with this. All of the interrogators in this case believed that sex abuse had happened. We call that interviewer bias. The questioners believe that they are there to validate the allegations and to elicit information that supports their preconceived notion of what happened."

"Why would they do that?" Facinelli asked.

"They start with the premise that the abuse happened and then they naturally want to protect the children. And that mindset is the result of lack of training or no training. The adult questioner should come into the interview seeking the truth," Guyer said, his voice resigned. "In the statements you sent to me, when one of the children denied abuse or said something inconsistent with abuse, the questioners just ignored it. They needed to explore that with more questions. Instead, they did everything to prove what they believed had happened. They repeated questions two or three times until the weary child eventually changed the answer. They offered rewards—a can of pop, things like that. They pressed a child to answer more questions after the child said that she didn't want to answer any more questions. You can't do that. They threatened one boy, telling him that his sister could be molested if he didn't disclose details about Joseph. I could go on and on with all of the coercive tactics, but I don't know how much you want to hear."

"I want all of your opinions."

"Okay then. Let me look at my notes." Facinelli could hear papers rustling on the other end of the line. "I don't know if I said this before, but there are so many leading questions. That's not how you question children of this age. You ask them open-ended questions like 'What happened?' That's how you get reliable information. It's what we call 'spontaneous recall.'"

"What happens if the child doesn't say anything?"

"You might suspend the interview or you might ask about a few innocuous details that could trigger a spontaneous memory. You could ask: 'What were you wearing that day?'"

"What if that still doesn't work?"

"Well, there are questions that can be asked that don't suggest an answer. 'Does your bus driver ever discipline you? Have you ever gotten in trouble for something you did on the bus?' That sort of thing. You try to get the child talking."

"How many interviews are appropriate?" Facinelli asked. Nina Zorich had been recorded four times and had been interviewed additional times when she hadn't been taped.

"The most reliable information comes from the first interview. Ideally, that should be the only interview, but sometimes that's not practical. So let me say, questioning sessions should be kept to an absolute minimum. The more a child is interviewed, the less reliable that child's statements become, particularly if the story changes or the child reveals new information."

Turning to another topic, Facinelli asked: "I'm wondering what you thought of the police interviewing the children in front of their parents."

"Oh, you can't do that. Now, that's not to say that a parent can't spend some time with the investigator and the child to allow them to feel comfortable with one another. They can have a conversation on a safe topic, even do an activity together. However, when it comes time to question the child about the alleged abuse, the parent needs to leave."

"I've read the statements," Facinelli said. "At times, the parent and the officer discussed details of the investigation in front of the child."

"I was appalled by that. The adults discussed their theories in the children's presence. That's a grievous departure from accepted interviewing methods. They were telling the children not only who the suspects were but what they believed the suspects had done. The adults had devised a conspiracy theory and then infused the children with that information."

Facinelli looked at his notes. He'd scribbled down Guyer's points as quickly as he could. For the next ten minutes, Facinelli reviewed what he'd written with Guyer, confirming quotes and adding details as the expert expanded on some of his earlier opinions.

"Well, I want to thank you again for reviewing the statements. Your comments will be an integral part of my article."

"I'm glad that you found my analysis helpful. Now, I have a favor to ask you," Guyer said.

"Sure, shoot," Facinelli said, trying not to convey his surprise.

"Well, these are some of the worst interviews I've ever read. If you have no objection, I'd like to use them in some of my classes and seminars as examples of how *not* to conduct interviews with young children."

"They're that bad?" Facinelli asked. "You don't need my permission. The statements were attached to court filings, so they're public records."

"Even so, I know that there are privacy concerns. I'll change the names of the children, of course," Guyer said.

After the two men said goodbye, Facinelli reviewed his notes again and prepared to call Ralph Underwager, the other psychologist to whom he'd sent the statements. Because Facinelli had read one of Underwager's books about interrogating young children, he expected that Underwager would be critical of the police in the Head Start case. He just didn't know how critical.

It didn't take long for Facinelli to find out. After Underwager took his call, the psychologist wasted no time in volunteering his outrage at the interviews. "There is no way these interrogations could have produced reliable and valid information. If the people accused in this case were convicted, it was a travesty of justice."

Two well-known psychologists had now provided scathing criticisms about the questioning of the Head Start children.

"I see," Facinelli responded.

Before Facinelli could say more, Underwager interjected, "I've examined thousands of hours of videotapes, audiotapes, and transcripts of children being interviewed. That being said, these are some of the worst I've ever seen."

"What I'd like you to do is to provide me with some examples of improper methods from the actual transcripts," Facinelli said. If he could provide details in his article, Facinelli hoped he could educate his readers about what had gone wrong in the interviews.

For the next thirty minutes, Underwager identified portions of transcripts and then critiqued the interviewer. He began by referencing the first transcribed interview of Nina Zorich, an interview conducted by Sally Miyara from Lorain County Children Services. The little girl repeatedly denied that there had been any inappropriate touching between her and Joseph. However, after the tape had been turned off and then restarted, the interviewer had asked, "Okay, who peed on your head?" Nina replied, "Um, Joseph." When the social worker asked her if anyone else did this to her, Nina replied, "You," indicating the interviewer.

Underwager told Facinelli that Miyara had exhibited interviewer bias by not accepting the little girl's initial denials. "If children are to be believed in sexual matters—you know they can't make this stuff up —why aren't this child's denials thought to be truthful?" Underwager paused before answering his own question. "Because denials don't fit the interviewer's preconceived notion of what happened. The denials are thought to be the result of shame or embarrassment. So the interviewer presses on until she gets what she wants."

Facinelli saw that Underwager's initial evaluation mirrored that of Guyer. However, Underwager's next comment provided more insight.

"You know, when this little girl said that Joseph peed on her head, she was describing sadistic or masochistic behavior."

"You mean where Miyara asked her a leading question about this happening?" Facinelli interrupted.

"Yes," Underwager agreed. Returning to his analysis, the psychologist said, "The act of urinating on someone is extremely perverse and very rare among the population in general. Pedophiles don't do that. I don't know of any instance in the literature in which a person who has been diagnosed as a pedophile has urinated on kids. They just don't do it."

"Meaning what?"

"Meaning that this girl's story, or the story that she's been led to tell, is probably fabricated. It's strong evidence that her story is untrue."

"Can we pause for just a moment as I finish writing down what you just said?" Facinelli asked. A minute later, Facinelli told Underwager to continue.

"There's another important psychological phenomenon going on in these interviews. It's called the majority effect and it's well established in the literature. In almost all of these interviews, the child is in a room with two adults and, in some cases, three adults. When the adults think that abuse occurred and ask questions that reveal that belief, the child is under great pressure to believe the same thing. Let's not forget that these adults are parents and police officers—authority figures that these young children want to please. Sometimes the pressure to conform can be overwhelming."

When Facinelli hung up the phone fifteen minutes later, he knew that his investigative piece would feature the improper interview techniques. If a jury had been told just a fraction of what he'd learned from these experts, he doubted that either defendant would have been convicted. The jurors would have understood that, despite the earnestness of their demeanor, the children could not be trusted. After many interviews over several months, their memories had been corrupted by suggestive and coercive questioning.

But he knew there was more to the story than just the inappropriate interrogation methods. He was equally troubled by evidence that had not been considered by the jury. Some of that evidence was known at the time of the trial but, for whatever reason, had never been presented. Other things had come to light only after the jury's verdict. Together, they formed a body of exculpatory evidence that raised considerable doubt about the defendants' guilt.

Facinelli was disturbed that neither defendant had introduced the attendance records of the Head Start children to determine if they had all been absent on the same day during the period that the abuse had allegedly occurred. The four child accusers testified almost uniformly that the other three were present at Joseph's house at the same time. (One boy had testified that only two others were present.) Because the children had also claimed that they had been abused on four separate occasions, the records should have documented four times when they were absent together.

When Facinelli obtained the records, he was startled by what they showed, or more precisely, what they didn't show. The four accusers were never absent on the same day. Two of the children were absent together, but only twice. One child had only missed two days of school during the entire four-month period. Facinelli went through all of the combinations and found that nothing in the attendance records supported the children's claim that they had been absent together— either at Joseph's house or anyplace else. Why hadn't the jury seen these records?

During the trial, Joseph Grunda was the only attorney who'd mentioned the attendance records. In his closing argument, he'd told jurors that the prosecutor hadn't proved his case when he'd not produced the attendance records to corroborate the children's absences and their stories. For Facinelli, this begged larger questions: Why didn't the defense submit the records themselves? The prosecutor's office had supplied photocopies of them to the defense about two months before trial. When Facinelli asked Bradley about this, Bradley told him that the prosecutor would have argued that they were part of a cover-up by Head Start officials and their introduction would only have hurt his case. Facinelli had studied the records and they looked authentic to him—different ink colors and dissimilar handwriting that reflected that they'd been recorded day by day at the hands of several teachers. Although not an attorney, Facinelli could not fathom how these records could have damaged the defense.

He'd also discovered that several of the children had not been able to identify Joseph Allen in the police lineup. Although it was not available to the defense attorneys at the time of the trial, a police report had detailed the children's reactions and misidentifications, and Facinelli had been able to get a copy of it and read it. In fact, Michael Osborne, the little boy who'd testified that Joseph had grabbed his arm near Nancy Smith's bus, had been given twelve opportunities to identify Joseph Allen and had failed each time. However, eight months later, when the prosecutor asked him to name the black man sitting at the trial table, the boy had told the jury, "Joseph."

In reviewing the court filings, Facinelli had read Bradley's motion for a new trial and the revelation that Marge Bronson, the first parent to allege sexual abuse, was a convicted felon. In a reply to the motion, Rosenbaum had disclosed that Emily Osborne, the State's first witness, had at one time been addicted to prescription drugs. In his filing, Rosenbaum had claimed that Osborne was not addicted at the time of the trial nor at the time she'd observed the events that had been the subject of her testimony. However, she was cooperating with authorities as they investigated a doctor and dentist who'd prescribed the medication for her. Facinelli, trained to ask questions, asked himself: What would the jury have decided if it had known this information?

For Facinelli, his investigative piece was beginning to take shape. Based on the mountain of information that he'd gathered, his investigative piece would require a multiple-day series in order to present it in a way that readers could digest. He could devote the first day to the improper questioning of the children and its ramifications. The second part could focus on the evidence that the jury had never heard. He was toying with a third part, one that would show how one parent's allegations had led to a community-wide hysteria that had culminated in the arrests and convictions of Smith and Allen.

This last part would find its underpinnings in a book that he'd read, *Sex Abuse Hysteria: The Salem Witch Trials Revisited* by Richard Gardner, MD. After he'd read this book, Facinelli had asked the author, a psychiatrist on the clinical staff at Columbia University, if he would review the Head Start children's interviews. Citing the press of other work, Gardner had graciously declined. Although disappointed, Facinelli was convinced that he needed to educate his readers about Gardner's opinions about sex abuse cases.

For the last ten years, Gardner had been a leader in ferreting out false sex abuse claims in child custody disputes, usually in situations where a mother claimed that a father had sexually abused their child to gain an advantage in a custody dispute. Although Gardner believed that 95 percent of intrafamily sexual abuse allegations were legitimate, he'd found that those arising from custody disputes were more likely to be false. Based on his investigations, three- and four-year-old children were the easiest to program for these claims. Before Gardner would agree to evaluate child sex abuse claims in this setting, he required equal access to the three central figures in the probe: the child/alleged victim, the parent accuser, and the accused parent. Gardner believed that in order to reach a sound opinion, he needed to elicit detailed information from each of these individuals.

In evaluating the child, the adult accuser, and the adult suspect, Gardner had developed a series of criteria that he believed pointed him toward the truth. One measure was whether the adult accuser (not just the accused) was willing to undergo a lie detector test. What would have happened in the Head Start case if Marge Bronson and other parents had been asked to take a polygraph examination?

When Facinelli considered Gardner's approach, his thoughts turned to Detective Cantu. Although Cantu had used leading questions in his interviews, he had been the only detective to question the child victims, the parent accusers, *and* the accused perpetrator, Nancy Smith. When Detective Andujar had been told to start fresh, he'd reinterviewed the children and their parents but ignored Smith. Likewise, Detective Miller had had no contact with Smith. Was it just a coincidence that only Cantu had doubted the children's stories?

Facinelli was also intrigued by Gardner's opinions about sex abuse cases arising in the setting of day care centers and preschools. Like others in his field, Gardner had been alarmed by the nationwide proliferation of these claims and he'd delved into many of them, including the celebrated McMartin day care case in California. Like the molestation allegations arising out of custody disputes, accusations arising out of nursery school and day care settings were often baseless.

According to Gardner, these cases followed a pattern. A single allegation from one parent often mushroomed into multiple accusations from many parents. In the McMartin case, the original accuser, a woman with significant psychological issues, had been convinced that her son had been molested at the school based on ambiguous findings. Her exaggerated and agitated response had fueled equally anxious and frantic behavior from other parents, culminating in dozens of claims, none of which led to a conviction after seven years of criminal prosecution. Gardner explained that one person's hysteria could spread to others like a contagious airborne disease, creating an atmosphere of mass hysteria where people accepted even preposterous details as true.

Facinelli could see that the Head Start case followed the model described by Gardner. One overwrought parent, Marge Bronson, had told her story first to the police and other public officials, then to other parents whose children she'd suspected had also been molested, and finally to the media, whose sensational stories snagged other parents, leading to more claims of abuse. For his third segment, Facinelli planned to trace how Bronson's astonishing accusations had fueled an entire community to believe as she did.

However, before he could complete his project, the newspaper's senior editors and its owners would give the prosecutor, Greg White, and his chief criminal assistant, Jon Rosenbaum, an opportunity to tell their side. They would disclose some of the disturbing aspects of Facinelli's investigation and then listen to the prosecutors' response.

CHAPTER 28
MEETING WITH THE PROSECUTOR
SEPTEMBER 26, 1996
TWO YEARS AFTER CONVICTION

Facinelli surveyed the faces in the newspaper's conference room. Around the table sat the prosecutor, Greg White, his assistant, Jonathan Rosenbaum; and the management of the newspaper: Arthur Hudnutt, the editor, Andy Young, the executive editor, and Arnold Miller, the managing editor. Although Young had given Facinelli his blessing to pursue the story and granted him a two-month leave from his column in order to pursue it, Facinelli sensed that Hudnutt had mixed emotions about his project.

For the last seventy years, the *Chronicle-Telegram*, through the Hudnutt family, had consistently promoted Republican candidates through the paper's editorials and news coverage. By criticizing the prosecutor's handling of the Head Start case, Facinelli's series would be attacking the county's lone Republican officeholder, a candidate whom the paper had wholeheartedly endorsed four times previously. For the *Chronicle*, this was uncharted territory. If White and Rosenbaum could defend the verdicts in the Head Start case, Facinelli feared that the publisher would spike the project.

Despite exchanging some preliminary pleasantries, the group appeared tense. Rosenbaum appeared to be the most uncomfortable, shifting about in his seat and staring at the tabletop. Although more at ease, Greg White punctuated his words with an occasional forced smile. After coffee had been delivered to the room, Arthur Hudnutt thanked the two prosecutors for meeting with them. He explained that the *Chronicle* was taking a second look at the Head Start case and wanted input from the prosecutors to fully understand some of the issues. He told them that Facinelli was researching the story, a statement that drew nods from the two prosecutors, who apparently already knew it. Because Facinelli had requested documents and interviewed a number of key people, including Rosenbaum, his project was not a secret. However, the substance of his findings was.

"Why don't you begin by telling us why you believe the verdicts were correct?" Hudnutt asked, tossing the prosecutors an easy question.

White glanced at Rosenbaum, who then launched into an impassioned defense of the case. He focused on the number of children who had come forward, the changes in their behavior after the abuse, and the corroborating physical evidence found at Allen's apartment. Hudnutt nodded as Rosenbaum made his points, causing Facinelli to fear that the head of the newspaper was being swayed by the prosecutor.

After Rosenbaum finished his polemic, Hudnutt told the prosecutors that the newspaper had asked two experts in the field of child sex abuse to review the children's interviews. "I won't pull any punches here. They were troubled by the way the interviews were conducted. They had serious questions about the reliability of the stories that emerged."

"Your experts are bogus," Rosenbaum shot back. "You can find experts to say anything."

Although he said nothing to defend the experts, Hudnutt seemed taken aback by Rosenbaum's defiance. At this point, the assistant prosecutor hadn't yet learned the names or the credentials of the experts who'd reviewed the statements, let alone their specific criticisms.

Trying to bring the discussion back to the details of the interviews, Hudnutt asked, "What about the initial interviews with the children— the ones that Detective Cantu tape-recorded. Did you ever listen to them before the trial started?"

"No. I listened to the tapes of the detectives who solved the case," Rosenbaum answered.

"You didn't think that these first interviews were important?" Hudnutt asked.

"Let's just say, Cantu is not the brightest guy around. Not only that, but his investigation was biased—he knew Nancy Smith. They played bingo together," Rosenbaum said. After a pause, he added, "His work was trash."

Facinelli rolled his eyes but did not dispute Rosenbaum's claims. The newspaper had obtained Cantu's performance ratings for the two years preceding the Head Start investigation. Three different evaluators had rated him as exceptional.

For the first time, Andy Young, the executive editor and Hudnutt's nephew, spoke. He'd read Facinelli's drafts of the Head Start articles several times and had been apprised of Facinelli's findings as the investigation progressed. "We've also reviewed guidelines for prosecutors published by the National Center for Prosecution of Child Abuse," Young said. "It's an arm of the National District Attorneys Association. Have you heard of it?"

"I'm a member of the association," White replied.

"Their guidelines state that someone knowledgeable about child interviewing techniques should listen to the police interviews before charges are filed. They do that in order to judge the quality of the prior interviews. Based on what Mr. Rosenbaum just said, it appears that no one in your office listened to the initial taped interviews before you charged Nancy Smith and Joseph Allen."

White took a deep breath and then exhaled. "All things being equal, we'd like to listen to the tapes in all of our cases."

The newspapermen caught White's meaning: in a perfect world where prosecutors were never pressed for time, things like that could be done, but that was not the real world.

White continued, "Before we charge an individual, we have two obligations. First, do we believe that the accused committed the offense? And second, is there enough admissible evidence to obtain a conviction?"

Young returned the prosecutor to the Head Start case, steering him away from the generalities of charging a suspect. "I want to stick with the guidelines for a moment. They advise that the prosecutor should talk directly to the children before making a charging decision. Was that done?"

White looked to Rosenbaum for an answer. His assistant said that he couldn't remember when he'd first met with the children; however, he'd conducted many interviews with them.

As Rosenbaum spoke, Facinelli remembered an earlier phone conversation he'd had with Rosenbaum about the case. When Facinelli had explained that he was calling about the Head Start case, Rosenbaum had admitted that he'd initially feared that the case would end in a directed verdict because the children were not responding to his questions. To avoid that, he'd "spent a lot of time getting the kids comfortable" in the company of a police officer and a parent. Besides multiple interviews, he'd taken them to the courtroom and "may well have" shown them the exhibits to refresh their memories.

Young continued with his line of questioning. "The guidelines also tell prosecutors to limit the number of interviews with the children." By the expression on the two prosecutors' faces, it was obvious that they were irritated by Young's persistent reference to these standards. Nevertheless, Young continued, "They also recommend that the children be interviewed one-on-one, that you avoid leading questions, and that you try to gather information by asking open-ended questions."

For a few moments, neither prosecutor spoke. Finally, White said, "You can criticize the police investigation, and, for that matter, you can find fault with us, but the bottom line is that this case has been reviewed by the Ninth District Court of Appeals and it upheld the verdict." Looking about the table, White made eye contact with several of the newspaper representatives as if to say this settled the matter.

Facinelli was not surprised by the prosecutor's response; he'd suspected that they would defend their tactics and the verdict. Hudnutt took over the questioning again.

"I understand that one of the detectives wrote that several of the children were unable to identify Joseph Allen in the live lineup at the police station. Have you read that report?"

"Absolutely," Rosenbaum said.

"Were the defense attorneys provided that report?"

"I notified both defense attorneys before the trial that some of the kids couldn't pick out Joseph Allen. After that, it was up to them to request the report."

Facinelli had read the prosecutor's filing and it disclosed that some of the children had failed to identify Joseph Allen from a photo lineup. It had not revealed that any of them had failed to recognize Joseph Allen at the live lineup.

More knowledgeable about the details of Facinelli's findings, Young took over the questioning again. "I want to ask you about the testimony of Michael Osborne. He identified Joseph Allen at trial as the man who'd grabbed his arm. Do I have that right?"

Rosenbaum nodded warily.

"However, the police report says that he was given many chances to identify Joseph Allen at the live lineup, but he kept picking other men."

Rosenbaum shook his head in disagreement. "That boy picked out everybody but Joseph Allen because he was afraid of him. In effect, he was choosing him."

Facinelli knew that the report did not bear this out. Of the five men in the lineup, Osborne had chosen three of them. Facinelli remained silent; he knew this meeting was not his show.

Rosenbaum continued, "Michael told his mother that Joseph had taught him how to hump. Have you read the transcript on this?"

Facinelli had read it, but not his editors. Young shook his head.

Rosenbaum continued, "Well, the boy could imitate Allen's slow Southern drawl, and before he'd come to the police station, he'd imitated Allen's pronunciation of the word 'humping.' When Michael was in the viewing room, we had all of the men say that word and Joseph Allen drew out the word. It was clear that the boy could mimic Allen's pronunciation to a T."

Again, Facinelli was not going to contradict Rosenbaum. Facinelli had read the report. The men in the lineup had been asked to say, "Don't tell nobody." Even after listening to the men's voices, Michael had not identified Joseph Allen as the man with whom he'd allegedly interacted.

"I think that's all of our questions for you," Hudnutt said. "Unless anyone else has questions for the prosecutors." None of them did.

After White and Rosenbaum left, Andy Young looked at Facinelli. "Can you incorporate some of the prosecutors' responses into your article?"

"Of course. I planned to do that," Facinelli responded. "Does that mean that the paper will run the series?"

Young looked at his uncle. Art Hudnutt had the last word. "Andy and I will discuss that after you leave."

CHAPTER 29
THE SERIES ATTACKED
OCTOBER 7, 1996
TWO YEARS AFTER CONVICTION

Paul Facinelli felt a sense of relief and pride as he drove to the newspaper's office this Monday morning. The previous day, the first installment of his three-part exclusive had hit the newsstands, and the initial reaction had been extremely positive. A few fellow journalists had called him at home to congratulate him on a job well done. Between them and his colleagues at the newspaper who'd previewed the pieces before they'd been published, Facinelli had heard nothing but praise.

After he sat down at his desk, colleagues continued to offer him their congratulations. Just as Facinelli finished his second cup of coffee, around eleven o'clock, his phone rang.

"Paul, we have a problem with your article," Andy Young, his boss said. "We need to talk now."

Facinelli could hear concern in Young's voice. "What's the issue?" Facinelli asked.

"It has to do with your expert Ralph Underwager. Let's just say that he's got baggage—lots of it. Just come to my office and I can explain."

When Facinelli entered Young's office, he saw a sheaf of papers about two inches thick on his editor's desk. "Greg White dropped these off this morning. They all deal with Underwager."

Over the next few minutes, Young explained that an upset Greg White had asked to see him earlier that morning. The prosecutor had handed Young a package that included articles and court decisions about Underwager. White had said, "As you might imagine, Jon is fuming about your use of Underwager in this series. He's a discredited hired gun and the newspaper has misled its readers by citing him as an authority."

Facinelli had expected that the prosecutor would be upset by the series—maybe even outraged—but he was confident that his research had been sound and that the questions he'd raised were legitimate. What could possibly be wrong? Underwager had published several books, authored and coauthored numerous articles, and rendered expert opinions in over two hundred fifty court cases.

"Let's start with the worst thing first," Young said as he handed Facinelli a photocopy of an article.

Facinelli saw that it was a 1993 article from a Dutch publication called *Paidika: The Journal of Paedophilia* and was an interview with Ralph Underwager and his wife, Hollida Wakefield.

"Just go to the highlighted part," Young said. "Underwager is quoted as saying that pedophilia is a responsible choice."

As Facinelli read that portion of the article, he felt physically sick. He looked up at his editor. "This doesn't make sense. Maybe he was misquoted."

"Yes, Underwager claims he was misquoted," Young replied. "He's published an article disputing the quote. He says that he and his wife have never asserted that sexual contact between adults and children can ever be viewed as positive."

"Well, what does he claim he said?"

"Here, you can read it yourself," Young said, handing Facinelli the article written by Underwager. In his defense, the expert explained what he'd actually told the interviewer: that if pedophiles claim that their behavior is acceptable, then they should come out in the open and take responsibility for their conduct. He protested that lawyers were now impeaching him through the *Paidika* article, implying that he and his wife approved of child molestation. His article made clear that neither he nor his wife should ever be linked to "those vile, reprehensible pedophiles."

Facinelli believed that Underwager had been misquoted. If this was Underwager's actual belief, why hadn't he stated it himself in any of his books or articles? No one who routinely testified in child molestation cases would make such a damaging public statement. It would forever doom him as an expert. There had to be a mistake here.

"Well, this article attacks Underwager as a person, but it doesn't touch his scholarship or his research," Facinelli said, hoping that he'd heard the worst.

"Well, there's more," Young said. "There's also an article published by the *Journal of the American Medical Association* that is very critical of one of Underwager's books. It claims that his references don't support his positions."

Facinelli sighed, realizing that these revelations had put the newspaper on the defensive. "What about the other experts that I quote in the article? Are there any documents that discredit Melvin Guyer or Richard Gardner?" Facinelli asked.

"No," Young said, "Just Underwager."

Facinelli nodded and exhaled deeply. Looking at Young uneasily, Facinelli asked, "You're going to continue to run the rest of the series, right?"

"We will," Young said. He shook his head before continuing, "I wish you'd never used Underwager as an authority. In hindsight, there were better choices available. Obviously, we'll run a story about the controversy surrounding Dr. Underwager. We owe that to our readers."

Facinelli wondered who would write that article; he doubted it would be him. He wanted time to carefully read and digest the articles about Underwager and hoped to have some input on the newspaper's response. "Can I take these?" Facinelli asked, pointing to the stack of documents about Underwager.

"Yeah, those are your copies. We'll talk more later," Young said.

For the next hour and a half, Facinelli read the documents about Underwager. He quickly realized that Underwager was engaged in an ongoing battle with the National Center for Prosecution of Child

Abuse, a project of the American Prosecutors Research Institute. The National Center provided prosecuting attorneys with critiques of Underwager's books and research and was determined to portray him as a shill for the criminal defense bar. Facinelli suspected that Rosenbaum had received these documents from that organization. For his part, Underwager had sued several of his most vociferous critics for libel, claims that were all dismissed early in the litigation. His lawsuits appeared to be a desperate attempt to restore his reputation. However, when the courts refused to take sides in the dispute, the attacks on Underwager continued and compromised his effectiveness.

When he finally pushed the stack of papers away from him, Facinelli realized that the controversy surrounding Underwager did not affect anything that he'd written. The attacks were about the man and not the opinions that he'd rendered about the Head Start interviews. And Underwager had not been his only source; Melvin Guyer's criticisms had been scathing, concluding that the interviews were some of the worst he'd ever read. Even the National Center for Prosecution of Children Abuse had published guidelines that underscored many of the same points raised by the *Chronicle*'s two experts. Facinelli saw no need to retract a single fact or alter his analysis in any way.

After the newspaper published the last installment of its three-part series, Facinelli and Young talked about the newspaper's response to Rosenbaum. Besides the materials on Underwager, Rosenbaum had also delivered an angry letter to the newspaper, blasting it for its unfair portrayal of the Head Start case. Young told Facinelli that the newspaper would not publish Rosenbaum's letter, but it would tackle the controversy surrounding Ralph Underwager.

On Thursday, two days after the last Head Start articles had been published, the *Chronicle* reported on Ralph Underwager. Running without a byline, the article explained that Underwager had filed a defamation lawsuit against a psychologist and a lawyer "who had been sharply critical of his views." It explained that Underwager's case had been dismissed and reviewed the substance of the controversy, including the quote from the *Paidika* article. Facinelli was both pleased and relieved that the newspaper had not retracted anything that he'd written.

Over the past several days, Facinelli had heard from a number of the newspaper's readers, and their comments were overwhelmingly positive. From their response, he believed that his articles had not only educated the public about the case but apparently changed views. In the court of public opinion, people now had significant doubts about the reliability of the jury verdict.

But where it mattered most—in the prosecutor's office—the article had achieved the opposite effect. Instead of causing a reexamination, it had only hardened the prosecutor's resolve to defend its actions. Jon Rosenbaum's lengthy response to the newspaper had described the two experts as "an affront to justice" and the articles a "continue[d] victimization of the children who were preyed upon in this case." He took aim at Facinelli, attacking his credibility and his views on gambling, prostitution, and narcotics, all of which the columnist had suggested should be legalized. However, the heart of Rosenbaum's polemic claimed that the series was biased and unfair. He complained that Facinelli's choice of facts had been decidedly one-sided, including only those that favored the defense while intentionally ignoring those that supported the jury's verdict.

A week had passed since the first article in the Head Start series had appeared in the paper. Facinelli again sat in his kitchen, sipping coffee and focusing on the paper's editorial page. Andy Young had written two editorials about the case. In the lead editorial, Young criticized the way in which the children's interviews had been conducted in the Head Start case, suggesting that the way in which the police had questioned the children had severely compromised its investigation. He urged the Ohio legislature to adopt rules that would require a judge to rule on the reliability of children's statements before trial. Refusing to back down, Young concluded that "the uncertainty that justice prevailed in the Lorain Head Start case is unsettling and intolerable."

Facinelli grimaced as he read the second editorial. His boss apologized for using Ralph Underwager as one of the experts in the first installment. Facinelli thought that this was unnecessary, particularly after the paper had already reported about the expert's ongoing battles with others in his field. Nevertheless, Young told readers that the paper should have known more about Underwager before allowing him to critique the interviews. Facinelli bristled as the editor explained that if the paper had vetted Underwager, it would have chosen someone else. Although Facinelli had not been named, it was clear that the blame had been placed at his feet.

The editorial, however, ended on a strong note. Young explained that the "controversy over Underwager should not detract from the series' impact." Irrespective of Underwager and his views, "the questioning of children in this case remains deeply troubling."

Setting the paper down, Facinelli thought about his journey over the last five months in reexamining the Head Start case. On a personal level, he was outraged by what had happened to Nancy Smith and Joseph Allen. He believed that they were the unfortunate victims of a hysteria that had caused otherwise reasonable and intelligent people to suspend reality and believe a story that was beset by inconsistencies and implausible details. He felt certain that the children's interviews were wholly unreliable.

Yes, he would return to writing his column, but he could not shake the belief that he had unfinished business. When the opportunity arose, he would continue his investigation. He could do no less.

CHAPTER 30
THE VIDEOTAPE

SEPTEMBER 21, 1997 - MAY 11, 1998
THREE TO THREE AND A HALF YEARS
AFTER CONVICTION

Paul Facinelli hadn't been able to let go of the Head Start story. For the better part of a year, he'd struggled with his next step. A month earlier, he'd decided to meet and talk with Joseph Allen at the Mansfield Correctional Institution. He wasn't sure why, but he wanted a face-to-face meeting with Allen. Perhaps it was to hear from him directly to evaluate his credibility, or maybe he was just curious. After Facinelli had contacted the prison authorities, they'd reached out to Allen, who was receptive to the interview.

The meeting had gone well. The two had talked in a large hall where prisoners and family met for scheduled social visits. Despite the noise from conversations occurring all around them, Facinelli and Allen were able to discuss the case for over an hour at a corner table. Soft-spoken and measured, Allen maintained his innocence throughout their conversation.

At one point, the conversation had turned to the police lineup, something Facinelli had covered in the second installment of the series.

"You know, they videotaped that lineup," Allen said.

Facinelli was unaware of this. He'd read the written police report detailing the children's reactions during the lineup, but he didn't know that it had been taped. If the session had been recorded, why hadn't the prosecutor shown it to the jury?

"Are you sure they were taping it?" Facinelli asked.

"Yeah, I'm sure. One of the cops had his camera going the whole time. You know, I seen the red light flashing when he turned it toward us."

"Any idea what it would show?"

"I couldn't see the kids or hear what they was tellin' the police, but I think they was having a hard time making a choice."

"Why do you say that?"

"Well, they was havin' us step forward like all the time. They'd have us take off our shirts, then tell us to put them back on. Then they had us say stuff, so the kids could hear our voices. It was probably an hour, and that's a long time to be standin' around there."

Facinelli nodded. He'd read the official police report about the lineup that had been authored by Detective Pete Rewak, one of the Lorain detectives who'd assisted in the Head Start investigation. Whenever a child failed to identify Joseph Allen, Detective Rewak had claimed that the child had appeared terrified of Allen. Facinelli was intrigued by what the videotape might show. Even if it didn't reveal anything startling, it would record the children's reaction to Allen unfiltered by Detective Rewak's spin.

"I'm going to check this out," Facinelli promised.

"If you get ahold of it, it'll show a lot—show you they got the wrong man," Allen said.

As Facinelli walked out of the prison and neared his car, he thought of another question. Had Allen told his attorney about the videotape? He shook his head, upset that he hadn't inquired. But did it matter at this point? Probably not.

When he returned to his office, he directed a Freedom of Information Act request to the Lorain police seeking a copy of the video. A few days later, he'd struck gold; the video did exist and the Lorain police had possession of it. After some wrangling, the police had delivered a copy to the *Chronicle*.

From the moment he'd inserted the tape into the VCR, Facinelli had watched dumbstruck. Seven children had paraded into the police viewing room, one at a time. Four had either identified the wrong person or claimed that Joseph was not in the group. Nina Zorich had initially identified someone else as Joseph Allen, but after help from her mother and leading questions by the two detectives, she'd finally picked Joseph Allen after almost ten tortuous minutes. Two boys had identified Joseph Allen quickly, causing Facinelli to wonder if they'd remembered his face after seeing it earlier in a photo lineup.

As soon as Pam Plas returned to the office, he would watch the video with her. Plas was a reporter with the *Chronicle* who'd been assigned to work on the article with him.

About an hour later, Facinelli and Plas were in a conference room watching the videotape together. After a few minutes, the monitor showed Nina Zorich and her mother, Marge Bronson, in the viewing room with Sergeant Russ Cambarare and Captain Cel Rivera, the head of the detective bureau. Looking like a princess, Nina was dressed in a cream-colored dress with large black polka dots and a matching jacket. Her long, wavy brown hair was set off by an explosion of golden ribbons tied to the top of her head, giving her the appearance of a fancy, gift-wrapped present. Wearing a loose-fitting, colorful print blouse, her mother, Marge Bronson, was equally well-groomed. Her thick black hair was piled high on her head as her daughter sat on her lap.

Of the two, only the mother looked apprehensive. She held her daughter to her chest like Nina was a life preserver, and her eyes were intense and focused. Her unease was reinforced by her constantly shifting body position. On the other hand, her daughter's expression alternated between solemn and bewildered. She lazily chewed gum while holding her right index finger poised on her lower lip. The daughter felt her mother's nervousness. "Why are you shaking?" Nina asked.

"I'm cold," her mother replied.

As the suspects cycled forward one at a time, Nina said, "It's him, Mama." However, Nina was referring to a man in the number three position. This was not Joseph Allen, who was the second from the left in a line of five men.

Captain Rivera said, "Take your time, Nina. Wait until we're done, okay?" When Marcus Logan had quickly identified Joseph Allen just a few minutes earlier, Rivera had not cautioned him to wait until he'd studied all of the suspects.

After viewing all of the men, first with their shirts on and then with them off (presumably to expose Joseph Allen's white spots and scars), the little girl appeared flummoxed.

Rivera spoke again. "You don't recognize nothing?"

Apparently convinced that the girl's fear was keeping her from identifying Allen, Sergeant Cambarare chimed in to reassure her. "The men can't see you. It's a magic mirror. You can see them, but they can't see you. We're going to put him in jail and you'll never see him again."

Pointing toward the glass, Nina whispered to her mother, "Is that them?" Her use of the word "them" did not make sense.

"Yeah, that's Joe. Right there," her mother whispered back.

Plas looked at Facinelli, holding her hands out in a gesture of disbelief. Wasn't it improper for a parent to influence a child like that in this setting? Understanding Plas's look, Facinelli stopped the video for a moment and then spoke. "It gets worse. Believe me, it gets worse." He, too, had been shocked when the police had not admonished Marge Bronson to keep quiet.

When he pressed the play button, the monitor came to life again. Bronson continued, "He's going to go back to jail and you won't have to worry and you can go outside and play again." Facinelli had no doubt that experts Underwager, Gardner, and Guyer would have recoiled if they'd heard a questioner promise a reward to a child for identifying a suspect.

"We're going to put him in jail and throw away the key," her mother said. To emphasize the point, she made a throwing motion with her right hand.

Holding her daughter close to her chest, she asked, "Okay, which one is he?" Not waiting for a reply, the mother shot her arm toward one of the suspects and, just as suddenly, brought it back down to her lap, the entire motion taking less than a second. "Now, remember, you just pointed to him," she said, even though she was the one who'd just done the pointing. Before her daughter could respond, Marge Bronson pointed in the direction of the glass for a second time—the motion taking even less time than the first one.

Immediately, Nina pointed straight ahead. Like hunting dogs that had just cornered their prey, the three adults looked intently at the little girl and her outstretched arm, trying to decipher which suspect she'd selected.

"What color shirt is he wearing, hon?" Rivera asked excitedly.

Nina answered with a word that was difficult to discern—either "black" or "plaid." Joseph Allen was wearing a green plaid shirt, while the man to his left wore a black shirt.

Rivera responded quickly. "Plaid? What color plaid, honey?"

Her mother echoed the question. "What color is the plaid shirt?"

Instead of answering, Nina pointed again, and this time, her mother grabbed her hand and guided it farther to the right until it clanked against the glass mirror.

Although the video did not show to whom her finger was directed, both Rivera and Cambarare reacted by saying the same thing, "Oh, black," as if she were pointing to the man in the black shirt. Rivera then said, "Did you say 'black' earlier?"

Still holding her daughter's hand, Marge Bronson also seemed surprised. "Black?" she asked. The mother then began pointing to the men, going from left to right, and describing the color of their shirts. "That's blue. That's green. That's black."

Talking into the telephone, Rivera said, "Have number three step forward." He paused for a few seconds. "Then step back."

Sergeant Cambarare asked, "Is that him?"

Nina made no response.

Captain Rivera asked, "Do you think that's him?" After a short pause, he asked, "Is there anyone else you want to take a closer look at?"

Holding her daughter's hand, Marge Bronson pointed it toward the glass. "Number two," the mother said.

"Do you want number two to step forward?" Rivera asked.

"Mm-hmm," the mother answered.

"Have number two step forward," Rivera said.

"He can't see you," Cambarare added.

"He can't see you, precious," her mother said as she flicked her own hand toward the glass.

"Is that Joseph, honey?" Rivera asked.

Nina nodded emphatically. After eight and a half minutes, she had finally identified Joseph Allen.

"What color shirt is he wearing?" Rivera asked, trying to confirm her choice.

"Blue," Nina responded.

"Blue?" Rivera asked, unable to hide his surprise.

"That's a green," her mother said.

"Green," Nina agreed.

"That's okay," Rivera said. Still intent on clarifying the girl's answer, he asked, "Which one?"

Nina pointed again.

Sergeant Cambarare spoke for her. "Green," he said. Then Cambarare asked a leading question. "Is he holding something?" In fact, Joseph Allen was holding papers in his left hand.

"Yeah," Nina replied.

For the next minute, the detectives asked Nina questions designed to confirm her choice. When they had concluded, her mother kissed and hugged her daughter, relief evident in her eyes.

Facinelli hit the stop button on the recorder and looked at Plas. "Can you believe that?"

Plas shook her head. "I wonder how the jury would have ruled if they'd seen that."

"You've only watched twelve minutes of a forty-five-minute video," Facinelli added. "Wait until you look at the three segments with Michael Osborne."

In his first series, Facinelli had addressed Michael Osborne's inability to identify Joseph Allen during the live lineup. From the police report describing the event, Facinelli had read that Michael had been called into the viewing room on three separate occasions and misidentified Joseph Allen on twelve attempts. At trial, his mother, Emily, had testified that he'd jumped back when Allen had stepped forward and had run crying from the room. The police report had not

THE EDGE OF DOUBT 267

mentioned the boy's fearful reaction, and Facinelli had wondered if it had happened.

Smiling at Plas, he hit the play button again and they focused on Michael's three appearances in the viewing room. During the first two, his mother had not accompanied him, although she'd testified at trial as if she'd been with him each time. More telling, the boy never exhibited any fear or upset. To the contrary, he seemed to be enjoying the experience and, at one point, grabbed one of the telephones in the viewing room (a dead one) and began mimicking Captain Rivera, telling the suspects to move forward and step back. At no time did he recoil, cry, or run out the door. The conclusion was inescapable: his mother had testified about something that had never happened. If the jurors had seen this video, would they have believed anything that she'd said? As the first witness, she'd set the tone for the entire case by claiming that Joseph had taught her son how to hump and had grabbed his arm near Smith's bus.

Facinelli stopped and then rewound the video to replay the last segment involving both Michael and his mother in the viewing room. When Joseph Allen was asked to step forward, the boy grimaced and said, "Ouch." At the same time, the little boy looked down at his right thigh where his mother's hand rested on it.

"Did she just pinch him?" Plas asked.

"It sure looks and sounds like it. Apparently, she was trying to give him a cue."

Despite the assist, Michael failed to identify Joseph Allen.

After the video had finished, Facinelli and Plas discussed their next steps. They would determine whether the prosecutor had divulged this video to the defense in any of the State's discovery filings. They'd also ask legal experts whether this evidence was exculpatory and should have been disclosed as such. They decided to seek out experts whose opinions were unlikely to be questioned: a law school professor and a veteran Cleveland prosecutor.

By reviewing the court filings in the cases, Facinelli learned that the prosecutor had reported the existence of the video recording. He'd included it on his witness list as the final item. Although the prosecutor had reported several things as exculpatory, including the failure of some children to pick Joseph Allen from a photo lineup, that list did not contain the video recording. How could that not be exculpatory? Didn't the video help Joseph Allen by casting doubt upon the children's subsequent courtroom identifications?

Prior to trial, neither defense attorney had sought any information about the children's failure to identify Joseph Allen in the photo spreads. When Facinelli called Bradley, he asked the defense attorney about the video included in the prosecutor's witness list. Bradley conceded that he should have insisted on seeing the videotape. However, he added that he should have been given a copy of the videotape immediately after the first child had testified in the courtroom. "I had demanded the prior statements of all witnesses, and, under the law, I was entitled to them. Because the children were both talking and making nonverbal gestures in the video recording, that was clearly a statement."

When Facinelli contacted Jack Guttenberg, a law professor and the associate dean at the Cleveland State University Marshall College of Law, Guttenberg said that the video recording "was clearly exculpatory" and noted there was "no doubt that it should have been listed in the exculpatory statement" and not just in the prosecutor's own list of witnesses. Seeking the opinion of a prosecutor who toiled in the trenches, Facinelli also presented this issue to Carmen Marino, the first assistant Cuyahoga County prosecutor. Marino was equivocal, suggesting that it was unclear whether Rosenbaum had met his obligation to disclose exculpatory material when he'd only listed it in his own witness list. However, Marino said that he would "have [personally] gone the additional step and notified the defense, [drawing] particular attention to it."

Both Guttenberg and Marino agreed with Bradley that the video constituted a prior statement and should have been turned over to the defense attorneys immediately after the first child had testified. Marino added, "The defense is entitled to all statements made to the police, regardless of how they're recorded."

It was now time to give Rosenbaum and White an opportunity to respond. It was no secret that the prosecutors were angry about Facinelli's original series. He'd heard from others that they viewed his stories as biased and unfair—nothing less than a hatchet job. Treading lightly, Facinelli and Plas sent written questions to the prosecutor's office, seeking comment on the video and why it hadn't been disclosed as exculpatory. Several days later, the prosecutor's office responded with a long, unsigned statement.

The prosecutor contended that the children had failed to identify Joseph Allen out of fear. Because Allen had threatened to kill them if they disclosed what he'd done to them, they were too frightened to point him out. "The refusal to identify a suspect out of fear is not exculpatory evidence but inculpatory," the prosecution wrote.

The prosecutor reiterated that he had disclosed the children's failure to identify Joseph Allen in a photo lineup and had conceded in his opening statement that some of them could not identify Allen during the live lineup. As a result, he argued that the defense had a full opportunity to explore and exploit this subject during its cross-examination of the State's witnesses. Next, the prosecutor summarized the evidence that supported the guilty verdicts. His statement concluded: "All the lawyers involved have raised suppression of excul-patory evidence. No court at any level has found any merit to such a claim when the complete record is considered."

As Facinelli pondered the prosecutor's response, the fact remained that the video had never been disclosed as exculpatory—something that would have alerted the defense to its importance. Although the prosecutor claimed that the children's failure to identify Allen was based on fear, Facinelli and others at the newspaper had watched the video and had reached different conclusions. The children did not appear frightened but, instead, looked lost and confused—as if they had been asked to solve a calculus problem and were staring at five multiple-choice answers.

When Plas and Facinelli met with Andy Young, Young remained committed to running their story. To give the prosecutor his due, the *Chronicle* would also publish the prosecutor's statement in its entirety.

By keeping the story in the public's eye, Facinelli hoped that he could change more than public opinion. He was convinced that the defendants were entitled to a new trial where the evidence, both old and new, could be analyzed by another jury. But was it realistic to think that these articles could lead to that result? That still seemed extremely unlikely.

May 11, 1998

The phone rang and Facinelli picked up the receiver. On the other end was a law clerk for attorney Brent English, a Cleveland lawyer specializing in defamation cases. A year earlier, Facinelli had been chosen to receive an award from the Association for Women in Communications for his investigative series on the Head Start case. When the *Chronicle* had reported on this honor, Rosenbaum had written to the group, telling it that Facinelli's articles "subverted the truth and [did] a tremendous disservice to victims of sex crimes, to those concerned with bringing sexual offenders to justice, to children, and to the entire criminal justice system." After questioning Facinelli's ethics, Rosenbaum had asked the organization to reconsider its decision.

The organization had delayed giving the award to Facinelli while it reviewed Rosenbaum's claims but had eventually bestowed the award on him. Facinelli had felt humiliated and angry about Rosenbaum's letter and contacted the defamation lawyer in order to explore his options. That had been months ago, and Facinelli had, to this point, been unsure about what he would do.

"You have one year to file a defamation lawsuit or else it's barred by the statute of limitations," the clerk explained. "The one-year time limit expires today. If you're going to sue Mr. Rosenbaum, we must file the lawsuit today."

Throughout his career, Facinelli had weathered criticism from upset readers, but Rosenbaum's letter to the Women in Communications had stung him like no other. "I'm going to talk to my wife and I'll get back to you within an hour." After discussing the lawsuit with her, he authorized the lawyer to file the lawsuit.

It was an unusual move. Once journalists filed a critical piece, they could expect angry denials and an occasional personal attack in response. It was an unwritten rule that journalists were required to stay above the fray and ignore criticism, regardless of how offensive or unwarranted it seemed.

Facinelli did not alert his editors at the *Chronicle* about his decision to file the lawsuit. When he arrived at the newspaper the following day, he was unable to log into his computer. A few hours later, he was summoned to a meeting with his editors and the publisher of the paper. Facinelli feared the worst.

The newspaper's publisher, Cooper Hudnutt, took the lead during the meeting. He told Facinelli that by filing the lawsuit, Facinelli had undermined his own objectivity and compromised the impartiality of the newspaper.

"We're calling for your resignation," Hudnutt said.

For over twelve years, Facinelli had worked at the *Chronicle*. He loved his job and desperately wanted to save it. He offered to withdraw the lawsuit, take a leave of absence, or forfeit his paycheck for a period of time. However, the publisher believed that Facinelli had crossed a line that required immediate severance from the newspaper. Refusing to resign, Facinelli told the group that if they wanted him to leave, they'd have to fire him. And that is what happened.

Over the coming years, Facinelli's lawsuit would eventually play itself out. Defended by the county's insurance company, Rosenbaum filed a counterclaim, alleging that he'd been defamed by the *Chronicle*'s series. Later, the trial court granted Rosenbaum's motion for summary judgment when Facinelli could not prove that Rosenbaum's statements had caused him any definite monetary losses. An appeal followed. The parties eventually agreed to dismiss their cases against one another with prejudice, meaning that neither could refile a claim in the future. However, Rosenbaum demanded that Facinelli and the newspaper agree in writing that the news articles published in the *Chronicle* "had portrayed an unbalanced and distorted picture by omitting many of the facts favorable to the prosecution or supporting the convictions in those cases." In the end, the official dismissal entry included that language.

Almost lost in this legal tussle was the fact that Nancy Smith and Joseph Allen remained in prison with no hope of a new trial. It was just as Marge Bronson had predicted years earlier, when Nina struggled to identify Joseph Allen in the lineup and Bronson told her daughter, "We're going to put him in jail and throw away the key."

Facinelli's articles had shone a light on the Head Start guilty verdicts, enveloping them in doubt and skepticism. Although those with entrenched views had not been swayed, others had. His impassioned effort had eventually cost him his job, but he had opened eyes and caused people to question. And wasn't that a journalist's highest calling?

PART
THREE

CHAPTER 31
THE CIVIL CASE
JULY 23, 1996
TWO YEARS AFTER CONVICTION

William Thomas Locke stared at the lawsuit papers and was not surprised. As the executive director of the Lorain County Community Action Agency, the organization that oversaw the operation of the Lorain County Head Start program, he'd been expecting this for nearly two years. He'd always suspected that the parents who'd accused Nancy Smith were driven by one thing—money. From his perspective, this lawsuit was further proof of that motive.

He'd never believed that Nancy Smith or Joseph Allen had molested any of the Head Start children. The allegations were too incredible for any sane person to believe. And after the verdicts, he did not keep these comments to himself. He'd told reporters that it was impossible for any Head Start student to have been secreted away from the school as alleged by the police and prosecution. He claimed that the bus mileage records showed that Smith had not deviated from her route. Likewise, he was convinced that the teachers had kept the children safe by meeting the buses at the time their students arrived. To top it off, they had employed bus aides, making it virtually impossible for a bus driver to be alone with the preschoolers. Never one to mince words, Locke had said that he was appalled by the jury's verdict.

Those statements had drawn the outrage of Head Start parents and prompted an editorial in the *Morning Journal* calling for his resignation. The Lorain-based newspaper had called his continued protestation about the defendants' innocence a "slap in the face to the people of Lorain County." The newspaper declared its confidence in the unanimous verdict and commended the efforts of Prosecutor Rosenbaum and the Lorain police. Patting itself on the back, the paper had claimed that the police investigation had been lackluster until the "parents turned to this newspaper for help." The county's other newspaper, the *Chronicle*, also criticized him, its editorial admonishing him for his failure to accept the "Allen-Smith verdict" because, unlike him, that jury had heard "all the evidence and found it compelling."

As Locke considered the lambasting he'd received two years earlier, he silently seethed. As a black man who'd lived in Tennessee for the first eleven years of his life, Locke did not share the white editors' confidence in the jury system. In his experience, white jurors either held openly hostile views toward black people or were influenced by subconscious biases that highjacked their objectivity when judging a person of color. The white jurors in the Head Start case had been asked to judge a black defendant who was allegedly dating a white woman. Of the four alleged victims, three were white. Could a predominately all-white jury render justice in this case? He doubted it.

His hands shook with anger as he read through the allegations in the lawsuit. The plaintiffs, three Head Start children and their parents, claimed that they were entitled to twenty million dollars in damages from his agency, Head Start, Nancy Smith, and Joseph Allen. They alleged that Smith and Allen had raped and molested the children while the Lorain County Community Action Agency and Head Start had been negligent in hiring, supervising, and retaining Nancy Smith, making them liable for the harms that Smith and Allen had caused.

Locke tried to regain his composure. He told himself that the two social agencies carried liability insurance that would provide them with a defense and pay a judgment if it came to that. However, he also realized that they had been sued for amounts that exceeded the amount of their coverage. He also knew that another lawsuit was probably in the offing—one likely to be filed on behalf of the fourth alleged child victim.

Nobody had told him that running an agency like this would be easy. Ever since Locke had taken over as director in 1988, there always seemed to be a crisis in progress or looming ahead. Although he answered to a board, he also had to placate politicians and Head Start parents, who frequently criticized his decisions and, on one occasion, had attempted to wrest control of the program from him.

His next step would be a simple one. His secretary would fax the complaint to Nationwide Mutual Insurance Company, the company that insured his nonprofit agency and Head Start. He knew the routine. The insurance company's brain trust would review the complaint and assign a law firm to defend them. If past experience was any guide, he expected the lawsuit to drag on for years.

August 5, 1996

After just a few minutes on the phone, Locke was reassured that the Lorain County Community Action Agency was in good hands. The young man on the other end was Dan Jaffe, an attorney with the law firm of Squire, Sanders & Dempsey, who along with others would defend both LCCAA and Head Start. Locke admired the way Jaffe could explain legal concepts in everyday language.

"We're the ones with the deep pockets, so I know that's why we were sued," Locke said. "But why'd they sue Smith and Allen? I mean, those two are in prison and have no assets."

Jaffe cleared his throat. "That's all true, but the plaintiffs want Smith and Allen to be included for strategic reasons even if they're locked away in prison. They want the jury to know about their criminal convictions, and if they're part of the lawsuit, it's easier to get that information before the jury."

"But the criminal case didn't make any findings against us," Locke protested.

"I know. That's one of our biggest problems. When the time comes for trial, I'll ask for separate trials. We don't want to be painted with the same brush as those two. But even if that fails, we can ask the judge to keep anyone from mentioning the criminal convictions during the trial. In legalese, it's called a motion in limine."

"You can do that?" Locke asked.

"I'm not saying that the judge will grant the motion, but we have a basis for it. Those convictions are extremely prejudicial and have nothing to do with whether Head Start was negligent in hiring or supervising Nancy Smith. And that's the issue as it relates to us."

Locke, too, didn't want to get mired in legal gobbledygook. "Can I speak frankly here?" he asked, his eight-year stint in the military influencing his choice of words.

"Of course."

"These claims are pure bullshit. I hope to God that Nationwide isn't planning to pay these people anything."

Jaffe did not immediately respond. "Well, I don't control their decision-making on this case. I can't guarantee anything. I wish I could."

Locke heard hesitation in Jaffe's voice and he decided to press him. "What does that mean?"

"Let's back up for a minute. We will do everything in our power to defeat these claims. We'll take depositions of everyone involved. We'll look at records. We'll hire a psychiatrist to evaluate the children's medical issues. We'll—"

"What can a psychiatrist do?" Locke interrupted.

"A psychiatrist can examine the medical records and evaluate the children through a psychological interview. I don't want to get too far ahead of myself here, but there's a possibility that a psychiatrist can tell us whether these children's original stories were reliable."

"So you're going to look at everything, right?"

"Everything."

"That's good. That's real good."

"Our plan is to get the case knocked out before it ever gets to trial."

Locke tried to keep the excitement from his voice. "Do you think you can actually do that?"

"I've done some preliminary research. Other than a few exceptions, governmental agencies are immune from civil lawsuits. Your agency receives almost all of its funding from state and federal sources. You're also required to have certain elected officials on your board. We'll argue that the Lorain County Community Action Agency is governmental in nature and should be entitled to immunity."

Locke took a deep breath. That was the best news he'd heard since the lawsuit had been filed. "What are our chances of getting it dismissed that way?"

Again, Jaffe paused a few seconds before answering. "I don't want to speculate on that. Let's just say that we've got a good chance and leave it at that."

Now it was Locke's turn to pause as he digested Jaffe's remark. "This is not a sure thing, is it?"

"No."

"What's Plan B then?"

"That's simple. The claims against LCCAA and Head Start are based on negligence. That means your employees had to be careless for hiring Nancy Smith or not supervising her properly. We know that she had no criminal record at the time that you hired her. Nothing to alert you that she had a propensity to molest children—so you weren't negligent in hiring her. Now, as for supervising her, if you had safeguards in place and had no reason to suspect that they weren't being followed, then you weren't negligent in that regard either."

"But jurors can ignore evidence. They can decide cases based on emotion and sympathy."

"That's the danger we face in this case," Jaffe said. "It's a problem that defense attorneys confront all the time."

As Jaffe's words sunk in, Locke remembered a letter that he'd received from the insurance company. "One last thing before we hang up—Nationwide sent us a letter telling us that our insurance doesn't cover the punitive damage claim. You know, the plaintiffs are seeking ten million dollars in punitive damages. That scares us. Nationwide also wrote that we might want to hire our own attorney to oversee our personal exposure in the case. Do we need to do that?"

"I can't really tell you what to do about that. Let's just say it wouldn't hurt to have your own attorney reviewing developments and advising you accordingly. We'll still do the work, but your attorney can review everything and make recommendations to you."

After the call ended, Locke pushed the suit papers away from him. One jury had already shocked him and damaged Head Start's standing and reputation in the community. Neither he nor the Head Start program could afford any more missteps. He'd involve the agency's personal attorney, Dennis O'Toole.

O'Toole was a forty-seven-year-old Lorain attorney who'd caught Locke's eye when he had represented the Lorain Metropolitan Housing Authority, another agency serving Lorain's impoverished community. He'd liked O'Toole from the start—an attorney he viewed as practical, personable, and street-smart. The man's winning smile could be deceiving. If he believed he had a strong case, he would not compromise for expediency. On the other hand, when clients had a losing case and needed to resolve the matter, he would let them know immediately. In sum, Locke trusted him.

And it wasn't just because of his legal knowledge. Locke knew a little about O'Toole's background. Although O'Toole's father was an attorney, he had not financed his son's legal education, refusing to loan him the money for law school. "Do I look like a bank to you?" he had told him. As a result, O'Toole had worked road construction jobs and sold furniture in order to pay for his legal education. About a year after O'Toole had passed the bar and joined his father's firm, the elder O'Toole passed away. Locke admired people like O'Toole, who'd been forced to fend for themselves and had succeeded.

Locke reached O'Toole by phone later in the afternoon. As the personal counsel for the agency, O'Toole was well aware of the allegations that had led to Nancy Smith's conviction. He'd told Locke to fully cooperate with the police and the prosecutor's office. Locke's employees had done just that, turning over records and meeting with the police whenever asked.

"I want you to be my eyes and ears about this case," Locke began. "You know how I feel about the criminal case. I've never believed that any of these things happened, and I don't want these parents to profit from this."

"How involved do you want me to be?" O'Toole asked.

"I want you to attend every deposition and hearing. I need you to review pleadings. I expect you to provide me with updates every couple of months, or sooner if something important occurs."

"All right. I can do that."

"I want you, not an associate, to monitor this case."

"I understand. It'll be my case and my primary responsibility. I may need to send an associate in rare instances when I have a conflict. Is that okay?"

"That works."

After Locke summarized his recent conversation with Dan Jaffe, the two ended the phone call. Returning to his desk work, Locke tried to review a grant seeking more funding for the Meals on Wheels program. After a few minutes, he gave up, his mind drifting to the civil lawsuit. How long would his energies be diverted by this case? If someone had told him that it would drag on for seven more years, he wouldn't have believed them. But that was his future.

CHAPTER 32
ATTORNEY DENNIS O'TOOLE
AUGUST 7, 1998
FOUR YEARS AFTER CONVICTION

"I already answered that question. Do you need a hearing aid?" the witness snapped.

"Here's how it works, Ms. Powell. This is your deposition," Dan Jaffe said, his voice calm after almost two hours of questioning. "You've taken an oath to answer my questions truthfully. In this proceeding, you're not permitted to ask me a question. And if I ask you a question in a slightly different form, you must answer it. Let's try it again: Did you read your affidavit before you signed it?"

Dennis O'Toole smiled inwardly as he watched his co-counsel, Dan Jaffe, wrestle with this most uncooperative witness, Elizabeth "Angel" Powell, who over the last few hours had not lived up to her nickname. The former Head Start bus driver and bus aide was more openly hostile toward Nancy Smith today than she'd been in the criminal trial four years ago. Several months earlier, she'd defied a subpoena and failed to show for her deposition. After that, she'd attempted to evade a process server, and this afternoon, she'd delayed the start of her deposition for over an hour while several attorneys tried to convince her that she was legally bound to answer questions.

O'Toole had attended hundreds of depositions over the last twenty years, and during that time, he'd never seen a witness as difficult as

Angel Powell. On several occasions she'd refused to answer, claiming she'd answered the question earlier when she had not. Once, she'd declined to answer because, in her opinion, the information sought was not "relative." She'd used a litany of responses to stop Jaffe from gathering information, ranging from "None of your business" to "That's all you're getting" to "I'll tell you in court." She'd also asked for several breaks to regain her composure when, by her own admission, she'd caught herself acting "cocky."

And there was nothing Jaffe or O'Toole could do to force her to answer. Unlike the courtroom, where the judge ruled instantly on objections and could compel a witness to respond, depositions were conducted without a judge. It meant that the attorneys and witnesses were on their own and had to find their own solutions when they disagreed. If a serious impasse occurred, an attorney could always file a motion with the judge for a resolution, but this could delay things for weeks, sometimes months. For that reason, the attorney asking the disputed question usually moved on to another topic, but not until both sides had squawked and postured "for the record."

O'Toole watched as Jaffe flipped a page on his legal pad to begin another line of inquiry. In keeping with his promise to William Locke, O'Toole had personally attended over twenty-five depositions in the Head Start civil litigation. From time to time, he'd ask some questions, but for the most part, he'd allowed Jaffe to take the lead. Although O'Toole was the more experienced trial lawyer, Jaffe was very organized, extremely well prepared, and tenacious. For those reasons, O'Toole was content to defer to the younger attorney. They almost always agreed on strategy, and their evaluation of witnesses rarely differed.

As they'd uncovered more and more of the factual underpinnings of the alleged events, they'd become convinced that neither Smith nor Allen had molested any Head Start children. When they'd compared the children's initial statements given to the police with their eventual trial testimony, they'd been shocked at the inconsistencies and changes. And now, four years later, their stories were still evolving.

Several months before, they'd deposed nine-year-old Nina Zorich. To their surprise, she now claimed that Nancy Smith had not left some of the children on the bus and then driven them to Joseph's house. Instead, she'd testified that Nancy had entered the school when she and her classmates were in gym and had taken several of them away, despite the presence of a teacher. When they returned to the school an hour or so later, Nancy instructed them to tell their teacher that they'd left for ice cream.

Marcus Logan now claimed that, on some occasions, his bus aide had left the bus before all of the children had exited. This had allowed Nancy Smith to take the remaining children to Joseph's home without the aide's knowledge. To Jaffe and O'Toole, both children's stories seemed inconceivable.

O'Toole returned his attention to Angel Powell. She was now railing against the Head Start management, particularly Glen Thaler, for granting Nancy Smith preferential treatment, and, in particular, not requiring her to have another adult on the bus with her at all times.

"How often did this happen?" Jaffe asked.

"It happened every day, every day after I started to complain. I told you that earlier. You need to start writing some notes down to remind yourself," she said, shaking her head in exasperation.

O'Toole knew that the most important questions were still to come. Jaffe had not yet asked Powell about the alleged incident involving Joseph Allen on Nancy Smith's bus. At the criminal trial, Powell had testified that Smith had stopped at a store to buy a soft drink, that Joseph Allen had attempted to board the bus, and that she'd repelled him with a tire iron. This story had even greater significance in the civil case because Powell claimed that she'd reported the incident to Glen Thaler, Head Start's transportation director. Because of this, the plaintiffs maintained that Smith's employers (LCCAA and Head Start) had been on notice that she was a rogue employee and she should have been fired or monitored more closely. Because her employers did neither, the plaintiffs claimed that they were negligent and responsible for what happened to the children.

Unbeknownst to Powell, Jaffe had secured a copy of her initial, two-hour taped interview with the police. In it, Powell had talked about the incident involving a strange black man who'd attempted to board the bus. At that time, she'd described him as a black male with a receding hairline. She'd also admitted that she'd later learned that the man was the father of one of the children, Cameron Taylor. In the tape, she acknowledged that the man had attempted to peek inside the bus to discover whether his son had boarded the bus that day.

Jaffe asked Powell to once again describe what had happened after Smith had gone into the store to purchase a soft drink. As she'd done at trial, Powell told of the harrowing attempt by Joseph Allen to enter the bus and how the children had screamed in terror and urged her to batter him with the tire iron. After she'd forced him off the bus, he'd later emerged from the store with Nancy Smith, arm in arm.

Turning to her first interview with the police, Jaffe confirmed with Powell that she had answered all of the detective's questions truthfully.

"Did you tell the detective that this man was Cameron Taylor's father?"

"I don't believe so. Also, I don't remember, so you need to listen to the tape."

"Did you tell the detective that the man was balding?"

"Don't remember."

"Did you also tell him that you hadn't met Cameron Taylor's father before that?"

"I don't remember."

Jaffe stood. "I want to go off the record and I will be right back."

When he returned, he carried a cassette tape deck and a cassette. After setting them on the table, he inserted the cassette into the machine. "Ms. Powell, I'm going to play for you a portion of your taped interview with police and I want you to tell me if you recognize your voice on the tape."

One of the plaintiffs' attorneys objected.

"I object too," Powell said, her face exhibiting both anger and surprise. "I don't want to hear it. We're not in the courtroom."

She glanced at the roomful of attorneys, apparently hoping one of the plaintiffs' attorneys would come to her rescue. When no one did, she said, "I'm taking a break. I'm not going to listen to the tape for two reasons. First, you didn't tell me you were going to bring it here, and second, we're not in a courtroom. So, if you want me to listen to the tape, I'm not going to. I'll sit out in the hall until tomorrow morning."

For the next few minutes, O'Toole and the other attorneys tried to explain to her that she was obligated to answer the questions and there was nothing improper about asking her to listen to the tape and identify her voice.

"Okay then. I want it to start at the beginning," Powell said. She then pointed a finger at Jaffe. "He might have cued up to some little bullshit on the tape and I don't want to hear that. Start it at the beginning. I'll tell you if that's my voice and then he can shut it off."

Thinking that the witness wanted to listen to the entire tape, one of the plaintiffs' attorneys said, "We might be here for three hours."

Sensing an advantage, Powell's face became animated. "We can be here until tomorrow morning. I have nothing to do today or tomorrow. I'll spend my day here. I don't care." She looked about the room, making eye contact with all of the attorneys except Jaffe, trying to gauge the effect of her threat.

Believing that the deposition was at a breaking point, O'Toole decided to weigh in. "Mr. Jaffe may ask questions differently than the other attorneys here, but each attorney is entitled to conduct the deposition in any manner he or she wants."

"I feel like I'm being badgered by Mr. Jaffe and I do feel like he's picking on me."

"You have every right to hire your own attorney if you want," O'Toole said.

"Everybody is treating me like I have no rights and I don't like that," Powell said.

"I think all the lawyers here just want to get through this—"

Powell interrupted O'Toole. "Did my rights stop four years ago when I took the stand and told my story to the judge and jury? That's the way it looks to me. That's when I lost all my rights."

O'Toole had seen witnesses behave this way before. When cornered, they'd lash out and play the martyr in an attempt to evade answering a question.

"Mr. Jaffe is going to give you a chance to explain your comments to the police," one of the plaintiffs' attorneys interjected.

"I think we need to stop this deposition until I get an attorney," Powell said.

For the next several minutes, Powell bantered with the attorneys. At first, she asked only to listen to the beginning of the tape to identify her voice. Anything more, she claimed, would allow Jaffe to cherry-pick parts of the interview out of context. "He's not going to give me these jerk-off questions like he's been doing all afternoon."

"I'd be happy to start at the beginning of the tape, but I don't think it makes sense for all of us to listen to it for two hours," Jaffe offered.

Hearing Jaffe's voice seemed to increase Powell's level of stress. "We're not going to play this tape," she said defiantly. "I'm going to walk out the door. When I come back—this time with a lawyer—we can go through this bullshit all again."

Ignoring her threat, Jaffe said, "Here's what I'm going to do. I'm going to play a specific part of the tape."

Powell thrust her fingers in her ears. "Go ahead and play it. I'm going to sit here with my fingers in my ears."

As Jaffe's hand edged toward the play button, Powell stood abruptly and rushed from the room. Turning to the court reporter, Jaffe stated, "Let the record reflect that the witness has left the room with her fingers in her ears and singing, 'La, la, la, la, la.'"

O'Toole and Jaffe exchanged knowing glances. How could anyone be convicted of a crime when part of the prosecution's case depended on a witness like this?

"I'll talk to her," O'Toole told the other attorneys. One of the plaintiffs' attorneys, volunteered to go with him.

About fifteen minutes later, they returned with Powell in tow, and despite the sullen expression on her face, she had agreed to listen to selected portions of the tape and respond to questions. After the first segment was played, she admitted that she could identify her voice but claimed that because of static, she could not understand most of the words. Listening to the same audio, O'Toole had heard Ms. Powell tell the detective that she thought the man who'd tried to board the bus was Cameron Taylor's father.

Undaunted, Jaffe played Powell another portion of the tape in which she described the man as having a receding hairline—a description that did not match Joseph Allen. Again, she insisted that the tape was too muffled for her to understand her words. This thrust and parry continued for the next ten minutes as Jaffe played parts of the tape and Powell maintained that she could not decipher the words.

Jaffe eventually moved on to another subject—Powell's two lie detector tests. "Now, I understand that you did take a lie detector test as part of the police investigation."

"It's not admissible, you said so yourself, so I'm not going to answer any questions about it."

"When you took the lie detector test—"

Turning to several of the plaintiffs' attorneys, Powell said, "I refuse to answer his question. He can sit there until he turns purple for all I care."

"It's getting very late and I don't intend to turn purple," Jaffe said. "I would suggest that we just reconvene the deposition in front of the judge because the witness is not being cooperative."

"I've been cooperative," Powell said. "You're just being a jerk."

"Let's take a one-minute break and let's talk," O'Toole said.

A few minutes later, the deposition reconvened, but the truce did not last. After another twenty minutes of spirited back-and-forth, Jaffe stopped the deposition. He told Powell that he would file a motion with the judge, Edward Zaleski, to have him supervise the deposition when it restarted at a future date.

It was well past seven o'clock when Powell and the plaintiffs' attorneys vacated the meeting room at O'Toole's office. When the room had cleared, O'Toole looked at Jaffe and raised his eyebrows.

"Well, that was interesting," O'Toole said.

"A jury will never believe anything she says," Jaffe replied. "But, of course, that's irrelevant when we're trying to get this case knocked out in a summary judgment motion."

O'Toole nodded. To prevail in a summary judgment, the judge was required to construe the evidence most strongly in favor of the party against whom the motion was directed. When they filed their motion, the judge would be obligated to view Powell's current story as true and disregard any inconsistencies between it and her earlier police statement. "It hardly seems fair," O'Toole said.

"I still think we can win our motion," Jaffe said. "We have a solid argument about governmental immunity. And if the court doesn't agree with us on that, we can still show that there's insufficient evidence to prove negligence. Even if everything Powell says is treated as true, our clients had no reason to suspect that Smith would intentionally hurt children. Yes, Nancy Smith broke some Head Start bus rules, but so what? It doesn't suggest that she might later commit crimes against these children. Breaking procedural rules and molesting children are two very different things."

"If she did molest any children, and I don't believe that she did," O'Toole added.

"I know," Jaffe said.

CHAPTER 33
THE PRISON VISIT

OCTOBER 25, 1998
FOUR YEARS AFTER CONVICTION

"Want to stick around for me, baby?" the prisoner called. "I'll be back in a couple of hours and then let's have some fun." O'Toole looked away from the group of ten or so women standing in the vestibule. They'd appeared just moments after O'Toole had walked through the prison's front entrance. Several were taking great pleasure in greeting him with lewd comments and outright propositions. Each comment was accompanied by laughter and derisive hoots from the other women—all of which was unnerving.

O'Toole did his best to ignore them, but he suspected that his embarrassment was apparent. Despite his attempt to look impassive, his face had reddened and his forehead was beaded with perspiration. He glanced at one of the guards, a heavyset woman in her forties who stood with her hands on her hips. She met O'Toole's eyes and smiled, apparently enjoying his discomfiture. A few moments later, another guard walked up to her and whispered something in her ear.

"Okay, women. You've had your amusement. The bus is here. Now line up and be quiet," the first guard said.

A minute later, the prisoners were gone. By then, O'Toole had checked in at the administrative office and was being led to an attorney-client conference room to meet with Nancy Smith.

He'd volunteered for this assignment several weeks before. The plaintiffs had filed a motion to take the depositions of both Nancy Smith and Joseph Allen. After the motion had been granted, the defense team had decided that one of them needed to talk to her about the deposition and discuss the questions that would likely be asked. In particular, they needed to know how she would respond to queries about the Head Start procedures regarding bus drivers and whether she'd followed them. It was a given that she'd be questioned about molesting the children and her relationship with Allen, but her answers regarding supervision would be critical to their efforts to get the case dismissed against LCCAA and Head Start.

Before O'Toole had left home that morning, he'd told his wife that he'd drawn the "short straw" and would be meeting with Smith in prison that day. She'd asked why he hadn't assigned this interview to one of the firm's younger associates. He'd shrugged before he'd kissed her goodbye.

The truth was O'Toole was curious. As a lawyer, he'd made his living by reading people: clients, witnesses, jurors, and even other attorneys. Over the years, he'd learned how to recognize deceit in its many forms, from blatant lies to half-truths to everything in between. In fact, he thought he was pretty damn good at it.

And that's why this meeting with Smith had piqued his interest. The children's stories, the police investigation, and the prosecution narrative were fraught with inconsistencies. Simply put, none of it made sense. He needed to talk to this woman, one-on-one, and carefully observe her demeanor—and that meant eye contact, facial expressions, and body language.

For most of the two-and-a-half-hour drive to the Ohio Reformatory for Women in Marysville, Ohio, he'd thought almost exclusively about the Head Start case. However, as he'd neared the prison, his mind had drifted to the two criminal trials that had initiated his legal career. The day after he'd been sworn in as an attorney, Judge Leroy Kelly had appointed him to defend a man accused of selling marijuana to an undercover agent. Because his client had been caught red-handed, he hadn't stood a chance. However, he'd been a quick learner, gaining an acquittal on his second trial—this time for a man accused of rape. But if these early criminal cases had taught him one thing, it was that he didn't want to earn his living this way. Instead, he'd developed his expertise in civil law, where his clients were more reputable and the work was less stressful. But here he was twenty years later, on his way to a prison to meet with an inmate.

Those had been his thoughts earlier that morning. As he followed the guard to the meeting room, he took in the dismal interior of the prison. From the outside, the building could have been part of a college campus, but the empty halls and barred windows reminded him where he was. He was escorted to a small meeting room, where he took a seat and surveyed the gray, windowless walls. He set his briefcase on a wooden table, opened it, and shoved it away, adding another scratch to the table's marred surface. The room's stale air smelled of cigarettes and body odor.

As he waited for Smith, he wondered what she would be like after four years in prison. He would not fault her if she was embittered, angry, or sullen. Perhaps she even blamed his clients for not helping enough during her criminal defense, though that seemed unlikely. Except for Angel Powell, the Head Start administrators and her coworkers had uniformly offered their support. After the jury rendered its verdict, William Locke had publicly expressed outrage at its decision.

O'Toole's thoughts were interrupted by a knock on the door. It opened and a woman guard peered in. A moment later, she ushered Smith into the room.

"I'll be outside if you need me," she said before she closed the door.

Dressed in a light blue denim shirt and dark blue jeans, Smith took the seat opposite him. Unlike O'Toole, she appeared relaxed and calm.

"I didn't need to read your letter to know why you are here," she began. "I receive all of the filings in the civil case."

Because she was representing herself in the civil case, the attorneys and judge were required to send her every pleading and journal entry. If she'd read those documents, she'd be aware of the most important developments in the case. And it appeared that she had.

"Then you know that the plaintiffs will soon be taking your deposition," O'Toole said.

Smith nodded. "And I will help you in any way possible."

O'Toole exhaled a deep breath and nodded. Before he could say anything, Smith continued, "I want you to know from the start that I did not touch any of those children. The charges against me were false. Totally false."

O'Toole nodded again.

"I would never hurt a child. I am a mother of four children. I could never have done those horrible things," she said. Over the next few minutes, she told O'Toole about all of the safeguards that were in place—precautions that made the prosecution's case border on the impossible. O'Toole knew all of the details, but he used this time to study Smith as she spoke, not bothering to write notes on his legal pad.

Smith had spoken with conviction and had looked him straight in the eyes when she'd insisted on her innocence. O'Toole had seen nothing in her manner that evinced deception, but he would defer his final judgment until they'd talked more.

For the next half hour, O'Toole asked about Head Start's rules and practices. They discussed the orientation sessions prior to her start, her job application references, and her unblemished criminal record at the time she was hired. Smith confirmed the practices Locke and his assistants had outlined for O'Toole earlier but told him other things too—how she'd done a practice run of the route with a Head Start supervisor before school had started, how they'd evaluated her driving skills from time to time, and the names of Head Start parents who'd ridden on her bus over the years.

As he talked with Smith, he could see that she was polite, articulate, and composed. Other than her initial claim of innocence, she hadn't strayed from answering his questions. Also, to her credit, she hadn't sought his sympathy, nor had she lashed out at anyone.

When they'd finished discussing issues related to her deposition, O'Toole asked her about the status of any further appeals. The previous year an attorney from Columbus had filed a petition to vacate or set aside her conviction, alleging constitutional violations and ineffective assistance of counsel. Judge McGough had denied the petition and the court of appeals had affirmed her decision.

"My attorneys tell me that we've exhausted all of the appeals. My only real chance to get out of here is parole, but that's not going to happen."

"Why is that?"

"I've been told that I have to admit to the crimes to have any chance for parole. The board won't consider releasing me if I'm still in denial about the crimes I supposedly committed."

O'Toole shook his head in sympathy.

"And I will not admit to crimes that I did not commit, even if that means I'll spend the rest of my life here," she said, her voice cracking for the first time.

O'Toole didn't know if he should respond with words of sympathy or encouragement; neither seemed adequate. Instead, he nodded and listened.

"Of course, I want desperately to be with my children. They need me. This is so difficult for them."

"I can't imagine," O'Toole answered.

"My youngest son is really struggling. He was twelve when I went to prison. I don't want to get into the details, but he needs some strong guidance. If I were with him, I know I could get him straightened out."

O'Toole realized that the prison sentence had ruined five lives—those of Nancy Smith and her four children—and perhaps more. Smith's sisters and brother had remained committed to her throughout her ordeal and, no doubt, were suffering for her. He'd always believed that the criminal justice system was designed to prevent wrongful convictions, but he was seeing firsthand that it didn't always happen. This family had been torn apart by a miscarriage of justice, but he was powerless to change that.

"I'm hoping that if I'm a model prisoner, I'll be released sooner."

"I would think so," he answered.

"Prison life doesn't really get easier over time, but I'm doing what I can to learn and grow. I've recommitted to my Catholic faith and I'm taking advantage of courses that interest me."

For the next few minutes, Smith told him about prison life and the ways she was coping. Despite the injustice of her situation, she'd found solace in her religion, serving as an assistant to the priest, routinely helping him prepare for communion. As a former floral assistant, she'd also completed a prison course in horticulture and was now assisting the instructor in teaching that course. A few months earlier, she'd learned the basics of watercolor painting.

Her children and siblings continued to visit as often as their schedules allowed. Although Smith had maintained a brave face throughout the meeting, she fought back tears as she talked about these visits. "I cry myself to sleep every night," she said. "That part doesn't get any easier."

After an hour, the guard knocked on the door. It was time to end the meeting.

As O'Toole walked through the prison's empty vestibule, he thought about what he'd learned that day. If he was any judge of people and their character, he had his answer. This woman had committed no crimes. She had molested no children. But he also realized that this was just part of what he'd discovered that day. He'd met a woman who showed strength and courage in the face of crippling injustice. And that was something he'd never forget.

CHAPTER 34
THE SETTLEMENT

MAY 21, 2003
NINE YEARS AFTER CONVICTION

From the tone of Dan Jaffe's voice, O'Toole suspected that bad news would soon follow. After they'd exchanged pleasantries, Jaffe cleared his throat. "Well, here's the reason for the phone call, and I know you won't be happy about this."

O'Toole knew what was coming. "Okay, how much?" he asked.

"Nationwide has agreed to pay each plaintiff one and a half million dollars," Jaffe said.

O'Toole didn't reply. It was a shock, but then again, it wasn't. He'd been aware that Nationwide had been negotiating with the plaintiffs' attorneys over the last few months, but he'd never expected that the insurance company would pay that kind of money on this case.

"It was a business decision, plain and simple," Jaffe explained.

"Explain it to me," O'Toole replied.

"Although you and I believe we could win this case at trial, the claims committee was not so sure. And if we lost, the verdicts would have been enormous. They didn't want to take that chance."

O'Toole was still shocked. He knew that insurance companies made decisions that defied logic—refusing to honor bona fide claims and paying others that had questionable merit. Why had Nationwide spent thousands of dollars in attorney and expert fees for seven years only to capitulate in the end? He and Jaffe had uncovered major inconsistencies and alterations in the children's stories. They'd hired a forensic psychiatrist from the Cleveland Clinic to examine each of the four children and review the police investigation and the children's prior statements. That psychiatrist, Kathleen Quinn, had concluded that the initial interviews had been tainted and, as a result, the children's accounts were unreliable.

Unlike the defense attorneys in the criminal trial, he and Jaffe would not have been surprised by anything the plaintiffs presented at trial and would have discredited the plaintiffs' witnesses through grueling cross-examinations. They were more than ready to try the case.

"We could have made them look silly," O'Toole lamented.

"Here is what concerned the claims people," Jaffe said, sidestepping O'Toole's assertion. "The jury would have learned that Nancy Smith and Joseph Allen had been convicted of sexually molesting these children and every appeal on those convictions had been rejected. We would have been forced to argue that the criminal justice system somehow got this all wrong. They weren't confident that we could do that."

O'Toole did not respond immediately, allowing the explanation to sink in. Technically, he and Jaffe did not have to prove Smith's innocence, only that their clients had no reason to suspect that Smith would molest children under her care. On the other hand, he realized that a jury, horrified by the crimes, would feel compelled to hold someone responsible. And it was just a small jump to conclude that someone at Head Start had failed to recognize the warning signs.

He understood why Nationwide was unwilling to gamble on a trial. Yet, if it was always the company's intention to settle before the case reached the courtroom, why resolve the matter now? They'd had an ideal opportunity to do that several years ago when they'd held a definite advantage.

Five years earlier, the trial court had granted their motion for summary judgment, finding that the Lorain County Community Action Agency was a governmental entity and entitled to immunity. In addition, Head Start was not a separate legal entity but just an extension of LCCAA. The judge in the case, Judge Edward Zaleski, had never ruled on the second part of their motion—that their clients were not negligent based on the undisputed facts. However, when Judge Zaleski concluded that they had immunity, both LCCAA and Head Start were dismissed from the lawsuit. The plaintiffs immediately appealed this decision to the Ohio Ninth District Court of Appeals.

O'Toole had believed that the immunity defense was a shaky one. The time to sue for peace was when this issue was pending in the court of appeals, when the plaintiffs were not sure if their claims would ultimately be allowed to proceed. That opportunity had been lost after the court of appeals had reversed Judge Zaleski's ruling, finding that LCCAA was a nonprofit corporation, not a political entity, not entitled to immunity, and sent the case back to Judge Zaleski for further proceedings.

"If Nationwide was afraid to let this case go to a jury, why didn't they try to settle the case when the case was in the court of appeals? The plaintiffs would have probably jumped at any offer," O'Toole said.

"Well, that's easy to say in hindsight," Jaffe replied, again deflecting blame away from Nationwide. "After we lost in the court of appeals, my orders were to refile the motion and force the trial court to rule on the negligence issue."

Jaffe had done just that. Again, he'd argued that their clients were not negligent because they had no reason to believe that Nancy Smith had any propensity to commit crimes.

The plaintiffs' attorneys had responded tenaciously. They'd focused on the Head Start rules that were either ignored or inadequate. A former bus supervisor provided an affidavit that it was the bus driver's responsibility to radio the office if they did not have an aide when the bus left the depot. If a driver did not notify the office, the bus would be without an adult aide—something they implied had occurred repeatedly with Smith.

They relied on Angel Powell's testimony that Smith made unauthorized stops and cursed at the children, many of whom seemed afraid of her. They'd also recycled Powell's story that Joseph Allen had attempted to enter the Head Start bus with Smith's blessing—something she'd reported to Glen Thaler, who'd failed to take appropriate action.

When questioned, none of the Head Start hierarchy could point to any procedures that could prevent a bus driver from dropping off a student at some place other than the school. Although it was based solely on his recollection four years after the events, Marcus Logan had signed an affidavit that once the bus arrived at the school, the bus aide often left before all the children had exited. The plaintiffs had also hired a safety "expert" who, upon review of all of the depositions, had concluded that LCCAA and Head Start were negligent.

Jaffe had filed a reply brief, gamely arguing that neither the breach of Head Start rules nor the episode described by Powell would have provided any notice that Nancy Smith was a potential child molester. He ridiculed the plaintiffs' arguments, characterizing them as requiring the Head Start management to be omnipotent with prophetic vision.

This time the trial court denied the motion, tersely concluding that it had found the defendants' arguments "unpersuasive." O'Toole realized that the judge's decision was probably more pragmatic than merit based. Judge Zaleski had been reversed once on this case when he'd found that LCCAA was a governmental entity and could not be sued. He did not want to be wrong and reversed a second time. The prudent and safer approach was to find that factual issues remained for a jury's determination, deny the motion, and allow the case to proceed to trial. Such a decision would ultimately put pressure on the defendants to settle the case, thus avoiding a trial that could last for weeks.

Three years had passed since Judge Zaleski had denied the defendants' motion to dismiss. Since then, the case had been set for trial numerous times, only to be repeatedly postponed. No longer willing to carry this potentially huge loss on its balance sheet, Nationwide had made its "business decision." The case was over and each of the four families would reap a very large financial reward.

As this realization set in, O'Toole thought of Smith and Allen in prison. Yes, justice was blind, but it could also be horribly subverted.

PART FOUR

CHAPTER 35

THE OHIO INNOCENCE PROJECT

JULY 25, 2006–FEBRUARY 21, 2007
TWELVE YEARS AFTER CONVICTION

F eeling a growing anxiety, the three women stopped talking as their car approached the entrance to the Ohio Reformatory for Women, where Nancy Smith was incarcerated. The three were all affiliated with the Ohio Innocence Project and had scheduled a visit with Smith. The trio was led by Jenny Carroll, the assistant director for the Ohio Innocence Project. The other two women were Whitney Sheff and Bobbi Madonna, second-year law students at the University of Cincinnati.

The Ohio Innocence Project, headquartered in Cincinnati, Ohio, was part of a nationwide network that championed the rights of the wrongfully convicted, seeking their release from prison and ultimate freedom. Ohio's only chapter was associated with the University of Cincinnati's law school and had been cofounded in 2003 by Mark Godsey, a former federal prosecutor who was now a member of the law school's faculty and a devoted wrongful-conviction activist. He and Carroll, a former public defender, were the Ohio Innocence Project's only attorneys. To spread the organization's reach, it hired eighteen UC law students each year to serve as fellows in the program. Sheff and Madonna were second-year law students and, like other fellows, were working as a pair on one case, an assignment that they'd have for the entire school year.

Sheff and Madonna had met in law school, become best friends, and together applied for fellowships at the Ohio Innocence Project at the completion of their first year. After their summer break started, they'd begun working there full-time, forty or more hours a week. Once classes resumed in the fall, they'd work there on a more limited basis.

They'd been attracted to the program for different reasons. Madonna hoped to become a prosecutor, while Sheff, who had Native American ancestry, had a keen interest in human rights. Both would be deeply changed by their involvement in the program and their interaction with Nancy Smith—enough so that Madonna would abandon her prosecutorial aspirations and seek a full-time position at the Innocence Project of Florida. But that was several years in the future.

"This will be difficult," Carroll reminded Sheff and Madonna as they walked toward the prison building. "Mark and I have visited many, many prisoners over the years, but none fills us with so much pain as Nancy. We feel her anguish."

Everyone at the Ohio Innocence Project was firmly convinced of Smith's innocence. Sheff and Madonna had quickly reached that same conclusion after reviewing the materials in Smith's file.

Carroll continued, "You can't imagine how agonizing this is for her. Back in 1994, she was a single mom raising four children, integrally involved in their lives. Then the impossible happened. She was sent to prison for crimes she didn't commit. Think about that. Suddenly, her children lose her in a miscarriage of justice. She's been their anchor and now she can't help them solve their problems and she can't share their joys. She is desperate to return and she sees us as her last chance. It's why she is so emotional when we meet with her."

What went unsaid was that the Ohio Innocence Project had reviewed Smith's case and determined that its chances of winning her exoneration were extremely slim. The court of appeals had found no irregularities during her trial and had affirmed the jury's verdict. The Ohio Supreme Court had refused to hear her appeal, something within its discretion. A few years later, a Columbus attorney had filed a petition for post-conviction relief claiming that her conviction should be vacated because of ineffective assistance of counsel and newly discovered evidence. From the vantage point of those in the Ohio Innocence Project, the brief had not been persuasive, not only in its organization and language, but in its failure to include enough supporting documentation. The court had denied Smith's petition, forever barring any further filings that raised the same arguments.

Because those avenues were now sealed, parole was the only possible path to Smith's freedom. This is what Carroll and the two law students intended to discuss with Smith.

Once inside the prison, the trio were directed into a large, noisy room where inmates were talking with family and friends at circular tables. Carroll spotted a vacant table in the corner and the group waited for Smith there. Sheff and Madonna had seen photographs of Smith taken during the trial and wondered what twelve years in prison would have done to her. When Smith joined them, the former conservatively dressed woman with smartly coiffed hair had been replaced by an older woman in plain prison garb with her hair cut short. Both students were struck by how sad she appeared.

After Jenny Carroll made the introductions, Madonna went to the vending machine and purchased a Lipton green tea for Smith.

"You've got to get me out of here," Smith said, looking at Carroll. Turning her gaze to the two law students, Smith explained, "My children need me. I mean they really need me. Since I've been in prison, the younger ones have been passed from house to house. My son—he was twelve when I was convicted. Anyway, he has a substance abuse problem now." Smith's lower lip began to tremble and she looked away, unable to continue.

As Smith cried, Carroll finished Smith's thought. Addressing the two law students, she said, "Nancy knows that if she hadn't been imprisoned, this would have never happened to him. She also knows that she could straighten him out if she were home. Am I right, Nancy?"

Smith nodded as she wiped away tears with her hands.

Instead of talking over her sobs, the three women sat quietly, responding only with sympathetic looks. When a guard walked over to a noisy table on the other side of the room, Carroll patted Smith's hand. For the next ten minutes, the three visitors watched as despair and hopelessness consumed Smith. When she could speak again, Smith begged, "You've got to promise me that you'll do everything you can to send me home."

Madonna and Sheff looked at each other, overwhelmed by the responsibility that they were about to undertake. They knew that they would be asked to organize the evidence and write the first draft of the letter that would go to the parole board. Their work would serve as the foundation for the final product that the Ohio Innocence Project would eventually file. Did they have the experience and skill to do that? They weren't attorneys, just law students who'd recently finished their first-year courses on contracts, real property, torts, criminal law, and civil procedure. Yes, they would be supervised by Jenny Carroll and Mark Godsey, and that was reassuring. Still, their preliminary work would have profound ramifications.

Carroll was the first to respond. "Our plan is to put all of our efforts into your parole bid. As you know, you'll be eligible for parole in several months. We'll send the board a large packet that includes a summary letter and many supporting documents. We'll tell them about you as a person, the miscarriage of justice that led to your conviction, and your accomplishments in prison." Glancing at the two law students, Carroll said, "Whitney and Bobbi are going to organize that information for Mark and me. They'll be contacting you from time to time—giving you updates and asking you questions."

"What are my chances?" Smith asked, her voice flat for the first time.

Carroll looked away before she answered. "I wish I could tell you that they'll release you, but I can't say that. There are unique factors in your case that make your release more compelling, but, to be perfectly honest, I just don't know."

Smith began to shake but did not cry.

"There's an important thing we need to discuss with you about your parole," Carroll said.

Smith looked up cautiously and waited.

"It has to do with the sex offender class that the prison has asked you to take," Carroll said.

Smith's eyes were no longer wary but were fiercely intense. Again, she made no reply, waiting for Carroll to continue.

"I am duty-bound to tell you this, no matter how unpleasant it may be to you," Carroll said, her voice even. As a public defender, Carroll had learned how to deliver hard news to clients, and she was using that experience to be unflinchingly honest with Smith. "You will have a much better chance for gaining parole if you take that class."

Smith's eyes flared, unable to hide her sense of betrayal.

Reading Smith's expression, Carroll replied, "I'm not telling you to take the class. Only you can make that decision. I'm just explaining the ramifications of that decision. That's all I'm doing."

"I am not a sex offender, and I am not going to take that class," Smith said, her voice low yet defiant. "I'll sit in prison for the rest of my life before I do that."

Smith's answer was not lost on either Sheff or Madonna. Here was an innocent woman languishing in prison, being forced to make a horrible choice—admitting to a crime that she did not commit or remaining true to herself and probably staying locked up.

The two had identical thoughts. If they were in Smith's place, would they have the courage to stand up for their innocence, or would they take the class—buckle for expediency's sake to escape this hell?

"We understand, Nancy," Carroll said. "We just needed to place that on the table for you."

Smith nodded, slumped in her chair, and began to cry again.

"It's a horrible choice, isn't it?" Carroll said, commiserating. "And it's terribly unfair." When Smith had regained her composure, Carroll said, "We will do everything we can for you."

"I know you will," Smith replied. "Will you be back to see me with updates?"

This time it was Madonna who replied. "Yes, we'll be back and we'll also call you every few weeks."

Sheff and Madonna walked back to the car without speaking, emotionally exhausted by what they'd just witnessed. It was Carroll who broke the silence. "Most attorneys never sit with an innocent person in prison. It will always stay with you."

Although Sheff and Madonna had been committed to helping Smith before this visit, they were determined to work unceasingly for her parole now. They could do no less.

Looking up from a file, Mark Godsey greeted Whitney Sheff and Bobbi Madonna, who took chairs across from him. The two law students waited for their instructions.

Godsey had accepted Smith's case shortly after he'd started the Ohio Innocence Project at the University of Cincinnati in 2003. Unlike most of the cases that the Ohio Innocence Project championed, Nancy Smith's case did not involve DNA evidence or the recantation of a key witness's testimony. He'd concluded that it screamed of injustice nevertheless.

Godsey had been approached by Martin Yant, a former journalist turned private investigator who was convinced that both defendants, Smith and Allen, were innocent. Yant had become involved in the case in 1996 when he'd been hired by Smith's family to uncover exculpatory evidence that they believed existed. He'd quickly exhausted the family's retainer but continued to work on the case for free, convinced that the pair had been wrongfully convicted.

Godsey was familiar with Yant's work from previous wrongful-conviction cases and believed that the investigator did solid and reliable work. After Yant had turned over his file, Godsey had quickly become a believer in Smith's innocence. Godsey had been appalled by the videotape of the police lineup involving Joseph Allen. He'd watched in disbelief as some of the parents apparently aided their children, while other children continually identified other men as Joseph. After that, he'd reviewed the children's inconsistent and unbelievable statements before trial and compared them to their very different testimony at trial.

He'd reviewed Smith's appeals and post-conviction filings and concluded that her best chance of release was through parole. With her first eligibility arising in a few months, he wanted to submit a comprehensive package as soon as that happened.

Godsey had no illusions, however, about their chances. The Ohio Parole Board granted parole in only about 10 percent of the cases it heard. More disturbing, no one knew why the board granted parole in some cases and not in others. The board decided each case behind closed doors, issuing a cryptic one-or-two-sentence explanation for its decisions in its minutes. Unlike judges and magistrates, its members were not required to provide detailed reasoning for a denial, thus shrouding their conclusions in secrecy.

Its critics claimed that the board lacked both transparency and diversity. Its members were almost all white men who were either former parole officers or former prison administrators and held well-entrenched biases about the prisoners who came before them. As a result, the board's decisions were seen as widely inconsistent and arbitrary.

"Many of us believe that there are some unwritten rules that dictate the board's decisions," Godsey began. "It's important that you understand them when you work on our letter to the board."

The two students nodded, their eyes intent and serious.

"The parole board assumes that every person in front of them is guilty. They can't fathom that innocent people are ever convicted. As a result, they believe that anyone who claims innocence is in denial and has not been rehabilitated. Nancy Smith will be penalized for her refusal to admit to the crimes and her failure to express remorse," Godsey said.

The two students looked confused. "Are we not supposed to mention all of the evidence that exonerates her?" Madonna asked.

"No, I want you to marshal that information, but, in the end, we will say that she was convicted on the flimsiest of evidence, that the children's testimony may have been tainted, and that the conviction occurred during a period of day care hysteria. We will make the argument that she was wrongfully convicted, but we will do so gently. We will suggest it but not be dogmatic about it."

For the next few minutes, Godsey outlined the other topics that they needed to address in the letter: that Smith had served the statutory minimum sentences for her crimes; that she would live with her brother if released; that she had secured a promise of employment at a garden nursery; that she had completed coursework in horticulture, food service, and other subjects; and that she had actively participated in many Roman Catholic organizations, serving as the personal assistant to the prison chaplain.

"You're going to have to explain away some minor prison infractions that Nancy incurred, too," Godsey said.

"Like what?" Madonna asked.

"When she was first incarcerated, she didn't understand all of the rules. Believe it or not, she violated rules for some very petty things, like possessing too many envelopes, having sweatpants, improperly positioning her television set, and failing to sign in," Godsey explained.

"You've got to be joking. We have to mention these things?" Madonna said.

"The parole board seems to have an unwritten rule that it will deny release to any inmate who has violated a prison rule. They apparently don't differentiate between minor and major infractions. We've heard that even something like excess commissary can lead to a denial of parole."

The two students exchanged confused glances.

Godsey explained, "That means too many bags of chips or cookies in the prisoner's cell."

Madonna and Sheff shook their heads in disbelief.

"I know it sounds ludicrous," Godsey said, "but these members have worked in the prison system forever. They believe that if an inmate can't follow the rules inside the prison, then the inmate won't follow the rules once released."

January 22, 2007

Godsey sat in his office reviewing the sixteen-page letter that Madonna and Sheff had drafted in support of Nancy Smith's bid for parole. In addition to the letter, they had attached thirty-one exhibits to support their assertions in the letter. It was Godsey's first look at the package. Jenny Carroll had reviewed it a half dozen times previously, sending it back to the students with edits and suggestions. After making some corrections and edits of his own, Godsey was pleased with the letter.

In this final draft, the students had summarized all of the exculpatory evidence, taking up almost two-thirds of the letter. It was a scathing indictment of the jury's verdict. However, in the end, the authors had attempted to soften their rhetoric by concluding that "it was not beyond the scope of possibility . . . that the crime did not occur." Godsey wondered whether this pullback would appease the board members.

Later that week, Godsey asked the students to come into his office to sign the official letter to the parole board.

"You did a great job drafting the letter and gathering the exhibits," Godsey told Sheff and Madonna. "By now, you two know this case as well as anyone in the office."

Sheff had felt an enormous sense of relief when they'd put the package into its final form. She and Madonna had done their part and they could relax.

Godsey continued, "We will have an oral hearing with one or two members of the parole board in a few weeks in Columbus. There's no requirement that the people advocating on Nancy's behalf be attorneys."

Sheff felt her stomach tense in anxiety. She knew what was coming.

"I'd like the two of you to make the presentation," Godsey said. "I'll accompany you to the hearing, but I won't say much, if anything. I have confidence that both of you will do a great job."

Sheff looked at Madonna, raising her eyebrows and showing her discomfort, but she did not decline the assignment. Madonna looked back at her and nodded. They would take on this challenge.

February 6, 2007

For the past two weeks, Sheff and Madonna had practiced their presentations with one another almost every day. One would interrupt the other with a question, trying to simulate a query from a parole board officer. In a final prep session, they'd given their talk to Mark Godsey, who'd made some minor suggestions. Because the hearing was set for eight in the morning, they had traveled to Columbus the day before and stayed at a hotel. Both Sheff and Madonna had a difficult time sleeping that night, convinced that any misstep could cost Nancy Smith her freedom.

When they arrived at the parole board offices the next morning, Madonna expected to be ushered into a large room where a full board of eleven members awaited them. Sheff envisioned a hearing in front of a smaller group in a conference room. Instead, they were led to a small conference room where one parole board member awaited their talk.

For Madonna and Sheff, their presentations were anticlimactic. The board member listened politely but asked few questions. There was something in his smile and manner that Madonna found patronizing, as if he were amused by them, thinking them naïve and unschooled in the penal system.

Despite this, they did a solid job. They were forceful throughout, never at a loss for words and always making eye contact with the parole officer. Godsey congratulated them on a job well done.

After they returned to Cincinnati, they would report to Nancy Smith and her family. Then they'd wait for a decision.

February 21, 2007

"I know that you'll be very disappointed by what I have to report," Mark Godsey told Madonna and Sheff after he'd summoned them to his office. "The parole board just denied Nancy Smith's application for parole."

The two law students were initially speechless, their minds refusing to accept Godsey's message.

"I don't know what to say," Madonna said. "I had such hope that the parole board would do the right thing. How do we explain this to Nancy and her family? This will destroy them."

"I feel like we let them down. I feel horrible," Sheff said.

"Did they even read what we wrote?" Madonna asked, her voice indignant.

Godsey shook his head. "I don't know."

"Do we know why they denied her parole?" Sheff asked.

"A spokesperson for the board issued a statement that the board believed that the nature of the crimes demanded that she serve more time. So obviously, the members didn't consider that she'd been wrongfully convicted," Godsey said.

"Did they say anything more?" Madonna asked.

"There's also something in the minutes that says one of the board members interviewed Nancy in prison. This board member told the others that Nancy was still in denial because she would not admit to the crimes."

Godsey had been through this before—many times. They failed more often than they succeeded. He'd witnessed this guilty reaction from other law students involved in the program. "You can't be discouraged," Godsey said. "You gave Nancy a terrific effort. You presented the arguments well. You hit all of the important points."

The two law students seemed on the verge of tears. Godsey continued, "Even when we lose, we have done something valuable for our clients. We have stood up for them. They've told me how important that is—just to have someone like you listen to them and believe in their innocence. I hear that from inmates all the time, even after a setback. They say it restores their faith in humanity."

Godsey paused for a moment, searching the two students' faces, hoping that some of his message was getting through. He began again: "There is incredible value in fighting for someone for whom no one else is fighting. Yes, it can end in bitter disappointment, but you fought for Nancy because it was the right thing to do. You should be proud of that. We are not giving up."

Sheff appreciated Godsey's words, but they could not ease her distress. She dreaded the next thing she had to do. She'd promised to call Nancy Smith's daughter, Amber Bronish, as soon as the parole board made its decision. Amber was in her late twenties and served as the point person for the Smith family, seeking periodic updates.

"I don't know how to tell you this, but the parole board denied your mother's application for parole," Sheff began when she called Amber.

At first there was silence on the phone, then she heard sobbing.

"I am so sorry," Sheff said. "I believe so strongly in your mother's innocence and I'm devastated by this result."

"Why are they making my mother suffer like this? They know that she didn't do any of those horrible things," Amber said.

"I don't know. I really hoped that I would be delivering good news to you."

"It's not your fault. I'm not mad at you. I'm so angry with the system. In America, how can innocent people stay locked up in prison? It's as if no one has the guts to admit to a mistake," Amber said.

"You can't give up," Sheff replied. "The Innocence Project will keep working to release your mom. They'll fight for her when she's eligible for parole again in 2009."

"We can't wait that long," Amber said. "I don't know how much longer my mom can survive in prison. I really don't."

"I'm so sorry," Sheff said before ending the call.

CHAPTER 36
AMBER BRONISH

FALL 2007 - FALL 2008
THIRTEEN YEARS AFTER CONVICTION

Amber Bronish had been fifteen years old when her mother was sent to prison. At the time, Amber and her siblings were too young to speak out for their mother, and they'd left that job to their aunts, their uncles, and their mother's closest friends. For the four Smith children, it was enough to try to survive in a world without their mom.

But things had changed after Amber reached adulthood. She'd gradually taken on the role of her mother's most outspoken and determined supporter. She visited her frequently and peppered her mother's attorneys with questions, always asking about their next steps. However, when the parole board denied her mom's bid for release, Amber sensed that her mom had reached her breaking point. If the attorneys couldn't help her, then maybe she needed to take matters into her own hands.

Married and busy with two children of her own, Amber wasn't sure where to start. However, she knew where she wanted things to end. Her goal was to get her mom a new trial and her freedom. Because of all the new evidence uncovered and developed since the original trial, Amber was certain that a new trial would end in an acquittal. However, the question remained: Who could help her? She thought of the Lorain police and their flawed and incomplete investigation. Could the police reopen their investigation? Would they consider searching for new evidence that would exonerate her mother? Amber didn't know, but she would start there.

Mentioning only that she was Nancy Smith's daughter, she left a voice mail for Lorain's chief of police, Cel Rivera. She knew it was unlikely that the chief or anyone from his staff would return her call, but she had no place else to turn. A few minutes later, Chief Rivera returned her call and invited her to come to his office the next day. After Amber hung up the phone, she sat in a chair, stunned by what had just happened.

Perhaps Chief Rivera's call should not have been surprising. Like Amber, the chief had experienced family upheaval in his youth. After his mother had died and his father was unable to care for him, he'd bounced between a Catholic orphanage and foster care. By his own admission, he'd been rebellious while in high school, eventually dropping out. He'd found his footing after enlisting in the army and serving in Vietnam. Returning to Lorain, he'd joined the police force and steadily climbed its ranks, becoming chief of police in 1994. At the time of the Head Start investigations, Chief Rivera had been the captain in charge of the detective bureau. He'd both supervised and helped in the investigation. And he'd overseen the infamous live lineup involving Joseph Allen.

When Amber entered his office, Chief Rivera stood, approached her, and then gave her a hug. Bald with a bushy mustache, the fifty-eight-year-old chief had a face that exuded both warmth and trust. After she was seated, he smiled and asked her why she'd come.

Amber came right to the point, insisting that her mother was innocent and that the police and the jury were wrong. She explained that her mother had recently been denied parole because she refused to admit that she'd molested the children or attend the prison's sex offender class.

The chief looked down at his desk, apparently gathering his thoughts. Returning his gaze to Amber, he said, "I can't really say that she is innocent, but it does trouble me that she continues to maintain her innocence—even when it goes against her own self-interest." He paused and cleared his throat. "Can I ask you a question? It's something I've always been curious about."

Amber nodded for the chief to continue.

"I've always wondered if the prosecutor offered your mom a plea bargain before trial," he said.

"Yeah, they did. If she pled guilty to lesser charges, she'd get only four years in prison," Amber replied.

Chief Rivera rubbed his chin. "You know, most guilty people would have jumped at that kind of deal," he said, more to himself than to Amber.

The chief shook his head as if unsure whether he should continue with his next thought. "For about three or four months, we felt like there wasn't enough evidence, and the assistant prosecutor, Jon Rosenbaum, kept calling and saying that he wanted the case. We kept saying it's too confusing and there's just not enough there."

Amber was surprised by the chief's openness. As they talked, Chief Rivera admitted that the system could make errors and perhaps it had made a mistake with her mother. However, he explained that her mom could not get a new trial unless there was new evidence.

"Those kids are all adults now, aren't they?" Chief Rivera asked.

Amber nodded.

"If they admitted that your mom didn't touch them, then you'd have enough new evidence to get her a new trial. Even if just one kid denies that she did anything, she'd get a second chance," Chief Rivera suggested.

"I could talk to them. They're all still in the area," Amber said.

"You'd have to tape them," the chief added. "And you'd need to do that secretly."

"Is that legal?" Amber asked.

"Yeah, it is," the chief said. "In Ohio, only one party has to consent to the recording, and that one person would be you."

"Would I be wired or something?" Amber asked, thinking of the cop shows that she'd watched on television.

"No, you'd carry a small tape recorder. Come back tomorrow and I'll give you one and show you how to use it. It's pretty simple," the chief said.

After Amber left his office, she reflected on what had just happened. She sensed that Chief Rivera had a guilty conscience. Although he'd been guarded in his responses, he'd said enough to reveal that he had serious misgivings about the case. Her mother's insistence on her innocence had unnerved him. He wanted to help them, and, apparently, he would.

In hindsight, it had been naïve to think that the former Head Start children, now young adults, would speak candidly to Amber. They had each received a 1.5-million-dollar settlement and would not say anything to undermine their claims' legitimacy. Approached at her workplace, one former complainant had told Amber that she could not remember what had happened to her fourteen years earlier. When Amber had phoned her the next day at her home, the girl's mother had answered and hung up on Amber. Amber and the chief assumed that the four claimants stayed in touch and it would be futile to contact the other three.

After that, Chief Rivera had suggested a second plan—a petition for clemency. He'd explained that the governor had the power to pardon anyone convicted of a crime if the governor believed that justice required it. The chief had made the initial phone calls to Columbus, downloaded the proper forms, and agreed to help Amber fill them out.

They met regularly, usually on Saturdays, to discuss what Amber needed to do. Their meeting on this day would focus on the summary statement that would accompany the petition.

"I've roughed out some things that you should include in your summary," Chief Rivera said. He then pulled a paper from a file folder and began to read, "'Nancy Smith has been incarcerated for almost fifteen years for crimes that she did not commit.'" Glancing up from the document, he said, "You'll also need to make it clear that your mom and Joseph Allen had never met and it was unfair that she was tried alongside a man who'd already been convicted of sex charges."

Amber rocked in her seat, convinced that the chief was not just suggesting what she should write but was revealing his own personal opinions.

"'The methods that the police used to interview the children are techniques that have been discredited,'" the chief said, reading again from his paper.

"You've said that I should include letters of support," Amber said. "Who would write those?"

"Well, first of all, I can write a letter expressing my own views," Chief Rivera replied. "If the Lorain detectives who investigated the claim wrote letters, that would carry a lot of weight. You should also contact the former prosecutor, Greg White. He's now a federal magistrate and that would be very helpful. You might try Judge McGough or the current prosecutor, Dennis Will, to see if they would write letters recommending clemency."

"How do I get them to do that?" Amber asked, wondering how she could convince these high-powered people to help her.

"Same way you got me involved. Call them, explain who you are, and ask if you can talk to them personally," the chief explained.

"Can I tell them that I have your support?" Amber asked. It was a good question—one that would reveal the chief's commitment to the project.

The chief did not answer immediately, and his pause was not lost on Amber. "I'm going to write my own letter with my own views. I'll do that for you," Chief Rivera said, sidestepping her question. "I'm working on my letter now. Next time we talk, I should have it ready."

October 10, 2008

Three months had passed since her last meeting with Chief Rivera. In the interim, Amber had told Mark Godsey, her mom's attorney at the Ohio Innocence Project, about her conversations with the chief. From her vantage point, Chief Rivera had revealed his innermost feelings about the case: insufficient evidence, an overzealous prosecutor, overwhelming outside pressures to solve the case, flawed interrogations, and gnawing doubts about her mother's guilt. Godsey had called the chief, eager to parlay Chief Rivera's concerns into a motion for a new trial. But the chief was much more cautious with Godsey than he'd been with Amber. He wouldn't criticize his detectives' investigation, nor would he opine that Nancy Smith was innocent.

After that, Amber was certain that the chief would never meet with her again. Her phone messages to him went unreturned. But two days earlier, he'd sent her an email, asking her to come in for a meeting. She'd readily agreed, but this time, she wanted confirmation that Chief Rivera believed in her mother's innocence. She decided to get proof; she'd secretly record their conversation.

Her heart beat wildly as she entered his office. She tried to look calm as she took her customary chair across from his desk. The chief explained that he still wanted to help her complete the paperwork for her mother's clemency petition. They began by reviewing the proposed summary that they'd discussed in earlier meetings.

"I've worked on my supporting letter for your package," Chief Rivera said. "Here is what I have thus far." The chief pulled out a paper and began reading: "'Over the years, this case has been spotlighted at various times. The question has been raised that Nancy Smith could be innocent of these charges. In all of this, Joseph Allen has often been forgotten. It is only natural to reflect on the outcome and to ask whether justice was truly served in this case.'"

The chief looked up from his paper and glanced at Amber before continuing. "'From every perspective, it seemed like the system did its job. But our system is not infallible and there are cases in which persons have been wrongly convicted. Is this one of those cases? I honestly don't know.'"

Amber was disappointed by the chief's words. He needed to take a stand on her mother's innocence. He should mention things like the detectives' improper interrogation techniques, the children's inconsistent statements, and the inappropriate lineup involving Joseph Allen. As these thoughts raced through her mind, the chief's words seemed to float above her, not registering. Finally, she focused on his words again.

"'Was this a travesty of justice and a living human tragedy? I have asked Lorain Police sergeant Mark Carpentiere to investigate new evidence brought forth by the family, but we have not been able to prove it.'"

Chief Rivera paused and looked to Amber for comment. "Is that all?" Amber asked.

"Well, no. I haven't completed the letter yet. The next part will get very personal. I'm just not sure how I am going to word it. I want them to know that there might have been a very tragic mistake made here. I'll tell them that if so, the police department and the prosecutors have to make it right."

Amber looked expectantly at Chief Rivera, hoping that he still had more to add. Picking up on her expression, the chief said, "I'll also definitely mention that your mom passed a polygraph test in 1993— that's an important piece of information that the governor should know."

Sensing that the meeting was nearing its end, Amber wanted to tell the chief one more thing. "I want you to know that my mom has no hard feelings toward you or the police department," Amber said.

Chief Rivera looked away, apparently moved by her mother's act of forgiveness. "I know you believe that your mom is innocent," he said. "And if that's true, how can the system ever make things right for her? You know, we're talking about taking fifteen years of someone's life away. I don't know how you ever fix something like that."

When the meeting came to a close, Chief Rivera suggested that they have future dialogues. As it turned out, Amber would meet with the chief six more times. Each time she would tape-record their conversation. She would eventually share the tapes with her mother's attorneys, Jack Bradley and Mark Godsey, and let them decide what to do with them. But for now, her work with the chief seemed like another dead end. If she hoped to succeed, she'd need him to contact the influential people and convince them to write letters of support. Although sympathetic to the family's plight, Chief Rivera was not going to do that. The family would have to seek another path.

CHAPTER 37
JUDGE JAMES BURGE

DECEMBER 20, 2008–JUNE 24, 2009
FOURTEEN - FIFTEEN YEARS AFTER
CONVICTION

Everyone seemed to agree that Judge James Burge was a maverick. Some described the outspoken judge as sui generis, a Latin legal term meaning "one of a kind." Although he had been in office for less than two years, Judge Burge had already earned a reputation as a bold and unpredictable jurist. For over thirty years, Judge Burge had been one of the county's most well-known and respected criminal defense attorneys. At age fifty-nine, he'd surprised the legal community by entering the crowded field to replace Judge Lynett McGough, who was retiring. He'd run a vigorous campaign, earned the highest rating of any candidate by the Lorain County Bar Association, and defeated his opponents in both the primary and then the general election.

Once on the bench, Judge Burge had garnered national attention almost immediately when a defendant facing the death penalty had filed a motion challenging the constitutionality of Ohio's lethal injection protocols. To aid in his decision, he'd ordered the state to produce detailed data about the injection process and the qualifications of the state's execution team. When the state refused to comply, he'd sought a ruling from the Ohio Supreme Court, which had upheld his request. After receiving the information, Judge Burge had found that two of the three drugs infused during the lethal injection process could cause extreme pain. As a result, he'd ruled that Ohio's current method constituted cruel and unusual punishment, and thus violated the Eighth Amendment to the US Constitution.

But on this day as he sat in his chambers, he was faced with a motion from an old case from Judge McGough's docket, one involving Nancy Smith. He knew very little about this case except that Smith had been convicted fourteen years earlier of heinous sexual crimes against young children and that the verdict had remained controversial ever since.

Of course, Judge Burge knew all of the attorneys involved in the case. Early in their careers, Jack Bradley and Burge had been law partners. They had parted amicably and pursued separate solo practices. As a criminal defense attorney, Judge Burge had frequently sparred with Jon Rosenbaum, and their arguments had occasionally been heated.

Judge Burge had read Bradley's motion and the prosecutor's response several times. Bradley's motion attacked Judge McGough's final judgment entry regarding her sentencing of Smith. In her entry, she had merely recorded that Smith had been found guilty of various crimes and then set forth the sentence for each offense. The Ohio Supreme Court, in a recently decided case, had interpreted the criminal rules as requiring a judge to precisely memorialize how a defendant had been found guilty—whether through a bench trial, a plea, or a jury verdict. It seemed to be a technical error that should have had no effect on Smith's case. In fact, the prosecutor argued that Judge Burge should just amend the entry to reflect that a jury had found Smith guilty and be done with it.

However, the analysis was not quite so simple. In the recent Ohio Supreme Court case, the court had ruled that the judge's sentencing order was not final or appealable until the entry contained this language. Bradley argued that the court of appeals never had the right to review the Smith case until the final journal entry stated that Smith had been found guilty by a jury. If this was true, then the trial court still had control over the case and could theoretically resentence Smith. This would have been of no consequence if Judge McGough had still been presiding over the case. In all likelihood, she would have amended the entry to reflect the jury's decision and retained her original sentences. However, she was gone and a former criminal defense attorney was sitting in her place.

After Judge Burge set the motion and briefs on the far edge of his desk, he looked about his office. On one wall hung a photograph of James Filiaggi, a person Judge Burge had defended in a capital murder case who had been executed by lethal injection the previous year. Judge Burge was unsure why he continued to confront himself with the man's photograph. Perhaps it reflected his uncertainty over the government's right to kill any of its citizens. Perhaps it was a reminder to temper justice with mercy. Perhaps he just wanted lawyers coming into his office to see the humanity in everyone, even a man who'd shot his wife at point-blank range.

Judge Burge's thoughts turned again to Jack Bradley, a lawyer still fighting to free a client whom he believed to be innocent more than fourteen years after her conviction. What did it say about Bradley that, after reading the recent Ohio Supreme Court case, he had retrieved the Smith file to see if Judge McGough had complied with the exact letter of the law? It told Judge Burge that Bradley was still haunted by the Smith case, something Judge Burge could understand. Bradley had undoubtedly handled several hundred, maybe several thousand, cases since then, but on the remotest of chances, he'd reviewed the judge's final entry searching for this mistake and had found it.

February 4, 2009

Judge Burge was convinced that, under the unique circumstances involving Smith and Allen, he had the right to resentence both defendants. He would explain that today in open court during a hearing on Smith's motion to resentence. At this point, however, he was unsure whether the original sentences were appropriate or whether he needed to change them. To decide, he would read the fifteen-hundred-page trial transcript and educate himself about what had happened fourteen years ago. Once he'd made up his mind, he'd summon the parties and their attorneys back to his courtroom and announce his decision.

June 24, 2009

Despite the spaciousness of Judge Burge's courtroom in the Lorain County Justice Center, the room felt cramped as spectators filled the benches and congregated in front of the double doors leading to the hallway. Any hearing involving the Head Start case always drew a crowd. Today's hearing was categorized as a status conference and the attorneys believed that nothing of consequence would occur. The controversial resentencing hearing was set for the following month. The attorneys surmised that Judge Burge had scheduled this status conference merely to discuss how that upcoming hearing would be handled.

The defendants, Nancy Smith and Joseph Allen, sat silently with their attorneys at one table, their expressions grim. George Koury, an assistant county prosecutor, sat impassively at another table, his hands clasped and resting on the table's surface.

Other than Bradley, the original attorneys in the case were no longer involved in it. Joseph Allen was now represented by a Sandusky criminal defense attorney, K. Ronald Bailey, who had been hired by the National Center for Reason and Justice. The NCRJ was a nonprofit organization that sought to free people it believed had been wrongfully convicted of sex crimes.

The prosecutor's office had undergone major personnel changes since this case had been tried. In 2002, Jon Rosenbaum had left the prosecutor's office, with neither Rosenbaum nor Greg White offering much of an explanation other than Rosenbaum's public statement that he was dissatisfied with the direction that the office was taking "on certain issues." A year later, White was appointed as the US district attorney for the Northern District of Ohio and resigned as the Lorain County prosecutor. Dennis Will, a former Elyria detective and assistant county prosecutor, had eventually been elected to the post.

Entering his courtroom from a door located behind his bench, Judge Burge sat down and surveyed the room. Trim and fit, the judge cut an athletic figure beneath his robe. A lifetime of weight lifting had broadened his shoulders and enhanced his five-foot-eight-inch frame. Gone was his trademark cigar, which he chewed when not in public. Today, his eyes were deadly serious, evincing none of the mischief that they often displayed.

His voice calm and measured, Judge Burge began by explaining that he had initially thought that he would enter new sentences for the defendants next month. To do this, he believed that he had to be as familiar with the case as his predecessor, Judge McGough, and this required him to review the entire trial transcript as well as the tape-recorded witness statements furnished to the defense attorneys during the trial.

Looking up from his notes, he paused for a moment. "Before I commence my analysis, I want to make clear that each detective, each law enforcement officer, who investigated this case is a personal friend of mine, and for each of them, I have the highest degree of respect.

"The matter was prosecuted by the Lorain County Prosecutor's Office, and by an assistant with whom I did battle for over twenty years. In reviewing his presentation of the case, it was clear to me that his motive was to do the best he could for the State of Ohio and for those witnesses who testified. He took advantage of every break he could get, as did the defense, as do all lawyers who are worthy to walk into a courtroom. I don't think in the course of my law practice that I ever received a favorable court ruling that I failed to accept, and that is all the assistant prosecutor did."

In another attempt to deflect any criticism away from the trial judge, the prosecutor, and the police, Judge Burge suggested that, in reviewing the transcript, he had the benefit of a more dispassionate look, not one caught up in the events of 1994. In addition, he noted that several key evidentiary laws had changed and that methods for inter-viewing young children had also evolved.

In reviewing the record, the judge explained that adults had testi-fied about hearsay statements allegedly spoken by the young victims. Although this was permissible in 1994 under a special rule of evidence, later cases had held this rule to be unconstitutional. Therefore, he believed that this evidence could no longer be marshaled to support the verdict.

Although Judge Burge had gone to great pains not to criticize Jon Rosenbaum in his opening remarks, his next comments took aim at the prosecutor, albeit indirectly. After listening to the tapes of the child witnesses and their parents, Judge Burge found that they were all exculpatory and should have been delivered to the defense well before trial. Although it went unsaid, it was Rosenbaum's responsibility to disclose all exculpatory evidence to the defense attorneys. The judge claimed that if the statements had been delivered in a timely manner, the defense could have transcribed them and offered them as substantive evidence to be reviewed by the jury.

Judge Burge had more to say about the interviews. "Although the police and social workers were doing their best—trying to seek justice for these children—they conducted these interviews in such a way that this Court, at least, would find the process to be so suggestive that the children's in-court testimony would be inadmissible."

To the casual observer, the judge's review of the evidence seemed esoteric and not germane to the issue of resentencing the defendants. But to the attorneys involved in the case, it was as if they could feel the earth shift beneath them. Had they heard the judge correctly? If the victims' testimony and that of their parents should not have been admissible at the trial, what evidence supported the verdicts? The answer seemed obvious. Stripped of this testimony, the prosecution's case crumbled.

Judge Burge continued, "And again, I don't believe that there was a human being in that courtroom in 1994 that was not there to do the best for his client, both defense counsel and counsel for the State of Ohio. Notwithstanding that, I have absolutely no confidence that these verdicts are correct. Therefore, pursuant to Criminal Rule 29(C), the Court will enter a judgment of acquittal on behalf of the defendant Smith and the defendant Allen, and this matter has an end. The defendants are each discharged, and their bonds will be ordered released."

It took a moment for Judge Burge's final statements to register with those assembled. When they did, Smith raised her hands over her face in astonishment before she began crying. Allen looked at his attorney and said, "Thank God." In unison, the defendants' family and friends began cheering.

As the defendants filed out of the courtroom, reporters followed them, seeking their reactions. Allen said, "I'll keep on praising God." A few minutes later, Smith told reporters that she would relish her time with her family and looked forward to finding a job.

Despite Judge Burge's statement that the case was "at an end," the prosecutor would undoubtedly appeal his decision. Why wouldn't he? Smith and Allen had been found guilty by a jury and their verdicts had been upheld by the appellate courts. The law was clear: a trial judge had no authority to overrule an appellate court, and that's exactly what Judge Burge had done—or so it seemed. The defendants' fate would hinge on what the appellate courts eventually decided, but for the moment, Allen and Smith were free.

CHAPTER 38
LIMBO
JANUARY 27, 2011 - JANUARY 29, 2013
FIFTEEN AND A HALF TO SEVENTEEN
AND A HALF YEARS AFTER CONVICTION

A year and a half later, the Ohio Supreme Court ended its opinion with these biting words: "Judge Burge patently and unambiguously lacked jurisdiction to vacate Smith's convictions and sentence when his authority was limited to issuing a corrected sentencing entry that complie[d] with Criminal Rule 32(C)." As Judge Burge set down the court's opinion, he felt not just the sting of those words but the injustice that flowed from them. The wheels of appellate justice had ground their way to a final disappointing decision: he had lacked the authority to either resentence or acquit the defendants. After correcting the deficient journal entry, he was required to send them back to prison under the terms imposed by Judge McGough years earlier.

The first appellate court to rule on the issue, the Ohio Ninth District Court of Appeals, had agreed with him. In a two-to-one decision, that panel had found that he indeed had jurisdiction to issue an acquittal under these unique circumstances. That court had affirmed his decision regarding Smith but reversed his decision regarding Allen. The appellate court noted that, after the jury verdict, Smith's attorney had filed a motion for acquittal, while Allen's court-appointed attorneys had not. That difference was enough to spell defeat for Allen. The court concluded that Judge Burge could not revisit a ruling on a motion that Allen's attorneys had never made. However, that oversight had become moot when the Ohio Supreme Court had ruled that Judge Burge had no authority to do anything except correct the final journal entry to reflect that the defendants had been found guilty *by a jury*.

As soon as he amended the journal entry, their freedom would come to an end. Unlike parolees who were returned to prison for violating the terms of their release, Smith and Allen had been model citizens since they'd returned to Lorain. They'd lived quiet lives, reintegrating themselves into the world of their families and friends. More important, Judge Burge was convinced of their innocence. Until his hand was forced, he would not resentence them.

Several miles away in his office, Jack Bradley was reviewing the same slip opinion issued by the Ohio Supreme Court. He'd likely be the one to give Nancy Smith the crushing news, assuming that a reporter had not already called her seeking her reaction.

Since her release, Bradley had kept in touch with Nancy, and he'd seen how she'd quickly become an integral part of her family's life. Her eight grandchildren, all born while she was in prison, could count on her to pick them up from school, babysit them, help them with schoolwork, and attend their events. Her youngest child, Chase, had been twelve years old when he'd been wrenched away from her. Raised in a number of homes, he'd turned to drugs to deal with the sadness of losing his mother. Now, with his mother's help, he'd overcome his drug addiction and was again gainfully employed. After her aunt had died, Nancy had taken on the role of the primary caretaker for her uncle until he, too, had passed away.

Bradley also knew that Nancy had supported herself as a painter and housecleaner. Her rekindled religious faith was still a guiding force in her life. She often volunteered at her church, serving food to the homeless and participating in other fundraising activities there. And this was the woman whom the legal system was determined to send back to prison. Except for Judge Burge, no other judge had shown the courage to admit the system's horrible mistake and try to correct it.

On a theoretical level, he understood why a unanimous Ohio Supreme Court had ruled as it had. At the core of the decision was the need for finality in the criminal justice system. If a trial court could vacate a jury's verdict after the case had wound its way through the appellate courts, could any judgment be final? If Judge Burge's decision had held, uncertainty and potential chaos might have overrun the system.

Yet, there had to be another path to freedom for Smith and Allen. What it was, he wasn't sure.

March 14, 2012

As he had done five years earlier, Mark Godsey was again reviewing a proposed filing with the Ohio Parole Board on behalf of Nancy Smith. However, this package was different from the first. Instead of a request for parole, the Innocence Project was filing an application for clemency, seeking either a complete pardon or a commutation of Smith's sentence. The full eleven-member parole board would hear the request, but it would not make the final decision. The board's job was solely to make a recommendation to the governor, who would ultimately make the determination.

After Judge Burge's acquittal and the Ohio Supreme Court's reversal of that decision, Godsey had convinced a New York City law firm, Davis, Polk & Wardwell LLP, to take on this case on a pro bono basis. Led by attorney Sharon Katz, the firm's five-lawyer team had prepared a 24-page memorandum in support of clemency, supplemented by 235 pages of exhibits. It was an impressive document, persuasive in its presentation and thorough in the affidavits, expert reports, and other records that supported its claims.

To date, Judge Burge had not scheduled a hearing for the resentencing of either Smith or Allen, but Godsey knew that it was only a matter of time before this happened. The problem was that it took months for a clemency petition to be processed to a final determination, and Smith could be back in prison before that happened. Godsey hoped to file the petition in the next few weeks, sometime during the first week of April. Once it was filed, the board would assign a parole officer to investigate the claim. Godsey questioned whether a nonlawyer could fully understand the issues presented, but that was the procedure. After that, the board would schedule a full hearing with its eleven members, hear testimony, and ask questions. At some future time, the members would make a recommendation to the governor, who was under no time constraint to rule on it.

Godsey had kept in close contact with Smith and knew how scared she was of being incarcerated again. As long as her freedom remained in perilous limbo, she would live in constant apprehension and anxiety. The parole board provided her with the best chance to retain her liberty, and he was convinced that their written presentation provided more than enough information for the board to recommend clemency.

January 29, 2013

Nine months after filing her petition for clemency, Nancy Smith was finally before the full eleven-member parole board to determine whether she was entitled to clemency or a reduction of her sentence. During that time, Judge Burge had not taken any action to correct the final journal entry. Today, Judge Burge had agreed to be one of Smith's first witnesses at the hearing and tell the board why the conviction against her could not be trusted.

Sharon Katz of Davis Polk would be Nancy Smith's lead attorney at this hearing. She and four of her colleagues had painstakingly put together the brief and supporting materials for clemency. Katz would not only argue the grounds for clemency but would call five witnesses to support it. One witness was Dr. Maggie Bruck, a psychologist and full professor of psychiatry at Johns Hopkins University who was poised to explain why the children's testimony was not reliable. Richard Gronsky, a veteran Lorain County assistant prosecutor, had been given the task of dissuading the board from recommending clemency.

After the hearing was called to order, the board's chairperson, Cynthia Mausser, asked each side to present opening statements. Katz told the members that they would find several aspects of this case "extraordinary." The first aspect was the conclusions of Judge Burge, an experienced jurist, who, after reviewing both the trial transcript and the children's taped statements, had felt compelled to acquit both defendants. Katz added, "He'd found that the children's statements were both contaminated and exculpatory. They should have been turned over to the defense well before trial."

She claimed that the second extraordinary thing was the findings of Dr. Maggie Bruck, a psychologist whose hundred-plus articles often investigated the pitfalls in questioning children, particularly in the course of a criminal investigation.

"She will tell you that she has reviewed all of the child interrogation tapes in this case and has found them wholly unreliable. They are permeated by bias," Katz said. "The jury in this case never heard expert testimony that analyzed these interviews. If they had, we have no doubt that we would not be here today. There would have been an acquittal."

Before completing her remarks, Katz outlined other deficiencies in the original case—the failure to call key witnesses or to offer exculpatory attendance and work records from Head Start.

Assistant Prosecutor Gronsky stood and addressed the panel. A tall, bulky man with short hair, he presented an imposing figure as he outlined the prosecutor's position. Gronsky stressed that a jury had judged the credibility of the witnesses and convicted Smith. He emphasized that every appeal had affirmed the jury's verdict. He claimed that the issues that Smith's attorneys were presenting today were just dressed-up versions of previous arguments that had been soundly rejected by the jury and the courts.

"We have been in touch with the retired judge who handled the trial, the former prosecutor, and Lorain's chief of police. That judge, Judge Lynett McGough, believes that there was sufficient evidence to convict the defendants and remains convinced of their guilt. However, she believes that Mrs. Smith has served enough of her sentence and is suitable for release."

Gronsky further explained that Lorain police chief Rivera and former prosecutor Greg White did not oppose releasing Nancy Smith for time served, a legal concept known as commutation. "However, as I have stated, Judge McGough, Chief Rivera, Gregory White, and the current prosecutor, Dennis Will, are all vehemently opposed to clemency. They all believe that the defendant had a fair trial that is supported by credible evidence."

When Gronsky finished his summary, one of the parole board members, Rich Cholar, seemed taken aback. "I'm sorry, this does not pass the smell test," he said, raising his eyebrows. Another board member nodded vigorously in support of Cholar. How could the prosecution claim that Smith had committed heinous crimes against children and yet agree to free her into their community?

Staring at Gronsky, Cholar continued, "It sounds as if the prosecution has some concerns about the basis of these convictions."

"We stand by the verdicts," Gronsky said. "No one knows if there would be a different result if this case were tried today. We realize that different juries can reach different results."

Smith's attorneys were not surprised by Gronsky's position. Over the last few months, they had had several conversations with the prosecutor, exploring ways that Smith's case could be resolved without returning her to prison. The discussions were preliminary, but they had talked.

Cholar looked at his colleagues as if to gauge their reactions. He sensed support from one other member, but the other nine sat in stony silence. When Cholar did not follow up with another question, the board's chairperson asked Katz to present her first witness.

In a reversal of his usual role, Judge Burge became Smith's first witness. The judge cleared his throat. "Let me begin by telling you that there is a difference between 'not guilty' and 'innocent,'" he said. After explaining that he had been a criminal defense attorney for decades before being elected judge, he said, "Many clients walked out of court with me having been acquitted. They weren't innocent. Seldom did I speak for an innocent man or woman." His voice broke as he tried to control his emotions. "Today I can."

By agreeing to testify at this hearing, Judge Burge would effectively end any further participation in Smith's criminal case still pending before him. Because his favorable testimony would align him with Smith's side, he would have to recuse himself from her case. Presumably, a visiting judge would be appointed to handle the resentencing and any other matter.

As he'd done in his courtroom three and a half years earlier, Judge Burge explained why he'd acquitted Smith after reading the transcripts and listening repeatedly to the taped interview of the children. "I became convinced that the children's testimony had become tainted by the way they were questioned. They then told incredible stories that could never have happened. I am personally ashamed by these verdicts."

After the judge finished his testimony, Katz called Dr. Maggie Bruck. Dr. Bruck was a diminutive, well-groomed woman, comfortable in this setting. Having served as an expert witness in several dozen trials, she'd developed the skills to communicate with laypersons despite a professional life in academia. She told the board that the interviews of the children were tragically flawed.

"Both parents and interviewers used highly suggestive techniques that are no longer used today," she explained. "They asked leading questions and repeated questions until the child changed an answer. They scolded children for answers that didn't fit the interviewers' preconceived notion of what happened and they rewarded answers that did."

For over an hour, Dr. Bruck provided the board with a tutorial on the proper way to interview young children in this setting and pointed out the techniques that should be avoided—most of which had been employed in the Head Start case. She also explained how allegations by one parent, if communicated to other parents by the media or otherwise, could create a hysteria that would lead to additional copycat claims. The panel members listened intently, but their questions showed that most of them had failed to grasp the significance of her testimony.

"Can you tell if the children were lying?" one member asked.

"That's not my job," Dr. Bruck replied. "I can tell you whether the interviews were improper and, therefore, unreliable."

"Well, if we are being asked to recommend a pardon, we need to know whether those children were telling the truth. We weren't at the trial to judge that for ourselves," the same member said.

"If a questioner suggests to a four-year-old child that something happened, that child will eventually believe that it did. The child is not lying when he or she repeats the story, but he or she is telling a story that is not true. These children were not lying, but they were complying by saying what they thought their parents and the investigators wanted them to say. Does that answer your question?" Bruck asked.

The member appeared confused but nodded. It was apparent that he was searching for a black-and-white response, and Bruck's answer had not given him that. Did the other members understand the significance of Bruck's opinions? Perhaps they dismissed her as a well-credentialed hired gun. If either of these things was true, the clemency effort was in trouble.

Katz presented the testimony of Detective Cantu, who told the board that he'd believed Smith was innocent before the investigation had been wrested away from him. Sherry Hagerman, a witness never called by the defense, told the panel that she had been Smith's bus aide on the day when one of the abuses had allegedly occurred. She was adamant that Smith had never deviated from her route and had delivered all of the children to the school. Two of Smith's daughters also testified, reiterating that their mom could never have committed these crimes. They implored the board to pardon her so that she could continue to be the wonderful mother and grandmother that she had always been.

As the hearing neared its conclusion, Katz asked Nancy Smith to address the parole board. Several times during the hearing, Smith had cried while listening to the testimony of others, and Katz knew that Nancy would have a difficult time controlling her emotions. Now fifty-five years old, Smith looked worn down by twenty years of struggling for vindication and fifteen years of life behind bars.

Speaking into a microphone, her voice shook with emotion. "I just want you to know that I honestly didn't commit these crimes," she said. She stopped as she covered her eyes with her hands, trying to conceal her tears. After a few moments, she regained her composure. "I am innocent and I really don't want to go back to prison."

That was all Katz wanted her to say. The parole board members could judge her credibility for themselves. But the parole board members had questions, and those questions would reveal how difficult it would be to convince them that Smith was entitled to a pardon.

A heavyset, balding member began the questions. "Why didn't you attend sex offender classes while you were in prison?"

Katz looked at one of her associates in bewilderment. Had this man listened to any of the testimony? Had he read their brief? More important, had he already dismissed any thought that Smith had been wrongfully convicted?

Before Smith could reply, another member said, "I had the same question." Other members stared fixedly at Smith, obviously intent on hearing her answer.

Smith took a moment before she replied. "I don't believe it would have benefited me because I am not a sex offender."

To Smith's defense team, this answer seemed obvious. Why had the board members felt it necessary to even ask? But these were not eleven jurors, everyday people from diverse backgrounds. These board members had spent their adult lives interacting with prisoners in and out of the prison setting. On a daily basis, they'd dealt with sociopaths, chronic liars, repeat offenders—people who said whatever was expedient to escape well-deserved punishment. As a result, the parole board members were a jaundiced crowd, wary of being conned.

"Were you offered a plea deal before your case went to trial?" asked another member, apparently interested in knowing how confident the prosecutor had been about the case before it went to trial.

"I was offered a plea deal but I can't remember the terms. I told my attorney that I wouldn't admit to a crime that I didn't commit," Smith answered.

Rich Cholar, the board member who'd quizzed the assistant prosecutor after his presentation, asked the next question. "Why do you think that you were prosecuted for the case?"

Smith shook her head. "I don't have an answer. I don't know. All I know is that this case has taken a toll on my life."

The defense had answered this question in its memorandum supporting clemency. The brief had outlined how people working in day care centers had been charged with sex abuse across the country at the time Smith had been prosecuted. Wherever these cases had surfaced, they had created a hysteria. In Lorain, the police department had felt intense pressure from parents and the media to prosecute someone for these alleged crimes. Also left unsaid was that the families of the Head Start children had benefited enormously from civil lawsuit settlements—another possible motivation for the initial claims. But Smith offered none of these explanations.

Another member probed in another direction. "If your sentence were commuted, you would still be required to register as a sex offender. Could you handle that?"

"I was forced to register as a sex offender after I was released a few years ago. When I sat at my dining room table and saw the notification card with my photograph on it, it was the most horrible and humiliating thing that has ever happened to me," she said, fighting back tears. "It's why I want a pardon, so I can move forward with my life with no restrictions."

The member pressed the question. "But what if all you receive is a commutation, then what?"

"I guess I would have to deal with it on a day-to-day basis," Smith answered, her voice quiet and resigned. "I just don't want to go back to prison."

After the hearing concluded, the defense team from Davis Polk talked privately.

"I think at least two of the members are with us," Katz said. "It's hard to read the other nine, but I am concerned."

"We only need six votes to get a recommendation for clemency. It's possible that we have that," another countered.

"Let's hope."

CHAPTER 39
THE DEAL
MARCH 9 - JUNE 4, 2013 EIGHTEEN AND A HALF YEARS AFTER CONVICTION

haron Katz knew that time was running out for Nancy Smith. If Smith did not receive clemency, which was essentially a forgiveness of her crimes, she would be sent back to prison. Six weeks had elapsed since the clemency hearing and the board had not announced its decision. Katz had hoped that the board would expedite its recommendation, but that apparently was not going to happen. Instead, the reality of a long wait was taking hold. She realized that it could be months before the parole board and then the governor acted upon Smith's petition. And when they did, there was no guarantee that either would grant the relief she'd requested. The only thing separating Smith from prison was Judge Burge who had, thus far, refused to hold the hearing to correct the faulty journal entry. But this stalemate was soon to end.

By testifying on Smith's behalf at her clemency hearing, Judge Burge had aligned himself with her side and was duty-bound to recuse himself from any further involvement in her case. This he had done. The day before, the Ohio Supreme Court had assigned a retired Stark County judge, Judge Virgil Lee Sinclair, to take over both the Smith and the Allen cases. Judge Sinclair's mission was simple: he was to hold the hearings that would amend the final journal entries and send both Smith and Allen back to prison.

The sixty-two-year-old Katz was determined to keep Smith out of prison. Except for a stint as a law clerk for a federal judge, she'd spent her entire legal career at Davis Polk. A litigator from the moment that she'd joined the firm, Katz had co-chaired the firm's pro bono committee for six years before she'd recently been placed in charge of it. Before that, she'd offered her legal skills to incarcerated women, helping them resolve custody, visitation, and other family law disputes. By all accounts, Katz was a premier attorney, well respected by her peers and skilled at overcoming the most challenging of legal obstacles.

Katz could also enlist the resources and talent of Davis Polk, a firm that had often garnered national and state awards for its pro bono services. If anyone had the ability to keep Nancy Smith out of prison, it was Sharon Katz and her team at Davis Polk.

Although she was uncertain about Smith's chances for clemency, Katz had strategically pursued another path with Assistant Lorain County Prosecutor Anthony Cillo, the head of the prosecutor's criminal division. Prior to the clemency hearing, the two had spoken about a sentencing agreement, a contract whose terms resolved a criminal matter, including the length of any prison term. Because it would supersede Judge McGough's original sentence, the sentencing agreement was a powerful alternative.

She and Cillo had exchanged some general ideas, but nothing had been finalized. Katz's ultimate goal was to reach an agreement that would release Smith from prison for the time she'd already served. With Judge Sinclair waiting in the wings, Katz felt an overriding urgency to negotiate and complete this agreement before the new judge corrected the journal entry and returned her client to prison.

Without any prompting, one of Katz's associates had taken the initiative to gather background information about Judge Sinclair.

Katz eagerly read the associate's summary. Just sixty-one years old, Judge Sinclair had retired from the bench a year earlier after serving as a county judge for seventeen years. Not only a practical judge, he was also a teacher, integrally involved in a program that taught newly elected judges how to do their jobs. He apparently was the lead faculty member for a required course on handling capital murder cases, a course that all judges were required to complete before presiding over this most serious type of criminal case.

When Katz read this, she assumed that he was tough on crime. This was confirmed when she read further. Upon retiring, he'd told a reporter why he'd become a judge and why he'd relished the role. "It allows you to make the community safer when you handle criminal cases and you put some of these really bad people that we deal with off the street for a long time."

Although Judge Sinclair was obviously smart and well regarded, Katz was concerned that this tough-on-crime judge would lump Nancy Smith as one of the "bad people" and be unwilling to release her after she'd only served fifteen years of her original sentence. However, she realized that she needed to focus first on the essential tasks ahead. As a New York lawyer, she was required to obtain special permission from the judge to appear in an Ohio courtroom on behalf of Smith. Next, she'd try to hammer out an agreement that would satisfy both the prosecutor and her client. Once this was accomplished, she and the prosecutor would go to Judge Sinclair and ask for his approval, something the law required.

June 4, 2013

Dressed in a black suit, her light brown hair styled short, Sharon Katz appeared relaxed and confident as she walked into the courtroom with Nancy Smith. Before she sat down, Katz smiled and whispered something to a Davis Polk attorney sitting in the front row. Poised, she looked straight ahead, waiting for the judge to enter the courtroom. A few moments later, Jack Bradley joined them as they waited for the proceeding to begin.

They were at the finish line. She'd negotiated an eight-page sentencing agreement with Assistant Prosecutor Cillo and it rested on the table in front of them. In it, Smith had agreed to give up any further right to appeal her conviction or to seek redress in a wrongful-conviction lawsuit. A few weeks earlier, Katz had filed a motion seeking a new trial for Smith, and this effort would be abandoned as part of the agreement. In return, the prosecutor had agreed to reduce each of the six charges against her to gross sexual imposition and recommend that she be sentenced to only twelve years in prison. Because Smith had already been incarcerated for almost fifteen years, she would be set free today if the judge adopted this agreement in open court.

Both sides had carefully crafted the document. The agreement gave Smith the right to continue with the pending clemency petition and did not require her to plead guilty to any charges in open court. In what would later turn out to be an extremely important provision, the agreement could be amended at any time if both parties consented in writing.

Katz and her team had also researched whether Smith would be required to register as a sex offender after the resentencing. They'd provided the judge with a memorandum that carefully explained that the law in effect at the time she was sentenced in 1994 had no such mandate and all subsequent laws could not be applied to her retroactively.

A few minutes earlier in chambers, Judge Sinclair had quizzed Katz and Assistant Prosecutor Cillo about the case and the sentencing agreement. Although the judge had conducted several telephonic status conferences with the attorneys, this was Katz's first in-person meeting with him. He asked probing questions and she quickly recognized that he was an intelligent, no-nonsense jurist. He'd concluded their conference by telling the attorneys that he would approve the agreement and commended them for working out an acceptable resolution.

Cameras began clicking as soon as Judge Sinclair took his seat behind the bench. The judge's long gray hair extended over his ears and flowed below his collar, giving him a youthful appearance. He took off his glasses and held them in one hand before he addressed Nancy Smith.

"Mrs. Smith, I want to make sure that you have reviewed this sentencing agreement with your attorney. Has she explained all of its terms to you?"

"She has," Smith replied in a quiet voice, her eyes looking straight ahead at the judge.

"And have you read it?"

Smith nodded.

"Have you knowingly, honestly, and intelligently reviewed this agreement before you signed it?"

"I have."

"Being satisfied that this is the case, the Court will adopt the sentencing agreement in its entirety. Pursuant to Criminal Rule 32(C), I will also amend the sentencing journal entry to reflect that you were found guilty by a jury."

As Judge Sinclair began to recite the changes and reductions in her sentences, Nancy Smith looked down, removed her glasses, and took a tissue to both eyes. While the judge continued with the sentencing, her chin twitched, and she repeatedly wiped tears from the corners of her eyes. Looking up from his notes, he told Smith that she would receive credit for the years that she'd already spent in prison and that her sentence had, therefore, been served in full. In his concluding remarks, he announced that Smith would not have to register as a sex offender —adopting in full Katz's legal analysis on this issue.

With that, Smith was free to return to her children and grandchildren. She rose and hugged her attorneys, first Katz and then Bradley. When reporters gathered around Smith, Katz told them that her client did not want to make a statement. Instead, Katz said, "Nancy Smith wants to thank all of the people who have supported her throughout this ordeal. She is going to move forward with the clemency and with her life."

"Is she admitting to these crimes?" one reporter asked.

"In this agreement, she merely acknowledged that a jury found her guilty of these crimes. That's all she has admitted to. She has not pled guilty in court and she has not pled guilty in any entry. As I said, we will continue to press for a pardon from the governor. This was the right move for Nancy today. She will not need to return to prison."

As Katz walked away from the Justice Center, she thought about what had just happened. She'd worked out a solid compromise that had saved her client from returning to prison. However, Katz was still troubled by the case. Despite all that had been revealed since the 1994 trial, the other side was still unwilling to admit that it had been wrong to prosecute Smith and Allen. In agreeing to the deal, the prosecutor had pressed for language that Smith had been "found guilty of all charges, beyond a reasonable doubt, upon sufficient proof," and that all reviewing courts had confirmed this.

Despite his insistence on these face-saving recitations, the prosecutor had, nevertheless, been willing to "commute" Smith's sentence to time served. Why? Apparently, it wasn't just the public and the media that had serious misgivings about the verdicts.

CHAPTER 40
A DIFFERENT RESULT
OCTOBER 1, 2013 NINETEEN YEARS AFTER CONVICTION

Joseph Allen sat slumped next to his attorney as he waited for Judge Lee Sinclair to take the bench and announce his new sentence in open court. After being free for four years, he would be returning to prison. Unlike Nancy Smith who had been released for time served, that would not be his fate. Instead, he'd ultimately been given the choice between serving two hundred years in prison on all charges or accepting a prison term of ten to twenty-five years for one count of rape. It was no choice.

On its face, it appeared that the prosecutor had treated Smith and Allen very differently. However, Prosecutor Will, through his chief criminal assistant, Anthony Cillo, had offered Allen a deal very similar to the one presented to Smith. Allen's charges would be reduced, new sentences would be imposed that were less than the time he'd already served, and he, too, would not be returning to prison. Allen had accepted this proposal and both sides had believed that he would be a free man. However, when the agreement was presented to Judge Sinclair, the judge would not approve it.

The sticking point was Allen's prior criminal history, including his conviction for sexual battery in 1985 and several complaints involving children and teens that never resulted in charges. By contrast, Smith had no prior record. As part of the negotiations, the prosecutor has insisted that Allen undergo two psychological examinations, including a sex offender risk assessment. In recommending Allen's release, the prosecutor had added a proviso: Allen was to be supervised.

Concerned for the public's safety, Judge Sinclair had nixed the deal. The judge reasoned that he'd been assigned to this case solely to resentence Allen and not to determine whether the man had been wrongfully convicted. For that reason, the judge felt compelled to consider Allen's prior criminal conduct.

After the judge had voiced his objections, the prosecutor and Allen's attorney, K. Ronald Bailey, had eventually drafted a new agreement—one that Judge Sinclair had signaled he would approve. From Judge Sinclair's vantage, the new agreement was still a significant reduction in Allen's sentence. Based on time served, Allen would be released from prison in ten years, and perhaps sooner if he was granted parole. For Allen, a man whom many believed to be innocent of all charges, it was a crushing development.

A few minutes after Allen and Bailey sat in their seats, Judge Sinclair took the bench. The judge looked around the courtroom before he spoke. Unlike the hearing four months earlier, the room was almost empty. Other than several reporters and Allen's two brothers, there were no other spectators. For a case that had garnered national attention, the lack of any outside interest was striking. The judge's voice was conversational as he began, "The prosecutor has dropped all charges except for the charge of rape in count one. On that count, the defendant will serve a term of ten years minimum and twenty-five years maximum pursuant to Ohio Revised Code 2907.02(A)(1)(b). He will be given credit for time served." He did not elaborate further.

Allen looked at his attorney, his eyes pleading, unable to hide his anguish. He rubbed the back of his right hand against his eyes, trying to wipe away the tears that would not stop.

As if nothing out of the ordinary were happening, the judge asked each attorney if they wanted to put anything else on the record. When they declined, he turned to Joseph Allen.

"Anything else from you, Mr. Allen?" Judge Sinclair asked. His tone was genial, like a waiter checking to see if a patron desired dessert.

"No, Your Honor," he responded, his voice barely audible but still respectful.

Allen's shoulders heaved and he hid his eyes behind his right hand. He drew in great gulps of air between soft, high-pitched cries. Bailey put his arm around him and expressed his sorrow, regretting that he had not achieved a better result.

Bailey's words were of little comfort. Allen continued to sob, his face a mixture of despair and resignation.

Two sheriff's deputies stood by him, their looks sympathetic. They inched closer, knowing that they needed to handcuff him and lead him out of the courtroom. Both looked reluctant to make the first move. When Allen's attorney stood, Allen grabbed his attorney's forearm, like a drowning man clinging to a life ring. After his attorney again expressed his sympathy, Allen released his grip.

Allen slowly stood from his chair, revealing a heavyset man now in his sixties. His untucked green shirt hung over his stomach, while his open collar was now stained with tears. A photographer's camera clicked in a steady whir as one deputy applied the handcuffs. Allen shook his head and looked at his brothers one last time before heading for the side door. One deputy gently placed his arm on Allen's back and guided him away.

Allen's two brothers walked from the courtroom and into the hall, where a reporter asked them for their comments.

One brother could not hide his anger. "I don't understand this. This is a travesty. Either way he went, they had him. They put him between a rock and a hard place. What kind of choice was that? Two hundred years or ten to twenty-five. That man has suffered enough for fifteen years. I can't believe the way they continue to do him."

When that brother paused, the other one jumped in. "What kind of stuff is this? He got railroaded. He went through enough hell already and we've gone through enough for him too. I put my house up for him now two times."

In the empty hallway, the first brother looked at the reporter, unable to disguise his bitterness. "The people should cry out about this. It's not right. It's just not right." If the public's interest in this hearing was any indication, that would not happen.

The two brothers turned and walked toward the elevators, unable to understand why their brother was returning to prison. If Nancy Smith was free, why wasn't their brother? No one—not the judge, not the attorneys, and certainly not the legal system—could ever explain that to them. Not ever.

PART
FIVE

CHAPTER 41
THE PHONE CALL

AUGUST 27, 2021
TWENTY-SEVEN YEARS AFTER
CONVICTION

When the phone rang at ten that evening, Mark Godsey was not sure whether he would answer it. As the director of the Ohio Innocence Project, he often put in long hours, and this night was no exception. When he picked up the receiver, the caller identified himself as Rocco Bronson Jr. By the tone of the man's voice, it was clear that he was agitated, maybe even hysterical.

"I have information about the Head Start case and I need to talk to someone about it now," Rocco Bronson said.

Godsey knew instantly who the caller was. Rocco Bronson was the brother of one of the Head Start children, Nina Zorich, whose mother had first made the sensational claims against Nancy Smith.

Eight years had passed since Judge Sinclair had approved the sentencing agreements involving Smith and Allen. Godsey had never felt satisfied with the result they'd achieved for Smith, even though the agreement had allowed her to stay out of prison permanently. Several months after her hearing before Judge Sinclair, the parole board had finally ruled on her clemency petition. Once again, it had been a very disappointing result. In a nine to two vote, the board had recommended against a pardon. Although the board's decision was not binding on the governor, he had taken no action on her petition. As a result, she remained a convicted felon.

Although he did not represent Joseph Allen, Godsey could think of nothing crueler than what had happened to that unfortunate man. Four years after Judge Burge's decision had released him from prison, Allen had been teased with a deal that would have granted him his continued freedom—only to have it snatched away at the last moment. Yes, there was much unfinished business with the Head Start case: first and foremost, the release of Joseph Allen, and then the exoneration of both defendants.

Through years of experience, Godsey had learned to be skeptical of calls like this. New witnesses surfaced all the time, claiming to have startling new information that did not pan out. Often the evidence was not new or was inadmissible hearsay, or, worse yet, was patently untrue on its face. "What is it that you want to tell me?" Godsey asked.

"I just read the stuff online about Nancy Smith and I'm freaking out," Rocco Bronson said.

Godsey assumed that Rocco Bronson was referring to the application for clemency that the Ohio Innocence Project had made accessible through its website. That cache of documents included a summary of the exculpatory evidence supported by affidavits, records, and reports.

"My mom coached my little sister to say all that stuff just to get money," Rocco Bronson said. There it was: concise and direct. Many had supposed Marge Bronson had manufactured the allegations against Nancy Smith and the man called Joseph to secure a large settlement, but there was never any direct proof. When she and the other parents sued Head Start, it added fuel to the speculation. But, then again, wouldn't any parent seek money damages if their child had been molested while participating in a preschool program?

"Go on," Godsey urged.

"I saw it with my own eyes. At six, I was old enough to understand what was going on. She told my sister what to say and practiced with her—telling her that if she got it right, we would get enough money to go to Disney World. She held Disney World over her head as a reward. I mean, I wanted to go to Disney World, too. What kid wouldn't?

"She'd tell my sister that if she didn't get the story right, the

'Cucuy,' which is slang for 'boogeyman,' would come to our house and kill our family and then her."

Rocco Bronson paused for a moment as if gathering his thoughts. "Here's the thing. Before I checked out your website today, I never knew what the exact allegations were against the defendants. Much of the weird stuff—you know, the sexual abuse that was alleged—my mom and her male friends had done that to us kids when we were little. Like they'd sexually abuse us with sticks and make us pee into bottles."

"You are talking about your sister, Nina, and you?" Godsey asked.

"Yes, both of us. I remember one occasion where a man was licking my sister's face all over and the man and my mom were laughing hysterically. They made me leave the basement and then I heard my sister scream. I was sexually abused several times by one of my mom's boyfriends, but I'd rather not go into the details."

Over the next few minutes, Rocco Bronson told Godsey that his mother had set up a school in the basement, complete with tiny desks, where Nina and several of the other alleged victims played games to sharpen their skills at telling their stories of abuse. The children would advance in the games if they repeated the allegations just as Marge Bronson had instructed them. She'd also posted a photograph of Joseph Allen on the basement wall and asked Nina to study it, point to it, and say it was Joseph.

"Can anyone else verify these things?" Godsey asked.

"My dad can," Rocco Bronson said. "His name is the same as mine except he's Rocco Bronson Sr. My mom and dad were divorced at the time, but he still came over to pick me and my older sister up for visitation. He attended birthday parties and other family events at my mom's house. He saw her coaching Nina and he heard my mom brag that she'd get paid when this was all over."

"Why are you telling me these things now?" Godsey asked. This man was an adult, probably in his early thirties. Why hadn't he volunteered this critical information earlier?

"Because my mom is doing the same type of thing with my wife and our little daughter," Rocco Bronson replied.

"I don't understand. You're going to have to explain that to me."

For the next fifteen minutes, Godsey listened carefully to Rocco Bronson's detailed account. Godsey soon understood that Marge Bronson had falsely claimed that her granddaughter, Rocco's toddler, had been sexually abused by Rocco's wife, Emily. She'd spread the claims of sexual abuse in an effort to gain custody of the little girl. Although doctors repeatedly found no evidence of sexual abuse, Marge Bronson had claimed otherwise to all who would listen.

She ultimately alleged that Rocco's wife had sexually abused the little girl during a visit supervised by Lorain County Children Services. This led to a sheriff's investigation that concluded that Marge Bronson had coached her granddaughter to make this false claim. Rocco Bronson suspected that his mother was trying to manufacture a claim against Lorain County Children Services for monetary gain.

"Anything else you want to share with me?" Godsey asked.

"Three of the kids in the Head Start case admitted that nothing happened and that the allegations were made up. One told me this at the time of the police investigation, another when we were teenagers, and a third told me when we were adults."

Godsey had always thought that the children had been manipu-lated and coerced into telling these stories but, after much condition-ing, they'd eventually believed them to be true. Rocco Bronson was saying something much worse: the victims knew that they'd lied.

"My mom has told them that if it's ever discovered that their claims are false, they'll have to give all the money back—besides being disgraced."

After the telephone conversation ended, Godsey knew that he needed to verify Rocco Bronson's claims. During their conversation, Rocco Bronson had disclosed not only that he and his wife were battling his mother for custody, but that they were also struggling with their own drug addictions. He had motives to lie.

Godsey decided to send Dr. Virginia Braden to Lorain to interview Rocco Bronson, Bronson's wife, and the people he'd mentioned. Braden had a PhD in criminal justice and had worked as a victims' advocate, private investigator, and behavioral analyst, serving private clients and law enforcement agencies. She'd done freelance work for the Ohio Innocence Project before, and he would have her investigate whether there was any merit to Rocco Bronson's revelations. Godsey had seen claims like Bronson's crumble under the scrutiny of an investigator. He would have to wait and see what developed, if anything.

Even if Dr. Braden corroborated Rocco Bronson's story, Godsey would have to overcome another obstacle, maybe an insurmountable one. Both Smith and Allen had signed sentencing agreements in 2013 that prohibited them from ever again challenging their convictions even if newly discovered evidence came to light. This meant that even if Rocco Bronson's claims had merit, his allegations could not serve as a basis for a new trial or a further appeal. The agreement, however, contained one exception, albeit a very unlikely one. If both the prosecutor and the defendants agreed in writing to modify the sentencing contract, it could be amended to allow for a further legal challenge. But what were the chances that this would happen?

As it turned out, things had changed in the prosecutor's office once again. J. D. Tomlinson, a former criminal defense attorney, had ousted the sitting prosecutor, Dennis Will, in the primary and then defeated the Republican challenger in the general election in 2020. One of Tomlinson's campaign promises had been to review the legitimacy of the Head Start convictions.

Since taking over the office, Tomlinson had assigned two of his investigators, two retired police detectives, to do just that. They'd studied the police reports, dissected the trial testimony, and reinterviewed key law enforcement personnel involved in the case. They'd been shocked at the things they'd found: the coercive interviewing techniques, the children's ever-changing and inconsistent stories, and the coaching by police and parents during Joseph Allen's lineup.

During their four-month review, the investigators periodically shared their findings with Tomlinson and one of his assistants. In the end, the four reached a unanimous conclusion: Smith and Allen were innocent of the charges. As an added wild card, Judge Burge, who'd resigned his judgeship in 2015, was now Tomlinson's chief administrator.

If ever the defense could mount a successful challenge, it appeared, for the first time, that the stars were finally aligned.

CHAPTER 42
JUDGE CHRIS COOK

DECEMBER 22, 2021
TWENTY-SEVEN YEARS AFTER
CONVICTION

Before he made any decision, Judge Chris Cook would proceed slowly and methodically, determined to gather the facts and probe the parties with pointed questions. A week earlier, Nancy Smith and Joseph Allen had filed a joint motion seeking permission to file a motion for a new trial based on recently discovered evidence. The prosecutor, J. D. Tomlinson, had answered the motion, stating that he would not oppose it. Rumors were swirling that if the court granted a new trial, the new prosecutor had no intention of retrying the defendants and would dismiss all charges. At last, it appeared that the case would soon be over.

That is, until Jonathan Rosenbaum, representing two of the alleged victims, filed a motion with the court to disqualify the prosecutor from the case and to appoint a special prosecutor to vigorously contest the defendants' motion. Rosenbaum, the former assistant prosecutor who had prosecuted the original case, was not going to allow the case to die without a fight.

The motion was Judge Cook's to decide because he had inherited all cases from Judge McGough's former docket. Understanding the magnitude of this case, he was committed to moving deliberately in order to "get it right." Judge Cook was the youngest of the six Lorain

County common pleas judges and was finishing his first six-year term. Despite being the most junior of the county judges, he had quickly proven himself capable in his new position. He had come to the job with a diverse legal background: former assistant county prosecutor, magistrate, city prosecutor, and a private civil practice that included frequent litigation. In addition, he was descended from a long line of distinguished Lorain County attorneys, being the fourth generation to practice in Lorain County.

Rosenbaum had been able to insert himself into the case by representing two of the alleged victims, Melissa Warner and Nina Zorich. Under an Ohio constitutional amendment known as Marsy's Law, victims had the right to be heard in judicial proceedings involving their perpetrators. In full-time private practice since 2005, Rosenbaum was still a pugnacious, no-holds-barred attorney who could dominate a hearing, despite being confined to a wheelchair. In 2008, a bullet had lodged in his spine during a shooting range accident, paralyzing him from the waist down.

Judge Cook had devoted his entire morning to reviewing the briefs and familiarizing himself with the case's long history. The defendants' joint motion alleged a sinister plot behind the original allegations against them. They maintained that Marge Bronson had orchestrated false claims against them for financial gain. The defendants supported this claim by submitting affidavits from two members of Marge Bronson's family: her son, Rocco Bronson Jr., and her ex-husband, Rocco Bronson Sr.

The defendants also asserted that, during the last year, Marge Bronson had falsely accused her daughter-in-law of sexually abusing her child. Marge Bronson had said these things in an attempt to gain custody of her granddaughter and perhaps seek damages in a complicated scheme against Lorain County Children Services. The affidavit of Rocco Bronson Jr. elaborated on these events, as did the affidavit of Dr. Virginia Braden, a private investigator who'd interviewed witnesses and reviewed records associated with this claim.

For good measure, the defendants also filed a recent affidavit from former detective Tom Cantu. In it, Cantu restated his opinion that the children's allegations were unfounded. However, he added a new wrinkle—his suspicion that the children had been coached for financial gain.

The final document attached to the defendants' motion was the thirty-three-page affidavit of Dr. Maggie Bruck, the renowned psychologist who'd testified at Smith's clemency hearing. Her detailed affidavit spelled out why the children's testimony was wholly unreliable.

Judge Cook knew the law on this issue. A judge could grant a new trial based on newly discovered evidence only if that evidence was so strong that it would likely change the result in the case and could not have been discovered at the time of the original trial. The defendants argued that their new evidence met that threshold.

However, to receive a new trial, the defendants had to first show that they had not relinquished this right when they signed their sentencing agreements in 2013. On their faces, the agreements prohibited any further challenges to their convictions, and that would include this bid for a new trial. To circumvent this, the defendants and the prosecutor had executed an amendment to the agreements that allowed for this new filing. The question for Judge Cook was whether this was legally permissible.

Rosenbaum's seventeen-page motion and brief argued that all of the attorneys in the prosecutor's office were disqualified from having any involvement in this case. He grounded his argument on ethical rules that prohibited attorneys from handling any matter in which they had a conflict of interest. In this case, Rosenbaum maintained that a conflict of interest existed because former Judge Burge, a public official who had previously presided over the case, was now a member of the prosecutor's staff. Because of this conflict, Rosenbaum asked the judge to appoint a special prosecutor, either Rosenbaum himself or someone from the Ohio attorney general's staff, to contest the defendants' motion for a new trial.

Although this was the gist of the motion, the brief was a furious tirade against former Judge Burge, whom Rosenbaum obviously held in the highest disdain. Rosenbaum claimed that Judge Burge's earlier attempt to free Smith and Allen had been "illegal, misguided, improper, personal, unethical, and perhaps corrupt."

Rosenbaum's opinion of Prosecutor Tomlinson was just as scathing.

He argued that Tomlinson's response in this case was a blatant violation of his oath of office and an abdication of his role to defend the public from crime. Rosenbaum characterized Tomlinson's response to the motion as arrogant and a rejection of "our entire system of criminal law and jurisprudence." He also suggested that Tomlinson and his staff should have taken action to reimprison Smith and Allen under their original sentences, because by filing their motion, they had repudiated their 2013 resentencing agreement.

As for the defendants' new evidence, Rosenbaum attacked Rocco Bronson Jr. as a convicted drug offender who would go to any lengths (even perjury and planting drugs) to discredit his mother in their custody dispute. What went unsaid was that Rosenbaum and the police had relied upon Marge Bronson, a convicted drug felon, to build their criminal cases against Smith and Allen twenty-seven years earlier. Relying primarily on personal attacks and emotional appeals, Rosenbaum had not supported his motion with any affidavits or other sworn testimony as would be customary.

He'd also failed to counter the affidavits of Rocco Bronson Sr., Thomas Cantu, Virginia Braden, and Maggie Bruck. Rosenbaum's failure to address Braden's affidavit about Marge Bronson's allegations against her daughter-in-law was particularly striking. In parsing out these claims, Braden had interviewed witnesses, reviewed medical records, analyzed the sheriff's investigation, and reported on the findings of Lorain County Children Services. Her affidavit recounted how Marge Bronson had manufactured a false story about her granddaughter's alleged sexual abuse and then coached her to tell that story—all to gain an advantage in a custody dispute and perhaps seek money damages from Children Services.

In a few minutes, Judge Cook would enter his courtroom to address the pending motions. Once again, the Head Start case had drawn a packed courtroom complete with newspaper reporters and videographers. All the parties and their attorneys were present, including Joseph Allen, who had been transported to the Justice Center from prison. Allen was represented by a new lawyer, Richard Parsons, a Columbus attorney who'd been hired to defend Allen by the National Center for Reason and Justice, a nonprofit organization that sought to free people it believed had been wrongfully convicted of sexual crimes. The organization had been involved in Allen's defense for a decade, first providing him with a private attorney, Ronald Bailey. After Judge Sinclair had returned Allen to prison, the organization had replaced Bailey with Parsons's firm.

Mark Godsey was advocating on behalf of Nancy Smith. Smith's former attorney, Jack Bradley, had been elected the mayor of Lorain the previous year and was no longer practicing law. Per the court's order, the prosecutor, J. D. Tomlinson, was also in attendance, along with an assistant prosecutor, Nicholas Celebrezze. The only attorney not physically present was Jonathan Rosenbaum, who was participating via Zoom.

As Judge Cook took the bench, he seemed confident and energetic. Trim and athletic with short-cropped hair, Judge Cook looked younger than his fifty-seven years. He began by reciting the case history and asking the attorneys to correct any inaccuracies in his chronology. Godsey offered the only correction—that Nancy Smith had not plead to lesser charges in 2013, but had instead agreed only to a resentencing agreement.

Judge Cook told the attorneys that he would address three issues today in the following order: potential conflicts of interest of the attorneys and him, the amendment to the 2013 sentencing agreement, and the motion for leave to file for a new trial. Of all the Lorain County judges, Judge Cook probably had the most experience in dealing with ethical issues affecting attorneys and judges which included conflicts of interest. Before he'd been elected to the bench, he'd prosecuted attorneys accused of ethical violations. In addition, he was currently the Vice-Chair of the Ohio Board of Professional Conduct, a board appointed by the Ohio Supreme Court to hear claims of ethical violations against both attorneys and judges.

Judge Cook began by disclosing his own potential conflicts in presiding over this case. He indicated that he'd been a county prosecutor early in his career, but not until after the Head Start case had been tried to a jury and then affirmed by the court of appeals. Later, he'd been associated with the law firm of Bradley and Giardini for several years. He explained that he had not been involved in the Head

Start case in either employment. He asked each side if it wanted to disqualify him from the case and neither did.

Judge Cook quickly turned to Rosenbaum's argument that all of the attorneys in the prosecutor's office were disqualified from representing the State of Ohio because former Judge Burge was now on its staff. Rosenbaum had cited a specific rule that, on its face, seemed to demand that result. Former judges and attorneys practicing in the same law firm were prohibited from handling any matter that the judge had presided over while a judge. However, Judge Cook took a more detailed look at the question and found that the prosecutor's office was not a law firm under the rules. As a result, he concluded that the rule only excluded former Judge Burge from participating but not anyone else on the prosecutor's staff.

Rosenbaum conceded that he "didn't disagree with the judge's analysis." However, he turned to a second rule that he believed required Tomlinson to step aside. That rule prohibited an attorney from representing a client if that lawyer's judgment would be compromised by "the lawyer's responsibilities to a third party"—in this case former Judge Burge. This argument was a stretch. It left unanswered a pivotal question: What responsibilities did Tomlinson owe former Judge Burge? Nevertheless, Rosenbaum pursued this argument aggressively.

His face looming in the video monitor, Rosenbaum said, "They've proven that they aren't going to advocate on behalf of the State or these victims. They've conceded in every possible way, shape, or form that they aren't going to fight this or adduce any evidence to give the Court an informed decision based on an adversarial process, and I think that disqualifies them."

Judge Cook responded by first praising Rosenbaum as one of the "most renowned and well-known prosecutors in Lorain County history." But, from his next comments, it was clear that he was not persuaded by Rosenbaum's argument.

"You say that the prosecutor is abdicating his responsibility. I guess I'm troubled by that phrase. We all know that prosecutors dismiss cases all of the time. They amend cases all of the time. And it seems to me that the role of the prosecutor is to do just that, to evaluate the case and make a decision based on what they believe justice requires."

Rosenbaum was not willing to concede the point. He argued that the case had been affirmed many times by various courts and, in his opinion, the defendants were not presenting any new evidence. He wanted Judge Cook to put the new evidence to the test through cross-examination of any witnesses who'd provided an affidavit.

"And this prosecutor's office is not going to do that. They're laying down for whatever reason. They're taking up where Jim Burge left off as a judge when he wrongfully acquitted these people with no review of the evidence." This last statement ignored the record. When former Judge Burge had acquitted the defendants in 2009, he'd prefaced it by explaining that he'd read the entire trial transcript and the children's transcribed statements from police interviews.

Unable to hide his disgust, Rosenbaum said, "But what's going on in this case now is a farce."

Judge Cook tried to interject a question, but Rosenbaum was not finished. After reminding the judge that Burge was Tomlinson's mentor, he attacked the former judge again. "Jim Burge's actions in this case are reprehensible. He disobeyed a direct mandate from the Ohio Supreme Court to resentence these people. Ignored it. Went down to the Adult Parole Authority and testified on behalf of Nancy Smith.

"Give me the chance to contest this evidence or appoint someone that will, and then make an informed decision. That's what we're asking for."

Judge Cook realized that Rosenbaum had never answered his question about a prosecutor's right to dismiss cases based on further investigation. He asked the question again and Rosenbaum agreed that the prosecutor had that power, but that it had to be exercised fairly.

Rosenbaum belittled Tomlinson, insinuating that his actions were arbitrary, almost whimsical. "A prosecutor cannot just walk in and say, 'Because I'm now newly elected—I'm the new guy—I have the pardoning authority to dump any case that I think, for whatever personal reason, deserves it.' There has to be a check and balance on that power, and that is the courts."

Rosenbaum's characterization of Tomlinson's behavior ignored that the new prosecutor had proceeded slowly and acted only after two veteran former detectives had reexamined the evidence over several months and reported their results to him.

Rosenbaum then attacked the defendants' new evidence, claiming that Rocco Bronson Jr. had been accused by the prosecutor of planting evidence on his mother. His voice incredulous, he continued, "Rocco Bronson was seven years old. Now all of a sudden, he's the basis to second-guess this? You know, the cases where people walk out of court, there's been retesting. There's been new DNA evidence."

Judge Cook responded that the defendants had presented more than just the affidavit of Rocco Bronson Jr., referencing the affidavits of Tom Cantu, Dr. Virginia Braden, and the "incredibly compelling report of Dr. Maggie Bruck."

Rosenbaum countered, "They did not meet with these children. They are in no position whatsoever to evaluate the children's testimony twenty-seven years later and offer an expert report. But think about it, can anybody go out and hire an expert to offer an opinion twenty-seven years later and say a conviction was no good?

"Detective Cantu was removed from this case because he was friends with Nancy Smith. He worked bingo with her," Rosenbaum claimed, repeating his charge that Smith and Cantu were friends, something Cantu vehemently denied. "But the fact that they have new affidavits from people who purport to have some kind of all-effective twenty/twenty hindsight is preposterous and should be contested in court."

Judge Cook had heard enough and was ready to move on to a new subject. "Now, well, we've turned the lens of potential conflicts on myself and on the prosecutor's office. Unfortunately, we now need to turn it on you." Cook paused before continuing, "How do you address the concern that you were the former prosecutor on this case? Your client was the State of Ohio. You are coming into court on behalf of two victims advocating a position contrary to your former client. Absent a waiver from the prosecutor's office that permits you to take on this representation, how do you appear in this court arguing against your former client in a case where you were lead counsel?"

Rosenbaum conceded that he'd received a nonbinding advisory

opinion from the Board of Professional Conduct that concluded that he had a conflict, but he'd disagreed with it. "I'm not arguing against my former client. I'm arguing in the exact same vein and the exact same way as I did for my former client."

Rosenbaum then proposed that he would withdraw if the court appointed someone else to contest the defendants' motion. "But I cannot leave these people and my former client hanging when Prosecutor Tomlinson is hell-bent on doing Burge's personal desires and dumping this case without any chance of an adversarial proceeding or anybody representing the State of Ohio."

Judge Cook quickly seized on the fallacy of Rosenbaum's argument. "You're making an assumption that because you're being consistent with the prior position of your client, that your former client can't change its mind. I mean, any client who has a lawyer who has represented him or her has a right to change their mind and seek new direction with their representation.

"And the lawyer doesn't get to say, 'No, client, you can't change your mind. I'm going to take a position adverse to what you want to do today because of what you wanted yesterday.' A client controls the relationship and the client controls the direction of the representation."

Leaving little doubt about his opinion on the issue, Judge Cook concluded, "Mr. Tomlinson is the duly elected prosecutor for Lorain County and it's his mandate, obligation, and responsibility to prosecute this matter as he deems appropriate. If the people of Lorain County disagree with his handling of this matter, he will be accountable down the road when he runs for re-election."

Turning to Prosecutor Tomlinson, Judge Cook asked, "Have you given Mr. Rosenbaum a waiver, permitting him to represent the victims in this case?"

"No, we have not," Tomlinson replied. "And, if I may, I would like to respond briefly to Mr. Rosenbaum." The judge nodded, signaling him to continue.

"I have signed all of the pleadings in this case. I am the attorney in charge of this investigation. Mr. Burge has not been involved in this review. We have screened him from any participation in this process," Tomlinson explained.

"I think I've heard enough on that issue. Let's turn to the sentencing agreement and the amendment that was recently filed," the judge said.

The defendants claimed that the agreement was a contract like any other and, pursuant to its terms, allowed the parties to modify it if they all consented.

Rosenbaum did not agree. "I think this contract analogy doesn't fit. It would be like I'm buying a car; I drive it into the ground, and then I turn around and say I want a new one."

Again, Judge Cook was not moved by Rosenbaum's argument. "If the dealership says 'Okay, no problem,' why is that an issue?"

After the defendants established that the 2013 sentencing agreement was not incorporated into a final journal entry, Judge Cook seemed confident that the parties could amend it to allow for the new motion. However, Rosenbaum continued to protest.

"It's not something that we just come to court and say, as a matter of contract, we're going to just undo it now because the new parties don't like it," Rosenbaum said indignantly. "That would destroy our system of justice."

"Let's move on to the final issue today—the motion for leave to file for a new trial," Judge Cook said. "Mr. Godsey, I will begin with you on this issue."

For the previous thirty minutes, Godsey had listened to Rosenbaum ridicule his new evidence, convinced that Rosenbaum was providing the judge with wildly inaccurate information. Rosenbaum had been doing what he did best: finding the weakest point in his opponent's argument and attacking it. In this case, he had zeroed in on the credibility and motives of Rocco Bronson Jr., but the defendants' new evidence was more than just that. As Godsey stood to address the judge, he was eager to provide the judge with the full story.

"Attorney Rosenbaum has claimed that none of our evidence is new, that we are rehashing things that have been litigated before. Let me respond to that. The most powerful piece of new evidence happened this year when the ringleader of what happened in 1993 and 1994 was found to have coached her granddaughter to make false allegations of sexual abuse. And we were following this as it was happening. And it is all detailed in the affidavit of Virginia Braden.

"A Lorain County sheriff testified that Marge Bronson's charges were unfounded, and he was able to determine that she had coached this child in a situation where Bronson could potentially have received a financial payout. And during an interview with the child, when the detective left the video recorder on and exited the room, the recorder caught the child practicing her crying and doing different things.

"How in the world do we get this until it happens? We couldn't have had this before trial," Godsey said, his voice tinged with indignation.

Godsey detailed how Rocco Bronson Jr. and his father had contacted the Innocence Project after they'd gone online and read the clemency petition involving Nancy Smith. "How could anyone have obtained an affidavit from Rocco Bronson Jr. back at the time of the trial? There was no way."

The judge interrupted, "What about the report of Dr. Maggie Bruck, are her findings new?"

Godsey explained that Dr. Bruck's report had been prepared at the time of Nancy Smith's clemency hearing in 2013. However, Godsey maintained that Dr. Bruck's findings should be viewed in a new light because they'd recently uncovered direct evidence that Marge Bronson had coached the children in 1993 and had hatched a very similar plot with her granddaughter this past year.

"What about Detective Cantu's affidavit? Is Attorney Rosenbaum correct that Detective Cantu has filed other affidavits that courts have looked at?"

Godsey conferred with Allen's attorney, Richard Parsons, before answering. "Apparently, as part of Joseph Allen's clemency petition a few years ago, Mr. Parsons filed an affidavit signed by Detective Cantu."

"But not considered by a court?" Cook asked.

This time Parsons responded. "To my knowledge, Your Honor, no, we've never presented it to a court."

"Anything else you want to add regarding your position?" the judge asked.

Godsey glanced at Tomlinson before returning his focus to the judge. "We have an admission in writing from the prosecutor and his staff that they've done an independent review of this case. They believe that our clients are innocent and the crime did not occur." Godsey paused to let this sink in. "This is unprecedented. This is an admission that could be used in court if this case were ever tried again. Imagine the power of a defendant's attorney saying, 'I've got it in writing from you that you've done your own investigation and my client is innocent.'"

Judge Cook responded, "I do not want to speak for Prosecutor Tomlinson, but if this Court grants a new trial for these folks, there ain't going to be a new trial. They're going to dismiss this case."

"That's true, but in looking at the motion for leave to file our motion, that's a powerful piece of new evidence that was not obtainable before," Godsey replied.

"I find it strange that you say this is unprecedented. Doesn't this happen whenever there is an exoneration of a person who has spent decades in prison?" the judge asked. "I read about it all the time. There's new evidence, the prosecutor admits that justice was not done, and the person is released."

"I think it's unprecedented that the defendants have a written statement to that effect when they ask for a new trial," Godsey answered.

"That's why I'm asking," Judge Cook said.

"It's not unusual for prosecutors to concede. I think this hearing is unprecedented. Usually when the defense and the prosecutor all agree, we go into court and the motion is granted. And so having to go through—"

Judge Cook interrupted Godsey and, for the first time, appeared irritated. "Don't I have an absolute obligation under Marsy's Law to hear from the victims and their counsel in this case?"

"I understand," Godsey said. "I'm not aware of any case where the prosecutor has agreed to a new trial and then we have to analyze all of these different issues."

"So you're saying I'm getting it wrong by having a hearing?" Judge Cook asked, seemingly upset by Godsey's remark.

"No, no, no. I'm not saying you're getting it wrong," Godsey said.

Up until this point, the judge had seemed to agree with the defendants' positions. But now Godsey had apparently riled the judge, and that was not good.

"It sounds like you don't like my hearing," Judge Cook said.

"Your Honor, if I—"

"I'm being facetious," Judge Cook said, his voice again conversational. "Essentially, by asking me to grant a new trial, I will have to vacate these convictions and make a big decision, not only for these defendants, but for the victims and the community. I want to err on the side of caution. It may sound trite, but with all due respect, whatever I do, I want to get it right."

When Judge Cook called on Tomlinson, the prosecutor confirmed that his office had done a thorough reinvestigation of the case and concluded that the defendants were innocent. "My intention is to dismiss these matters if the motion for a new trial is granted," Tomlinson said.

"Your Honor, may I interject?" Rosenbaum asked.

"You may."

Rosenbaum told the judge that at the trial, the defendants had claimed that the children had been coached or manipulated and that the jury had rejected that.

"That should count for something. And you don't get to retry and retry and retry the same arguments over and over again," Rosenbaum maintained.

Now Godsey wanted an opportunity to respond to Rosenbaum. He agreed that the defense had argued that the children were coached, but they'd had no direct evidence, making it easy for the prosecution to defeat the claim.

Godsey's voice became forceful. "Now we have new evidence from witnesses who were there who said, 'I saw it happen, and I heard Marge Bronson say, "I'm going to get paid when this case is over."' In addition, we have an incident in 2021 where Marge Bronson appears to have done the same thing.

"Mr. Rosenbaum keeps talking about Rocco Bronson and he's not credible for this reason or that reason. This is the Lorain County sheriff who investigated this and said, 'It's my opinion that she coached this child to make false accusations.' This has nothing to do with Rocco. That's bombshell evidence in 2021 that no one could have gotten in 1993."

Determined to keep the judge's focus on Rocco Bronson Jr., Rosenbaum said, "He planted drugs on his mother in order to get an advantage in a custody case. Mr. Tomlinson's own office is prosecuting that case," Rosenbaum countered. "How can they come into court and say that this new evidence is believable?"

"That goes to the weight of the evidence," the judge answered.

"I would welcome a hearing on Mr. Bronson's evidence," Rosenbaum persisted. "If I had done in this trial what these people are doing with Mr. Bronson's testimony, I would probably be disbarred. They're basically suborning perjury."

Judge Cook understood the parties' positions on the new evidence and could have ended the hearing at this point. However, he wanted Rosenbaum to answer a question that had no legal bearing on any issue before him. Cook wanted to know if Rosenbaum or the victims had any objection to Allen's being released based on time served.

Judge Cook began, "We know something happened in 2013. Somebody looked at this case and decided something needed to be done. Smith went home, and Allen did not," the judge said, revealing his suspicion that the prosecutor had questions about the legitimacy of the verdicts in 2013. "Let's say, hypothetically, that some or part of these crimes occurred. Nancy Smith spent fifteen years in prison and Mr. Allen has been incarcerated now for almost twenty-four years. Hasn't justice been served here?"

It was an insightful question. Rosenbaum's answer might reveal why he and the victims were so vehemently opposed to a new trial.

"I have no problem with them being released. I have an extreme problem with them being exonerated with a finding that this didn't happen. This would destroy these victims, if now everybody turns around and says that you weren't raped as a child. I agree that they served enough time. But there's a vast difference between being out of jail and being exonerated. Let them out."

Rosenbaum had provided one reason behind his clients' decision to contest the motion, but not the only one. If the court granted the defendants' motion, it would open the door to a wrongful imprisonment action that could conclude that the children's allegations had been fabricated—something that would lead to their ultimate disgrace. It would also tarnish the reputations of the police and prosecutors who had believed them and then wrongfully convicted two innocent people.

"I appreciate your candor," Judge Cook replied.

"But don't acquit them," Rosenbaum said.

Judge Cook's next statement was for the benefit of the media who would report on the hearing. "Let's make something clear. I can only order a new trial. If I do that, I am not exonerating either of them. Down the road, Ms. Smith and Mr. Allen would have to prove their innocence in a court of law in a wrongful imprisonment action."

The judge was distancing himself from what might occur in the future. If he granted a new trial and the prosecutor dismissed all charges, Smith and Allen would have the right to file an action for wrongful imprisonment under a special Ohio statute. In that action, the defendants would be required to present evidence to prove their actual innocence. If successful, they could then seek money damages from the State of Ohio.

Before Judge Cook concluded the hearing, he asked the attorneys if there were any other issues that needed to be addressed. Richard Parsons asked if the judge would consider bail for his client, Joseph Allen, while he awaited the court's decision on the motion.

"The State would not object," Tomlinson said.

The judge asked Rosenbaum if he wanted to be heard on this. Rosenbaum did. "Your Honor, Mr. Allen is a multiple-convicted pedophile. It would be a huge mistake to release him on bond."

Rosenbaum's response seemed to confuse the judge. "I thought I heard you say earlier, 'Let him out.'"

"If we're going to conclude that this matter is over and his sentence is up, that's fine. Let him out. But if this matter is not done and we haven't determined that he's served his whole sentence, he does not deserve to be let out on bond now."

Turning to Joseph Allen, Judge Cook said that he would consider allowing him to remain free on bond while he determined the motions, but he needed to get some information. Exhausted and worn down by twenty-five years in prison, Allen, now sixty-eight years old, sat with his head bowed. His drooping eyelids turned his eyes into mere slits, adding to his tired expression.

"Do you have any assets?" Judge Cook asked, trying to determine whether Allen had the financial means to flee.

"I do."

Allen's response surprised the judge, but Allen explained that he'd saved a few dollars from his prison jobs.

"Where will you stay?" Judge Cook inquired.

"With my brother," Allen replied.

"The Court will set bail at a one-hundred-thousand-dollar personal bond and you will be fitted with a GPS monitor. However, I want to make one thing perfectly clear. I may rule against you on your motion for a new trial, and, if I do, you will be returned to prison. I know that would be very difficult for you. But you understand that, don't you?"

"I do."

"I hope to make a decision within a week on whether I will allow your attorney to file a motion for a new trial. I will also rule on the motions to disqualify Prosecutor Tomlinson and to appoint a special prosecutor."

Everything Cook had done and said in the hearing suggested that he would grant the defendants' motion to seek a new trial and deny those filed by Rosenbaum. The signs were all there: the pointed questions that he'd posed to Rosenbaum, his off-the-cuff comments about the prosecutor's motivations for entering into the 2013 sentencing agreements, and his decision to allow Allen to remain free on bond while he decided the motions. However, in the world of the Head Start case, nothing was ever certain.

CHAPTER 43
THE DECISION
FEBRUARY 25, 2022 TWENTY-SEVEN AND A HALF YEARS AFTER CONVICTION

Two months had passed since Judge Cook had held his first hearing in the Head Start case. A few days after that hearing, Rosenbaum had faxed an entry withdrawing as counsel for the two alleged victims. Although he provided no reasons, he apparently conceded that he had a conflict of interest that barred his continued representation of these clients. Several days after that, Judge Cook had granted the defendants' motion to amend the 2013 sentencing agreement, opening the door for their motion for a new trial. At the same time, he'd denied Rosenbaum's motion to disqualify Tomlinson and had refused to appoint a special prosecutor.

There had been some scrambling after that. The two alleged victims had sought delays while they searched for new counsel. Once they had retained attorneys from the Ohio Crime Victim Justice Center, they filed motions asking the court to reconsider its earlier decisions, which the judge eventually denied.

Judge Cook had reached a decision on the motion for a new trial and had intended to announce it in open court three weeks earlier, only to postpone that hearing because of inclement weather. Although scattered snow flurries were forecast again, it would not be enough to sidetrack his decision for a second time.

Most observers believed that the judge would grant the defendants' motion for a new trial. When he'd given the defendants permission to file the motion, he'd explained his decision by issuing a ten-page opinion. In it, he'd written that "Smith and Allen ha[d] presented significant, probative evidence that justifie[d]" giving them permission to file a motion for a new trial. He'd also emphasized that, under the law, prosecutors had great discretion in determining which cases to prosecute and which ones to dismiss. Unless Judge Cook had a complete change of heart, it appeared that something momentous would soon happen in his courtroom.

When Judge Cook took the bench, he surveyed his courtroom. To his immediate left, a temporary table had been placed, where Joseph Allen and his attorney, Richard Parsons, sat. Allen, neatly dressed in a gray pinstripe jacket, exhibited a calm exterior. He looked far different from the man who, almost twenty-eight years earlier, had initially resisted scrapping his orange jail garb for street clothes. Next to them, at one of the two permanent trial tables, sat Mark Godsey and Nancy Smith. Smith's face could not hide her anxiety. She'd been devastated by legal rulings too many times to ever feel comfortable in a courtroom. Tomlinson and his assistant, Nicholas Celebrezze, sat at the trial table to the judge's right, separated from the two defendants' tables by a lectern.

The benches in the spectator gallery were filled and a sheriff's deputy stood guard in front of the double doors that led into the courtroom. Judge Cook guessed that most of those spectators were either family or friends of Smith and Allen, present to provide support. After obtaining permission from him, one of the local television stations had set up its cameras in the jury box to cover the proceedings. The stage was set for his announcement.

Judge Cook wasted little time in revealing his decision. As soon as he granted the defendants' motion for a new trial, several spectators murmured their approval, while others clapped their hands. Nancy Smith leaned toward her attorney, and while still seated, they embraced, his left arm wrapped around her shoulders. Except for hints of smiles, Allen and Parsons sat passively.

After that, events happened rapidly. Tomlinson moved to dismiss all charges against the defendants with prejudice. The phrase "with prejudice" was important because it meant that the State could never refile the charges. Cook granted the motion, culminating with the simple words, "The charges against Joseph Allen and Nancy Smith are all dismissed." And with that, it was done.

Tomlinson then glanced to his right, where the two defendants were seated. After clearing his throat, the forty-one-year-old prosecutor read a prepared statement, and he became emotional as he reached the end of his remarks. His voice shook as he apologized to the defendants. "On behalf of the State, I apologize for what was done to you and your families as a result of this ill-conceived prosecution."

As he delivered this apology, Nancy Smith was overcome by emotion and began to cry, dabbing at her eyes with a handkerchief. When Tomlinson was finished, the judge asked if any of the other counsel wanted to make a statement. Godsey indicated that his client wanted to speak.

Without mentioning Marge Bronson or the other parents specifically, Smith said, "I hope that one day you will answer for this. Not only did you make me a victim, but you made my children victims too. You took me away from them during the most crucial periods of their lives."

Thirteen years earlier, when Judge Burge had freed her with his unexpected acquittal, Smith had answered questions from reporters almost immediately after that hearing. At that time, she'd made clear that she did not hold the children responsible for what had happened to her—stating that "the children were victims of their environment." To her, that "environment" had always been the coercion of their parents.

Although Joseph Allen did not speak at the hearing, he stood with his attorney afterward and answered reporters' questions. Speaking in his deep Southern drawl, Allen told them that he was still very emotional about what had just occurred. "There's still some healing I need to get. It's been so long, you know."

Looking down, he shook his head and lamented the many injustices he'd endured. He told them how difficult it had been to be separated from his family, some of whom had passed away during his many years in prison. Still, he said, "Today is a bright day."

"Do you intend to file a lawsuit for your wrongful conviction?" one reporter asked.

"I suffered a lot," Allen said. "I'm going to do that."

Reporters also congregated around Nancy Smith, who told them that this ordeal had taken an enormous emotional toll upon her. Shaking her head, she said, "Twenty-eight years. Can you imagine what it's like to have that hanging over your head for twenty-eight years? Nobody knows what that was like."

The reporters asked her whether she, too, would file a lawsuit seeking compensation for her wrongful imprisonment.

"That is for another day," she replied.

Soon thereafter, Joseph Allen walked out from the Justice Center into the cold, snowy air. A few minutes later, Nancy Smith emerged with some of her family members. Still strangers, Smith and Allen walked away from the Justice Center in different directions, united only by the bizarre nightmare that they had been forced to share.

Doubt had both failed and saved them. At the beginning, the pair should have been protected by the requirement that their guilt be established beyond a reasonable doubt. Yes, there'd been important evidence that the jury had never heard or seen—for a variety of reasons. Despite this, the defense had presented enough evidence to establish reasonable doubt. They'd highlighted the children's wildly different descriptions of Joseph, the police's inability to locate the site of the alleged abuse, the flimsy evidence linking the two defendants, the children's inconsistent stories about the alleged abuse, and Smith's tearful testimony that she could never hurt a child. Nevertheless, in the end, hysteria had overpowered reasonable doubt, and they'd been convicted.

But doubt is a stubborn thing. It can force people to look at matters anew. After the Head Start convictions, public doubt crept in ever so slightly. First, there were letters to the editor in a local newspaper. That doubt was fed by a series of investigative pieces by an inquisitive and relentless columnist whose newspaper periodically raised questions about the reliability of the convictions. Doubt fully bloomed after a new judge thoroughly reviewed the trial transcripts and, motivated by a strong sense of justice, freed the pair from prison, albeit temporarily. By then, the public's doubt had been replaced by a growing sense that a grave injustice had occurred.

Yet the legal system remained intransigent, unable to admit its mistake or to take corrective action. For years, the Ohio Innocence Project and others worked tirelessly to release the defendants from prison and overturn their convictions. Those two goals were finally achieved in Judge Cook's courtroom on a cold, wintry day in February 2022, twenty-seven and a half years after their convictions.

Smith and Allen could now live the last chapters of their lives unshackled from the verdicts that had shattered them and their families. As in all controversial cases, questions would remain for some—particularly those who knew only bits and pieces of their agonizing story or were unwilling to accept the legitimacy of the new evidence. But those who understood the full narrative would see things differently—their opinions would never falter on the edge of doubt.

CHAPTER NOTES

NOTES ON CHAPTER ONE

Background information about Judge Lynett McGough came from an interview with a member of her staff, newspaper articles about her, her newspaper campaign ads, and the author's own personal experiences interacting with her, first as a fellow attorney and later as an attorney litigating civil cases assigned to her. The information about the three attorneys is based on the author's own observations of them in the courtroom. The statements made by the judge, the attorneys, and the two defendants are based on the trial transcript, pages 1285 to 1297. Nancy Smith's reaction and statements made while the verdict was being read are based on "Two Guilty in Head Start Sex Case" by Michael Higgins published in the *Chronicle-Telegram* (Elyria, OH) on August 4, 1994.

NOTES ON CHAPTER TWO

The background about Detective Cantu and his initial thoughts on the case are based on my phone interview with him that occurred on December 21, 2020. The dialogue for the meeting between Marge Bron-

son, Nina Zorich, and Cantu is based on the transcript of a taped interview of the trio that occurred on or about May 8, 1993. Most of the
chapter's dialogue is taken verbatim from that transcript. Other details
were gleaned from the initial incident report filed by Patrolman Swartz
dated May 7, 1993. The descriptions of Marge Bronson and Nina
Zorich are based on their appearance as recorded in the videotape of
the police lineup of November 4, 1993.

NOTES ON CHAPTER THREE

The background information about Alex Olejko and Cel Rivera is
based on the author's own knowledge—either personal interactions
with them or listening to stories about them from their friends and
colleagues. The author also relied upon the obituary of Alex Olejko,
published in the *Chronicle-Telegram* on September 9, 2009, and "Chief
Cel Rivera Retires Monday" by Carissa Woytach, published in the
Chronicle-Telegram on December 1, 2019. The author also talked with
Detective Cantu about this meeting.

NOTES ON CHAPTER FOUR

Much of the information for this chapter is based on my interview with
Detective Cantu conducted on December 21, 2020. Cantu's initial interviews with Marcus Logan and his father and Melissa Warner and her
mother are based on Lorain Police Department reports authored by
Cantu and dated May 31, 1993, June 3, 1993, and June 10, 1993.

NOTES ON CHAPTER FIVE

Detective Andujar's trip with Marcus Logan on August 2, 1993, is
documented in his police report of the same date. Detective Cantu's
investigation of the Moffitt home at 421 Fifteenth Street is documented
in his report dated June 3, 1993. Andujar's investigation of Richard
Jones and his home located at 1928 Lexington Avenue is documented
in his police reports dated June 18, 1993 and July 29, 1993. The
dialogue between Andujar and Marcus Logan regarding Marcus's

identification of Richard Jones from the photo lineup comes almost word for word from Andujar's recorded statement of Marcus Logan taken on July 22, 1993. The conversations between Andujar and Marcus Logan on August 2, 1993, and the conversation between Andujar and Stella Gilliam are fictional but are based on Andujar's summary of the visit in his report dated August 2, 1993.

NOTES ON CHAPTER SIX

Detective Miller's involvement in the case is based on his twenty-page report that summarizes his investigations into the Green Acres runaways, Hazel Parker's allegations against Joseph Allen, and his work on the Head Start case, including his interviews with Joseph Allen and his meetings with the alleged victims and their parents. The Lorain police's version of the in-person lineup of November 3, 1993, is based on Detective Rewak's report on this event. The author also watched the forty-five-minute videotape of this lineup many times. In addition, the author discussed the lineup videotape with Detective Cantu and two investigators from the Lorain County Prosecutor's Office who, at the request of the new county prosecutor, J. D. Tomlinson, reviewed the Head Start files in 2021 and 2022. The information regarding Allen's green station wagon is based on the Petition to Vacate or Set Aside Judgment and Sentence filed on behalf of Nancy Smith on September 20, 1996, and a copy of Allen's registration that was attached to that petition.

NOTES ON CHAPTER SEVEN

The information regarding the arraignment is based on journal entries filed in the criminal cases documenting the hearing. The gallery outbursts during the arraignments are based on an account found in "The Shame of Lorain, Ohio—Nancy Smith and Joseph Allen Convicted of Non-Existent Crimes" by Lona Manning, published in *Justice Denied: The Magazine for the Wrongly Convicted*, Issue 29 (Summer 2005).

NOTES ON CHAPTER EIGHT

Joseph Allen's letter referenced in this chapter was filed on March 29, 1994, and is reproduced word for word. The thoughts of the judge are fictitious but would accurately represent how a judge would typically react to a defendant's request for a change of a court-appointed attorney. All of the motions and documents referenced in this chapter are from *State v. Allen*, Case No. 93 CRO 44488. These include the following: Defendant's Motion for Discovery, filed November 19, 1993; Motion to Review Grand Jury Documents, filed on February 4, 1994; Motion for Change of Venue, filed on February 4, 1994; Motion to Appoint Expert Private Investigator, filed February 4, 1994; Motion to Dismiss, filed February 4, 1994; Court's Rulings on Motions, filed February 10, 1994; Motion to Reduce Bond, filed March 10, 1994; Court's Entry Denying Reduction in Bond, filed March 18, 1994; and Court's Entry Approving the Appointment of an Investigator, filed June 10, 1994.

NOTES ON CHAPTER NINE

The biographical information about Jack Bradley is based on the article "Lorain Defense Lawyer Jack Bradley Takes on Tough Criminal Cases" by Michael Sangiacomo, published in the *Plain Dealer* on December 16, 2016. The law regarding criminal discovery is based on former Rule 16 of the Criminal Rules of Procedure. Its uneven application in Ohio is detailed in the article "Criminal Discovery in Ohio: Civilizing Criminal Rule 16" by Charles L. Grove, published in the *University of Dayton Law Review*, volume 36, page 2.

The summary of the bill of particulars is taken from the bill of particulars filed on May 17, 1994, and the supplemental bill of particulars filed on June 2, 1994, in *State v. Smith*. The prosecutor's disclosure of exculpatory material comes directly from its answer to discovery filed in *State v. Smith*, State's Discovery Answers, page 6, filed on May 17, 1994.

Prosecutor Jon Rosenbaum's claim that Nancy Smith had a split personality is based on a brief that he filed to contest her motion for a new trial, State's Brief in Opposition to Defendant's Motion for a New Trial or Judgment of Acquittal, page 3, filed August 26, 1994, in *State v. Smith*.

The dialogue in the meeting between Jack Bradley and Nancy Smith is fictitious but is based on the actual events and law applicable to the case.

The cryptic description of the videotaped police lineup is pulled directly from the State's answers to discovery, State's Discovery Answers, page 5, filed on May 17, 1994, in *State v. Smith*.

NOTES ON CHAPTER TEN

The discussions of the motions are taken from the trial transcript, pages 3 through 17, either paraphrased or written verbatim. The conclusion that Elizabeth "Angel" Powell was not on the prosecution's witness list is the result of examining the prosecutor's discovery filings of May 17, 1994, June 2, 1994, July 20, 1994, and July 22, 1994, in *State v. Smith*. The claim that Jack Bradley represented Joseph Allen nine years earlier is not disputed and was referenced in the Petition to Vacate or Set Aside Judgment and Sentence filed in *State v. Smith* on September 20, 1996.

As to three of the four lay witnesses disclosed several days before trial, the Lorain police records verify that they were interviewed approximately nine months before trial. A Lorain Police Miscellaneous Report authored by Detective Pete Rewak details a November 5, 1993 interview with Marlon Howard. A Lorain Police Miscellaneous Report dated November 9, 1993 details an officer's conversation with Willie Mae Smith, who, after being shown Joseph Allen's photograph, claimed that she'd seen that man on Nancy Smith's bus. A report authored by Detective Rewak dated November 16, 1993, sets forth his conversation with Kathy Cole, who, after being shown Allen's photograph, claimed that she'd often seen this man waiting around the school at the time of the noon and five p.m. bus transfers.

NOTES ON CHAPTER ELEVEN

The account of jury selection is redacted and taken directly from the trial transcript, pages 19 to 231.

NOTES ON CHAPTER TWELVE

Each attorney's opening statement is either quoted verbatim or paraphrased based on the trial transcript, pages 232 to 251.

The author's claim that the Lorain detectives violated fundamental rules for questioning children in sex abuses cases is based on a number of sources. Four experts have reviewed the transcripts of the children's statements and concluded that they were extremely flawed. Kathleen Quinn, MD, a forensic psychiatrist, was critical of the interviewing techniques when retained by the defense in the civil lawsuit filed by four children and their parents. She authored four reports: Marcus Logan's, dated September 1, 1998; Nina Zorich's, dated September 1, 1998; Melissa Warner's, dated August 31, 1998; and Jason Gilbert's, dated September 1, 1998.

Maggie Bruck, PhD, a professor of psychiatry and behavioral science at Johns Hopkins Medical Center, wrote a scathing report dated January 25, 2013, about the interviews that was part of Nancy Smith and Joseph Allen's motion for a new trial filed on December 14, 2021. Melvin Guyer, PhD, and Ralph Underwager, PhD, reviewed the transcripts, and their opinions were included in Paul Facinelli's three-part series about the Head Start case published from October 6 through October 8, 1996, in the *Chronicle-Telegram*.

The author also read *Protocols for the Sex-Abuse Evaluation* by Richard A. Gardner, MD (Creative Therapeutics Inc., 1995).

The author's claim that Detective Miller's report differed from Prosecutor Rosenbaum's account about the Halloween mask is based on page 18 of Miller's report. On the same day that the children came to the police station to try to identify Joseph Allen from a lineup (November 4, 1993), Nina Zorich, accompanied by her mother, was also asked to identify objects seized from Allen's apartment. Miller wrote: "*Ninna* [sic] *was asked if Joseph ever wore a Halloween mask with black hair. Ninna* [*sic*] *was shown the mask and she said that Joseph was wearing that mask which she was showed* [*sic*] *in evidence item*

#10. *Ninna [sic] was asked if the eyes did anything on the mask* and Joseph [*sic*; Nina is meant] said yes, the eyes on the top snake lit up and the lights were pink in color. These officers pulled the pink eyes out of the mask before they were shown to the children." (Italics added.)

NOTES ON CHAPTER THIRTEEN

The questioning of Emily Osborne is based on the trial transcript, pages 251 to 285. The changes in Emily Osborne's stories about her son and the alleged encounter with Joseph Allen are based on a number of sources. Her original story is documented on page 9 of Detective Miller's twenty-page report dated November 8, 1993.

At trial, Emily Osborne was not truthful in describing the police lineup with her son, which is evident from watching the actual video-tape of the event. This is also borne out by the *Chronicle-Telegram* article about the videotape that was written by Paul Facinelli and published on September 21, 1997, titled "Tale of the Video Tape."

The changes in Emily Osborne's story about her son's interactions with his teddy bear are documented by reviewing her initial statement to Detective Cantu on May 28, 1993, recorded in his report dated May 31, 1993, and her statement to Detective Miller on October 30, 1993, set forth on pages 9 and 10 of his twenty-page report dated November 8, 1993.

NOTES ON CHAPTER FOURTEEN

The testimony of the witnesses is based on the trial transcript, pages 289 to 366. Jon Rosenbaum's assertion that Detective Cantu's investigation was "trash" is a quote from an article in the *Chronicle-Telegram* in an investigative series authored by Paul Facinelli published on October 6, 1996.

The author's claim that prosecutors had a duty to comb their cases for exculpatory evidence is based on *Brady v. Maryland*, 373 US 83 (1963), and several subsequent United States Supreme Court decisions that explained it. In *United States v. Bagley*, 473 US 667 (1985), the US Supreme Court explained that a prosecutor had a duty to turn over not only exculpatory evidence but evidence that could be used to impeach a prosecution witness, e.g. a prior inconsistent statement. The US Supreme Court ruled that if these nondisclosures were material, a new trial would be warranted. In defining what it meant by "material nondisclosed evidence," the court wrote: "Nondisclosed evidence is material only if there is a reasonable probability that, had the evidence been disclosed to the defense, the result of the proceeding would have been different. A 'reasonable probability' is a probability sufficient to undermine confidence in the outcome."

In *Kyles v. Whitley*, 514 US 419 (1995), decided after the Head Start trial, the US Supreme Court clarified the rule set forth in *Brady*. In *Kyles*, the court explained that materiality could be based on the cumulative effect of various nondisclosed pieces of evidence and not just on an item-by-item analysis.

The prosecutor's duty to search the State's evidence for exculpatory or impeaching evidence, implied in *Brady*, was made clear in *Kyles*. "The prosecutor, who alone can know what is undisclosed, must be assigned the responsibility to gauge the likely net effect of all such evidence and make disclosure when the point of 'reasonable probability' is reached. *Moreover, that responsibility remains regardless of any failure by the police to bring favorable evidence to the prosecutor's attention.*" [Italics added.]

The US Supreme Court also explained that the prosecutor's role in a criminal proceeding required disclosures of evidence favorable to the defense. "Such disclosure will serve to justify trust in the prosecutor as 'the representative . . . of a sovereignty . . . whose interest . . . in a criminal prosecution is not that it shall win a case, but that justice shall be done.'" This explanation quotes from *Berger v. United States*, 295 US 78, 88 (1935).

NOTES ON CHAPTER FIFTEEN

Elizabeth "Angel" Powell's claim that the Head Start case ruined her life is found in her deposition in the case of *NZ v. Lorain Head Start*, 96 CV 116729, Lorain County Court of Common Pleas, page 85. In that case, she testified that she underwent two polygraph examinations

(Powell deposition, page 175). A Head Start student named Amanda Lilly claimed that Powell (whom she referred to as "Angel") drove them to Joseph's house (Lorain Police records, report of Detective Andujar, July 15, 1993). When Melissa Warner identified the house where Nancy had taken her, she also claimed that "Eddie" and Powell were there (Lorain Police records, report of Detective Andujar, August 2, 1993). The testimony of Powell is either paraphrased, summarized, or taken verbatim from the trial transcript, pages 371 to 442. The direct examination of Ann Gilbert is either paraphrased, summarized, or taken verbatim from the trial transcript, pages 443 to 450.

NOTES ON CHAPTER SIXTEEN

The events described in this chapter are based on the trial transcript, pages 397 to 398 and 463 to 533.

NOTES ON CHAPTER SEVENTEEN

All dialogue is based on the trial transcript, pages 534 to 657, either word for word or edited slightly for clarity.

The claim that the police had not documented the episode involving Marcus Logan and his sister is based on Detective Cantu's report (pages 4 and 5) dated June 3, 1993; Detective Andujar's reports dated June 15, 1993, June 16, 1993, June 17, 1993, July 22, 1993, and August 2, 1993; and Detective Miller's twenty-page report dated November 8, 1993.

The distance between the bus parking lot and the Nativity School is 4.3 miles according to Google Maps.

NOTES ON CHAPTER EIGHTEEN

The testimony of Marge Bronson is based on the trial transcript, pages 680 to 748. Quoted sections are either verbatim or edited for clarity without changing the meaning of the statement.

The details of Marge Bronson's felony conviction are based on the Supplement to Motion for New Trial filed on behalf of Nancy Smith on

September 23, 1994; the State of Ohio's response, filed on December 2, 1994; and a certified copy of the United States District Court's journal entry memorializing Marge Bronson's sentence, filed on July 25, 1991, and attached to Smith's petition for clemency filed with the Ohio Parole Board.

The details of Marge Bronson's meeting with the social worker, Sandy Kelly, are based on Ms. Kelly's social work notes dated May 28, 1993, and attached as an exhibit to the Motion for New Trial or Judgment of Acquittal filed on behalf of Nancy Smith in *State v. Smith* on August 13, 1994.

The author's claim that Dr. Amy Richardson's records were received while Marge Bronson was testifying is based on the transcript, which shows that Marge Bronson took the stand at 2:30, the time of the fax transmission is printed as 2:48 p.m. on the faxed records, and Jack Bradley commenced his cross-examination of Marge Bronson at 3:30.

NOTES ON CHAPTER NINETEEN

The trial dialogues are based on the trial transcript, pages 749 to 1007, and are either word-for-word or edited slightly for clarity. The children's descriptions of Joseph's skin conditions are based on the transcripts of taped interviews. These include interviews with Marcus Logan on June 15, 1993, and July 22, 1993, and interviews with Nina Zorich conducted on or about May 11, 1993, May 13, 1993, May 31, 1993, and July 14, 1993.

The questions posed to Nina Zorich by the police about the mask are based on Detective Miller's police report, page 18, dated on or about November 8, 1993.

The details of Justin Frank's interview with the Lorain police are based on Patrolman Super's report dated May 29, 1993 and Detective Cantu's supplemental report dated June 15, 1993.

The law about the admissibility of a defendant's prior bad acts is based on Ohio Evidence Rule 404(B); *State v. Curry*, 43 Ohio St.2d 66 (1975); *State v. Carter*, 26 Ohio St.2d 79 (1971); *State v. Williams*, 134 Ohio St.3d 521 (2012); *State v. Burden*, 2013-Ohio-1628; and *State v. Morris*, 2012-Ohio-6151.

Joseph Allen's version of the Kelsey Calvin case is based on an article by Bob Chatelle and Emily Horowitz entitled "The Wrongful Conviction of Joseph Allen (and Nancy Smith)" published on the website of the National Center for Reason and Justice on June 1, 2012. A review of the court file in *State of Ohio v. Joseph L. Allen*, Lorain County Case No. 30644 (1985), includes a lengthy judgment entry denying Allen's petition for post-conviction release. After his imprisonment, Allen had alleged that he'd been denied his rights to compulsory process, to confront witnesses, and to be afforded effective counsel. In his entry, Judge Floyd Harris confirmed that he had several times explained to Allen that he could have his day in court and not plead guilty. At the sentencing hearing several weeks later, Judge Harris had been concerned because during the presentence investigation, Allen had told investigators that he was innocent and had pled guilty to "get it over with." At the sentencing, Judge Harris gave Allen the opportunity to withdraw his guilty plea and proceed to trial. Again, Allen "reaffirmed his desire to plead guilty and admitted his guilt." For those reasons, Judge Harris denied Allen's petition for post-conviction relief.

NOTES ON CHAPTER TWENTY

The events and testimony detailed in this chapter are based on the trial transcript, pages 1008 through 1055, and are either word-for-word or edited slightly for clarity. The statement that Detective Cantu doubted that any crimes had occurred is based on his police report dated June 3, 1993, and his affidavit that was attached to the defendants' Motion for Leave to File a Motion for a New Trial dated November 19, 2021, in *State v. Smith* and *State v. Allen*.

That Jack Bradley and Joseph Grunda had copies of Dr. Richardson's report and records involving Nina Zorich is based on pages 678 to 680 of the trial transcript. Bradley later included Dr. Richardson's report as an exhibit supporting his motion for a new trial filed on August 18, 1994.

The facts surrounding the first photo lineup involving Joseph Allen and Nina Zorich are based on Detective Miller's police report, found on page 9 of his twenty-page report.

The claim that a child interview can be corrupted by a number of factors is based on the studies cited in the New Jersey case of *State v. Michaels*, 264 NJ Super. 579, 625 A.2d 489 (1993) *affirmed* 136 NJ 299, 642 A.2d 1372 (1994); Dr. Maggie Bruck's lengthy thirty-three-page report dated January 25, 2013, and attached to the motion for a new trial filed on December 14, 2021; and the *Chronicle-Telegram* article on this subject authored by Paul Facinelli and published on October 6, 1996.

NOTES ON CHAPTER TWENTY-ONE

The trial testimony is based on the actual transcript (pages 1055 to 1174). Much is taken verbatim; other portions have been edited for easier reading. Mary Molnar's claims about the attendance records and her lack of an individualized preparation session with Jack Bradley are based on her affidavit dated August 31, 2011, and filed with Nancy Smith's application for clemency.

NOTES ON CHAPTER TWENTY-TWO

The trial testimony is based on the trial transcript, pages 1175 to 1218, and is either word-for-word or edited slightly for clarity.

The availability of other witnesses and the substance of their potential testimony are based on the Affidavit of Sherry Hagerman executed on August 18, 2011; the Affidavit of Susan Coates executed on June 24, 2011; the Affidavit of Kymberly Spangler executed on November 28, 2005; the Affidavit of Audrey Taylor Payne executed on June 25, 2011; and the Affidavit of Louis Payne executed on June 25, 2011. All of these affidavits were filed in support of Nancy Smith's Application for Clemency.

As to Joseph Allen and Eileen Andrews and her two daughters, Detective Mark Carpentiere stated in his report dated November 4, 1993, that he interviewed Donald Nickerson and Evona Winland, both of whom worked at Catholic Charities. Nickerson told the detective that until October 1993, Allen was at Catholic Charities almost every day with Eileen Andrews and her two daughters, ages seven and twelve. Allen would search recent donations for toys and take them with permission from Catholic Charities. According to Evona Winland, Allen often gave the toys to Andrews's two daughters or to other children who were there.

NOTES ON CHAPTER TWENTY-THREE

The account of the meeting between Jon Rosenbaum, Kathy Cole, and Donnetta Taylor is based on the affidavits of Cole and Taylor executed on August 17, 1994, and filed with Defendant Smith's Motion for New Trial or Judgment of Acquittal, as well as the State's Brief in Opposition to Defendant's Motion for a New Trial or Judgment of Acquittal filed in August 1993. The account of the trial on this day is based on the transcript, pages 1217 to 1254, and the article, "Two Found Guilty in Head Start Case" by Michael Higgins published in the *Chronicle-Telegram* on August 4, 1994.

NOTES ON CHAPTER TWENTY-FOUR

The author was guided by Jack Bradley's motion for a new trial and/or judgment for acquittal, which sets forth Bradley's thoughts about the errors that had occurred at trial. The author was also influenced by Bradley's remarks made on the April 8, 2012 episode of the television show *Dateline: Haunted Memories*, broadcast on April 8, 2012. However, as to Bradley's actual thoughts, the author has tried to put himself in the place of Bradley, particularly the feelings that typically well up inside a trial attorney after a jury decides in favor of the other party.

NOTES ON CHAPTER TWENTY-FIVE

The account of this oral hearing is based on the briefs in support of and in opposition to Nancy Smith's Motion for New Trial and/or Acquittal in *State v. Smith* and the transcript of the oral hearing held on

December 2, 1994. The thoughts of Judge McGough are re-created based on her comments during the hearing.

NOTES ON CHAPTER TWENTY-SIX

The author was aided by his interview with Paul Facinelli that occurred on April 9, 2021. Raymond Kandt's letters to the *Chronicle-Telegram* that are referenced in this chapter were published in the *Chronicle-Telegram* on March 31, 1988, June 25, 1988, August 10, 1990, February 20, 1991, August 12, 1994, December 11, 1994, August 18, 1995, May 12, 1996, and November 7, 1996. Facinelli's thoughts and the exact wording of his conversations with Michael Higgins are surmised by the author.

NOTES ON CHAPTER TWENTY-SEVEN

The author was aided by his interview with Paul Facinelli that occurred on April 9, 2021. Quotes from the two experts are taken verbatim or paraphrased for clarity from the article "Monsters or Victims" by Paul Facinelli, the article "Suggestibility, Techniques Can Hide the Truth" by Paul Facinelli, and "A Review of Tapes of Children's Interviews" by Paul Facinelli, all published in the *Chronicle-Telegram* on October 6, 1996. Much of the material for this chapter also came from "Contradiction—Cop Report About Lineup, Testimony About Lineup" by Paul Facinelli, published in the *Chronicle-Telegram* on October 7, 1996; "What the Jury Didn't Hear in Child Sex Case" by Paul Facinelli, published in the *Elyria Chronicle* on October 7, 1996; "Ember Turns to Wildfire" by Paul Facinelli, published in the *Chronicle-Telegram* on October 8, 1996; and *Sex Abuse Hysteria: The Salem Witch Trials Revisited* by Richard Gardner, MD (Creative Therapeutics, 1990). The author was also aided by the book *Protocols for the Sex-Abuse Evaluation* by Richard Gardner, MD (Creative Therapeutics, 1995).

NOTES ON CHAPTER TWENTY-EIGHT

The chapter is based partly on the recollections of Paul Facinelli. The quotes of Greg White and Jon Rosenbaum are either taken verbatim or paraphrased from direct quotes in the *Chronicle-Telegram* article "Interviews Did Not Follow Prosecutor Guidelines" by Paul Facinelli, published on October 6, 1996. The questions posed by the *Chronicle* management as described in this chapter are extrapolated from the prosecutor's answers quoted in the *Chronicle*'s article.

NOTES ON CHAPTER TWENTY-NINE

The magazine article "The Lost Crusade" by Andrew Putz, published in *Cleveland Scene* on April 19, 2001, details Facinelli's attempt to raise questions about the Head Start verdicts and the controversy surrounding Ralph Underwager and its effect on the series.

The legal struggles of Ralph Underwager were also set forth in the *Chronicle-Telegram*'s article of October 10, 1996, reporting on Underwager's alleged comments about pedophiles and the litigation it spawned. The *Chronicle-Telegram* revisited this issue in an editorial on October 13, 1996, entitled "Expert's Difficulty Doesn't Change Point."

Underwager's legal woes are also documented in a number of reported cases: *Underwager v. Salter*, 22 F.3d 730 (7th Cir. 1994); *State v. Swan*, 790 P.2d 610 (Wash. SC 1990); *Underwager v. Channel 9 Australia*, 69 F.3d 361 (9th Circ. 1995); and *State v. Franzke*, 795 N.W.2d 62 (Wisc. App. 2010).

NOTES ON CHAPTER THIRTY

The author watched the videotape of the lineup involving Joseph Allen many times. Facinelli's investigation regarding the videotape is documented in two articles: "The Telling Tape that the Defense Never Saw" by Paul Facinelli and Pam Plas, and "Kids' Behavior on Video Unlike Trial Description" by Paul Facinelli and Pam Plas, both published on September 21, 1997 in the *Chronicle-Telegram*. Facinelli's involvement in bringing the videotape to light is also described in the article "The Lost Crusade" by Andrew Putz (*Cleveland Scene*, April 19, 2001).

The prosecutor's written response to the videotape was published in the *Chronicle-Telegram* on September 21, 1997, in an article entitled "The Prosecutor's Office Responds to Our Questions in This Statement."

As to Facinelli's lawsuit against Jon Rosenbaum and Rosenbaum's counterclaim, "The Lost Crusade" provides many of the details. The Ohio Ninth District Court of Appeals decision in *Rosenbaum v. The Chronicle-Telegram*, Case Nos. 01CA00786 and 01CA007908, released on December 31, 2002, also sets forth many of the legal issues involved in the controversy. The final journal entry resolving this defamation case was attached as an exhibit in Rosenbaum's Motion to Disqualify the Lorain County Prosecutor's Office and to Appoint a Special Prosecutor in *State v. Smith* filed on December 21, 2021.

NOTES ON CHAPTER THIRTY-ONE

The response of William Locke, the Executive Director of the Lorain County Community Action Agency, to the Head Start verdicts is well chronicled: "Head Start Official Says Pair Innocent" by Joyce McCartney, published in the *Morning Journal* on August 5, 1994; "Locke Must Resign," editorial in the *Morning Journal*, published on August 8, 1994; "Parents Batter Locke" by Jeff Gallatin, published in the *Morning Journal* on August 8, 1994; and "Locke's Record Head Start Key," editorial published in the *Chronicle-Telegram* on August 12, 1994. Biographical information about Locke comes from the following sources: William Locke's obituary published in the *Morning Journal* on July 8, 2015, and "Black History Month: Who Were Hopkins and Locke?" LCCAA website, posted on February 11, 2021.

Conversations between William Locke and Attorney Dan Jaffe are fictional but are representative of conversations between an insured and an attorney hired by an insurance company to defend its insured. From 1978 to 1988, the author was frequently hired by insurance companies to defend its insureds and is, therefore, quite familiar with the tenor of those initial consultations. Jaffe declined to be interviewed by the author.

NOTES ON CHAPTER THIRTY-TWO

The questions and answers in Elizabeth "Angel" Powell's deposition are based almost word for word on her deposition taken on August 7, 1998, in the case of *NZ, et al., v. Lorain Head Start*. The testimony of Nina Zorich in the civil case is based on her deposition taken on July 2, 1998, pages 64 through 71. Marcus Logan's allegations in the civil case are based on his affidavit executed on February 11, 1998, and attached to his brief opposing the defendants' motion for summary judgment.

NOTES ON CHAPTER THIRTY-THREE

The account of Attorney Dennis O'Toole's prison visit is based on the author's interview with him on May 12, 2021. Despite the incarceration of Joseph Allen and Nancy Smith, the court granted the plaintiffs' motion to depose them in a journal entry dated September 11, 1998. As to Smith's coursework in prison, the author also relied on the Ohio Innocence Project's letter (page 11) of January 29, 2007, to the Ohio Parole Board that set forth Smith's accomplishments during her first few years of imprisonment. Dialogue in this chapter is derived from these sources and O'Toole's recollections.

NOTES ON CHAPTER THIRTY-FOUR

In the author's conversation with Attorney Dennis O'Toole on May 12, 2021, O'Toole stated only that Nationwide settled the civil suit for business reasons, although he and Attorney Dan Jaffe were prepared to try the case. O'Toole divulged no other details and Jaffe declined to be interviewed. The dialogue in this chapter between O'Toole and Jaffe is fictional but is derived from real events in the case: the defendants' first motion for summary judgment, the trial court's granting of the motion finding that LCCAA was a political subdivision, the Ohio Ninth District Court of Appeals' reversal of that decision, the defendants' second motion for summary judgment, the trial court's denial of that motion, and the trial court's journal entry setting forth judgments for each of the four plaintiffs in the amount of one and a half million dollars.

NOTES ON CHAPTER THIRTY-FIVE

The events described in this chapter are based on the following: the author's interviews with Mark Godsey, Bobbi Madonna, and Whitney Sheff Ellison; Letter in Support of Nancy Smith's Petition for Parole filed by the Ohio Innocence Project and dated January 29, 2007; "Ohio's Parole Board Undergoes Sweeping Reforms to Increase Transparency, Fairness" by Jeremy Pelzer, published on Cleveland.com on May 1, 2019; "Ohio Parole Board Member Quits, Calls Agency Toxic and Secretive" by Laura A. Bischoff, published in the Dayton Daily News on January 19, 2019; "Ohio Parole Board Under Fire from Victims, Inmates & Lawmakers" by Laura A. Bischoff, published in the *Dayton Daily News* on April 7, 2019. The conversations between Godsey, Sheff, and Madonna are fictional but are based on similar comments Godsey made to other law students involved in the Ohio Innocence Project after the court ruled against them. See *Blind Injustice: A Former Prosecutor Exposes the Psychology and Politics of Wrongful Convictions* by Mark Godsey, pages 53 to 54, published by the University of California Press (2017).

NOTES ON CHAPTER THIRTY-SIX

The author relied on the following sources: NBC News, *Dateline: Haunted Memories*, broadcast on April 8, 2012; "E-mail from Lorain Police Chief Shows His Misgivings About Head Start Case" by Brad Dicken, published in the *Chronicle-Telegram* on January 15, 2010; "Police Chief Says E-mail Wasn't His Opinion" by Brad Dicken, published in the *Chronicle-Telegram* on January 17, 2010; "Rivera Doubts Head Start Case in Tape" by Brad Dicken, published in the *Chronicle-Telegram* on March 17, 2011; "Lorain Police Chief Was Working to Free Bus Driver He Helped Lock Up" by Rachel Dissell, published by the *Plain Dealer* on March 16, 2011; "Smith's Daughter: I Didn't Release Tapes" by Brad Dicken, published in the *Chronicle-Telegram* on March 18, 2011; "Lorain Police Chief Cel Rivera Tried to Help Nancy Smith in Head Start Case" by Kelly Metz, published in the *Morning Journal* on March 23, 2011; "Lorain Police Chief Cel Rivera Announces Retirement After Serving as Chief for Twenty-Five Years" by Carissa Woytach, published in the *Chronicle-Telegram* on December 1, 2019.

NOTES ON CHAPTER THIRTY-SEVEN

The events described in this chapter are based on the following documents: Motion for Reconsideration of Sentence filed on October 1, 2008, in *State v. Smith*; State's Brief in Opposition to Defendant's Motion for Reconsideration of Sentence filed on October 22, 2008, in *State v. Smith*; Reply Brief to State of Ohio's Response filed on November 10, 2008, in *State v. Smith*; Journal Entry of February 4, 2009, in *State v. Smith*; court's opinion dated February 13, 2009, in *State v. Smith*; transcript of the hearing held on June 24, 2009, in *State v. Smith* and *State v. Allen*; "Interview with Nancy Smith" posted on YouTube video by the *Chronicle-Telegram* on June 24, 2009; "ACQUITTED" by Brad Dicken published in the *Chronicle-Telegram* on June 25, 2009.

NOTES ON CHAPTER THIRTY-EIGHT

The events in this chapter are based on Nancy Smith Clemency Memorandum and Exhibits filed with the Ohio Parole Board on April 6, 2012; "Lorain Bus Driver Tearfully Pleads for Freedom, Pardon before Ohio Parole Board" by Rachel Dissell, published by Cleveland.com on January 29, 2013; Affidavit and Report of Maggie Bruck attached to Smith's Motion for a New Trial Based on Newly Discovered Evidence filed on December 14, 2021; and Minutes of Parole Board Regarding Nancy Smith Clemency Petition, published on August 8, 2013. Because there is no transcript of the hearing, the author has re-created the testimony and questioning from available sources.

NOTES ON CHAPTER THIRTY-NINE

The events in this chapter are based on the following: *State v. Smith*, Motion for Pro Hac Vice Admission on behalf of Sharon Katz filed on March 18, 2013; *State v. Smith*, Memorandum of Law in Support of an Order That Nancy Smith Is Not Required to Register as a Sex Offender, filed on June 3, 2013; *State v. Smith*, Journal Entry for Sentencing, dated June 4, 2013, and filed on June 5, 2013; *State v. Smith*, Sentence Agreement of the Parties, filed on June 5, 2013; "Nancy Smith, Single Mother Wrongly Imprisoned for Fifteen Years, Is Exonerated" Davis Polk Website, posted March 29, 2022; "Sinclair to Retire After Eighteen Years on Stark County Bench" by Ed Meyer, published in the *Akron Beacon Journal* on November 9, 2012; "No More Prison Time for Nancy Smith" by Kaylee Remington, published in the *Morning Journal* on June 5, 2013; "Nancy Smith Hearing in the Head Start Case" posted on YouTube by the *Chronicle-Telegram* on June 4, 2013.

NOTES ON CHAPTER FORTY

The events in this chapter are based on the following: YouTube video of Joseph Allen's resentencing hearing and its aftermath on October 1, 2013; and Draft Opinion of Judge D. Chris Cook Granting Defendants' Motion for a New Trial, pages 19 to 23, dated February 3, 2022, in *State v. Smith* and *State v. Allen*.

NOTES ON CHAPTER FORTY-ONE

The events in this chapter are based on the following documents: Defendants' Motion for Leave to File a Motion for New Trial Pursuant to Rule 33(B), filed on December 14, 2021; Affidavit of Rocco Bronson, Jr., executed on November 19, 2021, and filed with that motion; Affidavit of Rocco Bronson, Sr., executed on November 20, 2021, and filed with that motion; Affidavit of Virginia Braden, executed on December 7, 2021, and filed with that motion; Expert Report of Maggie Bruck, PhD, dated January 25, 2013 and filed with that motion; and correspondence between author and Mark Godsey dated October 26, 2022.

NOTES ON CHAPTER FORTY-TWO

The events in this chapter are based on the Defendants' Joint Motion for Leave to File a Motion for a New Trial in *State v. Smith* and *State v. Allen*; Motion to Disqualify the Lorain County Prosecutor's Office and to Appoint a Special Prosecutor filed on behalf of two victims in *State v. Smith*; and the transcript of the proceedings on December 22, 2021, in *State v. Smith* and *State v. Allen*.

NOTES ON CHAPTER FORTY-THREE

The events described in this chapter were based on the following sources: "Charges Dismissed in Lorain County Head Start Sex Abuse Case" posted on YouTube by News 5 Cleveland on February 22, 2022; and "Interview with Nancy Smith" posted on YouTube video by the *Chronicle-Telegram* on June 24, 2009.

ABOUT THE AUTHOR

David Miraldi is an author, attorney, and artist hailing from Lorain, Ohio. With a career in civil law that spans over four decades, David has dedicated himself to championing the cause of the common man against insurance conglomerates and corporate giants.

A graduate of The College of Wooster (1975), David earned his law degree with honors from The Ohio State Moritz College of Law. Driven by an innate sense of duty, he returned to his hometown to practice alongside his father and brother, serving the community that shaped him.

An author with a flair for narrative nonfiction, David made waves with his debut book, "The Edge of Innocence: The Trial of Casper Bennett," which was crowned the 2018 Book of the Year by the prestigious International Rubery Book Awards. He further cemented his reputation as a storyteller with his sophomore release, "The Edge of Malice: The Marie Grossman Story," earning accolades from Kirkus Reviews as a "superbly crafted nonfiction drama" and receiving a shortlisting by Rubery for its 2021 awards.

Beyond the courtroom and the written page, David's creative spirit finds outlets through photography and music. His evocative photographs often grace local exhibits, and he generously donates the proceeds from their sales to charity. A pianist with eclectic tastes, David composes original pieces and has a predilection for classical, ragtime, and contemporary music. He is also a fitness enthusiast and engages in tennis, swimming, cycling, and gardening.

David shares his life with his beloved wife, Leslee, also a lawyer, and they are the proud parents of three children and doting grandparents to three grandchildren. They continue to make Avon, Ohio, their home.

ALSO BY DAVID MIRALDI

The Edge of Innocence: The Trial of Casper Bennett

The Edge of Malice: The Marie Grossman Story

The Edge of Doubt: The Trial of Nancy Smith and Joseph Allen